Baedeker

CH00735413

Greek Islands

www.baedeker.com

Verlag Karl Baedeker

SIGHTSEEING HIGHLIGHTS ★ ★

The list of sights on the Greek islands is long. But where are the highlights? Whether you want a fabulous beach, a major excavation site or a picturesque village – we've put together a list of what you should by no means miss.

1 ★ ★ Corfu
The landscape on the Ionian Islands is predominantly green – which doesn't mean that there are no beautiful coastlines or beaches. The main town of Corfu has a unique atmosphere that was strongly influenced by Venice.   ▶ **page 169**

2 ★ ★ Aegina
A visit to the Athenians' favourite island is worthwhile for the impressive Temple of Aphaia alone.   ▶ **page 126**

3 ★ ★ Mykonos
On the Greek Ibiza there's high life around the clock. The many beautiful beaches and the charming island town of the same name are also an attraction. The island is also the starting point for a trip to the once sacred island of Delos.   ▶ **page 313**

4 ★ ★ Delos
This little island is one large excavation site. As a shrine to Apollo it was a religious centre in antiquity.
▶ **page 220**

5 ★ ★ Santorini
This spectacular volcanic island with its wonderful villages clinging to the cliffs should not be missed, especially because of its magnificent sunsets.
▶ **page 370**

6 ★ ★ Patmos
The island has special religious significance since St John wrote the Book of Revelations here.   ▶ **page 329**

Mykonos Hora
Enchanting capital of the island of Mykonos

©Baedeker

Corfu

10 Chios

● 11 Athens

2 Aegina

3 Mykonos   6 Patmos
4 Delos

7 Kos

5 Santorini

8 Rhodes

9 Crete

7 ✶✶ Kos

The island of the famous physician Hippocrates, who was active here in the Asclepieion, is considered to be the birthplace of Western medicine.
► page 273

8 ✶✶ Rhodes

The first highlight of the island is the eponymous capital with impressive buildings of the Order of St John. But don't miss the fabulously situated Lindos either.
► page 336

9 ✶✶ Crete

Minoan excavation sites, picturesque villages, impressive landscape and many good beaches make Crete one of Greece's major vacation venues.
► page 187

10 ✶✶ Chios

The main attraction of this austere island, whose landscape is marked by contrasts, is the Nea Moni Monastery with its beautiful mosaics.
► page 162

11 ✶✶ Athens

In the Acropolis the capital of Greece has one of the world's most important historic sites.   ► page 138

BAEDEKER'S BEST TIPS

Here we have collected for you the most interesting of the many Baedeker tips in this book. Enjoy the Greek islands at their very best!

⊞ Simply delicious!
The excellent, extremely creamy Greek yogurt has to be tried. ▶ **page 80**

Greek yoghurt
… is delicious

⊞ Leather items galore
Skridlof Street in Chania on Crete is an excellent address for leather goods.
▶ **page 104**

⊞ The best view …
… of the ancient Acropolis of Athens can be seen from Filopappos Hill.
▶ **page 150**

⊞ Art in the Metro
Ancient finds that were discovered when the metro was built in Athens are displayed in some of the metro stations.
▶ **page 156**

⊞ Off to the »Caribbean beach«
Elafonisi beach on the west coast of Crete has Caribbean flair. ▶ **page 194**

⊞ Extreme Bar
An extremely rocking experience!
▶ **page 197**

Leather goods
A large selection of leather goods awaits visitors in Skridlof, a lane in Hania on Crete

Elafonisi
An unusual beach on
Crete's west coast

🚩 »Minoan« wines
The right place to taste good Cretan wines is the Minos winery near Arhanes on Crete. ► page 209

🚩 »Captain Corelli's Mandolin«
The plot of Louis de Bernières' novel takes place on Kefallonia, which makes it a great vacation read. ► page 264

🚩 Olive groves
Near Plomari on the island of Lesbos trails lead through olive groves.
► page 306

Olive trees ...
... mark the landscape on
many islands

🚩 Beautiful beach
Russian Beach on Poros is still a lovely and quiet beach. ► page 336

🚩 Cave trip
A trip to the Blue Grotto and the Grey Grotto on Skiathos is impressive.
► page 385

The traditional game of tavli is popular among young and old
▶ page 26

BACKGROUND

PRACTICALITIES

Price categories

Hotels
Luxury: over 200 €
Mid-range: 90–200 €
Budget: 40–90 €
For a double room

Restaurants
Expensive: over 15 €
Moderate: 10–15 €
Inexpensive: up to 10 €
For a main course

SIGHTS FROM A to Z

*An excellent Greek salad is served
in every restaurant*
▶ page 80

*Apella beach on Karpathos – just
what the holiday brochure promised*
▶ **page 257**

*Hart (currently removed)
and hind, the heraldic animals of
Rhodes, watch over Mandraki Harbour
in Rhodes Town*

Background

CONCISE AND CLEARLY WRITTEN:
FACTS ABOUT THE GREEK ISLANDS,
ABOUT THE COUNTRY AND ITS PEOPLE,
ITS NATURAL BEAUTY,
ITS ECONOMY AND EVERYDAY LIFE.

ISLANDS OF LIGHT

3,050 islands, every one of them bathed in enchanted light, from the Ionian Islands to the Cyclades, from Crete to the Sporades. Soft dawn on Corfu, glittering noonday sun on Chios and breathtaking sunsets on Santorini over an azure blue sea: the Greek islands intoxicate the senses.

Rhodes, the island of shining Helios, once boasted the bronze Colossus, a beacon that could be seen from far off. The god Apollo was worshipped in great temples as a figure of light on Delos. Even Dionysos needed the warmth of summer to ripen the grapes for his drinking bout with Ariadne on Naxos. On Lesbos, where Orpheus found his last resting place, the poetess Sappho, spellbound by light,

The largest Minoan palace
Knossos is a must for every vacationer on Crete

composed her verses, and Daedalus and Icarus fled the dark of the legendary King Minos' labyrinth on Knossos into spheres of light by means of the wings they made. Even the pragmatic Ulysses longed for the bright colours of his home island Ithaki.

Throughout the ages the Greek island world has served as a bridgehead between the cultural currents of the Orient and the West. The culture of the Cyclades in the Aegean with its characteristic idols in the third millennium BC was open to innovations that came from Asia Minor. Minoan society with its magnificent palace complexes and beautiful art on Crete in the second millennium BC, the first truly European civilization, profited from Egyptian cultural accomplishments. Greek antiquity, on the other hand, especially the ideas of Hellenism, travelled far into the Orient. The islands were not only vital sources of raw material, like the famous marble on Paros and Naxos, or merely trading bases with bustling ports for all sorts of agricultural products; they also produced art of the finest quality, such as the Venus de Milo, the Nike of Samothraki or the Laocoön group by Rhodian sculptors. Hippocrates, the father of medicine, was born on Kos; the philosopher and mathematician Pythagoras came from Samos, as did the philosopher Epicurus. The tragic poet Euripides was from Salamis. The heritage of antiquity has always attracted and enthused visitors, from Roman emperors to the crowned heads of the 19th century. In the periods

Greek salad
An essential part of any meal

Líndos
Picturesque Lindos on Rhodes with its wonderful location is one of the most beautiful places in all of Greece

Windsurfing
Surfers find excellent conditions in the Greek islands

Spectacular cliffs
High, vertical limestone cliffs give the western coasts of the Ionian Islands their unique look.
The Leucadian cliffs on Lefkada have been famous since antiquity.

Italian atmosphere
Many places in the Ionian Islands look as if they could be in Italy – here Corfu Town

Caribbean flair
on fabulous Elafonisi Beach on Crete

between ancient and modern times, the islands were subject to numerous foreign rulers: Byzantine emperors, the Venetians, Knights of St John, Turks, British and Italians came and went, leaving traces without having a lasting effect on the character of the islands, until finally in the course of the 19th and early 20th century they were united in a new Greek nation.

Sun, Sand and Syrtaki

The islands are full of scenic and historical contrasts, from the subtropical vegetation of the Ionian Islands to the bizarre karst landscape of the Cyclades, from the snow-capped peaks of the Ida mountain range on Crete to the volcanic landscape of Nisyros, from the remains of ancient temples on Aegina and Samos to the Gothic architecture of the Order of St John and Ottoman mosques on Rhodes, from the whitewashed cube houses and blue church domes of the Cyclades to the cultivated classical-style ship-owners' villas on Andros. There are wonderful broad beaches everywhere for sun worshippers, small isolated bays for loners, and watersports facilities for surfers and sailors. There are also attractive hiking trails to wind-swept heights with panoramic views, bustling ports with noisy nightlife as on Mykonos and quiet places of visionary revelations like the monastery of St John on Patmos. The hospitality of the islanders can be strained here and there by the excesses of modern mass tourism, but a glass of retsina or Samos wine combined with a tasty island meal and accompanied by music and dances like the ever-present syrtaki ignites the spark of Mediterranean life in everyone. Nights filled with scents and sounds belong to the revellers, the exuberant, the lovers and romantics – until morning, when Helios' sun chariot appears on the horizon and spreads its shining light over the thousands of islands, which gleam like precious pearls in the sea.

Mediterranean atmosphere
... eating outdoors in a taverna on a mild summer evening is part of the experience

Facts

The Greek islands are one of the main attractions of the eastern Mediterranean Sea. They have what many vacationers are looking for: sun and beautiful beaches. With their varying landscapes and cultures, the 3,050 islands together form an important economic region on the southeastern edge of Europe.

The spelling of Greek names is difficult since there is no standard transliteration of the Greek alphabet into Roman letters. In order to have consistent spelling in this guidebook at least, the **transliteration table** of the United Nations is used here (see p.99) for place names. The names of persons given in this book may differ from this principle if a different version is better known and more easily recognizable in English. Spelling often varies in Greece, too, and there are often different versions of the same name. Sometimes variations are listed.

Greek spelling

Nature and Environment

The Ionian Islands off the west coast of Greece are part of Balkan mountain ranges that run from northwest to southeast and still lie within the continental shelf, which has ocean depths ranging from about 100m to 600m (300ft to 2,000ft). To the west of the islands the shelf falls away sharply into the Inoussa Trench, which is up to 4,150m/13,600ft deep. Its ragged profile shows that it is part of an instable fault block system. When the Alps and the Balkans were pushed up in the Tertiary era, their margins crumbled into pieces whose edges are still in motion today. Many severe earthquakes in the course of history (since the 15th century more than 30 have been documented) bear witness to this; the Ionian Islands are the **earthquake centre of the Balkan peninsula**. Zakynthos, Kefallonia, Lefkada and Ithaki were severely damaged in the earthquake in 1953; the island of Kefallonia rose by 30cm–1m (12–40 inches).

Ionian Islands

? DID YOU KNOW …?

■ … the island of Gavdos is the southernmost point in Europe?

The Aegean islands are a continuation of the mountains of central Greece, which were the bridge to Asia Minor in the Mesozoic era some 170 million years ago. This applies, of course, to the rock from which they were formed as well; these are mainly crystalline stone and sediment. These slate rocks and the limestone and sandstone that in part metamorphosed to marble, as well as granite and gneiss, were formed in the Palaeozoic era as the so-called Cyclades massif. These mountains were subject to erosion and partly submerged as collapsed sections and eroded valleys were flooded by the sea. New calcareous deposits and sediment formed.

Aegean islands

In the later Pliocene epoch the Aegean folded mountains were raised again, above all by the drift of the large continental plates. The African Plate drifted northwards and caused the formation of the Alps

← *Meeting in a cafe to play tavli is not just for older people*

and the Carpathians. As the mountains were raised, more sections collapsed; in the Pleistocene era, which began around 2.6 million years ago, what remained of the mountain range sank again and was flooded for the most part. This subsidence created the middle and northern **Aegean Sea**, with the peaks of the sunken mountain ridges or new peaks caused by volcanic activity emerging as islands. The strong folding of the earth made the chalk brittle and slightly corroded, which promoted karst development, a characteristic of the islands.

Earthquakes and volcanoes in the Aegean

The earth's crust has not come to rest in the Mediterranean region. There are more or less noticeable earthquakes here every day, some with catastrophic consequences. These earthquakes are caused by continuous activity in the continental plates. In the case of Greece the **African Plate** moves from south to north at a speed of c 2.5cm/1in annually. In a zone marked by increased volcanic activity it sinks under the **Aegean Plate**, which in turn covers part of the Eurasian Plate. The islands of Aegina, Milos and Santorini owe their existence to the volcanic activity caused by this movement, which is presently only dormant.

During the severe eruption around 1600 BC on Santorini, huge amounts of pumice, tuff stone and ash were produced. The volcanic activity of that time was tied to severe earthquakes, which also severely damaged the island of Crete. The lava flowed for the last time in 1950. There have been catastrophic earthquakes in the Aegean in recent times as well: in 1856 on Crete, in 1926 on Rhodes and in 1933 on Kos.

Island Groups

Note

Here important characteristics, historical events and the tourist significance of individual island groups are summarized. Since Crete, the largest of the Greek islands, belongs to no group, it will be treated in more detail in the section »Sights from A to Z«.

Ionian Islands

The chain of Ionian Islands runs south along the west coast of Greece from the Albanian border in the north. The main islands are Corfu, Paxi, Lefkada, Ithaki, Kefallonia und Zakynthos. Kythira, which lies far away on the southeast tip of the Peloponnese, is also part of this group (it is administratively part of Attiki), but is not included in this section because it is completely different as a tourist destination. The islands in the Ionian Sea have a mild, rainy climate and lush Mediterranean or subtropical vegetation. This give them a **character untypical of Greece**. The architectural style from centuries of Venetian influence makes the islands look more Italian than Greek. The British period (1815–62) left its mark on culture and

Facts and Figures Greek Islands

© Baedeker

► Westernmost island: Othoni
► Easternmost island: Kastellorizo

Number
► 3,050 islands, of which 83 are always inhabited

Area
► 24,700 sq km/9,500 sq mi
(19% of the entire area of Greece)

Length of coastline
► 11,000 km/6,800 mi

Island groups
► Ionian islands
► Northern Sporadic islands
► Southern Sporadic/
Dodecanese islands
► Saronic islands
► Cyclades islands
► North and East Aegean islands
► Crete

Location
► Northernmost island: Thasos
► Southernmost island in Europe: Gavdos

Population
► 1.5 million

cooking as well. Only Lefkada and to a lesser extent Kefallonia, Zakynthos, Paxi and Ithaki were for a time part of the Ottoman Empire. Lefkada and Kefallonia especially still bear traces of oriental influence.

None of the islands have been left untouched by **tourism**. Corfu and Zakynthos were tourist venues of the European nobility 100 years ago already; today they are mainly visited by guests from Great Britain. The other islands have much less tourism; Lefkada is apparently not seen as an island despite its good beaches, and Ithaki lies in the shadow of the apparently more attractive islands, so it is possible to have a quiet vacation there.

The Ionian Sea got its name from the wanderings of Io (Aeschylus), or according to later sources from the Illyrian hero Ionios. The Ionian Islands were thus not named after the Ionian Greeks, who left Greece in the 11th–10th century BC, colonized the Anatolian coast and later gave this part of eastern Greece the name Ionia.
◄ Myth and history

Ancient finds go back to the Mycenaean period. The islands stepped into the spotlight of history when Corinth founded a colony on Kerkyra (Corfu) in 734 BC. In the 5th century BC Athens gained influence, and in the 2nd century BC the islands came under the control of Rome. At the end of the Byzantine period, the Fourth Crusade from 1203 to 1204 brought a turning point. Everywhere rulers from Italy claimed the inheritance of Byzantium. Gradually **Venice** got control of the islands: in 1363 Kythira, in 1386 Corfu, in 1479 Zakynthos, in 1500 Kefallonia and finally in 1684 Lefkada, which had been Turkish from 1467. Venetian rule lasted until 1797. In this time many people fled from the Turks to these islands. As a whole the islands can look back on a richer cultural heritage from these centuries than the rest of Greece; the tradition of icon painting continued here, for example. After a French intermezzo (1797–99 and 1807–10) and a spell of Russian influence (1800–07), the new **»Republic of the Seven United Islands«** became a British protectorate in 1815. Colonial power, although it provided infrastructure like roads and hospitals, was autocratic and repressive. Only in 1864, after long resistance, were the islands turned over to Greece. In World War II Italy occupied Corfu, and after Italian capitulation in 1943 German forces came.

Cypress trees mark the landscape of the Pantokrator mountain on Corfu

The Othonian Islands, officially the Diapondia Islands, are a small archipelago in the northern Ionian Sea and part of the Ionian Islands. The island group includes the inhabited islands Othoni, Erikoussa and Mathraki as well as the uninhabited Diaplo.

Othonian islands

The Saronic Islands include all the islands in the Saronic Gulf between Athens and Argolis in the Peloponnese, among them Salamina, Aegina, Angistri, Poros, many islets and rock cliffs as well as the Argolian Islands.

Saronic Islands

Among the »**Argolian Islands**«, the southernmost and westernmost group of the Saronic Islands, are all of the islands off the coast of the Argolis and in the Argolian Gulf, especially Ydra (Hydra), Dokos, Spetses, the islets Trikeri, Spetsopoula, Psili and Platia, as well as countless rocky outposts. The islands are located in the dry region of the Aegean, but despite low rainfall the vegetation is plentiful. On Aegina especially there are major historic buildings. Because of their proximity to Athens and the port of Piraeus, the islands with their idyllic harbour towns are a popular weekend goal for Athenians.

In antiquity the islands strewn around the Cyclades were called the Sporades, which means »scattered«. Today they are divided into the Northern Sporades and the Southern Sporades.

Sporades

The **Northern Sporades** are northeast of Evia (Euboea), after Crete the second largest Greek island, and east of the Pelion peninsula. They include Skopelos, Skiathos, Alonnisos and Skyros as well as about 75 smaller islands. There are few historic remains on the Northern Sporades, but the islands have pleasant scenery and wonderful beaches, which have been left relatively untouched by mass tourism.

The **Southern Sporades**, which lie off the southwest coast of Asia Minor (Turkey), are Patmos, Lipsi, Leros, Kalymnos, Kos, Nisyros, Tilos, Symi, Fourni and Ikaria. Sometimes Lesbos, Chios and Samos are included.

The Dodecanese, the »**Twelve Islands**«, are the southernmost of the Sporades, off the southwest coast of Asia Minor. The group includes the fourteen larger islands Lipsi, Patmos, Leros, Kalymnos, Kos, Astypalea, Nisyros, Symi, Tilos, Rhodes, Halki, Karpathos, Kassos and Kastellorizo as well as about 40 smaller islands. Rhodes Town is the administrative capital of the Dodecanese. Except for Rhodes these islands have little water and are mostly barren; they belong to Greece culturally and historically and to the Anatolian mainland geographically. The inhabitants live mainly from tourism, supplemented by agriculture and fishing. The Dodecanese islands, especially Rhodes, Kos and Patmos, are among the most popular tourist venues in Greece. Anyone who wants peace and quiet with authentic Greek culture should choose one of the smaller islands.

Dodecanese

History ▶   In antiquity the Dodecanese was a political unit. Only when incorporated into the Ottoman Empire in the 16th century did the islands, which had been combined into a Byzantine administrative district, receive a common political status through extensive self-administration. Italy occupied most of the islands in 1912. In the treaty of Lausanne in 1923 Turkey turned over the entire Dodecanese to Italy. After German occupation during World War II the islands were incorporated into the Kingdom of Greece in 1947.

North and east Aegean islands   The islands of Samos, Chios, Lesbos, Limnos, Samothraki and Thasos do not really form a group, since they are spread over the north and east Aegean Sea; they are »**individuals**«. They are fundamentally different from the other Greek islands. For one thing, their history was completely different; for another, their landscape is more luxuriantly green and has more fertile cultivated land than the rest of the Aegean islands.

History ▶   The history of this region goes back a long way. Thermi on Lesbos was settled as early as 2700 BC. As part of the Greek colonization, Aeolians came around 1100 BC to Lesbos, Ionians around 1000 BC to Chios and around 800 BC to Limnos. Thasos and Samothraki were colonized around 700 BC. The islands blossomed in the 7th and 6th century BC, when Lesbos was the home of the **singers Terpandros and Arion, Sappho and Alcaeus**, and Chios had an influential school of sculpture. After Persian rule (546–479 BC) the islands

Serifos Hora is the capitol of the Cycladic island with the same name

came under Macedonian, Ptolemaic and Roman influence from the 4th century BC onwards. After the Fourth Crusade in 1204 the islands came under Venetian, then Genoese control, followed by Turkish rule until 1912. In 1922–23, after the Greek-Turkish War, Lesbos and Chios took in many refugees. In the recent past Turkey has claimed, in part for its oil deposits, the Anatolian continental shelf of which Chios and Lesbos are a part.

The Cyclades are the **prototypical Greek islands**: barren rock with characteristic whitewashed cube-shaped houses stacked one above the other and tiny churches with blue domes. Their **name** derived in ancient times from the fact that the islands are arranged in a circle – Greek »kyklos« – around their religious centre, Delos. According to legend Poseidon pushed the mountains into the sea with his trident, where they took root in the deep. The archipelago consists of 23 large and about 200 small islands, all mountainous. Except for Naxos there is a lack of rivers that carry water regularly and of trees, due to the constant strong meltemi winds. In the 1970s **tourism** developed and is today the main source of income on the islands. Mykonos, Ios, Naxos and Santorini are sought out by foreign visitors during the high season, while the other islands are popular for weekend trips from Athens because they are so close. The smaller islands, especially those east of Naxos, are still relatively quiet. Tinos is often visited because it is the most important pilgrimage site in Greece.

Cyclades

The original inhabitants were the Carians, the bearers of the Early Bronze Age Cycladic culture (3200–2000 BC), whose so-called Cyclades idols were found on all of the islands. The Carians were pushed out in the late 2nd millennium BC by the Ionians from the northern islands and by Dorians from the southern islands. In the second half of the 1st century BC the islands were divided between the Macedonians and the Ptolemies, later becoming part of the Roman Empire and, after its partition, of the Byzantine Empire. Under Venetian and Frankish rule cultural and intellectual life blossomed. After the Turkish occupation in 1579, the islands largely kept their religious and cultural identity. They have been part of Greece since 1834.

◀ History

Flora and Fauna

Flora

Greece has some of the most interesting vegetation in Europe. Plants from southeastern Europe, the Near East and North Africa can be found here. Some of the islands also have great botanical variety, and even lush vegetation.

Mediterranean vegetation

The vegetation of the Greek islands has a typical Mediterranean character, with evergreen sclerophyllous plants and succulents; the trees reach only medium height. In the fertile lowlands and coastal regions up to about 800m/2,600ft there are mixed forests of oak, plane, Aleppo pine, carob trees and others, with frygana vegetation (garrigue) composed of holm oaks, Kermes oak, strawberry trees, mastic bushes, laurel, gorse, oleander and wild olive trees. In the moister west (Ionian Islands) this vegetation grows in higher regions as well (800m–2,000m/2,600ft–6,600ft). The further south, the more scant the frygana becomes.

In the drier islands in the southeast of the Aegean it gives way to sparse **dry vegetation** consisting almost entirely of juniper bushes, thistles, thyme, dill, peppermint and water-retentive succulents (including cactus, agave, opuntia). This dry frygana is used as a meagre pasture for sheep and goats. Anyone visiting the islands in the spring will be overwhelmed by the sight of flowering plants, as almost all blossom at the same time: mimosa, hibiscus, oleander, magnolia, anemone, bougainvillaea, diverse orchids and of course poppies.

Due to centuries of deforestation of the originally dense forests, many of the islands now have hardly any trees. The forests and macchia, destroyed by cultivation and over-pasturing, have been replaced

Olive trees have been cultivated for thousands of years

at best by **olive groves, fig plantations and vineyards**. Since wine, olive oil and figs bring in little income today, more and more of the old cultivated land is fallow. Frygana eventually takes over. Recently there have been efforts to reforest these areas. Cypresses and eucalyptus are also characteristic plants. Agave and prickly pear from Central America and date palms from North Africa have been introduced and also grow wild.

Important cultivated plants, along with olives, are grapes (including wine and table grapes, raisins and sultanas), citrus fruits (especially oranges and mandarins) and grain. In the past decades vegetables (early potatoes, cucumbers, tomatoes and onions) and fruits (apricots, peaches, apples, melons, bananas, figs and almonds) as well as flowers have also been cultivated.

Cultivated plants

Fauna

The early isolation of the Greek islands from the mainland in the history of the earth and the almost complete decimation of plant life have had an extremely detrimental effect on the variety of their fauna. Occasionally wild sheep, goats, donkeys and mules can be seen, as well as hares and rabbits, which are hunted by foxes, badgers, marten and feral cats. There are still some wild goats (Capra aegarus) on Crete. They are the ancestors of the European domestic goat.

Reptiles, too, are increasingly restricted in their habitat. This applies especially to the Hermann's turtle and the **loggerhead turtle**, a sea turtle that lays its eggs on various sandy beaches to be incubated by the sun. These beaches are now being protected by conservation laws (►Baedeker Special p.410). Geckos and various other lizard species, including the European green lizard, are common. Beware of snakes, especially the poisonous, aggressive viper and the protected Levantine viper, not only in the frygana brush but also in gardens and other sheltered places.

Reptiles

Bird life has been greatly reduced. In the mountains peregrine falcons and hawks can be seen, occasionally also bearded vultures, common kestrels and common buzzards. Partridge and quail, lapwings and magpies are common. Along the coasts black and white oystercatchers, terns and several varieties of seagull can be seen. The nuthatch, bunting and the colourful European bee-eater are also widespread. Pelicans can only be seen in a few refuges. Some varieties that are endangered and on the red list are still hunted.

Birds

The world of insects has great variety. This applies especially in the spring, when myriads of butterflies and bees swarm to the blossoms, and deafening cicada concerts can be heard. The poisonous rogalida spider and scorpions are dangerous.

Insects

Marine life The fauna of Greek waters has surprisingly few species, which is largely due to **over-fishing**, but recently also to **water pollution**; the yield hardly covers the needs of the island population. The most common varieties are the grey mullet, barbell mullet, mackerel, dentrex, perch, European hake, sardine, anchovy, Adriatic fish of the triglidae family and tuna. Squid (including calamares), octopus, different kinds of mollusc, lobsters, langoustines, shrimps and crabs are still plentiful.

Watersports fans should watch out for sharks and moray eels, especially along rocky coastline. Sea urchins and stinging jellyfish, too, can spoil a day on the beach. Dolphins can be seen now and again, especially from boats. Mediterranean monk seals live along secluded rocky coastlines and are in danger of becoming extinct. Corals and sponge colonies have been greatly reduced by water pollution.

Population · Economy

Population

Population, population density Only about 1.5 million of a total of 11.2 million Greek citizens live on the islands. With an average density of 84 people per sq km (217 per sq mi) the Ionian Islands lie above, and the Aegean islands with their 35 per sq km (90 per sq mi) far below the Greek average of 79 persons per sq km (204 people per sq mi).

Ethnic circumstances The homogeneity of the Greek population increased as a result of the political events after World War I, when about 1.5 million Greek refugees returned from Asia Minor and about 518,000 Turks and 92,000 Bulgarians left the country. The rural population of the islands is of Greek origin. After the **large exchange in population in 1922–23**, few members of the Turkish minority stayed on Rhodes and Kos. Since the collapse of socialist states in Europe, more and more eastern European immigrants, especially Albanians, have settled on the islands with their families. There are also nomadic Roma.

Rural exodus and migration Unlike the urban population on the mainland, the population is declining on most of the islands; some will be soon be completely uninhabited (e.g. Kastellorizo). Barren earth and the fragmentation of estates have made life so difficult that young people frequently prefer to look a better living on the mainland, in the industrialized countries of western Europe or overseas in the USA or Australia. The results are a dangerous **increase in the average age of the island population** and consequently a neglect of agriculture, which the elderly can no longer cope with. About 3 million Greeks live overseas. Recently there has been a turnaround, because many young Greeks are disappointed with city life and return to the countryside.

As in other southeastern European states, **patriarchal society** in Greece is in upheaval. For centuries the extended family has been the most important economic and emotional refuge for the individual; it gave security by taking care of people's needs in old age or when sick and out of work. This is being replaced, especially in the cities, by the nuclear family with one or two children. In connection with this the woman's role, which used to be restricted to child-rearing and the household, is changing. Political reforms are supporting this process. Women have been able to vote in Greece since the early 1950s, and since 1975 **equality of the sexes** has been anchored in law. In the 1980s parliament changed the laws on marital, family and divorce rights significantly – another important step towards equality. But the reality – at least in rural areas – is often a far remove from the opportunities and liberties promised to women by legal reforms. Men and women spend their free time apart. While he goes to the kafenion, she sits with the other women in front of the house. In spite of signs of dissolution, all members of the family have a

Two generations, two different worlds

strong feeling of belonging and a deep sense of family. Many Greeks come back to the islands from Athens and other cities on the mainland, or even from overseas, at Easter, for family festivities or on vacation.

Economy

Agriculture remains an important economic factor, even though its contribution to the gross domestic product has been declining for years. The islands belong to the less developed areas of Greece. There is hardly any industry. Agriculture is the most important source of income, followed by trade and commerce. While the smaller islands try to cover their own needs, the larger ones deliver their agricultural products to the mainland and overseas.

Agriculture **Major agricultural products** are olives (for oil and eating), wine, honey and beeswax, melons and early vegetables, cucumbers (Crete), tomatoes (Cyclades), sultanas, almonds and peanuts (Crete), table grapes and currants (Ionian Islands), cotton, tobacco, mastic (Chios), and fruit such as peaches, apricots, apples and pears. Livestock is raised in the mountainous areas. The sparse vegetation only supports sheep, goats and other small animals (especially poultry). The most important products are of course meat, milk and cheese, also wool, furs and leather. In some areas beekeeping (honey, beeswax etc.) flourishes. Mules and donkeys are still indispensable as working animals on some islands.

Fishing The Greek fishing industry faces massive problems. Over-fishing and water pollution have drastically reduced the catch in the last two decades. For this reason many businesses farm **marine fish** (especially bream and monkfish), shellfish and crustaceans. Because of the low regeneration rate and continued over-exploitation, fishing continues to be unproductive; thus fish is imported to cover the country's needs.

Sponge fishing Sponge fishing, once one of the major and most productive industries in the eastern Aegean, is shrinking due to pollution and the competitive pressure of synthetic sponges. The Greek sponge-fishing fleet was traditionally based on the islands of the Dodecanese; today it is worth mentioning only on Kalymnos.

Mining Mining (small and mid-sized businesses with up to 400 employees) is limited to small deposits of iron, manganese, nickel, chromium, zinc, lead and molybdenum (Evia and Milos). Since antiquity world-famous marble has been quarried on Tinos, Chios, Naxos and Paros. **Pozzolan**, a volcanic tuff earth from Santorini and Milos, was already used as mortar in antiquity for building ports, especially for underwater construction.

Water pollution has made natural sponges rare and expensive, so today the markets mostly sell synthetic sponges

Since 1981 Greece has belonged to the exclusive club of oil-producing countries. Two years earlier »black gold« was found off the coast of the island of Thasos. Along with petroleum, natural gas is also exploited. Several productive petroleum and natural gas fields have been discovered on the Asian shelf of the Aegean Sea. Both Greece and Turkey claim these fields, which has been the cause of tension between the two recently. The most important fossil fuel is lignite, which is mined on Evia. Domestic oil and natural gas make only a modest contribute to the country's needs, supplying 5% of the total demand. **Petroleum**

Trade and industry are based on the mining of clay for ceramics as well as on raising sheep and goats to make wool rugs, textiles and leatherwork. **Trade and industry**

The service industry has been by far the most important economic sector for a long time. More than half of all the working population is employed here. The Greek islands are among the classic holiday spots worldwide, and tourism has long been a major source of income. In the past three decades considerable amounts have been invested in tourist infrastructure. Every year more than **14 million tourists** flock to Greece. Two thirds of all the visitors come from EU countries, especially Germany and the United Kingdom. The pleasant climate together with good beaches, beautiful countryside and historical attractions have all contributed to the development of tourism, which is supported by the government. But the number of tourists has fallen gradually in the past years. In 2009 it was just under 15 million. As a result of the financial crisis the country was forced to accept a further reduction in the number of visitors. Two thirds of the visitors come from EU countries, mainly from Germany and Great britain. **Service industry, tourism**

Religion

Religious affiliation

Almost all Greeks belong to the Greek Orthodox Church, since every child of Greek Orthodox parents is automatically made a member and there is no formal means of leaving the church. The remaining few are Protestants, Roman Catholics (due to the Venetian heritage on the Cyclades and the Ionian Islands), Muslims and Jews.

Church structure

Despite regional differences for historical reasons and great geographical fragmentation, even the Greek islanders have managed to maintain their strong national identity. The Greek Orthodox Church has served as a uniting factor here, especially in difficult times, and its influence is unbroken in private as well as in public life. **Since 1833 the Greek Orthodox Church has been autonomous**, since 1850 it has been recognized by the ecumenical patriarchate in Constantinople (Istanbul in Turkey) as an independent national church (autokephalie), and since 1864 it has been the state church; the archbishop of Athens is the head of the church. Only the islands of the Dodecanese, which were united with Greece in 1912–13, and the monks' republic of Athos are subject to the spiritual jurisdiction of the patriarchate of Constantinople; Crete is a semi-autonomous church province and has a special position.

Priests

Greek priests with their black cassocks, long hair and characteristic beards are a common sight on the streets. Village life is hard to imagine without them. They are allowed to marry, but only before being ordained as a priest. If the wife of an ordained priest (pappas) dies, he may marry again, but married priests are not allowed to enter a monastery or to hold a higher ecclesiastical office. Thus most metropolitans are monks. Since the Greek Orthodox Church is a state institution, priests have the **status of government employees** – with a relatively meagre salary. They can supplement their income, however, through donations or fees for performing church services, such as baptisms, marriages and funerals. They often have to take extra jobs to support themselves. Social work like supervising youth groups or visiting the elderly is not part of the priest's duties. He only gets involved in social matters when someone fails to keep the traditional standards or breaks the law.

Church holidays

Since the Greek Orthodox Church uses the Julian and not the Gregorian calendar, holidays are one to five weeks later than in the Roman Catholic and Protestant churches.

Easter ▶

Easter is traditionally **a family-centred celebration**; Greeks who live on the mainland or even abroad come home for the holiday. The festivities begin with a procession on Good Friday. The climax of the feast comes in the night from Saturday to Easter Sunday: about one hour before midnight, believers gather in church. At midnight, when

Greek priests are highly respected

the priest announces the resurrection of Christ, all those present light their candles from the Easter light. There are fireworks and fire-crackers, and in many villages Judas is symbolically burned on a large bonfire. Following the midnight service, families gather to partake of the first Easter meal after the fasting period. There is an old tradition connected to hard-boiled red Easter eggs, which are knocked against each other: the person whose egg has the hardest shell and remains unbroken will have good luck for a whole year.

The Feast of the Dormition (Assumption) is celebrated on August 15. The unusual name comes from the fact that the Greek Orthodox Church does not recognize the doctrine of the physical assumption of Mary into heaven, as the pope declared it in 1952. The church dedicated to the Virgin Mary on the Cyclades island of Tinos, the centre of festivities on this holiday, is visited by thousands of believers. The day is celebrated with large festivals all over Greece.

◄ The Feast of the Dormition

? DID YOU KNOW ...?

■ ... that Easter is the most important holiday in the Greek Orthodox church?

History

The history of the Greek islands, which form a bridge between the Orient and the West, is marked by its many foreign rulers. Only the battle for independence in the 19th century allowed the Greeks to develop their own national identity.

From Prehistory to the Mycenaean Period

7th millennium BC	First signs of settlement
from 1700 BC	Minoan culture at its peak
from 1600 BC	Immigration of the Mycenaeans

Archaeological finds testify to settlements in the Aegean region from the 7th millennium BC (Cycladic culture). Common characteristics indicate a connection to the cultures of southwest Asia and make it possible to speak of a larger area of Neolithic culture. The excavation of axes and pottery on the mainland attest to a Copper Age during the 3rd millennium BC, especially on the Peloponnese.

Prehistory

The Minoan civilization, which was named after the mythical **King Minos**, developed on Crete around huge palace complexes. Seals, copper and bronze daggers and gold jewellery from the early 3rd millennium BC have survived in the ports in the east and in the vaulted tombs on the plain of Messara.

Minoan civilization

An urban civilization emerged around the royal court during the first cultural flowering, called the Old Palace Period after the **palaces of Knossos, Malia and Phaestos**. Its economic basis was intensive wine and oil cultivation and metalworking. The settlements on Crete during this phase appear to have been a relatively self-sufficient society that had little contact with other peoples, making it apparently unnecessary to fortify the palaces and cities. Examples of crafts of outstanding quality from this time have survived in the form of thin-walled vases painted in bright colours, named Kamares pottery after the site where they were first discovered.

◄ Protopalatial (Old Palace Period 2100–1700 BC)

? DID YOU KNOW ...?

■ ... that Minoan culture was the first advanced European civilization?

An earthquake probably destroyed the Cretan palaces around the 18th century BC. Their reconstruction marks the beginning of the Late Minoan Period. Knossos in particular was rebuilt on a more magnificent scale. Interest now shifted abroad, to the Mycenaean mainland and especially to the New Kingdom in Egypt.

◄ Neopalatial (New Palace Period 1700–1400 BC)

During this period the **Cyclades** came under the influence of Minoan rule on Crete (excavation sites: Akrotiri on Santorini and Fylakopí on Milos). Trade and contact with neighbouring peoples brought the **Linear scripts**, which replaced the old pictographic system of writing. Religious and social structures bore matriarchal characteristics. A

← *In 2004 Olympic flames also illuminated Knossos on Crete*

flowering of pottery and fresco painting in the so-called palace style developed in Knossos. The Mycenaean conquerors advanced to Crete around 1400 BC. The final destruction of Knossos in 1200 BC marked the end of Minoan civilization.

Mycenae (1600–1150 BC)

A number of different principalities were formed on the Greek mainland with the influx of new ethnic groups in the middle of the 2nd millennium BC. The most powerful was in Mycenae on the Peloponnese. In contrast to Crete, which was initially peaceful and self-sufficient, Mycenae was dominated by a hierarchical aristocracy of warriors under the leadership of a king, preoccupied with competition and seizing and settling land.

During the 15th century BC, the Greeks of the Peloponnese extended their sphere of influence all the way to Asia Minor, Crete and Melos. Extraordinary works of art were produced through a fusion with Minoan culture in the Late Mycenaean period from 1400 to 1150 BC. Beehive tombs with their burial offerings and fortifications are evidence of this today.

Archaic Greece

around 1000	Dorian migration
from 8th century	Greek colonization
594 BC	Solon takes control of the city state of Athens.

Dorian migration

The Illyrians triggered a migration of the Dorians at the end of the 2nd millennium BC. To avoid this threat, the peoples who had been living in the region of Greece until then moved to Asia Minor and the Aegean islands, where their culture flourished through contacts with the east. The Ionian **pre-Socratic** school of philosophy was the cradle of western philosophy. Rhodes experienced an economic and cultural upswing at this time as a staging post in long-distance trade between east and west.

Cultural achievements

After the storm of the Dorian invasion, things in Greece were quiet for about 400 years, between the 9th and the 6th centuries BC, enabling the **initial germ of Western culture** to develop. The Greek alphabet emerged around 850 BC, including not only consonants but, for the first time, vowels as well. It was adapted from the Phoenician alphabet, which can be seen both from the shapes and from the names of the letters. The **Homeric epics** composed in the 8th century made the transition from oral tradition to literature. They are also considered to be the forerunners of written history. During this early epoch the visual arts developed their own, geometric style.

Fundamental geographic conditions, i.e. the limited possibilities for urban expansion and the supply problem resulting from a shortage of fertile land, determined the further development of Greece. A wave of colonization resulted from numerous wars among the cities and the difficulty many cities had in providing their citizens with sufficient land. New territory was conquered by sea, while inland expansion was cautious. As a rule, settlement was confined to coastal areas. Among the most important new settlements were Kyme (the northernmost Greek city in Italy), Taranto (*c* 700 BC, colonized by Sparta), Syracuse (settlers from Corinth, *c* 730 BC) and Massilia (colonists from Phokaia, *c* 600 BC). By the end of the colonization period, the Greeks had founded over 700 cities and, according to an apt and much-quoted saying of the philosopher Plato, sat around the Mediterranean »like frogs around a pond«.

The great colonization

Rural Attica remained untouched by the wave of Dorian immigrants. During the first millennium BC government lay in the hands of the archons, who until the late 6th century BC were members of the aristocracy that owned almost all the land. In 594 BC, **Solon** was elected archon as a »reconciler« and invested with dictatorial powers to overcome the gap between the nobility and the peasants, who lived in debt bondage, and to avert the threat of civil war. Solon sought to create a social balance and to form the citizens into a community. During his rule, for the first time in history, the laws were written on tablets and displayed publicly. Some aristocrats wanted to restore their influence and initiated violent unrest, resulting in Peisistratos seizing power as a tyrant in 560 BC. The fortunes of a state were entirely dependent on the person of the tyrant, who like Polycrates on Samos could be brutal, or like Peisistratos in Athens could be a benevolent regent. **Cleisthenes**, the head of a long-banished aristocratic dynasty, the Alcmaeonidae, took over the leadership of a popular revolt against the tyranny of the sons of Peisistratos with his ideas for reform. With the help of Sparta, he was able to expel the tyrant Hippias, Peisistratos' second son, in 511–510 BC. Cleisthenes rearranged Attica's territorial and political structure and introduced the process of choosing legislators by lot. This new system of dividing the citizenry into ten phyle (»tribes«) gave them rights based not on their ties to noble dynasties but on divisions into administrative units.

City state of Athens

Classical Greece

490–479 BC	Persian Wars
around 450	Dominance and cultural pinnacle of Athens
432–404 BC	Peloponnesian War

Persian Wars (490–479 BC) As a result of his campaigns of conquest, all of Asia Minor had fallen into the hands of the first Persian Great King, Cyrus, by the mid-6th century BC. At the beginning of the 5th century, the Persians demanded recognition of their suzerainty from the Greek city states. This demand was rejected out of hand, especially by Sparta and Athens. In response, the Persians sent a naval expedition to Attica that was only stopped by the Athenians in 490 BC at the **Battle of Marathon**. Sparta was finally able to weld the now heavily armed city states into a fighting alliance in 481 BC. The Persian forces, however, penetrated a long way toward Thessaly and Attica before the Greeks won the **decisive naval battle at Salamis** in 480 BC. The Greek fleet pressed their advantage and defeated the Persians at the foothills of Mykale, making themselves safe from further attacks. In this naval battle some of the Cyclades islands made ships available to the Greek side, while others, which were occupied by the Persians, were forced to support them in battle.

Athens as a major power Within a few years of victory in the Persian Wars, Athens gained a position of supremacy in Greece. The basis for this was primarily the

The Acropolis shows the power of Athens in the Classical period

decision to build a fleet and the uniting of all major Greek cities in the Delian League to continue the campaign against the Persians. As **Sparta** had no interest in a policy of revenge against the Persian Empire, Athens took over the initiative of continuing the war and was able to bring those Greek cities that were formerly dependent on the Persians into her sphere of influence and bind them to her. Thus an empire grew that included almost all Greek city states of the Aegean, a major part of the Mediterranean area and the Black Sea region.

The period around 450 BC was a turning point in Athenian politics: the newly elected strategos (general) **Pericles** distanced himself increasingly from expansionist policies, turned to domestic politics and intensified the democratization of the state. After the aristocracy, who had dominated the Areopagus (council of elders) until then, had been deprived of power, the rights of the Areopagus itself were curtailed in 462–461 BC so that the executive branch of government was then also controlled by the assembly. Almost all government decisions were made by the assembly. The democratic principle of equality for all citizens, which however never applied to women, slaves or foreigners, was most clearly expressed in the principle of drawing lots to choose the nine archons, the highest magistrates. Nevertheless, a political elite, drawn from the ranks of aristocrats and large landowners, remained. One of the most important of these men was Pericles. His historic status comes from his balanced direction of the state, in which the security of the empire and the promotion of the arts and sciences had equal weight.

The age of Pericles

The expansionist foreign policies and »democratic« domestic politics of Athens led to an extraordinary cultural blossoming. Crafts and commerce enjoyed unprecedented prosperity, with goods from Attica being exported throughout the Mediterranean region. In Athens itself the impressive and still extant buildings on the Acropolis were constructed. The Parthenon and the Propylaea were erected during Pericles' rule in the years after 450 BC. The most important sculptor of classical Greece was active during this time: **Phidias**, the creator of monumental statues of Athena and Zeus. The Sophist school of philosophy influenced intellectual life, but branches of philosophy that were independent of the official culture developed. The most prominent unorthodox thinker of the period was certainly **Socrates**, who was seen as a spiritual father by almost all later Greek philosophers. Even when Athens lost its position as political leader through the victory of Sparta, it continued to flourish in cultural terms: **Plato** and **Aristotle** dominated the intellectual life of Athens in the 4th century BC. **Aeschylus**, **Sophocles** and **Euripides** brought tragic poetry to its zenith in the 5th century BC, and **Aristophanes** did the same in the field of comedy at the turn of the 4th century BC. The first important representatives of written history were **Herodotus** and **Thucydides**.

Cultural golden age

Peloponnesian War (432–404 BC) The **differences between Sparta and Athens** intensified in the 5th century BC. In 432 BC Sparta declared war on Athens. In the Battle of Syracuse on Sicily Sparta, which had allied itself with Persia in the meantime, defeated Athens. In 404 BC Athens was besieged and forced to capitulate. After the almost 30 years of the Peloponnesian War came a period of peace treaties among the Greeks and with the Persians. In 370 BC Theban troops forced Sparta to relinquish its almost 300-year hegemony in the Peloponnese.

Hellenism

| 359–336 BC | King Philip II of Macedonia gains control of Greece. |
| 336–323 BC | Alexander the Great conquers an empire. |

Philip II of Macedonia (359–336 BC) In the north of Greece in the 4th century BC rural tribes lived with kings at their head. One of these tribal leaders, Philip II, succeeded in making Macedonia a powerful kingdom through territorial expansion. In 340 BC the Macedonians moved against central Greece. A coalition of the major free city states under the leadership of Athens had to admit defeat in the summer of 338 BC at the **Battle of Chaeronea**. Philip II made a peace treaty in which the cities were allowed liberties, but he determined the foreign policy. With this power Philip II prepared to conquer the Orient and crossed the Hellespont in the spring of 336 BC. Soon afterwards he was assassinated in the city of Aigai, the capital of Macedonia.

Alexander the Great (336–323 BC) After the murder of Philip in 336 BC, his son Alexander ascended the throne and continued the campaign that Philip had begun. When Alexander died at the age of 33 in 323 BC, he left his successors, the rivalling Diadochi, territorial dominions that stretched from the Danube to the Nile and from the Adriatic to the Indus. The countless legends around the figure of Alexander give an idea of the status this warrior-king would later have as a role model. With all his endeavours to conquer the world, Alexander had little time to order the conglomerate of subjugated countries into a unified state. Even though Alexander's empire fell apart during the **Wars of the Diadochi**, his military campaigns had spread Greek culture and language over all the Middle East and Egypt. Hellenism, characterized by refinement in the arts and specialization in the sciences, left its mark on the ancient world.

Rhodes ▶ Rhodes was one of the cultural centres of that time; it resisted a siege by Diadoch Demetrios Poliokretes and as a victory monument built a 32m/105ft-high statue of the sun god Helios (292 BC), which as the **Colossus of Rhodes** was considered one of the seven wonders of

Kamiros on Rhodes is a good example of a Hellenistic city

the ancient world. As the trade hub for the entire eastern Mediterranean Sea, the island flourished economically and was a centre of art and science.

Roman Domination and the Byzantine Empire

63 BC	Greece is made a Roman province.
AD 395	Division of the Roman Empire
1204	Constantinople conquered by the Crusaders

After military success in the Adriatic the aspiring Roman republic made diplomatic approaches to Greece in the late 3rd century BC. However, the efforts of the Macedonian king **Perseus** to regain hegemony over Greece were not tolerated by Rome. The conflicts with Macedonia led in the end to its conquest: Macedonia was incorporated into the Roman-ruled territories in 148 BC. Only two years after Macedonia's defeat, the fate of all of Greece was decided with the defeat of the Achaean League.

Macedonia incorporated into the Roman Empire (148 BC)

Greece becomes a Roman province (63 BC)

Rome's goal was to occupy and transform the autonomous Greek city states into a Roman province. When Athens sided against Rome in its war against the king of Pontus in northern Asia Minor, Mithridates VI, the Roman general **Pompey** took away its special position and placed it under Roman provincial administration. The Greek states were now subject to the Roman province of Macedonia, which meant that Greek history became a part of Roman history for the following centuries. The **Ionian Islands**, however, had a special status: as an important base for the fleet they remained relatively independent during the 500 years of continuous Roman rule.

Division of the Roman Empire (AD 330 to c AD 400)

The Roman Empire was partitioned in the 4th century AD. From the day in the year AD 330 when the first Eastern Roman and Christian emperor, Constantine I, chose the ancient city of Byzantion to be his capital until the end of the 14th century, Greece was part of the **Eastern Roman Empire**.

Byzantium resolutely separated itself from Rome and introduced Christianity as the state religion in 391. The end of the Roman Empire came with its formal division in 395 by Theodosius. The Latin language and the Roman concept of empire increasingly lost importance, and Byzantium claimed the role of successor to the Greek culture of antiquity.

Remains of a Roman aqueduct on Lesbos

The onslaught of Germanic tribes that destroyed the Western Roman Empire also threatened Byzantium. The situation was stabilized under Justinian I; the Byzantine Empire was secured outwardly, and efforts were made to combine Christianity with Roman-style government internally.

Justinian I (527–565)

Justinian codified Roman law, closed the Platonic Academy in Athens and built the church of Hagia Sophia in Constantinople. The Byzantine Empire reached its greatest extent in the decades of his rule, but this splendour came to an end soon after Justinian's death.

The Arabs invaded the eastern Mediterranean in the 7th century, taking control of a large part of the Byzantine Empire and advancing as far as Crete, which remained Arab for almost a century and a half. The final schism between the Orthodox and Roman Catholic churches came in 1054. The death of **Theodora**, with whom the Macedonian dynasty also died out, plunged the empire into a violent crisis accompanied by civil wars. Its borders were also crumbling. Asia Minor became Turkish, while the Normans conquered southern Italy and crossed over to Epiros.

Early and Middle Byzantine Periods (c 600–1204)

In 1204 Crusaders and Venetians captured Constantinople. This was the end of the era of the Byzantine Empire, which the conquerors divided up amongst themselves. The Kingdom of Thessalonika and a series of principalities were founded by west European ruling houses, but larger sovereign kingdoms also emerged, like the Empire of Nicaea under Theodore I. In 1254, a major part of the Aegean region was incorporated into this successor state of the Byzantine Empire. Michael VII was finally able to recapture Constantinople in 1261. Once again, a Byzantine state was created, but only for a short while. Confusion in the royal succession and civil wars weakened the government, leaving it few resources to fight external threats.

Late Byzantine period (1204–1453)

Venetian Rule and the Order of St John

1204	Crete and the Cyclades come under the control of Venice.
1306	Conquest of Rhodes by the Order of St John
1386	Corfu falls to Venice.

In 1204 Crete and the Cyclades came under the control of Venice. At first the new rulers acted autocratically, but as Venetian rule became more moderate in the course of the centuries, Crete in particular gradually entered a period of cultural flowering that encompassed its monasteries, art and especially literature and painting, as well as the scien-

Crete and the Cyclades under Venetian control

ces. The painter Domenikos Theotokopoulos, called **El Greco** (▶ Famous Persons), probably came from Crete. However, the Venetians could not retain control over all the islands in the face of Ottoman expansion. In 1537 they lost the Cyclades, in 1669 Crete to the Turks.

Ionian Islands under Venetian rule

The Venetian state had more success in the Ionian Sea. In 1386 Venice took the island of **Kerkyra**, which was renamed Corfu; between 1482 and 1684 the Venetians took over the remaining Ionian Islands and ruled them until the demise of their city republic in 1797. Italian remained the official language on Corfu until 1852. While the Turks were a permanent threat to the Ionian Islands for many years, they were never able to conquer the whole archipelago. Corfu and Paxi are the only parts of modern Greece that were never occupied by the Turks. In the Venetian period many merchants, artists and craftsmen fled from the Turks to the islands. The Ionian school of painting, started by several Cretan artists after 1669, attained importance. As a whole the islands can look back on a richer cultural heritage from these centuries than the rest of Greece; the tradition of icon painting continued here, for example.

Rhodes and the Order of St John

In 1306 the Order of St John, the oldest of the religious orders of knights, drove the Byzantine governor from **Rhodes** with the approval of the pope and the help of Genoese pirates; they conquered the island in the face of bitter resistance in a three-year war. The order changed from an army of knights to a naval power that raided Muslim warships and trading vessels. In the years of the knights' rule the island, which had been on the periphery of historical events since the 7th century, gained importance. It became a military outpost of the West and an important station for trade between Europe and the Orient. The knights had to ward off attacks by the Turks again and again; finally in 1522 they were forced to surrender to a massive Turkish siege force. Rhodes as well as some of the neighbouring islands were turned over to the Ottomans after 200 years of rule by the Order of St John.

Ottoman Rule

| 14th–15th century | The Ottoman Turks conquer Greece |
| 1821–27 | Greek struggle for independence |

Conquest of Greece by the Ottomans (14th century)

The expansion of the Ottoman Empire changed what until then had been a world of small and medium-sized Islamic and Aegean states

The conquest of the Greek islands by the Turks began →
in the mid-15th century. Rhodes Town fell in 1522.

into a unified sphere of Turkish power. As often before, the consistent application of new weaponry and military technology – the Ottomans used firearms on a large scale for the first time – paved the way for a people to become a great power. Large parts of Greek territory had already come into Ottoman possession by the 14th century. The fall of Athens in 1456 only marked the end of Turkish conquests. The Venetians became the Turks' most important opponents in the Mediterranean. For a century they fought over maritime trading privileges and Greek territory. In the **Battle of Lepanto** a Venetian and Spanish alliance dealt the Turks a crushing defeat in 1571. However, the sultan was able to secure possession of all of Greece in the treaty of 1573, because the victorious alliance showed itself to be in discord and Venice proceeded tactically with great caution. Like all other peoples dominated by the Ottoman Turks, the Greeks had the status of semi-citizens. This meant extensive religious freedom and the preservation of their cultural identity. The Muslim ruling dynasty was able to integrate the subjugated peoples into its empire through a so-called blood tax, a levy of young men who were raised to be a military and government elite in the Janissary corps and in the court and administrative apparatus.

17th and 18th century

While the first decades of Ottoman rule were marked by a prosperous economy, the tax burden greatly increased in the 17th century as a result of internal crises in the Turkish empire. In order to escape the increasing exploitation of the rural Greek population by the Muslim ruling class, large numbers of serfs and the dispossessed formed robber bands. Sea trade brought about renewed economic growth by the 18th century. Greek merchants dominated the Black Sea trade and along with goods from western countries brought the ideas of the Enlightenment and national movements to their home country.

Greek War of Independence (1821–30)

Resistance to the sclerotic Ottoman regime was organized in secret societies. Supported by Greek merchants in Constantinople, the Fanariots, and the Orthodox Church, they initiated a national uprising. Particularly the Filiki Eteria (Society of Friends), founded in 1814 in Odessa and led by Prince **Alexandros Ypsilanti**, actively promoted revolts. In 1821, he crossed the Pruth River into Turkish territory with his corps of volunteers, giving the signal for the national uprising against the sultan. The Cyclades soon took part in the battle for independence. They took in many refugees from the islands off the coast of Asia Minor; the population of the islands, until then sparsely inhabited, grew to more than 20,000. Despite initial setbacks the movement declared independence in 1822 during the First National Assembly of Epidauros. The response in Europe was great, since the Greek desire for national self-determination struck a chord with contemporary romantic sentiment. Thus the English poet Lord Byron (▶Famous People) and King Ludwig I of Bavaria supported the Greek independence movement in word and deed. Writers such as

Friedrich Hölderlin and the painter Eugène Delacroix drew attention to the Greek cause. The intervention of Britain, Russia and France finally proved decisive in battle. This alliance utterly destroyed the Ottoman and Egyptian fleet in 1827 at the Battle of **Navarino**. **Count Ioannis Antonios Kapodistrias**, who was in the diplomatic service of the tsar, was elected the first Greek head of state and began to establish the government of the country from Nauplion. The Ottoman Empire recognized the independence of the Kingdom of Greece at the London Conference of 1830. Two years later the Cyclades were integrated into the newly founded independent Greek state.

Monarchy and Dictatorship (1830–1974)

1835–62	Reign of King Otto I
1862–1923	Parliamentary monarchy
1910–35	Venizelos era
1939–45	World War II
1967–74	Regime of the colonels

The state that was established as a hereditary monarchy in 1830 included today's southern and central Greece, Evia and the Cyclades, but not Crete and the Ionian Islands. When Kapodistrias fell victim to a family feud in October 1831, the major powers, who were determined to Europeanize a country that had been moulded by oriental influence for centuries, installed the still under-age Prince Otto of Wittelsbach as king in 1832. His rule found little sympathy among the Greek people. After a bloodless coup d'état in 1843, the king felt compelled to call a national assembly.

**Otto I
(1835–62)**

The Greek people found the foreign rule of the Bavarian king less and less compatible with the ideals of their struggle for liberation, but the overthrow of the king was only successful after British intrigues. All major military garrisons rebelled in 1862. Otto fled into exile to avoid a civil war. The protective powers agreed amongst themselves to **install, as King George, a Danish prince** of the anglophile house of Holstein-Glücksburg. In 1864, the Greek National Assembly adopted a new constitution that limited the rights of the king significantly and established a parliamentary monarchy. It rested on the sovereignty of the people and universal suffrage for men (women were not given the vote until 1952). In 1864 Britain finally turned the Ionian Islands, which were vital for their fleet and had been a British protectorate since 1815, over to Greece.

**Parliamentary monarchy
(1862–1923)**

The effects of unification with the Greek state were not all favourable for the islands: the centre of political, economic and cultural activities was moved to Athens. However a new source of income was developing, the most important branch of the economy today. Empress Elisabeth (Sisi) of Austria enjoyed staying on Corfu between 1861 and 1898 (▶ Baedeker Special p.180–183), as did Emperor Wilhelm II of Germany from 1907 to 1914.

Era of Venizelos (1910–35)
The dispute with the old rival Turkey over Crete escalated into war in 1897. Within a few months, the Turks stood at the gates of Athens. Through the intervention of the great powers, the war ended with the Treaty of Constantinople, which imposed harsh conditions on Greece. With the support of the nationalistically aroused masses, the military seized power in 1909 and in 1910 placed government in the hands of the leader of the Liberal Party, the Cretan **Eleftherios Venizelos**. Venizelos had set himself at the head of the »Great Idea« movement to enlarge Greece when he proclaimed the union of Crete with the Kingdom of Hellas in 1908; Crete did not officially become part of Greece until 1913.

World War I ▶
In a dispute over entering World War I massive intervention by the western powers prevented a burgeoning civil war and forced **King Constantine** to abdicate in 1917. As a result of World War I, Greece was able to add a substantial amount to its territory; the vision of a greater Greece that was based on ancient borders seemed to have become reality. However, large parts of this territory had to be returned when the war against Turkey was lost five years later. In 1920, the mood of the people once again turned to the royalists. Venizelos suffered a defeat in the parliamentary elections, while **King Constantine I** returned to the throne from exile in Switzerland.

Greco-Turkish War (1921–22) ▶
Greece lost the Greco-Turkish War of 1921–22, which it had begun without the backing of the great powers, and was forced to absorb an immense flood of refugees (about 1.5 million people). The only response to this social catastrophe was a fundamental land reform. In the **Treaty of Lausanne** of 1923, the border with Turkey was readjusted and Greece lost its settlements in Asia Minor. Italy got the islands of Rhodes and the Dodecanese, which it had taken from Turkey during the Italo-Turkish War in 1912 and occupied ever since.

The radical wing of the Venizelist party achieved the abolition of the monarchy in 1924, but the republic proclaimed in March proved to be as unstable as the parliamentary monarchy preceding it. The world economic crisis of the late 1920s had a particularly grave effect on Greece, which was highly indebted. The monarchy was reintroduced under General Metaxas with the help of a rigged referendum and, after twelve years, **King George II** once again took the throne.

World War II
At the beginning of World War II the axis powers, Italy and Germany, put pressure on Greece. In 1940 Corfu was bombed by Italy and conquered; until September 1943 it remained under Italian con-

trol. On **Crete Operation Mercury**, a bloody battle for the island, began in May 1941. After the conquest of Greece by the Germans, British troops had withdrawn to Crete. In the largest airborne operation in history until then, German paratroopers and mountain infantry conquered the island despite heavy losses. The **Cyclades** were also occupied by German troops, but experienced hardly any fighting. After the Italians declared a truce with the Allies, Germans reprisals began. In 1943 the **island of Corfu** was bombed by the German Luftwaffe and occupied; there was considerable damage. In November 1944 the last German troops left Greek territory – except for Crete and a few islands. Because of the naval battles in the Mediterranean Sea, German forces could not withdraw from Rhodes. In May 1945 the Germans surrendered to the British.

After the end of the war, a conflict that had long been smouldering between the old political cliques and the communists flared into a civil war. The British intervened in December 1944 and helped the conservative National Guard to win. The royalists gained a majority at the 1946 parliamentary elections and **King George II** returned from exile in Romania.

Civil War (1944–45)

New and old rulers: the dictator Papadopoulos (centre right) under portraits of the Greek king and queen, who fled into exile in 1967

1950s and 1960s	In 1947 the **Paris Peace Treaties** regulated territorial claims in the Balkans. Italy, which had occupied the islands of the Dodecanese since the Balkan Wars of 1912–13, was forced to return them, thus giving Greece its present territorial extent. From 1952 until the crisis of 1967 stable governments were in power. Greece joined NATO in 1952 and economic activity reached pre-war levels with financial help from the USA. In 1961 **Konstantin Karamanlis** signed a treaty of association with the EEC.
Regime of the colonels (1967–74)	The army staged a putsch on 21 April 1967. Colonels **Papadopoulos** and **Pattakos** established a reign of terror in Greece that elicited growing protests at home and abroad. Contrary to the provisions of the constitution, Papadopoulos ordered the abolition of the monarchy in 1973; he proclaimed a republic and named himself president. A budding economic upswing collapsed altogether in the oil crisis and worldwide recession of 1973. Violent student unrest in Athens induced the fall of the dictatorship. The attempt to bring **Cyprus** completely under Greek control provoked Turkish intervention. On 24 July 1974, in the face of war, the army turned over power to former prime minister Karamanlis, who had been called back from exile in Paris.

New Republic

1974	Plebiscite for the republic
2004	The party ND gains a parliamentary majority and Kostas Karamanlis becomes prime minister. The Olympic Games are held in Athens.

Plebiscite (1974)	With Karamanlis' »government of national unity« the political situation stabilized. The 1952 constitution was reinstated, with the exception of the clause on the form of state. On 8 December 1974, the Greeks decided in a free election to replace parliamentary monarchy by a republic. Still in the same year, Greece withdrew from **NATO** on the grounds that the alliance had been unable to prevent the Greek and Turkish conflict over Cyprus. June 1975 saw the ratification of a new democratic constitution that embodied basic rights. In 1979, the Greek government concluded a membership agreement with the European Community that took effect in 1981. Greece once again became a full member of NATO in 1980.
Present	The **Pan-Hellenist Socialist Movement (PASOK)** led by Konstantinos Simitis won the parliamentary elections of 1981. The central problem of Greece's foreign policy is still its relationship with Turkey: Cyprus is the bone of contention, as is the border of the mainland con-

Kostas Simitis won the parliamentary elections in 2000 as the leader of the PASOK party

tinental shelf in the Aegean. In 2002 the euro was introduced as the official currency. **Nea Dimokratia (ND)** gained a majority in the March 2004 elections and Kostas Karamanlis became prime minister. In August 2004 the **Olympic Games** were held in Athens. Karolos Papoulias (PASOK) has been president since March 2005.

The killing of a 15-year-old boy in December 2008 by a stray police bullet led to violent **unrest and looting** by youths in Athens and other cities. Decades of neglect of the educational system, socio-political lapses and high youth unemployment were behind the unrest.

In September 2009 the PASOK under GEorgios Papandreou won the elections. Only extensive support measures by the European Union and the International Monetary Fund could save Greece from **national bankruptcy** in 2010. But drastic tax increases and budget cuts had to be put throgh in return, albeit against heavy popular resistance. Pensions and salaries of public service employees were cut, the minimum wage was reduced and the retirement age was raised.

Art and Culture

What marks have the various foreign rulers left on the islands? What is an iconographic programme? How important are music and dancing to the islanders? What role does tradition play in their lives?

Art History

Visual art, poetry and philosophy are great and lasting achievements that have given ancient Greece its classical status in the history of Western civilization. While Johann J. Winckelmann, the founder of classical studies in the 18th century, still defined the classical period as the first millennium before Christ, the epoch-making discoveries of Schliemann, Evans and others in the late 19th century expanded our view of history far back into the second and even the third millennium before Christ through their discoveries of the Mycenaean and Minoan world.

Classical antiquity

In the transition from the Neolithic to the Bronze Age, between 3200 and 2000 BC, an independent culture developed on the Cyclades. The best known artefacts of this epoch are the marble idols that are recognizable by their slender bodies and geometric, strongly simplified facial features. They were not only used on the Cyclades but also exported to other parts of Greece.

Cycladic culture

The Bronze Age civilization on the island of Crete is named after the legendary **King Minos**. Among the important cultural achievements of the Early Minoan period (about 3300–2100 BC) are the production of bronze artefacts and the introduction of the potter's wheel. Minoan art reached its peak with the construction of large palaces. Profound political and economic changes on the island and the development of a priestly kingship were the social prerequisites for the monumental architecture that can be admired in Knossos, Phaestos, Malia and Kato Zakros. The upper floors of the multi-storey palaces, which were built on steep slopes, were reached by monumental flights of steps.

Minoan culture on Crete (c 3300 to 1400 BC)

The rooms of state were decorated with precious **wall paintings** of festivals, cult games and courtly life as well as paradise-like landscapes in which exotic animals romped. Besides the Minoan palaces, grand villas, presumably used as summer residences, have also partially survived on Crete, as well as shaft, passage and chamber tombs. The arts of the **potter and goldsmith, work in ivory, gem cutting and seal engraving** were well established. Ceramic art is comparatively well documented. The potter's wheel, introduced from Anatolia, and new firing techniques made the production of jugs with beak-shaped spouts possible. The vessels are decorated with drawings or reliefs. The Kamares style with abstract designs composed of spirals and stylized leaves, which was used after 2100 BC, was replaced around 1700 BC by a rich decor of natural-looking plant and marine motifs such as the reed pattern.

← *Masterly fresco in the Panagia Kera Church in Kritsa on Crete*

**Geometric art
(1050–700 BC)**

Art that can be described as Greek in a narrower sense of the word developed in the »dark« centuries after the **Dorian** invasion (around 1200 BC). The Geometric style is named after geometric line designs on pottery. Circumferential bands of patterns consisting of concentric circles or semicircles are typical for the Protogeometric phase; later friezes of triangles and rhombus shapes appeared, and the meander became the principal ornamental motif. During the course of the 8th century BC, in the Late Geometric style, pictures of people and animals increasingly appeared alongside the purely geometric patterns, which they gradually supplanted.

The scenes, for example entombment and lamentation of the dead, primarily had a connection to death, but there were also hunting and battles scenes and pictures of gymnasts, dancers and musicians. The types of vessels (amphorae, krater) changed during the Geometric period. Their individual parts (foot, belly, neck) became more pronounced and created tension by means of their varying proportions. The Attic workshops were the leaders, especially those in Athens. Early, small temples like the Heraion on Samos were erected in the Geometric period.

Archaic Art (c 700–500 BC)

**Monumental
sculptures**

The Archaic period saw the emergence of life-size statues, executed in marble or limestone, and usually painted in colour. The artists found inspiration for these monumental sculptures in Egypt and in oriental countries with which the Greeks traded. The precious marble used for these sculptures mostly came from quarries on the islands of Naxos or Paros.

Two types of figures predominate in Archaic monumental sculptures: the female clothed statue, the **kore**, and the naked youth, called **kouros**. The hallmarks of the early type of kouros are frontal representation of the figure and stylized treatment of the body that emphasizes its joints. The three-dimensional and anatomically correct depiction of the body increased in the later period even though the frontal, slightly forward-stepping stance of the figure, with the arms held to the side of the body and fists clenched, remained obligatory until the 6th century BC. An especially impressive kouros figure can be seen in the archaeological museum in Samos Town.

**Pediment
sculpture**

When stone became established as the building material for temples and treasuries during the 7th century BC, large-scale relief figures also developed as architectural decoration for pediments and entablatures. The Temple of Artemis (600 BC) on Corfu, one of the first sanctuaries built completely stone, already had two sculpted pediments and metopes with reliefs. Characteristic of this early phase of relief sculpture ist that the figures were in relatively flat relief.

Amphora (around 450 BC) in the red-figure style →

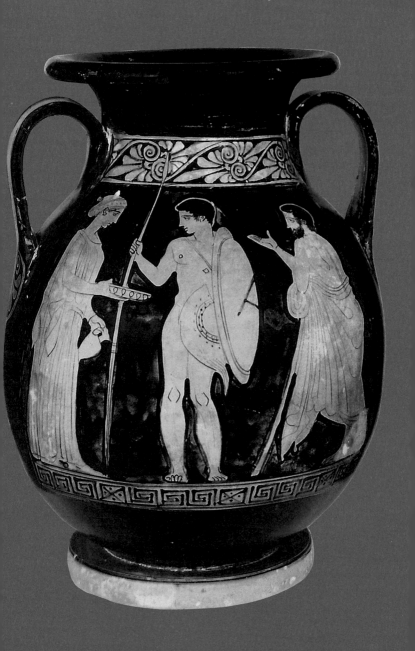

Basic forms of Greek Temples

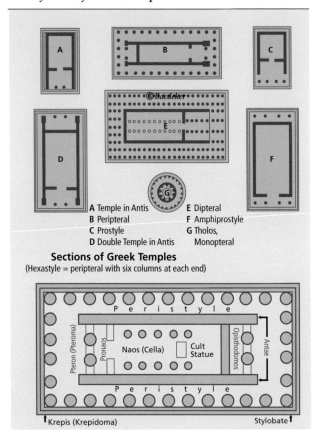

A Temple in Antis   E Dipteral
B Peripteral   F Amphiprostyle
C Prostyle   G Tholos,
D Double Temple in Antis   Monopteral

Sections of Greek Temples
(Hexastyle = peripteral with six columns at each end)

Peristyle

Pteron (Pteroma) · Pronaos · Naos (Cella) · Cult Statue · Opisthodomos · Antae

Peristyle

Krepis (Krepidoma)   Stylobate

Vase painting
Black-figure pottery ►

Pottery production presented a picture of great diversity at the start of the Archaic period. The Cyclades, the eastern islands including Rhodes, and Athens were the centres of ceramic art. The details were engraved with a hard stylus, and those within the contours of the silhouette figures were often very delicately executed. The motifs in the vase paintings reveal regional differences. Usually themes from **Greek mythology** were the subject of the pictures, which are characterized by the representation of several figures, juxtaposed as in a frieze their heads at the same height. The vase painting of the eastern islands mainly shows animal friezes and the total impression of the décor is more ornamental and flatter than in other areas of Greece.

Red-figure pottery ►

The red-figure style developed a little later. It worked with the same colour contrasts as the mature black-figure pictures, only reversed:

now the background was black and the figures retained the reddish colour of the clay. The drawings within the contours were no longer incised but rendered in glossy black or matt lines. The figures of such illustrations gain in plasticity compared with the black-figure silhouettes.

The Greek Temple

The stone monumental temple is considered to be one of the major accomplishments of ancient Greek art. The beginnings of temple construction date back to the 9th century BC. The simplest form of temple – not a gathering place for the faithful but rather a place for cult images – derived from a basic form typical of a Greek dwelling (megaron). In the early temples the windowless, rectangular inner chamber of the temple, called the naos or (in Latin) cella, stood on a base of undressed stone. The entrance to the cella was usually on the east side, with the image of the deity opposite on the west wall. It was not until the second half of the 7th century BC that marble or limestone was used for all parts of the structure.

From an early period various temple forms developed. The simplest type is the temple *in antis*, in which the portico, the pronaos, is formed by the protruding walls of the naos, called antae. Two columns supporting the pediment stand between the antae. If the rear of the naos also has a porch (opisthodomos), then it becomes a double anta temple, e.g. the core of the Temple of Aphaia on Aegina. When the porch of such a temple has a row of columns in front of it supporting the pediment – as can be seen on the Acropolis in Athens in the east cella of the Erechtheion – then it is termed a prostylos or prostyle temple. If the row of columns is repeated at the rear of the structure, it is then called an amphiprostylos, like the Temple of Nike on the Acropolis of Athens. **[Temple forms]**

The most striking form of Greek temple after the second half of the 7th century BC is the peripteros, where the cella is surrounded on all sides by a colonnade, the peristasis or peristyle. The porch on the entrance side corresponds to the opisthodomos at the other end. The classic proportions, used since the 5th century BC, called for the sides to have twice the number of columns of the ends, plus one; the ratio at the Athenian Parthenon is 8:17. If the temple has a double row of columns all around, then the peripteros becomes a **dipteros** (e.g. the Olympieion in Athens). If the inner row of these two is missing it is a pseudodipteros with a large space between the cella and peristyle. **◄ Peripteros**

Next to the rectangular temple, the form of the round temple (tholos) only plays a minor role. It consists of a cella with a perfectly round ground plan, surrounded by a circle of columns. Individual temples vary, however, not only in their overall plan but also in the forms and proportions of columns and entablature. **◄ Circular temples**

Classical orders of columns

Doric order ▶ The oldest Greek stone temples follow the Doric order. The characteristic of these buildings is a ponderous and squat impression. This is due in part to their relatively thick columns, tapering towards the top with between 16 and 20 flutings in their shafts and standing without a base directly on the stylobate, the top step of the temple platform. The Doric capital, consisting of a circular convex moulding (echinus) and a square slab (abacus), bears the architrave and the frieze of sculpted triglyphs and flat or sculpted metopes. The **tympanum** is framed by horizontal and raking (diagonal) cornices. Reliefs are found on the metopes and on the tympanum. When limestone was used to build a temple instead of marble it was stuccoed and then painted. Since the colour has remained in only a few places, they were thought to be a »classical« white when Greek art was rediscovered in the 18th century.

Ionic order ▶ The Ionic order is particularly suited for large temples as found on Samos. An Ionic temple appears more graceful and elegant than a Doric temple, both in its individual parts and in the total impression. The columns stand on a base, while narrow ridges between the fluting stress their vertical character. The characteristic elements of the capitals are the volutes, scrolled at both ends. Above the tripartite architrave a frieze without triglyphs runs around the outside.

Corinthian order ▶ The Corinthian order is the same as the Ionic, except for the capital. The Corinthian capital has sculpted decoration in the form of large, deeply lobed acanthus leaves that encompass its round body. Tendrils curve up to the corners of the concave abacus. The Corinthian order was particularly widespread during the time of imperial Rome, where the composite capital, which was composed of the Ionic and Corinthian orders in combination, was developed and richer decorations were added.

Classical Art (490–330 BC)

The Archaic period ended with the fall of the Peisistratids (510 BC) and finally with the Persian Wars (490–479 BC). What followed was the Classical century, the absolute zenith of Greek culture, whose centre in the areas of visual art, poetry and philosophy became more and more closely identified with Athens. The extent to which Athens was the centre of the Greek world around 450 BC is shown in the concentration of effort employed to extend the Acropolis in the age of Pericles.

Phidias The cella of the **Parthenon temple** (447–438 BC) was planned to hold the giant gold and ivory statue of Athena Parthenos made by the Athenian sculptor and architect Phidias, who was famous during his own lifetime. Pericles had placed him in charge of the building of the temple. He designed all the sculptural decoration for the Parthenon – 92 metopes, a 160m/525ft frieze and the two immense pedi-

ment reliefs. However, Phidias gar-
nered most of his fame for his
monumental statue of Athena Parthenos, of which only Roman copies are extant.

Hellenistic Art (323–27 BC)

The cultural period between the
death of Alexander the Great (323
BC) and the creation of the Roman
province of Achaia (27 BC) is designated as Hellenistic. During these
three centuries, Greek art spread as

Rhodian artists created the famous Laocoön group (copy in the Grand Master's Palace in Rhodes Town)

far as Asia and was in turn perme-
ated by oriental influences. The flourishing capitals of the newly independent parts of Alexander's empire, chiefly Alexandria and Pergamon, emerged as new centres of art alongside the cities of the Peloponnese and the coast of Asia Minor.

Architecture

The trading cities and their Hellenistic rulers, desiring a lavish display of their power, were the motor for the creation of Hellenistic architecture. Marketplaces, the focus of city life, were now laid out according to a plan and adorned with public buildings. Not only palaces but also private homes were furnished with expensive
decorations: sculptures, wall paintings and mosaics. Hellenistic
builders used mainly the Ionic and Corinthian orders in their temples. Just after 300 BC the complex of the Asclepieion on Kos was begun. It was expanded in the 2nd century to an extensive terraced
complex. On Rhodes the Temple of Athena Lindia was given an elaborate ensemble of stairways and halls.

Sculpture

Sculpture underwent a change in style from the late Classical to the
Hellenistic period under **Lysippus** and his school. An increased psychological and dramatic content becomes noticeable in the course of
the 3rd century BC, a preference for diagonal tensions and complex
twisting of the body, which had been studied in exact anatomical detail. This can especially be observed in famous works like the figure
of **Nike of Samothrace** (190 BC; Louvre, Paris; ► photo p.368),
which is originally thought to have been a monument celebrating the
victory of Rhodes over Antiochos III of Syria. The forward motion
of the body is accompanied by a spiral twisting that leads the viewer
around the statue.

Venus de Milo, Laocoön and his Sons

The two major developments of the following period are represented
by two world-famous works: the *Aphrodite de Melos*, better known as
the *Venus de Milo*, created at the end of the 2nd century BC (Paris,

MARBLE BEAUTY

Milos can boast of being the place where one of the most famous ancient works of art was found, but it is a long time since the island has owned this outstanding statue.

The farmer **Georgios Kentrotas** stared in astonishment at the gleaming white parts of a marble figure that he found in April 1820 while ploughing his stony farmland below the town of Tripiti on the island of Milos. Little by little Kentrotas unearthed a marble statue that had split into two pieces. The arms had broken off and the left hand held an apple. Without a doubt it was a life-size statue of the goddess Aphrodite. The farmer, of course, talked about his find and soon it came to the attention of a Frenchman who was staying on the island. It was decided quickly to acquire the statue for **France**. Without much ado a deal was made with the farmer Georgios. However, when the secretary of the French ambassador arrived on Milos in May 1820 in order to pick up the Venus he found out that the **Turkish rulers** had offered a better deal and were at that very moment loading the statue onto a ship as a present for a prince in Constantinople. The secretary intervened on the spot, insisted on his contract with the farmer Georgios and was finally able to acquire the statue for a substantial increase in price – but without the arms, which were lost in the fracas and never found again. After the French ambassador decided to make a present of the enchanting goddess to King Louis XVIII, Venus de Milo (Italian for Milos) arrived in Paris in February 1821.

Bad luck for Milos

The Venus de Milo embodies the **late Hellenistic ideal of beauty** with her slender figure, a robe draped around her long legs, her naked torso and full breasts, narrow shoulders and delicate head with hair parted in the middle. But Milos can only boast of being the statue's place of origin. It now stands in the Louvre and is daily surrounded by crowds who pay tribute to the goddess of eternal beauty.

Venus de Milo: a world-famous masterpiece of Hellenistic art

Louvre) ►Baedeker Special p.58), and *Laocoön and his Sons*, (original in the Vatican Museum in Rome, a copy in the Grand Master's Palace in Rhodes Town on Rhodes). Only the marble copy of this sculpture made in the 1st century BC by three sculptors of the isle of Rhodes, Hagesandros, Polydoros and Athanodoros, has survived. *Laocoön and his Sons* unites principles of the Classical approach, e.g. frontal positioning, with inner and external dynamics typical of Hellenistic statuary.

In the Hellenistic period mosaic art blossomed, especially through the use of coloured tesserae, as on the sacred island of Delos. The mosaics of Dioskourides from the island of Samos give an idea of the scope of Hellenistic visual arts.

Mosaic art

Roman Period
(2nd–1st century BC to 4th century AD)

In the Roman period new elements were added to the Hellenistic tendencies: personal characteristics in portrait art and historical subjects on reliefs. Greek portraiture until then was usually a full-length statue of a person in a more or less idealized form. Sculptors now began to model facial features as individually and realistically as possible. In the fourth century AD reliefs were strictly frontal, a feature which was dominant in Byzantine art, especially in icons.

Sculpture

A number of architectural styles were slightly modified under Roman rule, and a number of typically Roman building types, like the triumphal arch, aqueduct and baths, were adopted.
Moreover, Roman mastery of vaulting techniques made larger and more daring structures possible than during the era of Hellenism. Greek Classical forms, however, remained the favoured style.

Architecture

Marvellous Roman mosaic floors have survived not only on the Greek mainland, but also on the larger islands. Most of them can be seen in archaeological museums. As wall paintings in private dwellings have been lost, the mosaics alone convey an impression of domestic life in Roman city and country residences.

Mosaics

Byzantine Period
(4th–15th centuries AD)

The founding of Constantinople in AD 330 and the **division of the Roman Empire into western and eastern (Byzantine) parts** 65 years later brought to the eastern Mediterranean region a new cultural era that lasted until the Byzantine Empire fell in 1453. The art that was created in Greece at this time was influenced by Christianity.
It is therefore not surprising that the architects, painters and sculptors of the Byzantine era no longer sought and found their inspira-

tion in ancient Greek art, but rather in the Christian art of late antiquity. Along with extant churches, monasteries and numerous smaller collections, the Byzantine Museum in Athens above all gives a comprehensive picture of this cultural epoch.

Painting and mosaics

Byzantine painting ranges from monumental to miniature, from icons to frescoes, mosaics and woven tapestries. There are countless examples of Byzantine sacred art. Miniatures decorate medieval manuscripts, e.g. on Patmos; magnificent mosaics have survived on Chios. The **Iconoclastic Controversy** (726–843) played a decisive role in the development of iconography, as the question of whether or not Christ and the saints could be portrayed led to a regular civil war. The supporters of icons won in the end but had to develop a strict canon of figures.

Architecture

Basilica ▶

The first churches on Greek soil were built when Christianity was adopted as the state religion in the 4th century. The dominant form of early Christian church buildings was the basilica. In this type of building, which developed out of the Roman market basilica, the nave is flanked by one or two lower aisles on each side. The altar is at the east end while the entrance, with a narthex and often an atrium too in front of it, is in the west.

Crossing dome ▶

In the course of the centuries, ecclesiastical architecture developed away from a longitudinal orientation and towards a central ground plan with two axes of equal length. A new type became established in the 9th century throughout the Byzantine trading area: the church with a dome crossing. Above the four arms of the cross-shaped church, which were usually equally long with barrel vaults, rose a central dome. The sanctuary is separated by a stone screen which later evolved into the **iconostasis** (wall of icons). On either side are two smaller apses for liturgical purposes, called the prothesis and the diaconicon. Accordingly, as a rule the church has three apses on the east side. In the west an outer porch (exonarthex) was often added to the narthex. The decoration of the church was governed by an **iconographic scheme** guided by the concept that the church interior should reflect the heavenly hierarchy.

Art during the Ottoman Period (15th–19th centuries)

The almost 400-year rule of the Ottoman Turks in Greece began in 1456 with the capture of Athens. Post-Byzantine art on the Balkan peninsula no longer had the significance of the art of past centuries, but Turkish rule allowed enough latitude for Byzantine-influenced art to continue. On Crete, which belonged to Venice from 1204 to 1669, secular buildings such as harbour and defensive architecture as well as prestigious residences show Venetian influence. In the 16th century the Venetians brought art on Crete into contact with the Renaissance.

Mural in the Monastery of St John on Patmos

The traditional methods of building in Greece were characterized primarily by the climatic conditions and the materials available locally. Thus white-washed cube-shaped houses were typical of the Cyclades, one-storey square houses with flat roofs the dominant type on Lindos (Rhodes). On the other hand, the various occupying forces also left their mark on Greek architecture. The influence of Frankish rulers is apparent in the old part of town on the Cyclades island of Naxos, and English and French influences are evident in the Ionian Islands, especially on Corfu.

Music

The roots of modern Greek music lie in Byzantine sacred music and in the folk song, which developed different characteristics during the centuries of Turkish rule. An example of this are the so-called **klepht and bandit songs**, melancholy music about the longing for freedom and bitter resistance battles in the mountains. The singers of klepht songs are accompanied by a lyre or a pan flute.

Italian opera had great influence on the development of music in the 18th and 19th centuries; it was spread through the Italian occupation of the Ionian Islands in the early 18th century. That led to the development of the **Ionian School**, whose spiritual father was the first major modern Greek composer **Nikolaos Mantzaros** (1795–1872).

Alan Bates and Anthony Quinn in »Zorba the Greek«: totally opposite characters

WHEN ZORBA DANCES THE SIRTAKI

The famous novel »Zorba the Greek« by the Cretan writer Nikos Kazantzakis was the basis for the Michael Cacoyannis hit film of the same name with Anthony Quinn in the title role.

»A stranger of about sixty, very tall and lean, with staring eyes, had pressed his nose against the pane and was looking at me. He was holding a little flattened bundle under his arm. The thing which impressed me most was his eager gaze, his eyes, ironical and full of fire. At any rate, that is how they appeared to me. As soon as our eyes had met, he seemed to be making sure I was really the person he was looking for...« Thus begins the strange encounter between a young English writer and a man named Alexis Zorba, and two more contrasting men could hardly be imagined. The one, educated, introverted and rather more at home in his books than in real life; the other, full of a lust for life and a fierce passion in all that he does, a man that primarily lives from his gut and heart. It is the story of a friendship between men told in front of the backdrop of everyday Cretan life in all its harshness, but also in all its poetry and unspoiled archaic beauty. The author of this story, **Nikos Kazantzakis**, was a native of Crete and, great as his attachment to his homeland was, he was also an extremely cosmopolitan spirit and a sharp-sighted critic of his fellow countrymen. Although he was no longer unknown as a writer in Greece, his novel about Alexis Zorba published in 1946 made him instantly world famous.

What many do not know is that Alexis Zorba is not a pure invention of Kazantzakis, but that he actually existed. The real Zorba was named Giorgos and was a miner. Their paths crossed in the year 1916. The writer spent several months together with the Macedonian miner in the Peloponnese digging for lignite – the true-to-life antecedent for the mining project in the novel. Hardly anyone

could have imagined that Giorgos Zorba or, more precisely the Zorba that Kazantzakis made of him, would go down in world literature as the hero of a novel! The success of the novel, however, was only the prologue for even greater popularity that the story of these two men would garner through the film version.

With *Zorba the Greek*, director **Michael Cacoyannis** succeeded in creating a film in 1964 that drew people to the cinemas in droves and was heaped with praise by the critics. *Zorba the Greek* quickly became a classic in film history. The film was shot on the original locations on Crete, primarily in the little fishing village of Stavrós on the Akrotiri Peninsula. Many things that appear to be genuine Greek in the film turn out on second glance to be a (clever) deception, such as the **sirtaki** that Anthony Quinn so captivatingly dances. Because the ac-

tor could not be expected to learn the complicated Cretan folk dances during the short period during which the film was shot, he was only required to dance a simple version to **Mikis Theodorakis'** music. Most holidaymakers incorrectly believe the sirtaki is a traditional dance. It would not be news to anyone who has seen more than one film made from a book that Cacoyannis' film simplified a lot of the novel. Naturally, Cacoyannis created characters of the main figures that border on being overdrawn clichés. The fact that they appear so convincing is thanks to the excellent cast. But it was the star, **Anthony Quinn**, who won over the audience most of all. Quinn seemed so tailor-made for the role of this master of the art of living that the actor and the role became one for the audience – Quinn was not acting Zorba, he was Zorba.

Increased urbanization led to the growth of western influence in the area of musical entertainment in the early 20th century. Contemporary music was a mixture of folk songs, Byzantine and Turkish music, Italian-influenced kantades from the Ionian Islands and finally imports from other countries, like tango, which was popular in the 1920s.

Rembetiko developed in the 1920s in the poor neighbourhoods and taverns of Piraeus. The lyrics of these songs are about the lives of social outcasts, pickpockets, their drug use, their daily problems, love and pain. The songs are accompanied on a type of bouzouki that was created specially for this music, the baglama, made out of a hollowed-out pumpkin, a piece of wood and some wires as strings. Today rembetiko is one of the pillars of Greek folk music. Along with the pop-

The lyra is present in every musical performance.

ular bouzouki, the music was also played on a santouri, a trapezoidal guitar and various woodwind instruments.

Customs

Customs and folklore

It is still occasionally possible to see people (mainly older ones) wearing folk costumes on festive occasions, particularly in rural areas. One component of the men's folk dress is the »fustanella«, a short kilt trimmed with small bells and coins, usually worn together with a white shirt and an embroidered waistcoat. On Crete, men still often wear the characteristic pleated, black baggy trousers (vraka) and a black headscarf. Old costumes are also sometimes worn on Karpathos, in the south of Rhodes and on Corfu. The colourful uniform of the former royal bodyguard, the **Evzones** – the »finely girded« – which was derived from Albanian folk costume, is still worn today by, among others, the guard of honour at the national monument in front of Parliament in Athens.

Folk dance

Music and dance have always gone hand in hand in Greece. Because of the variety of cultural development in the country there are about 150 local dances, but they are performed less and less often. Choreographically there are two major dance forms today: the measured movement of the **syrtos** (»round dance«) and the tempestuous, occasionally almost acrobatic **pidik dances**. Each island and every region of the mainland has developed its own style and variations. Greek circle dances in which the dancers hold hands or a handkerchief have only recently been danced by mixed couples; originally they were performed with the sexes separated. The syrtos, in which the steps are performed with dragging feet, is very popular. The tsamikos, a war dance from Thessaly with heavy, stamping steps, and the kalamatianos, which goes back to antiquity, are very popular. The cheerful ballos, a dance for couples, is also still performed. Many people consider the syrtaki to be the epitome of the Greek folk dance, but it was actually dreamed up in Hollywood for the 1964 movie ***Zorba the Greek***. Since Anthony Quinn had trouble mastering the chassapiko, a simpler version was created for him to the music of Mikis Theodorakis – the syrtaki (►Baedeker Special p.62/63).

Syrtaki

Famous People

Why did the poet Byron join the Greek battle for independence? How did El Greco get to Spain? Why did the novel *Zorba the Greek* become so famous? Here are short tributes to some people connected to the Greek islands.

ΔΟΜΗΝΙΚΟΣ ΘΕΟΤΟΚΟΠΟΥΛΟΣ
EL GRECO

Lord Byron (1788–1824)

Poet

George Gordon, 6th Baron Byron, followed in the footsteps of his ancestors while still a schoolboy at Harrow and student at Trinity College, Cambridge, leading a wild life marked by debts and numerous love affairs. He inherited his title and Newstead Abbey near Nottingham in 1798, and took his seat in the House of Lords in 1809, by which time he had already published verses and begun the work that first made him famous, ***Childe Harold's Pilgrimage***. Between 1809 and 1811 he travelled extensively in southern Europe, including Greece, and the Levant, conceiving the wish to help liberate Greece from Turkish rule. After his return to England he was a celebrated society figure, but scandals and a short failed marriage soon caused him to be ostracized. His path then took him to Italy and later to Greece. As a passionate supporter of the Greek independence movement he raised his own brigade of 500 men. He spent the last months of the year 1823 on Kefallonia and lived in a small house in Metaxata; from here he travelled to Mesolongi on the Greek mainland, where he died of malaria at the age of 36 without seeing serious military engagement. In Greece he was a hero, but his notoriety at home prevented a burial in Westminster Abbey.

Daskalogiannis (d. 1771)

Freedom fighter

The freedom fighter and national hero Ioannis Vlachos, called Daskalogiannis (»Jannis the Teacher«) because of his education, came from Anopolis on the Sfakia Plateau in Crete. This rough, impassable mountain terrain was never really subdued during the centuries of foreign rule – neither by the Saracens, Venetians and Turks nor by the Germans. The ship-owner Daskalogiannis was the leader of a rebellion against the Turks in 1770–71, but had to surrender to them in the fortress Frangokastello when they promised peace negotiations and amnesty for his fellow fighters. The Turks lured him to Iraklio, where the local pasha had him skinned alive – in front of a mirror and in the presence of his brother, who consequently lost his mind.

Epicurus (342/341–271 BC)

Philosopher

Born on the island of Samos, the philosopher started his own school in Athens in 306 BC. Epicurus' philosophy, which was transmitted in three extensive teaching letters and numerous fragments, concentrates on this life with the goal of mankind's spiritual happiness. His works examine the three thematic spheres of epistemology (with perception as the basis), physics (based on Democritus' teaching on the movement of atoms) and ethics (with serenity and virtue as the fundamental principles). His teaching, Epicureanism, was received well

← *El Greco was famous far beyond the borders of Crete*

in late antiquity, but later lost its popularity. To the Romans already the term »Epicurean« had undertones of an unscrupulous sensualist.

Euripides (around 485–406 BC)

Poet The tragedian Euripides was born on the island of Salamina and was the founder of the psychological drama, the character tragedy. His dominant theme was Protagoras' aphorism: »Man is the measure of all things«. In his tragedies, the gods no longer control the destiny of man, but rather man acts independently, lives his own life and struggles through personal conflicts. Of his 70 or more dramas (according to some sources he wrote more than 90), 18 have survived intact and are performed to this day, including *Alcestis*, *Electra* and *Orestes*. Euripides' work was a major influence on the development of drama throughout Europe. Almost all Euripides' great plays have served as the basis for modern works by, among others, Corneille, Racine, Goethe, Schiller, Grillparzer and Sartre.

El Greco (c 1541–1614)

Painter El Greco (»the Greek« in Spanish) was born as Domenikos Theoto-kopoulos around 1541 near Iraklio on Crete. He learned icon paint-ing as a child in his homeland. As a young man he moved to Venice, where he worked in Titian's studio and later went to Rome. Since his name was so difficult to pronounce he was called Il Greco. From 1577 he lived in Toledo, where he painted mainly for clerics and no-blemen. Along with his religious works, he created numerous com-pelling portraits and landscapes. His style is characterized by elon-gated, sinuous figures, expressive colouring and unreal light effects that imbue his paintings with an impression of the ethereal and the supernatural. El Greco died in 1614 in Toledo.

Hippocrates ▶Baedeker Special p.279–281

Nikos Kazantzakis (1883–1957)

Nikos Kazantzakis was born in Iraklio on the island of Crete. He studied law in Athens and afterwards philosophy and political sci-ence in Paris, returning to Greece after his studies. His literary works – descriptions of his many travels, stories, novels and poems – are marked by penetrat-ing descriptions, fresh, original language, abundant lyricism and profound philosophical insight. Kazant-zakis gained international fame with his 1946 **novel** *Zorba the Greek*, which is set on his home island of Crete. The poet translated works by Homer, Dante, Goethe, Shakespeare, Nietzsche, Rimbaud and Garcia Lorca into Greek. Kazantzakis held a ministerial post from 1945 to 1946 in Greece, and died in 1957 in Freiburg in Germany; he was buried on the Martinengo Bastion of the old city wall of Iraklio, because the church had refused to have a free thinker buried in a consecrated cemetery.

Pythagoras (c 570–497/496 BC)

No mathematical equation is more famous than the theorem, $a^2 + b^2 = c^2$, which was named after the philosopher Pythagoras but probably known before his time. Pythagoras himself left no writings and his students were sworn to secrecy. He left his birthplace, Samos, around 530 BC, allegedly to escape the tyranny of Polycrates, and founded a philosophical and religious society of Pythagoreans in Croton in southern Italy. He was venerated by his disciples even during his lifetime as a perfect sage. The Pythagoreans considered numbers to be the essence of all things, as the principle of a »world harmony«.

Philosopher

►Baedeker Special p.298–299

Sappho

Eleftherios Venizelos (1864–1936)

The lawyer and statesman Eleftherios Venizelos, who was born in 1864 in Murnies on Crete, is greatly venerated by his fellow Cretans because of his struggle to bring about the union of Crete and Greece. He founded the Greek Liberal Party and became prime minister of his country for the first time in 1910. He created the modern Greek state through far-reaching domestic reforms. Internationally, he worked for the union of all Greeks and the territorial expansion of Greece by military means. The two Balkan wars (1912–13) did actually bring about a considerable increase in territory and the ultimate annexation of Crete. His further attempts at expansion failed, due to the resistance of the Turks under Mustafa Kemal Pasha (Ataturk). After a failed coup against the government of Tsaldaris, Venizelos went into exile in Paris, where he died in 1936.

Politician

Practicalities

WHICH ARE THE
BEST BEACHES?
WHERE ARE LIVELY
FESTIVALS HELD?
HOW DO YOU
SAY THANK YOU
IN GREEK?

Accommodation

Hotels

Prices Hotel prices vary depending on the season. Bear in mind that at least 16% tax is added to the listed room prices. When compared to west European standards of comfort and prices, Greek hotels – both higher-class and low-end accommodation – often provide poor value for money.

Price per double room

- Luxury: more than 200 €
  Mid-range: 90–200 €
  Budget: 40–90 €

When planning a trip to Greece during high season (from June to September), it is advisable to **book rooms in advance**.

Categories Hotels are officially divided into six categories. They range from luxury hotels (L) to comfortable (A) and mid-range hotels (B, C). At the bottom of the scale is basic accommodation (D, E).

Holiday Apartments

Holiday apartments Holiday cottages and apartments for self-caterers are available on all Greek islands. Travel agencies at home and in Greece can make the arrangements. There are also fine old houses or cliff dwellings (for example on Santorini) that the Greek National Tourist Organization (EOT) has restored. When a ferry arrives in an island port, providers of accommodation are usually waiting to offer their rooms.

Rural holidays Anyone who wants to spend a vacation in the simple but hospitable atmosphere of a farmhouse should try a rural holiday. This kind of accommodation is on offer in, for example, Petra on Lesbos and in several villages on Chios. A brochure is available from the Greek National Tourist Organization (▶Information).

▶ USEFUL ADDRESSES

CAMPING

▶ **Panhellenic Camping Association**
Solonos 102
GR-10680 Athens
Tel. 2 103 62 15 60
Fax 2 10 5 22 27 23
www.greececamping.org

HOTELS

▶ **Chamber of Hotels of Greece**
Stadiou 24
GR-1056 Athens
Tel. 2 10 3 23 71 93
Fax 2 10 3 22 54 49
www.grhotels.gr

YOUTH HOSTELS

www.hihostels.com

Youth Hostels

Young travellers will want to take advantage of the cheap accommodation in youth hostels. Most youth hostels are open all year, but reservations are recommended, and essential in the high season. Reservations, especially for groups, are only valid when paid in advance. The length of stay for individuals in a youth hostel is limited.

Camping

Most campsites in Greece are controlled by the Greek National Tourist Organization. The sites are classified: cat. A = excellent facilities, cat. B = good facilities, cat. C = adequate facilities. Camping outside campsites on roads, parking lots, open land or in rest areas is prohibited.

Arrival · Before the Journey

Many European cities have regular daily flights to Thessaloniki or Athens, most operated by **Olympic Airlines and Aegean Air**. From the UK and Ireland budget airlines offer various options for getting to Greece, including direct flights to the islands. Easyjet has the biggest range, with flights from UK airports to Corfu, Crete, Mykonos, Rhodes and Santorini; jet2.com flies to Corfu, Crete and Rhodes. A number of North American cities, especially New York, have direct connections to Athens, but there are no direct flights from the US west coast. Travellers from Australia are best advised to take a flight to a major European hub such as London, Amsterdam or Frankfurt and from there a connecting flight to Greece. **By air**

Almost all Greek islands can be reached by air from Athens. Changing planes in Athens and Thessaloniki is uncomplicated since baggage is checked through. From Iraklio **Sky Express** flies to a number of islands. Scheduled flights that involve changing planes are often not much more expensive and are usually more frequent than direct charter flights. Moreover, charter flights are only available in the summer to islands with an established tourist industry, while scheduled flights go to other islands as well.

For those who like the idea of driving all the way to Greece, the route on the Balkan highway (Autoput) passes through Slovenia, Croatia, Serbia and Macedonia. Allow 2–3 days to get from Venice to Athens. Transit visas for Serbia and Montenegro can be obtained from their diplomatic missions. EU citizens do not need a visa for travel through Slovenia, Croatia and Macedonia, but must present a passport. **By car**

⏵ USEFUL ADDRESSES

ATHENS AIRPORT
Tel. 21 03 53 00 00
www.aia.gr

OLYMPIC AIRLINES

▶ **In Athens**
Headquarters
Syngrou 96
GR-11741 Athens
Tel. 21 09 66 66 66 (reservations)
www.olympic-air.com

▶ **In Australia**
64 York street, Sydney NSW 2000
Tel. 13 00 086 152
olympicairlines.sydney@worlda-
viation.com.au

▶ **In Canada**
80, Bloor Street West, Suite 502,
Toronto, Ont. M5S 2V1
Tel. 416 964 27 20
admin.yyz@olympicairlines.ca

▶ **In UK**
11, Conduit St., London W1S 2LP
Tel. 871 20 00 500
reservations@olympicairway-
s.co.uk

▶ **In USA**
70-00 Austin Street
Forest Hills, NY 11375
Tel. 800 22 31 226
oausa@olympicairlines.us

FERRY LINES AND AGENCIES

▶ **Timetables**
www.gtp.gr
www.greekferries.gr

▶ **Ferry Lines**
Minoan Lines
www.minoan.gr

ANEK
www.anek.gr

Ventouris Ferries
www.ventouris.gr

Superfast Ferries
www.superfast.com

▶ **Agencies**
Euronautic
Tel. (09 11) 9 26 69 15

Ferries Anyone who wants to avoid driving through Slovenia, Croatia, Serbia and Macedonia, but doesn't want to do without a car, can use one of the many **ferry connections between Italy and Greece**. Ferries run from the Italian Adriatic ports of Trieste, Venice, Ancona, Bari and Brindisi to Igoumenitsa, Corfu and Patras. From Igoumenitsa and Patras drive to Athens, then on to Piraeus to catch ferries to almost all of the Greek islands. There are fewer inter-island connections, and then only in the high season. The most popular crossing for drivers from western Europe, from Venice to Patras, takes about 26 hours, with a further 3–4 hours' drive from Patras to Athens.

By train If you are already on the continent, there is a train connection from Munich via Budapest to Thessaloniki and on to Athens (travel time app. 50 hrs). There are regular trains from Vienna via Budapest and Belgrade to Athens. The long and expensive trip from London to Greece by rail, via Paris, Brindisi and Patras or alternatively via Munich as above, cannot be recommended except for out-and-out railway fans, those unwilling to travel by air, and holders of an Inter-Rail pass who are spending some weeks travelling through Europe.

Entry/Exit Requirements

Greece is party to the Schengen Agreement, so there are no border controls for those arriving from other Schengen states. However, visitors arriving from the UK or Ireland require a valid **passport** (children's passport for children under 12 years). A residence permit (automatically granted to British and Irish citizens) is required for stays beyond three months.

Documents

If a passport has stamps from North Cyprus it is possible that entrance to Greece will not be permitted. European national **driving licences and vehicle documents** are recognized. Vehicles are required to have an oval national identity sticker or European vehicle registration plates. It is recommended to have an international green insurance card.

Those planning on taking along their pets to Greece are required to have an **EU Pet Passport** with proof of a rabies vaccination. Information for UK travellers can be found on the DEFRA website http://www.defra.gov.uk/animalh/quarantine/pets/index.htm, in Ireland from http://www.agriculture.gov.ie/index.jsp?file=pets/travel.xml. The animal must also be identified either with a transponder or a clearly recognizable tattoo.

Pets

Citizens from EU countries may take unlimited goods out of Greece for private consumption. But there are certain amounts that, when exceeded, might along with other criteria be taken to indicate commercial importation. These are: 800 cigarettes, 400 cigarillos, 200 cigars, 1 kg of smoking tobacco, 10 litres of spirits, 20 litres of fortified wines or liqueurs, 90 litres of wine and 110 litres of beer. Travellers by air or sea may also take goods valued up to 430 €, for sea and car travellers up to 300 €. For children under the age of 15, the limit is 175 €.

Customs duty
◄ EU citizens

The following tax-free amounts are for travellers over 18 years from non-EU countries, for example Canada. 200 cigarettes or 100 cigarillos or 50 cigars or 250g/0.55lb of smoking tobacco; furthermore, 2l/1.8qrt of wine and 2l/1.8qrt of sparkling wine or 1l of spirits with more than 22 vol % alcohol content or 2l/1.8qrt of spirits with less than 22 vol % alcohol content, 50g/1.76oz of perfume and 0.25l/9oz of eau de cologne, 500g/1.1lb of coffee or 200g/7oz of instant coffee, 100g/3.5oz of tea or 40g/1.4oz of tea extract. In addition, gifts in value up to 45 € (23 € for children under the age of 15) are duty free.

◄ Entry from non-EU countries

Import/export bans ▶ Greece does not allow the import of plants, radio equipment or weapons of any kind, including self-defence sprays. Persons under the age of 18 may import neither tobacco products nor spirits and children under the age of 15 are not allowed to import coffee.

See above for EU citizens. The unlicensed export of antiquities and archaeological finds is rigorously prosecuted. Replicas of antiquities can be freely exported.

Beaches

The Greek islands have many beautiful beaches and bays. The bathing season is from April to November; the average water temperature from June to September (whether southern or northern exposure) is between 19 and 23°C (66–73°F). As the evening breeze can often be quite fresh, it is recommended to take some warm clothing along.

Natural beaches These open beaches lack any kind of facility and safety feature, such as warning signs, marking buoys and nets.

EOT beaches The beaches cared for by the Greek National Tourist Organization EOT (▶Information) are extremely well equipped with features such

Porto Katsiki on Lefkada: breathtaking beach at the foot of steep cliffs

as changing cubicles, snack bars and playgrounds, as well as restaurants, dance clubs and a wide selection of sports facilities.

The **hotel beaches** are well cared for and their services are good because they are subject to state inspection, though lifeguards and first-aid stations are not the rule everywhere.

Many of the beaches along the Mediterranean are no longer as clean and untouched as they were 20 years ago. This applies first and foremost to beaches near built-up areas, especially in the Saronic Gulf, where the **water quality** has been affected heavily by ship traffic and waste water from the Athens metropolitan area. Swimming at beaches near the city is not recommended (in places officially prohibited).

i | The finest beaches

- Ios, Mylopotas beach: in a wonderfully wide bay, popular mainly among young people
- Crete, Elafonisi beach: a breathtaking beach with beautiful greenish-blue water, reminiscent of the Caribbean
- Lefkada, Porto Katsiki: fabulous beach at the foot of steep cliffs
- Lesbos, beach at Valera: 10km/6mi long sand and pebble beach
- Skiathos, Koukounaries: lined by umbrella pines, in the southeast of the island, regularly voted as one of the three most beautiful beaches in the world

Children in Greece

Travellers who take children to Greece will very quickly realize that the little ones are warmly welcomed everywhere. The beaches, especially those with sand, are the main attraction for children. Thus most of the beaches on the northern coast of Crete are ideal because they are flat and especially suited to children. Along with swimming and splashing, boat rides are always fun. Ice cream is also available on many beaches.

Bear in mind that youthful skin needs special **sun protection**. The strong rays of the sun demand a sun cream (waterproof!) with a high sunscreen factor. Larger hotels and apartment complexes usually offer their young guests a variety of supervised activities. All Grecotels, for example, have children's clubs.

Electricity

As a rule, the power mains supply is 220 volts a/c; onboard ship, it is often 110 volts a/c. Standard continental plugs are usually the norm, adaptors can be obtained from most electrical supply stores.

Emergency

▶ USEFUL TELEPHONE NUMBERS

IN GREECE

▶ **Tourist Police**
Tel. 1 71
The most important contact point for tourists is the tourist police, who provide general information and tips for accommodation in English.

▶ **Police**
Tel. 1 12

▶ **Road Assistance Service**
Tel. 1 04 00

▶ **First Aid**
Tel. 1 66

▶ **Red Cross**
Tel. 1 50

▶ **Pharmacy**
Tel. 1 07

▶ **Road Traffic Police**
Tel. 21 05 23 01 11

▶ **Fire Department**
Tel. 1 99

Etiquette and Customs

Clothing   Like other Mediterranean peoples, the Greeks attach great importance to proper dress. Tourists who stroll through towns or villages or eat out in swimming clothes attract unfavourable attention. The dress code in churches and monasteries is far, far stricter. Long sleeves, long trousers and for women below-the-knee skirts and no hats are expected, even though many places will loan guests appropriate clothing. Evening clothing is normally not especially elegant, but in higher-class hotels formal clothing is worn in the evening.

Taking photos   If you have chosen a local person as the main motif of a photo, it is a good idea to gain permission through a couple of gestures first. It is forbidden to take photographs of military facilities. Taking pictures in museums with a portable camera is permitted almost everywhere, but special permission is necessary for taking pictures using a tripod and/or flash. Taking photos is not allowed in churches.

Tips   Service charges are included in the bill in hotels, restaurants and cafés. An additional gratuity, for example, rounding up the bill, is still always welcome. In taxis, too, the fare is generally rounded up (about 10%). At Easter and Christmas taxi drivers, hairdressers etc. expect a cash »gift«.

Food and Drink

Greek cooking, in its basics, is rather plain and offers – so say the critics – not much variety. It is dominated by a few basic ingredients – olive oil, tomatoes, garlic, onions, lamb, goat and chicken meat, sheep's and goat's cheese and whatever vegetables are in season. For a long time the food in tourist centres consisted of monotonous mass cooking with gyros, souvlaki and tzatziki. Now there is a trend toward more authentic Greek cooking.

Greek food

Tavernas are traditional Greek restaurants with simple furnishings since most people eat outside in the summer. Food is eaten at plain wooden tables. In an increasing number of restaurants along western European lines in the tourist centres, the tables are nicely decorated and lighting makes for a pleasant atmosphere, but the quality of the food is not always better than in the simple tavernas.

Tavernas, restaurants

The coffee house (kafenion) plays an important role in the daily life of the Greeks. It is not only where drinks are served, but also a gathering place to have a conversation, play games and do business. Coffee is always accompanied by a glass of water (nero); ouzo, an aniseed liqueur, often by cheese, olives and other appetizers (mese).

Kafenion

Breakfast (proyevma) in the hotels usually corresponds to western European standards and is normally eaten between 8am and 10am. Lunch (yevma) is served as a rule from noon to 3pm, the evening meal (dipno) generally after 8pm. Many tavernas serve cooked meals from mid-day through to midnight. In the tavernas all of the food will be brought at the same time if not otherwise specified. In Greece it is customary to write only one **bill** per table. But in the tourist centres asking for separate bills is not unusual. The menus are usually in English and Greek.

Mealtimes

The typical Greek **breakfast** is quite modest. A cup of coffee or a glass of milk is usually accompanied by a couple of slices of white bread with butter or margarine and jam (usually either apricot or strawberry). A really varied breakfast buffet can only be found in the upper-grade hotels. **Lunch** is also of minor importance. The natives make do with small meals or snacks. **The evening meal is the main meal** and is rarely eaten before 9pm in restaurants, usually even later. But foreign guests do not have to adjust to this timetable. Most restaurants serve cooked food all day from noon until late in the night anyway. For Greeks the most

Eating habits

---

i PRICE CATEGORIES

- The price of a main dish

Expensive: more than 15 €
Moderate: 10–15 €
Inexpensive: up to 10 €

important thing is to go out in the evenings with the whole family and friends. Everything is ordered at the same time. Starters, salad, fish and meat dishes all arrive on the table at the same time and everyone helps themselves. Bread is always served with meals. Bear in mind that no one in Greece thinks it important to get the meal to the table hot.

Greek Specialities

Hors d'oeuvres   Along with the appetizers that are served with an aperitif – usually the aniseed liqueur ouzo – there are dishes with prawns and mussels, seafood or rice-filled vine leaves as well as salads. Don't forget the tzatziki (yoghurt with chopped cucumber and garlic) and baked zucchini.

Soups   When soups are served, they are very filling. A favourite is fasolada, a traditional Greek white bean soup. Fish (psarosoupa) and meat soups are usually seasoned to taste with lemon juice.

Meat   Lamb or mutton (arni) are preferred and are often served roasted or grilled. Meat grilled on an upright rotisserie (gyros) and skewered meat (souvlaki) are very popular with tourists.

Bakes   Bakes like pastitsio (macaroni and minced meat) and moussaka (potatoes and aubergines) are widespread.

Vegetables   Typical garden vegetables are artichokes (anginares), aubergines (melitsanes), courgettes (kolokithakia) and Greek bell peppers (piperies), which are often cooked with minced meat or in oil. Horta, a wild vegetable similar to spinach, is very popular and is served blanched and seasoned with lemon juice.

Salads   Choose between lettuce, tomato salad and a farmer's salad (horiatiki) made of cucumber, tomatoes, olives and sheep cheese, often advertised as **»Greek salad«**.

Fish   Seafood is popular despite the high price. Along with bream (tsipoura), sole (glossa), red mullet (barbouni) and tuna, squid (kalamarakia), octopus (oktapodi) and shrimp (garides) are also on the menu. Some restaurants let guests choose their fish and prepare it as they like.

Dessert   Baklava (pastry with a nut filling and soaked in syrup) and krema (semolina) are typically Greek. Good Greek cheese is produced from sheep's or goat's milk, which are also used to make excellent yogurt (► Baedeker Tip) .

The ever-present Greek salad looking its best

Drinks

The most widespread drink is wine (krassi). Grapes for red wine (mavro krassi) and white wine (aspro krassi) are cultivated. Both dry and sweet wines are made.

Inexpensive retsina wines are resinated so they will keep longer (krassi retsinato), thus gaining their characteristic tangy taste. They stimulate the appetite and are very easily digestible.

In addition, there are a number of unresinated red and white wines that comply with EU standards and are identified by the letters »V.Q.P.R.D.«.

Of the Greek dry white wines and a few red wines on the islands, which as a rule are not worth mentioning, the wines of Crete, Kefallonia (Robola), Zakynthos (Verdea) and Rhodes (Lindos) should be noted. The white Muscatel from Samos is excellent.

Beer is getting more and more popular in Greece. Mythos is a well-known Greek brand.

The national drink **ouzo** is an aperitif; it is usually diluted with water, which gives it a milky appearance. Cretan raki – not to be confused with the eponymous Turkish liqueur – is made from pressed grape skins and is quite strong. The bark of the mastic tree is used to make a mastic liqueur (masticha). Greek cognac (koniak) is fruity and relatively sweet. Metaxa is a brandy that comes with 3, 5 and 7 stars; the more stars the better. A speciality from Corfu is a liqueur made from kumquats (dwarf oranges).

Greek coffee (ellinikos kafes) is drunk from small mocca cups after the grounds have settled. It is prepared in a whole gamut of ways according to strength and sweetness; gliki vrasto (with a lot of sugar),

Wine

Retsina

Unresinated wines

Wine-growing areas

Beer (byra)

Spirits (pnevmatodi pota)

Coffee, tea (kafes, tsai)

vari gliko (strong and sweet), elafro (light). Metrio (medium strength, medium sweet) is very popular. About the only »cosmopolitan« type of coffee available is Nescafe, called ness (with milk: »me gala«). The cold version – a frappé with thick foam and ice cubes – is something akin to Greece's national non-alcoholic drink. Tea (mavro tsai) is brewed from tea bags, but peppermint tea (tsai menda) or camomile tea (chamoumili) are also available.

Non-alcoholic drinks The non-alcoholic drinks available everywhere include water and the usual soft drinks known world-wide. Fresh-pressed juices are worth recommending.

Health

Medical help On the islands medical care is provided by hospitals and health centres (Kentra Ygieias), which treat tourists free of charge. UK and Irish residents are covered by reciprocal EU schemes. The **European Health Insurance Card (EHIC)** has been in use in the EU since 2005. Even with this card, a portion of the doctor's fees and costs for medicine often has to be paid by the patient. In such cases, request detailed receipts (apodixi) of the costs incurred. Enquire about possible reimbursement procedure when obtaining the card.

Pharmacies Pharmacies can be recognized by a round sign with a cross over the entrance as well as the word »ΦΑΡΜΑΚΕΊΟ« (»FARMAKEIO«). As a rule, pharmacies are open Monday to Friday from 8am until 2pm. Each pharmacy will know which other pharmacies have emergency hours.

Holidays, Festivals, Events

 CALENDAR OF EVENTS

HOLIDAYS

New Year's Day (1 January)
Epiphany (6 January)
Independence Day (25 March)
Kathari Deftera
(Shrove Monday)
Good Friday
Easter (most often later than in the
Roman

Catholic and Protestant
churches; dates: p.83)
Labour Day (1 May)
Pentecost
Feast of the Dormition of Mary
(15 August)
Ochi Day (28 October):
  Day of the No (»ochi«)
  to Italy's ultimatum in 1940

Christmas (25–26 December)

▶ **Saints' feast days**

Almost every town on the Greek islands has a patron saint, who is honoured with a festival on his or her name day. The festivities usually begin with a mass. In some towns there are colourful processions followed by lively celebrations. The following are the biggest saints' festivals.

6 JANUARY/EPIPHANY

▶ **Everywhere**

Blessing of the waters in memory of the baptism of Christ

FEBRUARY

▶ **Everywhere**

Carnival. The carnival celebrations reach their high point in the seventh week before Greek Easter. There are elaborate parades in the island capitals.

25 MARCH

▶ **Everywhere**

National holiday with military parades

APRIL/MAY

▶ **Everywhere**

Easter is the most important church holiday in Greece. Especially colourful Easter festivities take place in Oia (Santorini) and Olympos (Karpathos; on Easter Tuesday). Easter is celebrated on the first Sunday after the first full moon after the vernal equinox (21 March), which usually results in a later date than in the Western churches. ▶ Background, Religion.
Easter dates:
2012: 15 April; 2013: 5 May

▶ **Everywhere**

23 April: Feast of St George;

festivals in many places; special celebrations on Limnos and Kos (horseracing; singing and dancing)

MAY–OCTOBER

▶ **Rhodes**

Rhodes Town: Greek folk dancing in the old theatre and other performances, also in the Grand Master's Palace

MAY

▶ **Everywhere**

1 May: Labour Day with parades everywhere, flower festivals and excursions into the countryside

▶ **Kalymnos**

Sponge divers begin their season

▶ **Ios**

Omiria: three-day festival in honour of the poet Homer (cultural and sports events, art exhibits etc.)

▶ **Ionian Islands**

21 May: anniversary of the unification of the Ionian Islands and Corfu with Greece (1864); big parades especially in Corfu Town

JUNE

▶ **Rhodes**

21 June: midsummer night fire festival in Katakolo

▶ **Crete**

End of June: feast of the Klidona in Piskokefalo and Krousta

JULY

▶ **Corfu**

Early July: fair with folklore in Lefkimmi

▶ **Crete**

Mid-July: wine festivals in Dafnes and Rethymno (one week long);

raisin festival in Sitia

► **Kos**
Hippokratia: theatre, concerts, folk art

► **Crete**
Renaissance festival in Rethymno: theatre, concerts in the medieval fortezza

AUGUST

► **Lefkada**
Lefkada Town: international folk-lore festival with dance and music programme by artists from all over the world

► **Corfu**
11 August: festival in honour of St Spyridon with solemn processions

► **Crete**
Community festival in Anógia: high-class competition for lyres, dance and singing

► **Lefkada**
Karya: Lefkadian wedding, using traditional costumes

► **Zakynthos**
Zakynthos Town: international event for medieval and folk theatre (mid-August)

► **Everywhere**
15 August: Feast of the Dormition of Mary, for which many Greeks return to their home towns. Celebrated enthusiastically with music and dance, especially on Tinos, Corfu, Lesbos, Crete and Paros (fish and wine festival)

► **Zakynthos**
Zakynthos Town: 24 August, Feast of St Dionysios with procession and fireworks

AUGUST/SEPTEMBER

► **Santorini**
International Music Festival: Greek and foreign music groups perform classical music

SEPTEMBER

The Hippocratic Oath is re-enacted during the Hippokratia festival staged in August in the Asclepieion in Kos

► **Corfu**
Corfu Town: Corfu Festival with concerts, ballet, theatre and opera performances

► **Kefallonia**
Argostoli and Lixouri: international music and folk dance festival

► **Zakynthos**
Zakynthos town: cultural festival

► **Kythnos**
8 September: Anniversary of the church dedication that attracts pilgrims from all over Greece to the church Panagia Kanala

OCTOBER

Information

 USEFUL ADDRESSES

GREEK NATIONAL TOURISM ORGANIZATION

► **Internet**
www.eot.gr

► **In Australia**
37–49 Pitt Street
Sydney, NSW 2000
Tel. 2 92 411 663/4/5
Fax 2 92 412 499
E-mail: hto@tpg.com.au

► **In Canada**
1500 Don Mills Road, Suite 102
Toronto, Ontario M3B 3K4
Tel. 416 968 22 20
Fax 416 968 65 33
E-mail: grnto.tor@on.aibn.com

► **In UK**
4 Conduit St
London, W1S 2DJ
Tel. 0207 495 93 00
Fax 25 78 27 29
E-mail: info@gnto.co.uk

► **In USA**
Olympic Tower
645 Fifth Avenue, Suite 903
New York, NY 10022
Tel. (001212) 4215777
E-mail: info@greektourism.com

REGIONAL TOURISM OFFICES

► **Dodecanese**
Archipiskopos Makarios/Papagou
GR-85100 Rhodes
Tel. 22 41 04 43 30,
Fax 22 41 02 69 55
www.ando.gr/eot

► **Ionian Islands**
Alykes Potamou
GR-49100 Kerkyra
Tel. 26 61 03 76 38
Fax 26 61 03 02 98
E-mail: eotcorfu@otenet.gr

► **Crete**
Papa Alexandrou E 16
GR-71202 Iraklio
Tel. 28 10 24 61 06
Fax 28 10 24 61 05
E-mail: drkritis@otennet.gr

▶ **Cyclades**
Thymaton Sperchiou 11
GR-84100 Ermoupolis (Syros)
Tel. 22 81 08 67 25
Fax 22 81 08 52 75
E-mail: pna@notioaigaio.gov.gr

▶ **Northern Aegean Islands**
J. Aristarchou 6
GR-81100 Mytilini/Lesbos
Tel. 2 25 10 4 25 12
Fax 2 25 10 4 25 12/3
E-mail: eotpytva@otenet.gr

▶ **EOT offices on the islands**
▶ Sights from A to Z
Many of the Greek islands have no
tourist information offices. On
some of the Cycladic islands there
are offices, in which case they are
located right at the harbour in the
local administrative building.

INTERNET

▶ **http://www.greece-island.info**
General practical information and
descriptions of individual islands

▶ **www.greekhotel.com**
Hotel recommendations on various islands. Some may be booked
online.

▶ **www.culture.gr**
Homepage of the Greek ministry
of culture with almost all museums and archaeological sites as
well as a detailed calendar or
events.

▶ **www.greeceindex.com/**
A site with more than enough
information for any trip

▶ **www.gtp.gr**
Website of »Greek Travel Pages«:
ferry schedules, hotels, airlines and
much more

▶ **www.greektravel.com/
greekislands**
This site is part of a network of
sites on everything Greek; they are
maintained regularly and kept up
to date.

EMBASSIES IN GREECE

▶ **Australian Embassy
in Greece**
Level 6, Thon Building,
Cnr Kifisias & Alexandras Ave,
Ambelokipi, Athens
Tel. 2 10 870 40 00
http://www.ausemb.gr/

▶ **British Embassy in Greece**
Ploutarhou 13
GR-10675 Athens
Tel. 21 07 27 23 00
http://ukingreece.fco.gov.uk/en/
Email: consular.athens@fco.gov.uk

▶ **Canadian Embassy in Greece**
Genadiou 4
GR-11521 Athens
Tel. 21 07 27 34 00
canadaonline.about.com/od/
travel/a/embgreece.htm
E-mail: athns@international.gc.ca

▶ **Irish Embassy in Greece**
7 Leoforos Vasileos
Konstantinou 106 74, Athens
Tel. 2 10 723 27 712
http://www.embassyofireland.gr
Email: athensembassy@dfa.ie

▶ **US Embassy in Greece**
Leoforos Vass. Sofias 91
11060 Athens
Tel. 21 07 21 29 51
http://athens.usembassy.gov/

GREEK EMBASSIES AND
CONSULATES

▶ **Consulate General in Australia**
219 Castlereagh Street

Sydney, NSW
Tel. 2 92 64 91 30
http://greekconsulate.org.au
Email: info@greekconsulate.org.au

► **Consulate General in Canada**
365 Bloor Street East, Suite 1800
Toronto, Ontario M4W-3L4
Tel. 416 515 01 33
www.greekembassy.ca

► **Embassy in Ireland**
1 Upper Pembroke Street
Dublin 2

Tel. 1 67 67 25 4-5
E-mail: dubgremb@eircom.net

► **Embassy in UK**
1a Holland Park
London W11 3PT
Tel. 72 21 64 67
www.greekembassy.org.uk

► **Consulate General in USA**
69 East 79th Street
New York, NY 10021
Tel. 212 988 55 00
www.greekembassy.org

Language

In general visitors to Greece will find a local person who speaks English, but in rural areas it is best to know at least the rudiments of Greek.

Communication

Modern Greek is essentially different from **ancient Greek**, even though the number of words whose spelling has remained unchanged since the time of Homer is surprisingly large. However, even with these, the deviation in pronunciation from the academic pronunciation of ancient Greek is very marked. The change in pronunciation holds true for both variants of modern Greek and they are considerably dissimilar from each other in grammar as well as in vocabulary: **Dimotiki** (demotic Greek, the colloquial language of the people) and **Katharevoussa** (»purified« official and written language).

Modern Greek

In the past all official notices, signs, timetables etc. were written in Katharevoussa, an artificial language based largely on ancient Greek. Since 1975, however, Dimotiki has been the official language. It is the product of a long evolution of the language and long ago established itself in modern Greek literature, as well as in the entertainment section of the newspapers.

Greek Alphabet

Letters	Transcription	Pronunciation
A α (alpha)	a	a
B β (beta)	v	v

Γ γ (gamma)	g	gh, before e and i: y (as in Engl. »you«)
Δ δ (delta)	d	th (as in Engl. »that«)
Ε ε (epsilon)	e	short e
Ζ ζ (zeta)	z	z
Η η (eta)	i	i
Θ ϑ, θ (theta)	th	th (as in Engl. »thing«)
Ι ι (iota)	i	i
Κ κ (kappa)	k	k
Λ λ (lambda)	l	l
Μ μ (mu)	m	m
Ν ν (nu)	n	n
Ξ ξ (xi)	x	ks
Ο ο (omicron)	o	o
Π π (pi)	p	p
Ρ ρ (rho)	r	r
Σ σ, ς (sigma)	s	s (as in »sister«)
Τ τ (tau)	t	t
Υ υ (epsilon)	y	ee
Φ φ (phi)	f	f
Χ χ (chi)	ch	ch: as in Scottish »loch«
Ψ ψ (psi)	ps	ps
Ο Ο (omega)	o	o (short)

Letter combinations

αι	e	e (as in »bet«)
αυ	av	ow (before voiced consonant or vowel)
αυ	af	af (before unvoiced consonant)
γγ	ng	ng
γκ	g	g (at the beginning of a word, rarely in the middle)
γκ	ng	ng (in the middle)
ει	i	ee
ει	i	when unstressed like y
ευ	ev /ef	ev /ef (as in αυ)
μβ	mv	mv
μπ	b	b (begins word, rarely in the middle)
μπ	mb	mb (in the middle)
ντ	d	d (begins word, rarely in the middle)
ντ	nt	nd (in the middle)
οι	i	ee
ου	ou	oo

The spelling of Greek names and terms is a bit of a problem because there are no hard and fast rules for their transcription into Roman script. In order to achieve uniformity in this guide, **a UN transliteration table was used**. The table above shows which Greek letters correspond to which Roman letters. But in addition there are a few special features. Thus »γγ« is written using Roman »ng« and »μπ« is written using »B« at the beginning of a word (otherwise »mp«). The letters »αυ« are transcribed as »av« before vowels (and sometimes before consonants), before consonants and at the end of a word always »af« (the same for »ευ« and »ηυ«). The letters »ου« are written »ou«.

Greek spelling

SHORT LANGUAGE GUIDE

Useful Phrases

Yes / No	ne / óchi	Ναί / Όχι
Maybe	'issos	Ίσως
Please	paraka'ló	Παρακαλώ
Thank you (very much)	efchari'stó (pol'í)	Ευχαριστώ (πολύ)
Sorry!	sig'nómi!	Συγγνώμη!
Pardon? What do you want?	o'ríste?	Ορίστε;
I don't understand you.	ðe sass katala'véno.	Δε σας καταλαβαίνω.
Please repeat that.	na to ksana'péete, parakaló.	Νά το ξαναπείτε, παρακαλώ.
Do you speak … English?	mi'late … anggli'ká?	Μιλάτε … αγγλικά;
I only speak a little Greek.	mi'ló 'móno ligo elliniká.	Μιλώ μόνο λίγο ελληνικά.
Could you please help me?	bo'ríte na me voi'θísete, paraka'ló?	Μπορείτε να με βοηθήσετε, παρακαλώ;
I would like …	'θelo …	Θέλω …
Do you have … ?	'échete … ?	Έχετε …?
How much is it?	'posso 'kostisi?	Πόσο κοστίζει;
What time is it?	ti 'ora 'ine?	Τι ώρα είναι
Today / Tomorrow	si'mera / 'ówrio	Σήμερα / Αύριο

Greetings and Meetings

Good morning!	kali'mera (soo / sas)!	Καλημέρα (σου / σας)!
Good afternoon!	kali'mera! / 'cherete!	Καλημέρα / Χαίρετε!
Good evening!	kali'spera!	Καλησπέρα!
Good night!	kali'nichta!	Καληνύχτα!
(general greeting)	'yassas!	Γειά σας!
Hello!	yassu!	Γειά σου!

| Goodbye! | a'dio! | Αντίο! |
| Cheerio! | 'yassu! | Γειά σου! |

On the Road

left / right	ariste'ra / ðek'sya	αριστερά / δεξιά
straight ahead	ef'θia	ευθεία
near / far	ko'nda / makri'a	κοντά / μακριά
How far is it to …?	'posso ma'kria 'ine ya …?	Πόσο μακριά είναι γιά …?
I would like to hire …	'θelo na ni'kyasso …	Θέλω να νοικιάσω …
… a car	… 'ena afto'kinito	ένα αυτοκίνητο
… a bicycle	… 'ena po'ðilato	ένα ποδήλατο
… a boat	… 'mia 'varka	μία βάρκα
Excuse me, where is …?	Paraka'ló, pú 'íne …?	Παρακαλώ, πού είναι …

At the Petrol Station

Where is the next petrol station, please?	'pu 'ine, paraka'lo, to e'pomeno vensi'naðiko?	Πού είναι, παρακαλώ, το επομένο βενζιναδικό;
I would like … litres …	θelo … 'litra …	Θέλω … λίτρα …
… regular petrol.	… ven'sini.	… βενζίνη.
… diesel.	… 'dizel.	… ντίζελ.
… unleaded	… a'molivði	… αμόλυβδη
Fill up, please.	ye'miste paraka'lo.	Γεμίστε παρακαλώ.
Check the oil, please.	ekse'taste, paraka'lo, ti 'staθmi tu lað'yoo.	Εξέταστε, παρακαλώ, τη στάθμη του λαδιού.

Breakdown

My car has broken down.	'epaθa zim'ya.	Έπαθα ζημειά.
Could you please send me a tow truck?	θa bo'russate na mu 'stilete 'ena 'ochima ri'mulkissis?	Θα μπορούσατε να μου στείλατε ένα όχημα ρυμούλκησης;
Where is the next garage?	'pu i'parchi e'ðo kon'da 'ena siner'yio?	Πού υπάρχει εδώ κοντά ένασυνεργείο;

Accident

Help!	vo'iθya!	Βοήθεια!
Look out! Careful!	proso'chi!	Προσοχή!
Please, call quickly …	ka'leste, paraka'lo, 'grigora	Καλέστε, παρακαλώ, γρήγορα …
… an ambulance.	… 'ena asθeno'foro.	… ένα ασθενόφορο.
… the police.	… tin astino'mia.	… την αστυνομία.

»Now, if only one of us knew how to ask where the beach is ...«

| ... the fire department. | ... tin pirosvesti'ki ipire'sia. | ... την πυροσβεστική υπηρεσία. |
| Please give me your name and address. | 'peste mu to 'onoma ke ti ðiefθin'si sas, paraka'lo | Πέστε μου το όνομα και τη διεύθυνσή σας, παρακαλώ. |

Eating Out

Where is a good restaurant?	u i'parchi e'ðo 'ena ka'lo pestia'torio?	Πού υπάρχει εδώ ένα καλό εστιατόριο;
Is there a cosy taverna around here?	i'parchi e'ðo ta'verna me 'aneti at'mosfera?	Υπάρχει εδώ μια ταβέρνα με άνετι ατμόσφαιρα;
Please reserve a table for 4 for this evening.	kra'tiste mas ya 'simera to 'vraði 'ena tra'pesi ya 'tessera 'atoma, paraka'lo.	Κρατήστε μας για σήμερα το βράδυ ένα τραπέζι για 4 άτομα, παρακαλώ.
May I have the bill please?	θelo na pli'rosso, paraka'lo.	Θέλω να πληρώσω, παρακαλώ.
knife /fork	ma'cheri / pi'runi	μαχαίρι / πηρούνι
spoon	ku'tali	κουτάλι

Shopping

| Where do I find ...? | pu θa vro ...? | Πού θα βρω ...; |

a pharmacy	'ena farma'kio	ένα φαρμακείο
a bakery	'ena artopo'lio	ένα αρτοπολείο
a food store	'ena ka'tastima tro'fimon	ένα κατάστημα τροφίμων
the market	tin ayo'ra	την αγορά

Accommodation

Could you please recommend …?	bo'rite na mu si'stissete …, paraka'lo?	Μπορείτε να μου συστήσετε …, παρακαλώ;
… a hotel	… 'ena ksenoðo'chio	… ένα ξενοδοχείο
… a guesthouse	… 'mia pan'syon	… μία πανσιόν
I booked a room with you.	'eðo se sas 'eklissa 'ena ðo'matyo.	Εδώ σε σας έκλεισα ένα δομάτιο.
Do you still have a room free …	'echete a'komi 'ena ðo'matyo e'lefθero …	Έχετε ακόμη ένα δομάτιο ελεύθερο …
… for one night? ?	… ya mya 'nichta ?	… γιά μια νύχτα;
… for two days? ?	… ya 'ðio 'meres ?	… γιά δύο μέρες;
… for a week? ?	… ya mya vðo'maða ?	… γιά μια βδομάδα;
How much does the room cost with …	'posso ko'stisi to do'matyo me …	Πόσο κοστίζει το δομάτιο με …
… breakfast?	… proi'no?	… πρωινό;
… half board?	… 'mena 'yevma?	… μένα γεύμα.

Doctor

| Could you recommend me a good doctor? | bo'rite na mu sis'tissete 'enan ka'lo ya'tro? | Μπορείτε να μου συστήσε έναν καλόγ ιατρό; |
| I have a pain here. | 'echo 'ponnus e'ðo. | Έχω πόνους εδώ. |

Bank

| Where is a bank? | 'pu 'ine e'ðo mya 'trapeza? | Πού είναι εδώ μια τράπεζ |
| I would like … to exchange British pounds for euros. | 'θelo na a'lakso … li'ra ang'glias se evró. | Θέλω να αλλάξω … ελβετικά φράγκα σε ευρ |

Post

What is the cost of …	'posso ko'stisi …	Πόσο κοστίζει …
… a postcard …	… mya 'karta	… μια κάρτα
… to England/America/ Ireland/Canada?	… ya ti ang'glia/ameri'ki irlan'dia / kana'das?	… γιά τη Γερμανία/ Αυστρία / Ελβετία;
one / two stamps, please.	'ena / 'ðio grammat'osimo/ grammat'osima, paraka'lo.	Ένα / δύο γραμματόσημο γραμματόσημα, παρακα

Signs

ΑΝΔΡΩΝ	Gentlemen	ΓΥΝΑΙΚΩΝ	Ladies
ΕΙΣΟΔΟΣ	Entrance	ΕΞΟΔΟΣ	Exit

Numbers

0	mi'ðen	μηδέν	19	ðekae'nea	δεκαεννέα
1	'ena	ένα	20	'ikossi	είκοσι
2	'ðio	δύο	21	'ikossi 'ena	είκοσι ένα
3	'tria	τρία	22	'ikossi 'ðio	είκοσι δύο
4	'tessera	τέσσερα	30	tri'anda	τριάντα
5	'pende	πέντε	40	sa'randa	σαράντα
6	'eksi	έξι	50	pe'ninda	πενήντα
7	e'fta	εφτά	60	e'ksinda	εξήντα
8	o'chto	οχτώ	70	evðo'minda	εβδομήντα
9	e'nea	εννέα	80	og'ðonda	ογδόντα
10	'ðeka	δέκα	90	ene'ninda	ενενήντα
11	'endeka	ένδεκα	100	eka'to	εκατό
12	'ðoðeka	δώδεκα	200	ðia'kosya	διακόσια
13	ðeka'tria	δεκατρία	1000	'chilia	χίλια
14	ðeka'tessera	δεκατέσσερα	2000	'ðio chi'lyaðes	δύο χιλιάδες
15	ðeka'pende	δεκαπέντε	10 000	'ðeka chi'lyaðes	δέκα χιλιάδες
16	ðeka'eksi	δεκαέξι	1/2	to/'ena	το / ένα
17	ðekae'fta	δεκαεφτά		'ðeftero	δεύτερο
18	ðekao'chto	δεκαοχτώ	1/4	to/'ena 'tetarto	το / ένα τέταρτο

Κατάλογος φαγητών · Menu

προινώ	proin'o	**breakfast**
καφές (σκέτο)	ka'fes ('sketo)	(unsweetened) coffee
καφές με γάλα	ka'fes me 'yala	coffee with milk
καφές φίλτρου	ka'fes 'filtru	filter coffee
τσάι με λεμόνι	'tsai me le'moni	tea with lemon
τσάι από βότανα	'tsai a'po 'votana	herbal tea
σοκολάτα	soko'lata	chocolate
χυμό φρούτου	chi'mo 'frutu	fruit juice
αυγό μελάτο	ow'yo me'lato	soft-boiled egg
ομελέτα	ome'leta	omelette
αυγά μάτια	ow'ya 'matya	fried eggs
αυγά με μπέικον	ow'ya me 'beiken	egg with bacon
ψωμί / ψωμάκι	pso'mi / pso'maki	bread / rolls
τοστ	'tost	toast

κρουασάν	krua'san	croissant
φρυγανιές	frigan'yes	zwieback / rusk
βούτυρο	'vutiro	butter
τυρί	ti'ri	cheese
λουκανικό	lu'kaniko	sausage
ζαμβόν	sam'bon	ham
μέλι	'meli	honey
μαρμελάδα	marme'laða	jam
γιαούρτι (με καρύδια)	ya'urti (me ka'riðya)	yogurt (with walnuts)

ορεκτικά / σούπες	orektik'a / 'supes	**Hors d'œuvre / Soups**
ποικιλίαελιές	e'lyes	olives
φέτα	'feta	white sheep's cheese
μελιτζάνα σαλάτα	meli'dsana sa'lata	aubergine salad
ντολμαδάκια	dolma'ðakya	stuffed wine leaves (cold)
γαρίδες	ga'rides	shrimps
γίγαντες	'yigandes	large white beans
σαγανάκι	saga'naki	baked cheese
σκορδαλιά	skorðal'ya	purée of potato, garlic and oil

Say »please« and »thanks« in Greek, and the waiter will be happy to bring another table

σπανακόπιτα	spana'kopita	spinach pasty
ταραμοσαλάτα	taramosa'lata	purée of roe
τζατζίκι	tza'tziki	yogurt cream dip with cucumber and garlic
τυρόπιτα	ti'ropita	cheese pasty
κοτόσουπα	ko'tosupa	chicken soup
κοτόσουπα αυγολέμονο	ko'tosupa owgo'lemono	chicken soup with lemon and egg
ψαρόσουπα	psa'rosupa	fish soup
λαχανόσουπα	lacha'nosupa	vegetable soup
φασολάδα	faso'lada	bean soup
μαγειρίτσα	mayi'ritsa	traditional Easter soup
σαλάτες	sa'lates	**Salads**
(ν)τοματοσαλάτα	tomatosa'lata	tomato salad
αγγούρι	an'guri	cucumber
χοριάτικι (σαλάτα)	chor'yatiki (sa'lata)	village salad
μαρούλι σαλάτα	ma'ruli sa'lata	iceberg lettuce
λαχανοσαλάτα	lachanosa'lata	coleslaw
πατατοσαλάτα	patatosa'lata	potato salad
άγρια χόρτα	'agria 'chorta	wild herbs salad
λαδολέμονο	lado'lemono	lemon-oil sauce
ψάρια	ps'arya	**Fish Dishes**
αστακός	asta'kos	lobster
γαρίδες	ga'rides	shrimp
χταπόδι	chta'podi	octopus
μπαρμπούνι σχάρας	bar'buni 'scharas	grilled red mullet
γλώσσα τηγανητά	'glossa tiyani'ta	fried sole
μύδια	'midia	mussels
καλαμαράκια	kalama'rakya	small squids
μπακαλιάρος φούρνου	bakal'yaros 'furnu	stockfish from the oven
σολομός	solo'mos	salmon
κακαβιά	kakav'ya	bouillabaisse
καραβίδες	kara'vides	large scampi
χριστόψαρο	chris'topsaro	Zeus faber
σκουμπρί	skum'bri	mackerel
τσιπούρα	tsi'pura	gilthead seabream
φαγκρί	fan'gri	dentex
τόνος	'tonnos	tuna
ξιφίας	ksi'fias	swordfish
φαγητά με κρέας	fayit'a me kr'eas	**Meat Dishes**
άρνι ψητό	ar'ni psi'to	lamb roast
άρνι στο φούρνο	ar'ni sto 'furno	lamb from the oven

βοδινό φιλέτο	voði'no fi'leto	fillet of beef
γαλοπούλα ψητή	galo'pula psi'ti	roast turkey
γύρος	'yiros	meat from the rotisserie
κατσίκι	kat'siki	kid
κεφτέδες	kef'tedes	meatballs
κοτόπουλο ψητό	ko'topulo psi'to	roast chicken
κουνέλι	ku'neli	rabbit
μιξτ γκριλ	'mikst 'gril	mixed grilled meat
μοσχάρι κοκκινιστό	mos'chari kokkini'sto	braised veal
μοσχάρι ψητό	mos'chari psi'to	roast veal
μπόν φιλέ	bon fi'le	fillet
μπριζόλες χοιρινές	bri'soles chiri'nes	pork chops
μπιφτέκι	bi'fteki	grilled minced meat
παιδάκια αρνίσια	pai'ðakya ar'nisia	lamb chops
παστίτσιο	pa'stitsyo	macaroni soufflé with meat
σουτζουκάκια	sudsu'kakya	rolls of minced meat
σουβλάκι(α)	su'vlaki	skewered meat

λαχανικά	lachanik'a	**Vegetable Dishes**
ντολμάδες	dol'maðes	stuffed vine leaves
λάχανο	'lachano	white cabbage
αγγινάρες	angi'nares	artichokes
μελιτζάνες γεμιστές	meli'dsanes yemi'stes	stuffed aubergines
ντομάτες γεμιστές	to'mates yemi'stes	stuffed tomatoes
πιπεριές γεμιστές	piper'yes yemi'stes	stuffed bell peppers
τουρλού	tur'lu	mixed vegetable stew
φασολάκια	faso'lakya	green beans
μουσακάς	mussa'kas	aubergine, mince and potato bake
πιπεριές τηγανητές	piper'yes tigani'tes	fried bell peppers
κολοκυθάκια	koloki'θakya	zucchini
φασόλια	fa'solya	white beans
πατάτες τηγανητές	pa'tates tigani'tes	chips / french fries

επιδόρπια	epid'orpia	**Desserts**
φρούτα	'fruta	fruit
παγωτό	pago'to	ice cream
μπακλαβάς	bakla'vas	puff pastry in syrup with nut filling
μπουγάτσα	bu'gatsa	puff pastry pocket filled with vanilla cream
κρέμα	'krema	semolina pudding
ρυζόγαλο	ri'sogalo	rice pudding
σταφύλια	sta'filia	grapes
καρπούζι	kar'puzi	watermelon
πεπόνι	pe'poni	honeydew melon

Greek coffee: don't fail to try it

ροδάκινο	ro'ðakino	peaches
μήλο	'milo	apples
αχλάδι	ach'laði	pears

Αλκοολούχα ποτά	alkoo'lucha pot'a	**Alcoholic Beverages**
άσπρο κρασί	'aspro kra'si	white wine
κόκκινο κρασί	'kokkino kra'si	red wine
ρετσίνα	re'tsina	resinated wine
χύμα	'chima	wine from the barrel
ξερό	kse'ro	dry
ημίγλυκο	i'migliko	semi-sweet
ούζο	'uso	anise-flavoured liqueur
τσίπουρο	'tsipuro	marc liqueur
(μια) μπύρα	(mya) 'bira	(a) beer

μη αλκοολούχα ποτά	mi alkoo'lucha pot'a	**Non-Alcoholic Beverages**
φραππέ	frap'pe	cold Nescafé with thick foam
ελληνικος καφές	elini'kos ka'fes	Greek mocca
τσάι	tsai	tea
πορτοκαλάδα	portoka'laða	orange lemonade
λεμονάδα	lemo'naða	lemonade
(μια καράφα) νερό	(mya ka'rafa) ne'ro	(a jug of) water
μεταλλικό νερό	metalli'ko ne'ro	non-carbonated mineral water
σόδα	'soda	soda water

Literature

Fiction **Louis de Bernières**: *Captain Corelli's Mandolin*. Vintage, 1998. A love story set in the horrifying events of the Italian and German occupation of Kefallonia from 1940 to 1943. A very worthwhile read and a stirring epic, filmed in 2000 on Kefallonia, directed by John Madden.

i The Best Books

- Nikos Kazantzakis: *Zorba the Greek*. Faber and Faber 2008. The world-famous novel, filmed with Anthony Quinn in the title role, about the friendship of two very different men, one an intellectual writer and the other a vigorous working man.
- Lawrence Durrell: *Reflections on a Marine Venus*. Faber and Faber 2000. Poetic introduction to the landscape, inhabitants and customs of the island of Rhodes, where Durrell worked as a press attaché after World War II.

Lawrence Durrell: *Prospero's Cell*. Faber and Faber 2000. The poet, who lived on Corfu in the 1930s, describes the landscape and shows great insight into the lives of the local people, their everyday life, religion and festivals.

Stuart Harrison: *Aphrodite's Smile*. HarperCollins 2004. Romantic suspense on the Greek island of Ithaca. Just the thing for vacation reading.

Stratis Myrivilis: *The Mermaid Madonna*. Efstathiadis 1992. One of the most admired of modern Greek writers sets his tale in a fishing village on his native island of Lesbos at the time when the Greek population was being expelled from Turkey.

Travel **Gerald Durrell**: *My Family and Other Animals*, Puffin 2006. A funny account by the naturalist and brother of Lawrence Durrell of a childhood on Corfu, and his passion for the plants and animals of the island.

Henry Miller: *The Colossus of Maroussi*. Minerva, 1991. Sensitive account of Henry Miller's stay in Greece in 1939 and of the people he met there.

John Mole: *It's all Greek to Me! A Tale of a Mad Dog and an Englishman, Ruins, Retsina – and Real Greeks*. Nicholas Brealey, 2006. A modern glimpse into rural Greek life.

Non-fiction **John Camp and Elizabeth Fisher**: *Exploring the World of the Ancient Greeks*, Thames and Hudson 2002. A concise historical study of the development of Greek culture from the Bronze Age to the Christian era.

Diane Farr Louis and June Marinos: *Propero's Kitchen*, Pedestrian Publications 2000. Recipes from the Ionian Islands, from Corfu to Kythera.

Curtis Runnels and Priscilla Murray: *Greece before History,* Stanford University Press 2002. An account of early Greece since the Stone Age, with a good deal of information on the Cycladic, Minoan and Mycenaean cultures.

Media

Radio and Television

The state radio and television company, Elliniki Radiophonia Tileorassi (ERT), comprises Hellenic radio (Elliniki Radiophonia, ERA) and Hellenic television; three channels: ET1, NET and ET3).

There are a number of private television stations besides ERT, like ANT 1, Mega, Alpha, Alter and Star. The foreign TV stations that can be received with a terrestrial antenna are CNN, TV5, Euronews and RAI. BBC World and Sky News are available free-to-air on the Astra satellite, as is Deutsche Welle TV, which has an extensive English-language service.

Television

Take your choice: English-language newspapers and periodicals are available here, too

Newspapers and Magazines

Foreign periodicals The major English-language newspapers and magazines are available usually a day late in the main towns on the islands and in tourist centres.

Greek foreign-language newspapers *Athens News* (daily), published in Athens, provides information about what's going on in Greece and abroad and includes information of interest to tourists. To keep up with the news on Corfu read *The Corfiot* (monthly) and, on Lefkada, the English-language monthly *Planet Lefkas*.

Money

Euro The euro has been the currency of Greece since 2002.

ATM machines The simplest way to obtain money is from ATMs, which can also be found in rural areas. Money can be withdrawn by using a normal debit or credit card – together with the secret PIN.

 CONTACT DETAILS FOR CREDIT CARDS

In the event of lost bank or credit cards you can contact the following numbers in UK and USA (phone numbers when dialling from Greece):

▶ **Eurocard/MasterCard**
Tel. 001 / 636 7227 111

▶ **Visa**
Tel. 001 / 410 581 336

▶ **American Express UK**
Tel. 0044 / 1273 696 933

▶ **American Express USA**
Tel. 001 / 800 528 4800

▶ **Diners Club UK**
Tel. 0044 / 1252 513 500

▶ **Diners Club USA**
Tel. 001 / 303 799 9000

Have the bank sort code, account number and card number as well as the expiry date ready.
The following numbers of UK banks (dialling from Greece) can be used to report and cancel lost or stolen bank and credit cards issued by those banks:

▶ **HSBC**
Tel. 0044 / 1442 422 929

▶ **Barclaycard**
Tel. 0044 / 1604 230 230

▶ **NatWest**
Tel. 0044 / 142 370 0545

▶ **Lloyds TSB**
Tel. 0044 / 1702 278 270

On the Greek islands the usual international credit cards are accepted by banks, major hotels, and upscale shops and restaurants. Car rental agencies require them or request a security deposit. In case of loss, contact the credit card company or bank immediately

Credit cards

The banks are open Mon–Thu 8am–1.30pm, some (at least during high season) also on Sat 8am–1pm.

Opening hours of banks

Museums

Museums and archaeological sites have varied opening hours; these are listed in the descriptions of the individual sites in this guidebook. As a rule archaeological sites are open between 9am and 3pm. Many museums are closed on Mondays, some on Tuesdays as well. They are either open half days or closed on 6 January, Shrove Monday, Easter Saturday, Easter Monday (Easter dates: ► Holidays, Festivals, Events), Pentecost Sunday, August 15 and October 28. Most archaeological sites and museums are closed on 1 January, 25 March, Good Friday, Easter Sunday, 1 May and at Christmas. Admission is generally charged, except for school children and students with student IDs.

Opening hours

Post and Communications

Die Greek post offices are run by the Hellenic Post, Ellinika Tachidromia (ELTA). It is not possible to make telephone calls in a post office. Greek post boxes are yellow. Post offices are generally open Monday to Thursday from 8am to 2pm and Friday until 1.30pm.

Post

A picture postcard or a normal letter to other countries in Europe costs 0.70 €. It is best to purchase stamps from the post office because they cost more in other places, such as kiosks, hotel receptions and souvenir shops.

Stamps

The **Hellenic Telecommunications Organization (OTE)** is responsible for the telephone system in Greece. Phone calls can be made from kiosks, tavernas and hotels, but it is expensive. Card payphones are common. Cards are available from OTE, from kiosks and supermarkets.
The entire 10-digit **telephone number** has to be used for local calls as well. There are no area codes in Greece. All landline telephone numbers begin with 2, mobile numbers with 6.

Telephoning

USEFUL TELEPHONE NUMBERS

COUNTRY CODES
▶ **To Greece**
Tel. 00 30

▶ **From Greece**
to Britain: tel. 00 44
to Ireland: tel. 00 353
to USA and Canada: tel. 00 1

INFORMATION
▶ **Inland**
Tel. 1 51

▶ **Foreign**
Tel. 1 61

Prices and Discounts

The euro has definitely had an impact on the level of prices in Greece, especially because it is so easy to raise prices massively in restaurants and the tourist trades. Expect prices similar to or lower than those in the UK, depending on where you are staying. As accommodation is the most expensive item, it is definitely cheaper to travel off season when it is possible to bargain over the price, particularly in the case of longer stays.

WHAT DOES IT COST?

Double room **Simple meal** **Cup of coffee** **Glass of beer** **1 litre of petro•**
from 40.00 € from 5.00 € 2.00 € 2–3.50 € 1.20 €

Sailing

Arrival Persons arriving from abroad in their own yachts wishing to cruise Greek waters must first of all be equipped with a customs clearance and put in at a major port classified as a port of entry and departure. Boats from EU member states are not subject to inspection by port officials. Boats from outside the EU, however, are subject to this inspection and require a transit log that gives entitlement to six months of sailing in Greek waters. A passport control is carried out on all passengers arriving by private yacht from abroad, with foreign passengers classified as »in transit«.

⏵ USEFUL ADDRESSES

▶ **Hellenic Sailing Federation (EIO)**
Marina Delta Falirou
Athens
Tel. 2 10 9 40 48 25
Fax 2 10 9 40 48 29
www.eifo.gr

▶ **Piraeus Port Authorities**
Tel. 2 10 4 51 13 11/9

▶ **Greek National Weather Service (EMY)**
Athens
Tel. 2 10 9 69 93 16/7/8/9 (24 hours)

The brochure »Sailing Sports«, with information on regulations governing entry into the country, boat charters and marinas, is available from the Greek Tourist Board (▶Information).

Sailing

Shopping

The Greek islands offers a wide variety of things to take home as souvenirs, especially handcrafted items. Souvenir shops sell the usual assortment, although nowadays many items are mass produced on the mainland or abroad and quality has become a rarity. The largest selection is in the tourist centres and larger towns.

Watch out for mass production!

The export of antiques (e.g. icons) is strictly prohibited, but it is possible to buy and export copies of antiques (including frescoes, icons, jewellery) like the ones sold in museum shops such as in the National Museum of Archaeology in Athens.

Antiques

Ceramics are offered in all price categories, from poor imitations of antique vases to good replicas and the most exquisite products from the island of Paros. Plates from Lindos and ceramic vessels from Arhangelos (both on Rhodes) are well known. There are also typical wares on Sifnos.
Pay attention when buying ceramics: most of the items cannot be washed since the colours are only painted on and not fired in. Marble, onyx and alabaster, copper and brass goods, icons and olive woodcarvings also make popular souvenirs. Alabaster copies of Greek statues of the gods are very reasonably priced.

Crafts

Embroidery, lace and leather goods, especially bags, are also popular. Weaving has a long tradition among the folk arts on Skyros, Karpathos and Rhodes. Works with ancient themes are created exclusively for tourists.

Textiles

With such a range, choosing is difficult

Food, alcohol   There is a large selection of **sweets**: the best known are thyme honey from Thasos as well as loukoumia (fruit jelly pieces), chalvadopitta (wafers covered with honey, almonds or other nuts) from Syros. There is a large supply of dried fruits, pistachios, almonds and walnuts. Among the **spirits** ouzo, an aniseed liqueur, is well known; the best brands are supposed to come from Lesbos. Other tasty souvenirs are cheese, olive oil and herbs.

> ## ! *Baedeker* TIP
>
> ### Leather items galore
>
> Skridlof Street, the »leather street«, in Hania on Crete is known for good leather products. The shops here have a huge selection of bags, shoes and gloves. Shoes can also be custom-made.

Gold jewellery   On islands where cruise ships stop, like Mykonos and Santorini, there is a great selection of gold jewellery. Rings, necklaces and bangles are cheaper than in many European countries.

Icons   Icons are also a popular souvenir. In many places local artists will custom paint icons from ancient pictures.

Sponges   Natural sponges are still sold on Kalymnos and the neighbouring Dodecanese islands. The sponges with a regular structure are the most expensive.

Sport and Outdoors

Boats and angling equipment are available in almost all coastal towns.   Angling

►Beaches   Beaches

There are mountain bike stations, which also offer day trips, on several islands including Corfu, Crete and Rhodes. Bikes can be rented in almost all of the larger tourist centres.   Cycling

Diving in the sea with breathing equipment is prohibited – except at a few places – in order to protect cultural treasures. In regions that are excepted the rules made by the Director for Aquatic Finds in the Ministry of Culture must be followed precisely. A list of the excepted regions and their current regulations, as well as information about underwater fishing, is available at the Greek National Tourist Organization (► Information). In any case, it is advisable to first enquire about the local regulations from the proper harbour authorities.   Diving

The game of golf has come relatively late to Greece. There are good courses on the islands of Corfu, Crete and Rhodes.   Golf

The Greek islands would be ideal **hiking regions** if there were marked trails and good maps. However, these either do not exist or are simply inadequate. Several travel companies offer guided hiking tours on Greek islands; consult travel agencies for more information. Sometimes good hiking guides are available locally, for example on Samos and Kefallonia.   Hiking

The Greek Equestrian Club has information on horseback riding.   Horseback riding

The local branches of the **Greek Alpine Club** maintain a number of mountain shelters, most of them at an elevation between 1,000m and 2,000m (3,300– 6,600ft), for example at Dirfys on Evia, Levka Ori and Psiloritis on Crete. Information about the shelters in the mountains is provided by the Greek Tourist Board and the Greek Alpine Club (►Information).   Mountain climbing

There are water sports centres that rent boats and offer **sailing** courses in the larger holiday resorts. More information: ►Sailing

Tennis courts usually can be found at hotels and in the area of beaches. There are tennis courts owned by clubs in Crete, as well as on Corfu and Rhodes.

Hiking on Crete

● ADDRESSES

ANGLING

▶ **Greek Fishing Association**
Moutsopoulou, Piraeus
Tel. 2 10 4 51 57 31

DIVING

▶ **Greek Diving Association**
Athens
Tel. 2 10 9 81 99 61

GOLF

▶ **Hellenic Golf Federation**
Post office Box 70003
GR-16610 Glyfada
Tel. 2 10 5 29 77 77
www.hgf.gr

HIKING

▶ **Hellenic Federation of Mountaineering and Climbing**
Dragatsaniou 4, Athens
Tel. 2 10 3 23 41 07

HORSEBACK RIDING

▶ **Olympic Equestrian Centre**
Dimtriou Ralli 37
Markopoulo, Attica 19402
Tel. 2 29 90 4 93 50
Fax 2 29 90 4 96 17
www.hef.gr

MOUNTAIN CLIMBING

▶ **Greek Alpine Club (EOS)**
Milioni 5, Athens
Tel. 2 10 3 64 59 04
Fax 2 10 3 64 46 78

ROWING

▶ **Hellenic Rowing Club**
Voukourestiou 14, Athens
Tel. 2 10 3 61 21 09

SAILING

▶ **Helenic Sailing Federation (EIO)**
Marina Delta Falirou, Athens
Tel. 2 10 9 40 48 25
Fax 2 10 9 40 48 29
www.eifo.gr

▶ **Helenic Yachting Server**
www.yachting.gr

TENNIS

▶ **Helenic Tennis Federation**
Ymettos 297, Pangrati/Athens
Tel. 2 10 7 56 31 70
Fax 2 10 7 56 31 73
www.efoa.org.gr

WATER SKIING

▶ **Greek Waterski Association**
Thrakis 60, Ilioupolis
Tel. 2 10 9 94 43 34
Fax 2 10 9 94 05 21
hwsf@ath.forthnet.gr

WINDSURFING

▶ **Greek Windsurfing Association**
Filellinon 7, Athens
Tel. 2 10 3 23 36 96
www.ghiolman.com

Water skiing For those who want to learn to water ski, there are many schools on the Greek islands, for example on Chios, Corfu, Crete, Kythira, Lesbos, Mykonos, Patmos, Poros, Rhodes, Skiathos and Spetses.

Windsurfing There are surfing bases on most of the islands during the high season. They are often on the beaches of large hotels.

Time

Greece is in the Eastern European Time Zone (EET = GMT + 2 hours). Summer time (daylight saving) begins and ends on the same days as in the rest of Europe (last Sunday in March and October respectively), so Greece is two hours »ahead« of Britain and Ireland the whole year.

Eastern European Time

Transport

By Car

Many of the larger towns on islands are connected by paved, but often very winding and narrow roads. Many remote villages in the island interiors are still only accessible on unpaved roads. In general, it is best not to drive at night because the verges of the roads are usually unmarked and very irregular; instead of a shoulder there is often a deep ditch, and even good roads can have large and deep potholes. There are still gravel roads, particularly on the smaller islands. The road network has been expanded at great expense and according to plan during the last decades and effort is being made to improve and expand it further.

Road network

For the most part, international traffic regulations are in force in Greece. Offenders face drastic fines even for parking violations.
Multi-lingual police officers wear an armband with the words »Tourist Police«. Sounding a horn in the city is prohibited. Seatbelts are mandatory when driving and cell phones may only be used with a hands-free system. Driving at night with sidelights only is permitted in brightly lit towns. The sign »priority road« means no parking. The alcohol limit is 50mg per 100ml (0.5 per mille).

Traffic regulations

Speed limits for personal vehicles, also with trailers (and motorcycles over 100 cc): in towns 30–50kmh/19–31mph, outside towns 70kmh/44mph or 90kmh/56mph, on national roads 110kmh/68mph and on motorways 120kmh/75mph. Driving too fast can result in heavy fines and possible loss of the driving licence.

Speed limits

Diesel and the usual grades of unleaded petrol, as well as motor oil (normal and super) are found almost everywhere and, infrequently, LPG. Carrying canisters of fuel in the car is prohibited.

Petrol

Besides the international car rental firms, whose reservation systems are dependable, local servicesoffer cars for hire, especially in Athens,

Rental cars

Piraeus and the larger tourist centres on the islands. Car rental firms are represented at the international airports; hotel receptions also arrange car rentals. The rental rates are relatively high. Apart from rental cars – including jeeps and vans for five to seven people – local rental agencies rent motorcycles, motor scooters, mopeds, bicycles and mountain bikes. The pre-condition for hiring a vehicle is possession of an international driving licence. A national driving licence is sufficient if issued in an EU country. When renting check the insurance benefits carefully, for example the deductible on full coverage.

Breakdown services
The **Automobile and Touring Club (ELPA)**, call tel. 1 14 00, maintains a patrol service (OVELPA), which gives assistance to foreign drivers. The vehicles are yellow, with the sign Assistance Routière. In case of a breakdown, wave a yellow cloth or open the bonnet to attract attention. There is a fee for the service. On-the-spot service and towing to the next garage are without charge for British drivers with AA (www.theaa.com/breakdown-cover/european-breakdown-cover.jsp) or RAC (www.rac.co.uk/web/breakdowncover/european) European breakdown cover.

Taxis
Taxis have the international sign »Taxi« on the roof and will stop when a person waves or calls from the side of the road. There are large numbers of taxis available in the larger cities, found in all places heavily frequented by the public (airports, bus stations, etc.) as well as in front of large hotels and museums. The **charge** for a trip in a taxi is cheaper than, for example, in the UK. Additional fees are charged for entering the taxi at bus and train stations, harbours and airports; also for each piece of luggage over 10kg/22lbs and trips between midnight and 5am. There is an additional charge at Easter and Christmas. Negotiate the price before entering a taxi for an excursion. A more reasonable alternative to the usual taxis in some tourist

 USEFUL ADDRESSES

BUS TRAVEL

▶ **KTEL**
Tel. 28 10 22 17 65
www.ktel.org

RENTAL CARS

▶ **Internet reservations**
Avis: www.avis.com
Budget: www.budget.com
Europcar: www.europcar.co.uk
Hertz: www.hertz.com

Sixt: www.sixt.com
(for USA: www.sixtusa.com)

AIRLINES

▶ **Olympic Air**
www.olympicair.com

▶ **Aegean Air**
www.aegean.com

▶ **Sky Express**
www.skyexpress.gr

Excursion boats stop at all the larger islands

centres are the **taxi limos**, which take passengers until the car is full. Sometimes a little patience is needed before the taxi sets off.

Ferries

There are regular passenger services to the Greek islands, with almost all lines sailing to the islands from Piraeus. There are fewer connections between the islands and then mainly within the island group. The prices are reasonable. Boating excursions to beaches and the outlying islands are offered in many coastal towns. Ship timetables are very much dependent on the weather. Travel can be restricted for days when the winds are strong. More information: ►Arrival · Before the Journey

Buses

The Greek islands have an extensive network of bus routes run by the **Greek bus company KTEL**, but smaller towns often only have one or two buses a day. The traffic hubs are, of course, the larger cities. Buses arrive at and leave from various bus stations within one town for various destinations.

Dense network

There are buses running to excavation sites and beaches as well. English bus timetables are available in the larger tourist information offices (► Information). Most buses pick up passengers who wave for them to stop. Bus fares are quite cheap. Buy tickets at the bus station in advance; in small towns pay when boarding the bus.

Flights

Greece has a good network of domestic flights, with Athens at the hub. The Greek operators **Olympic Air** and **Aegean Air**, Athens Air and Sky Express fly to many of the islands. More information: ►Arrival · Before the Journey. Since many flights are full during the high season it pays to book beforehand and in time.

Domestic flights

Travellers with Disabilities

Hotels, restaurants, museums etc. on the Greek islands are generally not barrier-free. The Hellenic Chamber of Hotels' official guide contains listings of disability-friendly accommodation. It is available at the offices of the Greek National Tourist Organization EOT ►Infor-

mation). The website http://gogreece.about.com/od/disabledtravel/
Disabled_and_Handicapped_Travel_Greece.htm also provides useful
information.

When to Go

Climate

As on the Greek mainland, there are basically only three seasons on
the Greek islands: a relatively short spring from March to mid-May
when the vegetation explodes, a long, hot and very dry summer from
the middle of May until October, and a cool, wintry rainy season
from November to March. Greece is well known as a sunny holiday
destination. The average sunshine hours vary between 2,500 and
3,000 a year. In some areas it shines 300 days a year. The average
temperature during the warmest months (July August) fluctuates
between 26°C and 30°C (79–86°F), but temperatures up to 40°C/
104°F are not unusual. The heat and summer dryness increase to the
south.

Ionian Islands   The Ionian Islands, due to their western location and the influence
of the sea, **are more temperate than the Aegean islands** – the winters
are a bit warmer and the summers not so hot; above all they get a
relatively large amount rain for Greece. As the »bad« weather is
limited to a few days when the amount of
rainfall is relatively high, the Ionian Islands
have more sunny days and fewer overcast days
than eastern Greece.

This applies especially to **Corfu**; with its
1137mm/45in of precipitation it gets as much
rain as some parts of western Europe, and the
island with its four months of little or no rain
is unusually green for Greece. The summer
temperatures (up to 40°C/104°F) are easy to
bear because of the almost constant northwest
wind called the maistros. Water temperatures
go up to 24°C/75°F. The best times to go to
the Ionian Islands are from April to late June
and September to October; except for the dry
summer months – late May to late August –
rain gear is recommended.

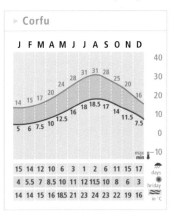

▶ Corfu

J F M A M J J A S O N D

Aegean islands   The Aegean island climate is characterized by **a very dry summer
with sub-tropical temperatures**, a relatively mild winter rainy season
and above all northerly winds all year round. Spring on the Aegean
islands is famous. After the plentiful rainfall from December to

March, flowers blossom for several weeks with an intoxicating scent. Summer begins in late April or May and lasts until October. Rain falls only sporadically during this time. In the months of June to September there is almost no rain. There are drought-like conditions with longer heat waves and temperatures up to 40°C/104°F. In late September or October there are local, sometimes violent thunderstorms, which bring the longed-for rain. The rainy season lasts from November to March.

In the summer months strong, dry winds often blow from the north across the Aegean Sea. These are called the Etesian or **meltemi** winds. The winds increase until early afternoon and decrease toward evening. In the southern Greek islands (Cyclades and Crete) moist, warm winds in winter and spring called **sirocco** blow from the south and make for humid weather. These winds can bring dust from the Sahara that falls over the islands.

The sea cools during the winter and warms up again in May to about 18°C/64°F. By August the **water temperature** has reached 25°C/77°F and then begins to sink again. The surface water in the eastern Mediterranean region is relatively warm into late autumn and keeps the winters mild; in October the water temperature is still around 20°C/68°F.

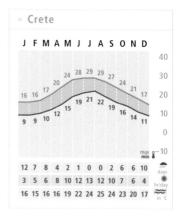

▸ Crete

	J	F	M	A	M	J	J	A	S	O	N	D	
max	16	16	17	20	24	28	29	29	27	24	21	17	
min	9	9	10	12	15	19	21	22	19	16	14	11	
	12	7	8	4	2	1	0	0	2	6	6	10	days
	3	5	6	8	10	12	13	12	10	7	6	4	hr/day
	16	15	16	16	19	22	24	25	24	23	20	17	in °C

When to Go

The best time to travel to Greece is in spring, from about the second half of March to the end of May or early June, as well as in autumn, during the months of September and October, sometimes even until the beginning of November. The summer months (mid-June to the start of September) are very hot, particularly in the large cities, but the dry air and the north winds blowing constantly across the Aegean, the meltemi, make it quite bearable. From mid-November until the end of March, the weather is rainy. The months of March, April and May are mild and nature blossoms. The summer offers ideal conditions for visiting one of the many outdoor theatre or folklore performances as well as wine festivals with wine tasting. It is recommended, even in summer, to take along warm clothing because it can become quite cool in the evenings on the sea and in the mountains. The temperature becomes mild once again from October, with the fine weather often lasting into November, but the first rainfall can be expected then.

Tours

YOU DON'T KNOW
WHERE TO START?
OUR SUGGESTIONS WILL
HELP. READ ON FOR
SOME ESPECIALLY
INTERESTING ISLAND TOURS.

TOURS THROUGH THE ISLAND WORLD

These three island tours include various types of island, from the »less Greek« Ionian Islands to the picture-postcard islands of the Cyclades, which the Greeks use to advertise for visitors. Allow plenty of time for the tours, since they need some organizing.

━━ **TOUR 1**   **The Other Greece**
This tour covers a uniquely green islands that have been influenced by Western culture for centuries.   ▶ **page 116**

━━ **TOUR 2**   **Picture-postcard Island World**
This tour introduces you to the definitive Greek island of the coffee-table books.   ▶ **page 118**

━━ **TOUR 3**   **Between East and West**
This tour introduces two historically significant islands: Patmos and Rhodes.   ▶ **page 120**

Ferries: island tours are impossible without them

The streets of Corfu Town are a relaxing place to stroll

©Baedeker

✳ Corfu

Igoumenitsa

TOUR 1

Preveza

✳ Lefkada

✳ Kefallonia

✳ Zakynthos

✳ Andros

✳ Samos

TOUR 2

✳✳ Mykonos

✳ Patmos

✳✳ Delos

✳ Kalymnos

✳ Paros

✳ Naxos

✳✳ Kos

✳ Ios

✳ Nisyros

e houses of Thira on
ntorini seem to cling
the cliff

✳ Symi

✳✳ Santorini

TOUR 3

Rhodes

The Avenue of the
Knights in Rhodes
Town gives an im-
pression of the life of
the Knights of
St John

Travelling the Islands

It takes a bit of organization to travel around the Greek islands. However, since every island has its own character it is worthwhile to see not just one island, but to visit the neighbouring ones as well. While almost all islands can be reached by ship from Piraeus, they cannot always be reached from other islands. The best connections are within the island groups. The following suggestions are therefore based mainly on island groups.

Means of transportation

When travelling by ship, check the **ferry** schedules beforehand. When arriving on a certain island check for further connections right away. Information on ferry schedules is available on the website Greek Travel Pages www.gtp.gr. Island hopping is possible with your own car or with a rental car hired locally, but this is only recommended for the larger islands, since the smaller ones have few roads and the car ferries are very expensive. When travelling without a car, either rent one on each of the larger islands or use local buses or taxis – in which case plan some more time. About 26 islands are **accessible by air**, most of them from Athens and Iraklio, a few from Thessaloniki and Rhodes. Charter flights go to about half of the islands.

Tour 1   The Other Greece

Start: Corfu   **Finish:** Zakynthos
Duration: at least two weeks

This tour explores the Ionian Islands, which have a special place in the Greek island world. For one, the landscape is dominated by the colour green; moreover centuries of Western influence, especially from Venice, give them their own character.

★★
Corfu

When visiting ➊ ★★ **Corfu** plan to stay about three days. Consider spending the first night in Corfu Town with its Venetian architecture. The towns on the west coast with their beautiful beaches, e. g. Glyfada or Agios Georgios, are well suited as starting points for further exploration. A visit to the ★★ **Achilleion**, which was the vacation home of two crowned heads, is almost a must. A drive through the north of Corfu to the picturesquely located ★★ **Paleokastrítsa**, the remains of the fortress ★ **Angelokastro** and in the extreme northwest of the island to the impressive ★ **Cape Drastis** takes about one day. Follow the coast road to the popular vacation resort town Kassiopi. If there is time, make a side trip to ★ **Pantokrator**, the highest mountain on the island. Otherwise follow the coast road to get back to Corfu Town quickly.

From Corfu take the ferry to ➋ **Igoumenítsa** on the Greek mainland.
Then follow the E 55 with its beautiful views of the picturesque
coastal landscape. 20km/12mi
southwest of ➌ **Preveza** cross the
causeway and bridge to the island
of ➍ ✱ **Lefkada**. For non-swim-
mers one or two days are enough
to explore Lefkada – along the west
coast the beaches are for the most
part untouched. Tourism is con-
centrated around Nydri on the east coast, while the towns of Agios
Nikitas and Vasiliki are closer to the beaches. The village of Karya
makes for a charming excursion, and another leads to the southwestern peninsula, to ✱ **Cape Lefkatas**. The incredibly beautiful beach at
✱ **Porto Katsiki** is definitely worth a stop.

✱ Lefkada

✔ DON'T MISS

- Corfu Town: beautiful Venetian-style town
- Lefkada: fabulous Porto Katsiki beach
- Zakynthos: Shipwreck Beach – picture perfect

Ferries run from Nydri or Vasiliki on Lefkada to the neighbouring island to the south, ➎ ✱ **Kefallonia**. The ferry port is ✱ **Fiskardo**, one
of the most beautiful towns in the Ionian Islands and the best place

✱ Kefallonia

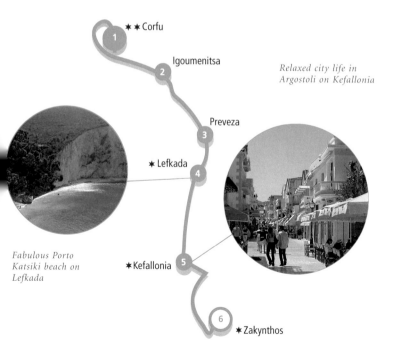

✱✱ Corfu

Igoumenitsa

Relaxed city life in Argostoli on Kefallonia

Preveza

✱ Lefkada

✱ Kefallonia

✱ Zakynthos

Fabulous Porto Katsiki beach on Lefkada

to spend the night. There are ferry connections from Fiskardo to Ithaki. The drive to the island capital of Argostoli goes past the picturesque Assos and ✷ **Myrtos Bay**, which is framed by high cliffs. From there cross the entire island towards Sami.

A tour of the ✷ **Melissani Cave** here is worthwhile; the lake in the grotto enchants visitors with its display of colours. Travel on to Skala via Poros, where tourism is slowly arriving. The monastery Agios Andreas with its museum is worth a stop. Return to the island capital via Metaxata.

✷
Zakynthos

From Pesada on the southwest coast of Kefallonia take the ferry to Agios Nikolaos in the northeast of ❹ ✷ **Zakynthos**. From here boat trips run along the coast to the fascinating ✷ **Blue Grotto** and the wonderful ✷✷ **Shipwreck Beach**. A visit to the mountain village of ✷ **Anafonitria** with the eponymous monastery is also worthwhile. From there turn south on the road that runs parallel to the west coast, take a side trip to Keri with its picturesque locale and then continue to the lively ✷ **island capital Zakynthos**. There is an impressive view of the town from Bochali Hill.

Tour 2 Picture-postcard Island World

Start: Andros   **Finish:** Santorini
Duration: 1–2 weeks

No other group of islands has influenced our image of holidays in Greece as much as the Cyclades, the subject of this tour: bare islands with white villages and domed churches, with the blue sea as a backdrop. This impressive picture matches the reality.

❶ ✷ **Andros**, the second-largest Cyclades island after Naxos, still cultivates a native Greek lifestyle, since tourism has not really arrived. The former fishing village Gavrio on the west coast is the port of arrival. Go past the tourist centre Batsi and the ancient capital Paleopolis to the fertile Messaria valley with the fortress-like Panachrantou monastery. To the northeast lies the modern ✷ **capital of Andros**. The neo-classical patrician houses here are a reminder of wealthy ship-owners who built their summer villas here. Back in Gavrio take the ferry to Tinos.

Upon arrival on ✷ **Tinos** in ✷ **Tinos Town**, the ✷ **Evangelistria church**, an important place of pilgrimage, draws all eyes with its

✓ DON'T MISS

- Mykonos: beautiful capital of the island with the same name
- Delos: the ancient centre of the Apollo cult is a must for all archaeology buffs.
- Santorini: the town of Thira is breathtakingly situated on this spectacular volcanic island.

commanding position above the city. Make sure you visit the well-tended monastery Kechrovounio north of Tinos and the sculptors' village **Pyrgos**.

The next stop is the most visited island of the Aegean, ❷ ✳✳ **Mykonos**. It has few important cultural sites, but its traditional island architecture makes an enchanting setting. Mykonos is also the starting point for a boat excursion to the neighbouring island of ❸ ✳✳ **Delos**, the ancient centre of the cult of Apollo with impressive excavation sites.

✳✳
Mykonos

On the trip to Naxos a stop on ❹ ✳ **Paros** is possible. This island has been famous for its marble since antiquity, and marble quarries can still be seen today. The picturesque capital ✳ **Parikia**, the port of arrival, has one of the oldest churches in Greece, the ✳ **cathedral of Katapoliani**.

✳
Paros

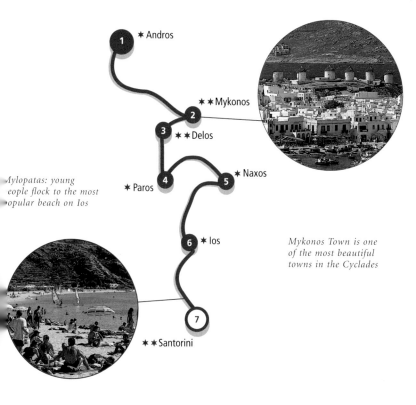

✳ Andros

1

✳✳ Mykonos

2

3   ✳✳ Delos

4   ✳ Paros

5   ✳ Naxos

6   ✳ Ios

7

✳✳ Santorini

Mylopatas: young people flock to the most popular beach on Ios

Mykonos Town is one of the most beautiful towns in the Cyclades

✳   The largest island in the group, ❺ ✳ **Naxos**, is worth a longer stay
Naxos   because of its charming scenery. The view through the ✳ **Marble Gate** of the ✳ **main town of Naxos**, which nestles picturesquely on the slopes of a mountain, is impressive. The restful vacation resort Apollonas in the north of the island is a 50km/30mi drive away.

✳   Those who plan to spend their vacation on the beach should head
Ios   for the island of ❻ ✳ **Ios** to the south with its beautiful sandy beaches. ✳ **Mylopotas Beach** south of ✳ **Ios-Hora** is very popular among young people.

✳ ✳   The final stop and highlight of every tour of the Cyclades is
Santorini   ❼ ✳ ✳ **Santorini**, whose unique landscape makes it one of Greece's most attractive sites. Just the arrival in the giant, almost completely enclosed volcanic crater, with white houses clinging to the edge, is an unforgettable experience. The wonderful capital ✳ ✳ **Thirá** is the main destination on the island.

Tour 3 Between West and East

Start: Samos   **Finish:** Rhodes
Duration: 2–3 weeks

This tour includes two islands rich in history: Rhodes with its medieval capital and the seat of the Order of St John, and Patmos, where St John is supposed to have written the Book of Revelation. The Turkish west coast seems close enough to touch.

✳   The ports of arrival on ❶ ✳ **Samos** are the tourist resort ✳ **Pytha-**
Samos   **gorio** on the southern coast and the pretty capital, ✳ **Samos-Hora** in the northeast. It is advisable to disembark in Pythagorio in order to find accommodation for two nights. The archaeological highlight is the ✳ **Heraion of Samos**, 9km/5.5mi west of Pythagorio. Sunbathers and swimmers plan a stop at the many beaches on the southern coast. The houses of ✳ **Samos Town** are grouped beautifully around the harbour bay. The most important sight here is the kouros in the archaeological museum. From Samos Town drive along the north coast to the former fishing village of Kokkari and the second-largest town on the island, Karlovasi. Make side trips to Vourliotes and Manolates.

✳ ✳   A highlight of every island tour in the southeastern Aegean is
Patmos   ❷ ✳ ✳ **Patmos**, where the evangelist John is supposed to have written down the Book of Revelation. From the lively port village of Skala either walk or take the bus up to the ✳ **Monastery of the Apocalypse** and on to the ✳ ✳ **Monastery of St John**, which offers a wonderful view of the island.

From Kos Town (or by ferry from Mastihari) cross to the island of the sponge divers, ❸**Kalymnos**, which has had little contact with tourism as yet. Above the harbour the whitewashed houses are stacked up on the sloping ground. Make an excursion to the beach resorts Myrties and Massouri on the picturesque bay along the west coast.

✔ DON'T MISS

■ Rhodes: in the capital of Rhodes stand impressive medieval buildings of the Order of St John.
■ Rhodes: picturesque Lindos has a beautiful location and an impressive acropolis.
■ Patmos: the massive Monastery of St John is the religious centre of the island.

Guests arriving in ✳ **Kos Town** on ❹✳✳ **Kos** are captivated by the cheerful holiday atmosphere and the charming urban panorama. Plan on spending at least two nights here in order to explore the island, which takes about one day. Follow the street that runs southwest across the island to Kefalos. Detours lead to the beach resorts Marmari and Mastihari on the north coast or the mountain villages Zia, Pyli or Antimachia. The archaeological highlight is the ✳✳ **Asclepieion** southwest of Kos town, which was once dedicated to the god of healing.

✳✳
Kos

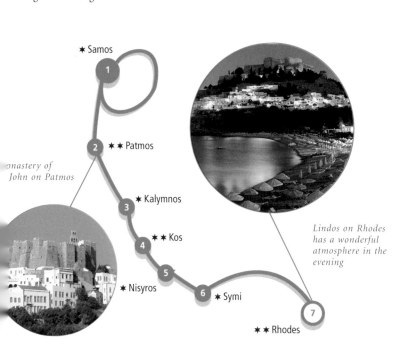

✳ Samos

1

2 ✳✳ Patmos

nastery of
John on Patmos

3 ✳ Kalymnos

4 ✳✳ Kos

5

6 ✳ Symi

✳ Nisyros

7

✳✳ Rhodes

Lindos on Rhodes has a wonderful atmosphere in the evening

The fast boats from Rhodes and Kos stop on the beautiful island of **★**
6 ★ Symi and sometimes also on Nisyros. The pretty **★ village of**   **Symi**
Symi, which sprawls up the slope around a deep bay, is a popular
destination from Rhodes, while the volcanic island of **5 ★ Nisyros**
often gets visitors from Kos.

The last stop and highlight of the island tour is **7 ★★ Rhodes**. The   **★ ★**
island capital **★★ Rhodes Town** with its medieval centre is one of   **Rhodes**
the main tourist attractions of the island. Plan to stay for three nights
on Rhodes in order to enjoy the beauty of the island. The east coastal
road leads from Rhodes Town southwards and soon reaches the tourist centre of Faliraki with its long beach. After the beach resort of
Kolymbia comes **★ Tsambika Beach** with its fine-grained sand below
the monastery of the same name.
Pass the largest town on the island, Arhangelos, to get to **★★ Lin-**
dos, a picturesque town with an impressive acropolis in a wonderful
setting. After a side trip to the attractive church in Asklipeio cross
the island to the west coast at Apolakkia. Now head northwards
again to Rhodes Town past the villages of Monolithos, Kritinia and
Skala Kamirou to the beautifully situated ancient city of **★ Kamiros**.

← *Sunset at Hania harbour on Crete*

Sights
from A to Z

A SUMMER EVENING ON
THE SHORES OF ENCHANTING
LAKE VOULISMÉNI IN ÁGIOS NIKÓLAOS ON CRETE,
THE APPROACH TO AN OLD ISLAND HARBOUR
SEEN FROM THE DECK OF A SHIP, SUNSET WITH A
VIEW OF THE LAGOON ON VOLCANIC SANTORINI –
EXPERIENCES TO REMEMBER

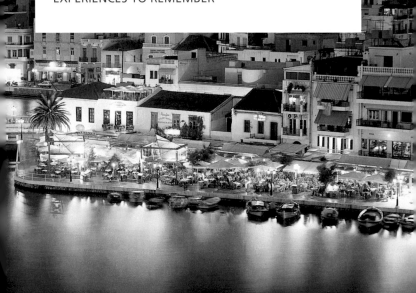

Aegina · Éjina

J/K 9

Greek: Αίγινα
Area: 83 sq km/32 sq mi
Population: 13,500

Island group: Saronic Islands
Altitude: 0–532m/1,745ft
Capital: Aegina

Aegina in the Saronic Gulf is a fertile, hilly island with a number of volcanic peaks. Most of the coastline is steep and there are hardly any sheltered bays. The mild climate and low precipitation make the island a favourite destination of Athenians for summer holidays – no wonder, since the island is right at their doorstep. More and more international guests are showing up, too. A visit to the island is worthwhile for the Temple of Aphaia alone.

Island of divine origin
The inhabitants' main source of income is agriculture, especially the cultivation and export of their excellent pistachios. Fishing is also a significant earner. According to legend **Aeacus**, the son of Zeus and Aegina, is the clan father of the Aegineans.

What to See on Aegina

Aegina (Αίγινα)
The main town on the island, Aegina (population 6,000), occupies gently rising ground around a wide bay on the northern west coast,

 VISITING AEGINA

INFORMATION

Tourist information
Leonardou Lada, Aegina Town
Tel. 22 97 02 77 77
(tourist police)

GETTING THERE

Connections by ship to Piraeus and Galatas on the mainland and to the islands of Angistri, Poros, Spetses and Hydra.

WHERE TO EAT

▶ **Moderate**
Agora
Aegina Town
Street parallel to the harbour, behind the fish market hall
Excellent fish dishes at acceptable price

WHERE TO STAY

▶ **Mid-range**
Aeginitiko Archontiko
Ag. Nikolaou/Thomaidou 1
Aegina Town
Tel. 22 97 02 49 68
www.aegnitikoarchontiko.gr
13 rooms. The hotel in a 19th-century residence has a roof garden with bar.

▶ **Budget**
Artemis
Kanari 20
Aegina Town
Tel. 22 97 02 51 95
www.artemishotel-aegina.com
24 rooms. Pleasant house; all rooms feature a balcony

on the site of a larger ancient city. The small harbour with fishing boats and yachts is lined with tavernas and cafes; there are nice restaurants in narrow Panagia Irioti Street behind the harbour. From the harbour, which is protected by a pier, there is a beautiful view of the smaller islands Metopi, Angistri, Moní and the mountains of Epidauros.

On Colóni Hill north of the town there is an 8m/26ft-high Doric **Colóni** column from the Temple of Apollo by the harbour (460 BC). Traces of pre-Mycenaean and Mycenaean settlements were found under the temple and, to the west, two smaller temples thought to have been dedicated to Artemis and Dionysos. Archaeological finds from the 3rd millennium BC up to Roman times, particularly those from the temples of Aphaia and Apollo, are displayed in the interesting **archaeological museum**. Opening hours: Tue–Sun 9am–3pm.

Aphaia, the daughter of Zeus, was venerated as a protector of women in this over 2,500-year-old temple on the east coast of Aegina

Temple of Aphaia ✶✶ The drive to the Temple of Aphaia (13km/8mi east of Aegina) on the east coast of the island leads through wooded and cultivated hill country. It passes the Church of Ágii Theódori (1289), which was built using material from ancient temples and is decorated with frescoes, and after 8km/5mi the **medieval island capital of Paleohora**, where there are about 20 chapels dating from the 13th to 18th centuries. The ruins of the medieval citadel rise above it. Further on is the village of Mesagró, and then a steep path leads to the temple. The Temple of Aphaia (5th century BC), dedicated to a deity associated with Artemis who was regarded as a protector of women, rests on the foundation of a shrine of the 6th century BC and was designed as a peripteros with 6 : 12 columns. The pronaos and opisthodomos – here there is a stone altar – were enclosed by antae walls with two columns between. The roof of the cella is supported by two rows of columns. 23 columns of yellowish limestone with parts of their original plaster covering have survived, especially on the eastern main façade and the sides attached to it. There are several monolithic columns. The roof and sculpture decorations were made of marble from Pentelicon. The irregularities in the floor of the cella and the fact that the opisthodomos is divided are unusual. In the floor there are holes in which screens used to rest.

Temple of Aphaia Plan

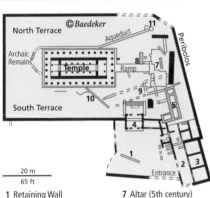

20 m
65 ft

1 Retaining Wall
2 Stoa
3 Priests' building (5th century)
4 Propylon (5th century)
5 Priests' building (7th century)
6 Altar (5th century)
7 Altar (5th century)
8 Altar (7th century)
9 Propylon (5th century)
10 Peribolos (7th century)
11 Cisterns,
   Sphinx column

The pediment sculptures are now in the Glyptothek in Munich, other sculptures in the archaeological museums of Athens and Aegina. The sacrificial altar was in front of the whole width of the east front and connected to it by a ramp, while south of the east front is a small propylon with octagonal columns. The whole of the sacred site was levelled with earth and buttressed, in part by natural rocks and in part by walls built of stone blocks. Remains of Late Neolithic settlements were discovered in the area (4th–3rd millennium BC). Opening hours: April–Oct daily 8am–7.30pm, Nov–Mar 8.30am–5pm.

To gain an overview of the construction history of the Temple of Aphaia, visit the **archaeological museum** to the left of the entrance. There is a magnificent view from the temple grounds over a large part of the Saronic Gulf all the way to the mainland coastline.

Below the Temple of Aphaia the road winds through pine forests to the coast. After 3km/2mi Agía Marína, the island's tourist centre, extends around a beautiful bay with sandy beaches. Modern hotels and many cafes, tavernas and souvenir shops characterize the town today. There are quieter places to swim below the road to Pórtes.   **Agía Marína**
(Αγία Μαρίνα)

Mount Óros (532m/1,745ft) is the most striking summit on the Saronic Gulf. The way to the top is a difficult path from Marathon (6km/4mi south of Aegina). The view from the peak takes in almost all of the island and the Saronic Gulf.   **Óros**

✶ Amorgós

O/P 11

Greek: Αμοργός
Area: 120 sq km/46 sq mi
Population: 1,900

Island group: Cyclades
Altitude: 0–826m/2,710ft
Capital: Amorgós Hóra

For people who enjoy hiking and spending their holidays far from the madding crowd, the easternmost Cycladic island of Amorgós is the place to go, even though it has already been discovered by tourists.

There are numerous donkey trails around Katápola and the main town, Amorgós. The two best hiking routes go to Moní Hozoviótissis on the east coast and via Minóa above Katápola to Moní Valsamitis.   **Easternmost**
Cycladic island

▶ VISITING AMORGÓS

INFORMATION
Tourist information
In travel agencies in Katápola
www.amorgos.gr

GETTING THERE
Ships to Piraeus on the mainland as well as to the other Cycladic islands

WHERE TO EAT
▶ Moderate
Mouragio
Katápola
Tel. 22 85 07 10 11
This restaurant close to the square serves good Greek cooking.

WHERE TO STAY
▶ Luxury
Aegiális
Aegiáli, tel. 22 85 07 33 93
www.aegialis-amorgos.com
32 rooms. This hotel, situated between two sandy bays just outside Aegiáli, offers nicely furnished rooms with a magnificent sea view.

▶ Mid-range
Amorgós
Katápola
Tel. 22 85 07 10 13
10 rooms. Comfortable guesthouse by the harbour

Amorgos Map

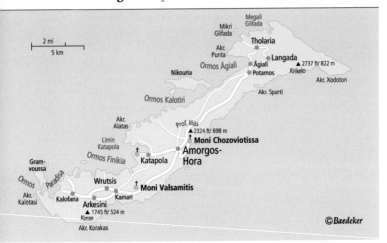

Several bays with sand or pebble beaches on the north and northwest coast are suitable for swimming. The barren, rocky island with attractive scenery is 33km/21mi long and between 2km and 6km (about 1–3.5mi) wide. The rocky cliffs on the southeast coast rise spectacularly to 800m/2,625ft above the sea; the northwest coast is more gentle and has two deep bays: in the north Aegiáli Bay and in the south Katápola Bay with the island's principal port. The remaining inhabitants of the island live from some agriculture and livestock, and increasingly from tourism.

What to See on Amorgós

Katápola
(Κατάπολα)

The quiet Katápola is the **main port** and a popular tourist venue on the island. Stroll along the long, tamarisk-lined beach promenade and, at least in the low season, enjoy the peaceful island atmosphere. With numerous holiday rooms and several tavernas, the inhabitants have adapted to tourism. The Monastery of Panagía Katapolianis, built on the foundations of an early Christian basilica, is worth seeing. A temple to Apollo is supposed to have stood here in antiquity.

Minoa

On the south side of the bay on Muntiliá Hill are the remains of the city of Minóa (a 30-minute walk from Katápola); it was probably founded by Cretans in the 2nd millennium BC. There is a spectacular view from the top all the way to Náxos.

Amorgós
Hóra

The island's old capital, Amorgós Hóra (population 300), is located 5km/3mi from Katápola at an altitude of 400m/1,300ft. Its white Cycladic houses in narrow lanes, over 40 family chapels and the remains of a 13th-century Venetian castle nestle around the rocks. Ancient spolia are set into many house walls. Outstanding examples of Cycladic art have been uncovered on Amorgós, some of which can be seen in the Goulandris Museum in Athens. Next to Zoödóhou Pigis Church the **archaeological museum** displays examples of Geometric, Archaic and Classical art.

The famous Byzantine Panagia Hozoviótissa Monastery, daringly built 360m/1,180ft above the sea on a steep cliff face, is most impressive. Its architecture is unusual for the Aegean. The monastery can be reached on foot in about 30 minutes from Amorgós Hóra. It was originally founded in the 9th century; the present building was funded by **Emperor Alexios Komnenos** in AD 1088. In the monastery valuable icons and parchment manuscripts can be seen. There is an impressive view of the sea from the terrace.

Hozoviótissis
(Χοζοβιότισσα)

Aegiáli, the second port on the island on the eponymous bay northeast of Amorgós, is quieter than Katápola but also well visited. The local attraction is the sandy beach with its tamarisk trees. To the northwest there are some smaller isolated sand and pebble bays.

Aegiáli
(Αιγιάλη)

The Monastery of Panagia Hozoviótissis clings like a bright swallows' nest to the rock face

Astypálea (Αστυπάλεα)

Western Dodecanese island
The island of Astypálea (population 1,100) has little water and is the westernmost of the Dodecanese islands. Even though Astypálea has been part of the Dodecanese since 1830, it was controlled from the Cyclades in the past. Its landscape and culture also betray its proximity to these islands: barren hills without vegetation and white houses. Approximately 200 small churches and chapels are scattered around the island. Most of them were founded by private citizens and many are in ruins today. Livestock, fruit and vegetable farming give the inhabitants a modest income. Tourism has not yet developed much. There are enough hotels, private rooms to let and some nightspots, yet few beaches.

Sights
The picturesque **principal town, Hóra**, the island's main attraction, sits majestically above the harbour on barren rock. More than two decades ago it was a ghost town, but since more and more foreigners have bought and renovated abandoned houses, some Greeks have returned too. The eight windmills near the town square have also been restored. Hóra is dominated by a Venetian fortress, of which only the outer walls still exist. It was built between the 13th and 16th century. Below Hóra to the west is the fertile **Livadi Valley**, the main farming region on the island. The **pebble beach of Livadi** is shaded by tamarisk trees and is the most popular beach on the island.

A Venetian fortress dominates the town of Astypálea

✶ Ándros

Greek: Άνδρος
Area: 380 sq km/147 sq mi
Population: 10,000

Island group: Cyclades
Altitude: 0–994m/3,261ft
Capital: Ándros Hóra

Luxuriantly green Ándros, the northernmost and, after Náxos, the second-largest of the Cyclades, is still pretty much undiscovered as a holiday destination. The relatively modest tourist trade is mostly concentrated on the beaches around Batsí and Gávrio on the west coast.

At first sight Ándros, which is 40km/25mi long and up to 16km/10mi wide, presents a barren aspect with its bare and rough mountain slopes. The coastline is uneven but there are some beautiful beaches. Nevertheless Ándros is **one of the most fertile islands in the Cyclades**. Long valleys with lush vegetation are a charming contrast to the barren mountain slopes. The four mountain ranges that cross the island from west to east have marble deposits. An unusual amount of water permits intensive agriculture (citrus fruits, tomatoes, grain, olives) in the deep valleys south of Mount Pétalo. Red-tiled roofs make the island look more like the mainland than a Cycladic island and show the prosperity of the inhabitants. Since the 19th century Ándros has been the home of several Greek ship-own-

Ship-owners' island

▶ VISITING ÁNDROS

INFORMATION
Tourist information
Gávrio
Information booth at the harbour
Tel. 22 82 02 51 62
www.androsweb.gr

GETTING THERE
Ferries to Rafina on the mainland and to the islands Amorgós, Donousa, Iráklio, Kéa, Koufonisia, Kýthnos, Mýkonos, Náxos, Páros, Sýros and Tinos.

WHERE TO EAT
▶ **Inexpensive**
Parea
Plateia Kaïris

Ándros Hóra
The taverna at the entrance to the old town offers Greek dishes along with a beautiful view of the beach.

WHERE TO STAY
▶ **Mid-range**
Paradise
Ándros Hóra
Tel. 22 82 02 21 87
www.paradiseandros.gr
38 rooms, 3 suites. This hotel at the southwest entrance to the town has spacious, well-appointed rooms; there is a magnificent view from the dining room; regular shuttle bus to the beach.

Andros Map

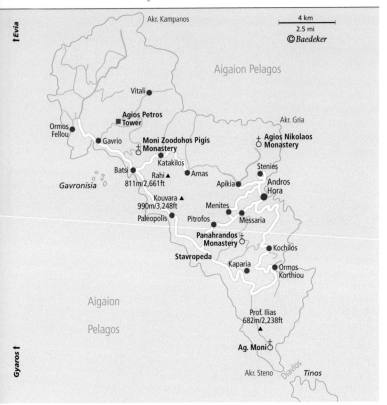

Akr. Kampanos

4 km
2.5 mi
©*Baedeker*

↑ Evia

Aigaion Pelagos

Vitali ●

Akr. Gria

Agios Petros
■ **Tower**

Ormos
Fellou ●

● Gavrio

Moni Zoodohos Pigis
✝ **Monastery**

✝ **Agios Nikolaos**
○ **Monastery**

Katakilos

Batsi ●

Rahi ▲
811m/2,661ft

● Arnas

Stenies ●

Apikia ●

Andros
Hóra ●

Gavronisia

Kouvara ▲
990m/3,248ft

Menites ●

Paléopolis ●

Pitrofos ●

Messaria ●

Panahrandos ✝
Monastery ○

● Kochilos

Stavropeda

Kaparia ●

● Ormos
Korthiou

Aigaion

Pelagos

Prof. Ilias
682m/2,238ft
▲

↑ Gyaros

Ag. Moni ○

Akr. Steno

Diavlos

Tinos

---

ing dynasties. Thanks to plentiful tax income and many foundations the »ship-owners' island« is one of the wealthiest Cycladic islands today.

✳ Ándros Hóra

City The main town, Ándros Hóra (population 1,500), spreads over a rocky ridge between two bays on the east coast. It was founded in the Middle Ages on the fortified islet off the eastern point of the narrow spit, where the Venetians built the town as a fort in the sea (kastro). Its image of a wealthy, quiet, picture-postcard town comes from well-tended streets, patrician homes and several churches. The street signs reveal who is responsible for the prosperity: wealthy ship-owners who built their summer villas here. Not only the coherent urban architecture but also the generous cultural and social facilities are the

Ándros Town stretches out along a ridge that reaches into the sea

fruits of their work. The town is crossed by a marble-paved main street as well as numerous covered alleys and steep steps. The main beach, Niborío to the north, can be quite full during the high season.

★
Kastro

The tour of the old town begins in its western part at the little **Plateia Kaïri** with its acacia and plane trees, a marble fountain (1818) and some tavernas and cafes. Steps lead down from the square to the north and south beach. From Plateia Kaïri enter the old town kastro with its neo-classical patrician houses through the archway. Pass the stately houses and St George's Church at the east end and go to Plateia Afani Nafti. In the centre is the massive »monument to the simple sailor«. This bronze figure of a sailor looking towards the sea with his right hand raised was created by Michael Tombros. There is a small maritime museum (open only sporadically) with some ship models. An arched bridge leads to the fortified island with remains of the Venetian defences. The new town with its bustling main street lies within. The terraced cemetery on the road to Mesaria is worth a look. There are some elaborate tombs of influential shipping families, many shaped like temples, in its upper parts.

> ## ! *Baedeker* TIP
>
> ### A speciality ...
>
> ... of the island is »froutalia«, an omelette with potatoes and sausage, which is mainly served in the interior, for example in the village of Katakilos, 5km/3mi from Batsí.

Archaeological Museum

The Archaeological Museum of Ándros on Plateia Kaïri was donated by the shipping magnate Basil Goulandris. The exhibitions concentrate on the excavations of Zagora (Geometric period) and Paleopolis. The museum's centrepiece is the *Hermes of Ándros*, probably a copy made in the 1st century BC of a marble statue by the famous sculptor Praxiteles (4th century BC). Opening times: Tue–Sun 8.30am–3pm.

Museum of Modern Art

From Plateia Kaïri steps lead north down to the **Museum of Modern Art**, which was also donated by the Goulandris shipping dynasty. This modern building holds sculptures, pictures and installations by 20th-century Greek artists. Works by the avant-garde sculptor Michael Tombros (1889–1974) dominate the collection. Opening hours: May–Sept Mon–Sat 10am–2pm, 6pm–8pm, Sun 10am–2pm; Apr, Oct Mon, Wed–Sat 10am–2pm; Nov–Mar Mon, Sat, Sun 10am–2pm; internet: moca-andros.gr.

Other Sights on Ándros

Apikia (Αποικία)

About 6km/4mi northwest of Ándros in Apikia, where there is a fine panoramic view, Sariza mineral water is bottled. It can be sampled in the well-house. A beautiful hiking trail leads from Apikia to **Moní Agiou Nikolaou** 3km/2mi away. A special attraction in the domed church is an exquisite icon of its patron, St Nicholas, which was fashioned in the 17th century by a nun from gold and silver thread and her own hair, and decorated with pearls.

Mesaria Valley

From Ándros the large and fertile Mesaria Valley traverses the island. Here there are unique **dove towers** and in the pretty town of Mesaria the Taxiarchis Church dating from 1158. The oldest and largest monastery on the island, **Panagia Panahrandou**, founded in 961 by the later emperor Nikephoros Phokas, lies 4km/2.5mi south of Mesaria at an elevation of 800m/2,600ft. The fortress-like complex and the Byzantine domed church are worth seeing.

Gávrio (Γάυριο)

The Bay of Gávrio served as a sheltered anchorage even in antiquity. The fishing village Gávriois the island's main port now, and many ferries stop here. It has several hotels and tavernas and a small beach. About 2km/1mi to the northeast, near Agios Petros, is a massive **Hellenistic tower** (3rd–1st century BC), which is 20m/65ft high and has a circumference of 21m/70ft. It was probably used as a watchtower and a refuge for the island population, and as protection for the nearby iron-ore mines. There is a magnificent view from the tower.

Zoödóhou Pigis

East of Gávrio at an elevation of 300m/2,600ft is the Convent of Zoödóhou Pigis (»life-giving spring«). The convent church, which was founded in 1325, possesses a beautiful marble iconostasis, frescoes and valuable icons. One treasure, a 300-year-old silk tapestry from Constantinople, depicts the Virgin Mary as the source of life.

The former fishing village of Batsí is now a lively holiday centre and especially popular among British tourists. There is ample accommodation here and tavernas as well as several sandy beaches south of town. From Batsí it takes about four to five hours to climb Mt Kouvara (990m/3,200ft) or Mt Rachi (811m/2,660ft).

Batsí
(Βατσί)

The ancient capital of Ándros (500 BC to AD 800) lay on the west coast near the hamlet of Paleopolis (»old city«), 8km/5mi south of Batsí, and flourished into the Byzantine period. There are a few remains of the acropolis and the port. Most of the finds from here are in the Archaeological Museum of Ándros, including the famous *Hermes of Ándros*.

Paleopolis
(Παλεόπολη)

Batsí: popular beach resort on Ándros

★★ Athens · Athína

Greek: Αθήνα
Altitude: 40–277m/130–900ft

Nomos (prefecture): Attica
Population: 730,000

The capital of Greece, the cradle of Western culture, is an exuberant metropolis where the past and present seem to blend into each other. Athens with its world-famous Acropolis and important museums is a must for every visitor to Greece – on the way to Piraeus and the Greek islands.

National capital
As in ancient times, Athens is once again the spiritual and cultural as well as the economic centre of Greece. Athens has been the capital of Greece since 1834. The metropolitan area is the focal point of trade and industry in Greece; all banks, most large companies and the shipping lines have their headquarters here. Piraeus is a major port. Since gearing up for the **Olympic Games** of 2004, Athens has radiated a new lustre. The transport infrastructure was extended, repaired and improved. Zones of traffic calming were created with new footpaths, especially in the inner city, that connect the important sights and the old quarter, Pláka.

History
The development of Athens began with the union of various settlements (synoikismos) in the Attica region under King Theseus in the 10th century BC. **Solon** succeeded in temporarily easing social tensions in the 7th century BC through his reforms. After his death, conflicts soon broke out again and paved the way for the tyrannies of **Peisistratos** and his sons (560–510 BC). Their rule weakened the power of the aristocracy – an important prerequisite for the development of Attic democracy, which in turn encouraged the rise of Athens to be a leading economic and cultural power in Greece. The city state experienced its golden age under **Pericles** (443–429 BC). The turning point was the **Peloponnesian War** (431–404 BC), in which Athens lost a struggle for supremacy in Greece to its rival Sparta. Sulla led the Romans in their conquest of the city in 86 BC. The invasion of the Germanic Heruli in AD 267 put a sudden end to Athens' greatness, however. Sacked several times during the barbarian invasions, Athens was finally reduced to an inconsequential provincial town of the East Roman or Byzantine Empire and did not flourish again until it came under Frankish rule in the 13th century. In 1458 the Ottoman Turks took Athens, and the city remained Turkish until the 19th century. In the **War of Independence** (1821–33) Athens was hotly contested. In 1834, King Otto I, a Bavarian, made Athens the capital of the Kingdom of Greece and employed German and Danish architects to develop it. In 1896 the first modern **Olympic Games** were held. Vast new districts were created after the Greek-Turkish War of 1923, when some 300,000 refugees

VISITING ATHENS

INFORMATION

Tourist information
Amalias 26 a
Tel. 21 08 70 70 00, 21 08 70 71 81
www.greece-athens.com

Airport office:
arrivals concourse
Tel. 2 10 3 33 07
Fax 2 10 3 33 06

GETTING AROUND IN ATHENS

Although Athens sprawls over an area of more than 400 sq km/150 sq mi, the places of interest to tourists are confined to a small district. Most sights are within easy walking distance of each other. Express bus lines and Metro line 3 connect Eleftherios Venizelos Airport, 27km/17mi east, with the city centre. 3 Metro lines, a tram, minibuses and the yellow trolley-buses serve the inner city.

SHOPPING

Athens has a broad range of goods for sale: from cheap souvenirs to major international fashion labels and renowned jewellers. The main shopping area is in a triangle bordered by Sýntagma, Monastiráki and Omónia squares. Ermou, the main shopping street in Athens, is mainly given over to fashion, shoes and cosmetics. One of the most pleasant places to walk around is Pláka, the traffic-calmed old quarter, with its picturesque narrow lanes. All sorts of souvenirs are sold here, from sponges to icons, copies of famous Greek statues and various objects made of marble, alabaster and onyx. Most of these are cheap mass-produced items of poor quality, but works of good quality can also be found. The quarter with the most elegant shops and the trendiest clubs is Kolonaki on the southern slope of Lykavittós Hill. Fashions by international and Greek designers, jewellers, antique shops and a number of art galleries can all be found here. Craftwork is sold at Monastiráki Square and Avissinias Square, where a flea market is held on Sundays.

GOING OUT

There are vast numbers of pubs, bars, clubs and discos in Athens with music to suit every taste, from rock to Greek folk music. Tourists are usually drawn to the traditional music tavernas in the Pláka. In the clubs, where appropriate dress is usually required for entry, things don't really get moving until after midnight, which is why they stay open until sunrise, particularly at weekends.

WHERE TO EAT

► Expensive

① *Symposio*
Erechthiou 46
Makrigianni
Tel. 21 09 22 53 21
Modern Greek cuisine using regional organic products in a garden restaurant with a view of the Acropolis

② *Daphne's*
Lysikratous 4
Tel. 21 03 22 79 71
Small restaurant in a neo-classical building of 1840 with murals and ceiling paintings; frequented by celebrities; beautiful inner courtyard with remains of an ancient wall; light Greek and international cuisine with regional dishes; reservations recommended.

► Moderate

③ *Tou Psara*
Erechthiou 16

Tel. 21 03 21 87 33
Best fish taverna in Pláka in a historic
building with shady courtyard; the
house wine is from the barrel.

④ *Thespidos*
Thespidos 18
Popular taverna directly below the
Acropolis with outside seating on
different levels

► Inexpensive
⑤ *Platanos*
Diogenous 4
Tel. 21 03 22 06 66
Romantic taverna with traditional
cooking on the small, idyllic Palea
Agora Square; popular with locals and
tourists.

Luxurious Grande Bretagne

⑥ *Xynos*
Geronda 4
Tel. 21 03 22 10 65
One of the oldest garden tavernas in
Athens; typical of Pláka, very popular
with the locals.

WHERE TO STAY
► Hotel prices in Athens
Luxury: from 200 €
Mid-range: 100–200 €
Budget: up to 100 €

► Luxury
① *Grande Bretagne*
Plateia Sýntagma
Tel. 21 03 33 00 00
www.grandebretagne.gr
262 rooms, 59 suites. Athens' most
traditional luxury hotel stands directly
opposite the parliament building. This
magnificent hotel is furnished with
antiques and has, among other things,
a fin-de-siècle ballroom and a winter
garden.

② *St George Lycabettus*
Kleomenous 2, Kolonaki
Tel. 21 07 29 07 11
Fax 21 07 29 04 39
www.sglycabettus.gr
154 rooms and suites. This idyllic
hotel stands serenely on the slope of
Lykavittós in the exclusive Kolonaki
district. Many of the rooms and the
swimming pool on the roof have a
marvellous view of the city.

► Mid-range
③ *Athens Acropol*
Pireos 1
Tel. 21 05 23 11 11
www.classicalhotels.gr
167 rooms. On noisy Omónia Square.
Well-appointed rooms along with a
restaurant, bar, gym and panorama
terrace.

⑤ *Omiros*
Apollonos 15
Tel. 21 03 23 54 86
Fax 21 03 22 80 59
www.omiroshotel.com
37 rooms. Peacefully located, small
hotel in the midst of Pláka. The
rooms are functionally furnished. The
roof garden has a superb view of the
Acropolis.

► **Budget**
④ *Arethusa*
Metropoleos 6–8
Tel. 21 03 22 94 31
www.arethusahotel.gr

87 rooms. The hotel is centrally
located close to Sýntagma. Large
rooms, some with terraces offering a
view of the Acropolis; restaurant on
the roof terrace.

⑥ *Adonis*
Kodrou 3
Tel. 21 03 24 97 37
26 rooms. Small hotel, quietly situated
in Pláka; rooms with balcony; view of
the Acropolis and Lykavittós over
breakfast in the roof garden.

from Asia Minor fled to Athens. The integration of these refugees remained a problem for decades. The city was once again the venue
for the Olympic Games in 2004. In 2008, after the death of a young
boy hit by a stray bullet fired by a policeman, young people started
violent riots (►History).

✶ ✶ Acropolis

The rock plateau of the Acropolis (»high city«) was the most suitable
place in the Attic plain for its purpose, originally a fortress of the
kings of Athens and a cult site. This religious centre of ancient
Athens gained its Classical appearance during the time of Pericles
and has become a **monument to Western culture**. In spite of the destruction wrought over the centuries, the buildings still radiate
something of the splendour of the age of Pericles, when Athens was
the intellectual, artistic and political centre of the Greek world.

⏲
Opening hours:
April–Oct daily
8am–7pm Nov–
Mar Tue–Sun
8am–5pm

All buildings of the Archaic period (7th and 6th century BC) were
destroyed in 480 BC by the Persians, including the Temple of Athena.
The remains of the old temple were torn down in 406 BC. During
reconstruction Themistocles used column drums and pieces of the
architrave that are still visible in the north wall. After 467 BC Cimon
altered the southern perimeter, building the straight length of wall
that still exists today. **Pericles** went on to beautify the site with Classical buildings. The Parthenon, Propylaea, Temple of Athena Nike
and Erechtheion were all built between 447 and 406 BC. The only
later ruins – dating from the early imperial Roman period – are
those of a circular temple dedicated to Roma and Augustus in front
of the east end of the Parthenon.

Building history

Athens Map

Platia Omonia ③
National Archaeological Museum

German
Archaeological
Institute

City Hall

Platia Kotzia

Pireos

Sofokleous

Piraeus

Platia
Koumoundourou

Evripidou

Diplou

Sari

Sofokleous

Market Hall

Agios
Athanasios

Kyriaki ✕

Ministry of
the Interior

Agii Theodori
Platia

Klafth-
monos

Athens
Municipal
Museum

Athinas

Paleologou

KERAMEIKOS

Sari

Ag. Anargiri

Agia
Chrisospiliotissa

Ermou

Agii Asomati

Karaiskaki

Menandrou

Miaouli

Agios
Georgios

Agia
Irini ✕

Platia
Ag. Irinis

Kolokotroni

Evangelistria

Lekka

Perikleous

Pl. Monastiraki

Pantanassa
Church

Ermou

Kapnikarea

Ermou

Kerameikos Cemetery, Iera Odos

Stoa of
Zeus

Adrianou

Tsisdarakis
Mosque

Pandrosou

Mitropoleos

Grand
Mitropolis

Temple of Hephaestus
Temple of Ares

Métroon

Stoa of
Attalos

Library of
Hadrian ⑤

Platia Palea
Agora

Platia
Mitropoleos

Little
Mitropolis

Odeon
Bouleuterion

Vissariou

Roman
Agorá

Adrianou

Apollonos ⑤

Agora

Agii Apostoli

Tower of
the Winds

Agios
Andreas

Nikodimou

Hill of the
Nymphs

PLAKA

Pritaniou ③

Flessa

Adrianou

Metamorfosis
tou Kottaki ⑥

Kanellopoulos
Museum

ANAFIOTIKA

Centre of
Folk Art and
Tradition ⑥

Areopagus
Hill

Metamorfosis
tou Sotiros

Erechtheion

Theorias

Beulé Gate   Propylaea

Acropolis

Stratonos

Filopappos Hill
Pnyx

Nike-Temple

Parthenon

Museum

Agia Ekaterini ②

Odeon of
Herodes
Atticus

Thespidos ④

Lysikratous

Lysikrates
Monument

Theatre of
Dionysus

Hadrian's
Arch

Tiras

①

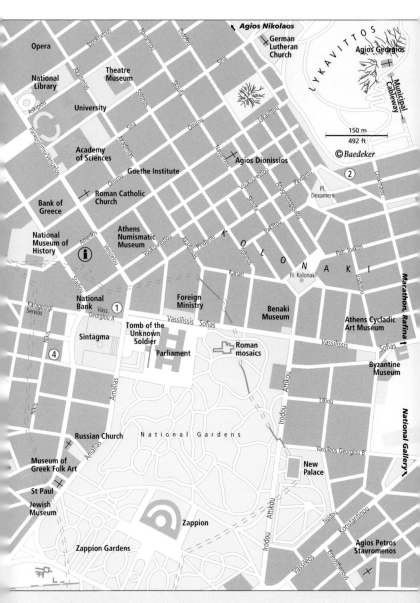

Opera

National Library

Theatre Museum

University

Academy of Sciences

Goethe Institute

Roman Catholic Church

Bank of Greece

National Museum of History

Athens Numismatic Museum

Agios Nikolaos

German Lutheran Church

LYKAVITTOS

Agios Georgios

Municipal Cableway

150 m
492 ft

© Baedeker

Agios Dionissios

Pl. Dexameni

K O L O N A K I

Pl. Kolonaki

Marathon, Rafina

National Bank

Sintagma

Tomb of the Unknown Soldier

Parliament

Foreign Ministry

Roman mosaics

Benaki Museum

Athens Cycladic Art Museum

Byzantine Museum

Russian Church

Museum of Greek Folk Art

St Paul

Jewish Museum

National Gardens

New Palace

Zappion

Zappion Gardens

National Gallery

Agios Petros Stavromenos

Vassilissis Sofias

Vassileos Georglou B'

Where to stay

① Grande Bretagne
② St George Lycabettus
③ Athens Acropol
④ Arethusa
⑤ Omiros
⑥ Adonis

The Acropolis, the »high city« of ancient Athens, towers above the Agora

Propylaea ✱ Today, the entrance to the Acropolis is south of Beulé Gate. The gate is named after its discoverer (1853), the French archaeologist Ernest Beulé. It was built in AD 267 out of the remains of buildings that were destroyed during the raid by the Heruli. Mnesicles had the tall Propylaea built between 437 and 432 BC. On the natural rock are steps, the lowest one of grey Eleusinian marble, while lighter-coloured Pentelic marble was used for the other buildings. The central part of the Propylaea is a gate wall with five doorways, which increase in width and height from the sides to the centre. The columns in the centre doorway are one metope further apart than the others. To the west is a deep portico, its central doorway bordered by 2 : 3 Ionic columns. The front of this portico, on the other hand, consists of six Doric columns which supported the pediment. While the west portico rises in an imposing manner, the east portico, which is also borne by Doric columns but is shorter and lower, appears modest when seen from the Acropolis.

Agrippa Monument Adjoining the west portico are wings, including the Pinacotheca, which contained a collection of panel paintings. In front of it is a marble plinth, the Agrippa Monument. It was named after Caesar Augustus' son-in-law, whose quadriga was set on it in 27 BC.

Acropolis Plan

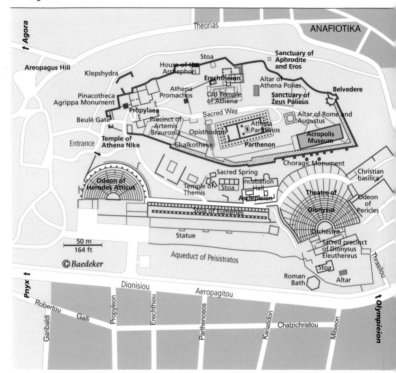

The Acropolis rock gradually rises behind the Propylaea. Beyond the ✱✱ shrine of Artemis Brauronia and the Chalkothek, in which bronze **Parthenon** offerings and weapons were stored, is the Parthenon. The Temple of Athena Parthenos, the Virgin Athena, constructed from 447 to 439 BC is the masterpiece of the architects Iktinos and **Phidias**, whom Pericles entrusted with overall supervision of the Acropolis building programme. This temple was based on an earlier, narrower building. The Parthenon was given a broader base, with eight columns at the ends instead of the previous six, and 17 instead of 16 columns on its sides. Its Doric columns are 10.43m/34ft high and have a diameter at the bottom of 1.90m/6ft 3in, at the top of 1.48m/4ft 10in. The entasis (swelling) of the shafts and the curvature of the base (slight rise towards the middle) are visible. The state treasure was probably stored in the first of the two temple chambers, whose ceiling was supported by four Ionic columns; in the other stood the gold and ivory statue of **Athena Parthenos** by the famous sculptor Phidias.

The sculptural decorations (432 BC) of the Parthenon were equally ◄ Sculptures famous: the two pediments, the Doric metopes and the Ionic frieze

running around the upper part of the cella wall. Parts of them are held in the Acropolis Museum and some in the Louvre in Paris, but most of them were taekn to London by Lord Elgin after 1801, which is why they are called the **»Elgin marbles«**.

★ ★
Erechtheion

The Erechtheion in the north of the Acropolis was constructed from 421 to 406 BC. It incorporated several very ancient shrines, which explains the complicated ground plan of the new building. The eastern part was occupied by a temple for the wooden cult figure of the patron of the city, Athena Polias. In the western part of the building the tomb of King Erechtheus, as well as that of Cecrops, the first king of Athens, were under the **caryatid porch**, which projects to the south of the Erechtheion, its entablature supported by six figures of maidens (caryatids or »kore«) instead of columns. The mark of Poseidon's trident was in the ground of the north hall. The north and east halls have six Ionic columns each. On the exterior of the cella wall, above delicate palmetto ornamentation, is a frieze of grey Eleusinian marble bearing white marble figures.

South Side of the Acropolis

★
Theatre of Dionysos

The south wall of the Acropolis offers a superb view of the Theatre of Dionysos, which was built in a natural hollow on the slope, in association with the cult of Dionysos. The earliest building phase went back to the 6th century. Around 330 BC the theatre was given the stone seating that can still be seen today, accommodating some 17,000 spectators. The rows are divided into three tiers by horizontal aisles. In the first row are the inscribed **seats of honour**. The spectator gallery included an orchestra paved with slabs and a stone barrier to separate it from the animals used in the games in Roman times. The stage building adjoining to the south was remodelled repeatedly. The reliefs depicting scenes from the Dionysos legend, dating from Roman times and re-used in a 5th-century bema, the orator's platform, are striking. The significance of the Theatre of Dionysos is that it was built when **tragedy** was first being introduced. The first drama was presented in 534 BC, probably still in the Agora, by Thespis, who travelled through the country with his theatre troupe in »Thespian carts«. It was in this theatre that the works of the three Attic tragedians Aeschylus, Sophocles and Euripides were first performed as part of the Dionysos cult. Thus European theatre originated here. Opening hours: Apr–Oct 8am–7pm, Nov–Mar daily 8.30am–5pm.

Eumenes Stoa

West of the Theatre of Dionysos stands the 163m/535ft Stoa of Eumenes, built by King Eumenes II of Pergamon (197–160 BC). Eumenes' building served as a spacious place to promenade for visitors to the Dionysos sanctuary and Theatre of Dionysos. The hall

The Dionysos Theatre below the Acropolis is regarded as the cradle of European drama

had two storeys with Doric capitals outside, Ionic capitals inside on the ground floor and Pergamene capitals on the upper floor. As the stoa is built against the slope, a retaining wall reinforced by pillars and round arches was constructed. The arcades, originally covered with marble slabs, are still visible today.

The existence of a spring on a narrow terrace above the Stoa of Eumenes caused the Asclepieion, the sanctuary of the healing god Asclepius, to be located here from 420 BC. In the right-angled area directly by the Acropolis rock stood a 50m/165ft-long, two-storey hall for the sick to lie in. Attached to it was a cave with a spring that is still regarded as having curative powers.

Asclepieion

Adjacent to the Stoa of Eumenes to the west is the Odeon. It was built in AD 161 by Herodes Atticus (AD 101–177), one of the great patrons of antiquity, who rose to high office under Roman emperors. During the Athens Festivals noted artists perform here in **plays and concerts**. There is a good view of the theatre on the way up to the Acropolis. Only open for performances.

**★
Odeon of
Herodes Atticus**

The new Acropolis Museum (Dionisiou Areopagitou 15), which opened in 2008, was designed by the **Swiss architect Bernard Tschumi** in collaboration with the Greek architect Michalis Photiadis. It holds the most valuable collection of Greek art in the world. The museum is an architectural masterpiece. Form and function are connected here in a unique harmony. The four-storey structure has glass outer walls and allows continuous views of the place of origin of its exhibit pieces: the Acropolis. The floor beneath the porch roof con-

**★ ★
Acropolis
Museum**

The best view ...

... of the Acropolis can be seen from Filopappos Hill, site of the tomb of the ruler Filopappos, who came from Komagene in southeast Anatolia, was banned to Athens from Rome and died here in AD 116. The Athenians gave him this preferential site for his tomb out of gratitude for his donations.

sists for the most part of glass bricks, which make for a clear view of the extensive remains of this part of Athens, which were exposed when the area was excavated for the construction of the museum.

The exhibits on the second floor stand in a large open room so that there is an unobstructed view from all sides. At the end of the ramp the visitor is greeted first by the reconstructed limestone pediment of the archaic Hekatonpedon, which in 570 BC stood on the site of the later Parthenon. The next exhibits are grouped thematically. After

✱
Korai ►

the Parthenon comes the Erechtheion and its Korai (7th-5th century BC), figures of women dressed in a peplos (draped garment) and later in a more elaborate chiton. The third theme is the propylaia, followed finally by the Nike temple. In each department large models show what the various structures looked like in various phases. Finally there is a model of the Acropolis during the Middle Ages.

Fourth floor ►

✱
Parthenon Frieze ►

The fourth floor faces in the same direction as the Parthenon on the Acropolis. Here a full-scale concrete replica of the beams has been constructed and the Parthenon frieze was attached to it. The difference between the original and the replica of the part that is still in the British Museum can be seen clearly (opening times: Tue–Sun 8am–8pm; www.theacropolismuseum.gr)

⊙

✱ Agora

⊙
Opening hours:
Apr–Oct daily
8am–7.30pm,
Nov–Mar daily
8am–5pm, museum
from 11am

A good impression of the whole Agora (ancient market place) can be had from the path that runs along the north slope of the Acropolis and the Areopagus. At the north entrance to the Agora on Adrianou street a display board shows the site as it looked in ancient times. From Mycenaean times to the end of the 7th century BC the area served as a burial site; it was used as an agora from the time of Solon in the 6th century BC. In the following millennium the place was the centre of public life in the city.

✱
**Stoa of Attalos/
Agora Museum**

The 116m/380ft-long stoa was built by **King Attalos II of Pergamon** (159–138 BC). The two-storey stoa (a stoa is a long colonnaded building) was faithfully reconstructed in 1953–56 to serve as the Agora Museum. The front has Doric columns below and Ionic columns above. The hall is divided into two parts by Ionic columns and houses the Agora Museum. A wealth of finds from the excavation site are displayed in the entrance hall and the room behind it. In the entrance hall the series of exhibits begins at the southern end with a colossal statue of Apollo Patroos (4th century BC). Also on display

Highlights Athens

Acropolis
The most famous building in the country was once both the centre of political power and a religious cult site.
► page 146

Lykavittós
A superb view of the metropolitan sea of lights and the Acropolis comes free with the meal when dining in the Orizontes restaurant on »Wolf Mountain«.
► page 158

National Archaeological Museum
The National Archaeological Museum presents the largest collection of ancient Greek works of art in the world.
► page 156

Acropolis Museum
The new museum offers unusual views of outstanding exhibits.
► page 149

are a painted Ionic capital dating from the 5th century BC, a female figure (opposite column 4; 4th century BC), flanked by two herms and sculptures from the Temple of Hephaestus (opposite column 11). The long main room presents a large collection in chronological order of finds which are less important as works of art than as testimony to life in antiquity. The collection begins with pieces from the Neolithic third millennium BC. From the Mycenaean period (1500–1100 BC) there are vases and grave goods, including two ivory boxes with reliefs of gryphons and nautiluses. From the early Iron Age (11th–8th century BC) the display includes 9th-century graves with their contents. The magnificent 9th-century BC Protogeometric and Geometric vases are from the same period. Beyond oriental-style ✱ vases is a mould used to cast a bronze statue in the Archaic period ◄ Geometric vases (6th century BC). Many of the exhibits illustrate daily life in the Classical period, the 5th century BC, including inscriptions, a device for drawing lots for public offices, and pot sherds used as tokens in ostracism courts (»ostrakon« means »pot sherd«), one with the scratched-in name of Themistocles.

Three tall tritons mark the Odeon of Agrippa, which stands in the **Odeon of** centre of the Agora north of the middle stoa. It was built in 20 BC **Agrippa** by the **Roman commander Agrippa** and contained a square room with a stage and 18 rows of seats for about 1,000 spectators. The entrance was on the south side. In the 2nd century AD a new entrance was created in the north. Walk west from here to get to the buildings on the west side.

On the southwest side of the Agora is the **Tholos**, a round building **Metroon** with a diameter of 18m/60ft. Erected about 465 BC, it served as the meeting place of the 50 prytanei. To the north stands the Metroon,

Agorá Plan

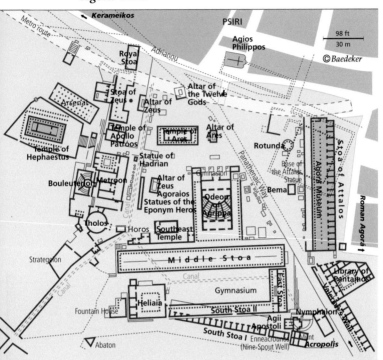

the temple to the mother goddess, behind which is the **Bouleuterion** (5th century BC); here the Council of the 500 met. The next building – also only the foundations – is the **Temple of Apollo Patroos** (4th century BC), whose statue is now in the Stoa of Attalos. Athens' oldest register of inhabitants and their status was found in an annexe. The **Stoa of Zeus Eleutherios**, who protected the freedom of the city, occupies the northwest corner of the Agora up to the Metro station. It was probably built around 430 BC by Mnesicles. In front of it on a round base is a statue of Zeus Eleutherios.

Royal Stoa

The Royal Stoa was built soon after 480 BC. It was the **seat of the Archon Basileus**, the magistrate who inherited all the cult functions of the earlier kings. Among them was to try the crime of impiety. The trial of **Socrates**, who was sentenced to death by poisoning, was probably held here.

★ ★
Temple of Hephaestus

From the Tholos a path leads to the top of the Agora, which is dominated by the Temple of Hephaestus (Hephaisteion). It was located close to the district of blacksmiths and craftsmen and dedicated to the deities of blacksmiths and the arts, Hephaestus and Athena. It is **one of the best-preserved Greek temples** because conversion into a Christian church in the 5th century saved it from destruction. A Doric temple built in the late 5th century BC, at about the same time as the Parthenon on the Acropolis but considerably smaller, it has a Classical ground plan of 6 : 13 columns. The damaged pronaos frieze shows battle scenes, the west frieze battles between Lapiths and centaurs; in the centre, the Lapith Caeneus is being battered to the ground by two centaurs. Despite the lack of space, the cult image of Hephaestus and Athena, created by Alkamenes and set up in the cella in 420 BC, was surrounded by columns. When the temple was converted into a Christian church dedicated to St George, the wooden roof was replaced by the present barrel vault.

✳ Pláka

The old quarter, Pláka (»slab«), lies between the north slope of the Acropolis and Odos Ermou and Filellinon/Amalias streets to the east. Of course it is a large tourist attraction today and seems to consist

The Hephaisteion on the Agora hill is one of the best-preserved temples in the country

only of tavernas and souvenir shops, yet its alleys and squares with modest neo-classical houses, a few tiny Byzantine churches and ancient monuments have a pleasant atmosphere. Today Pláka is a **protected heritage area**; pedestrian zones have been established and night clubs banned. Pláka is not large, and is best explored by just drifting from one pretty corner to the next. The following description is recommended as a walking tour.

Plateia Monastiráki

The area around Monastiráki Square is one of the most colourful in Athens; street traders and rustic tavernas contribute to the atmosphere. Its name »little monastery« comes from the **Pantanassa** a 17th-century former monastery church. Two ancient bazaar streets lead off the square: to the west Ifestou, to the east Pandrosou, where there is a flea market on Sundays. Behind the Tzisdarakis Mosque (today housing a **ceramics collection** (opening hours: Mon and Wed–Sun 9am–2.30pm) are the Corinthian columns of the **library** built by Emperor Hadrian after AD 132. This building was a large colonnaded courtyard, whose outer wall is marked by exedra (semi-circular bays). Part of the west side is extant. The middle room in the east wing served as a library (opening times:Apr–Oct daily 8am–7pm; otherwise Tue–Sun 8.30am–3pm).

Tower of the Winds

Eolou – a street with a beautiful view of the Acropolis and its north walls with re-used column drums – leads to the Tower of the Winds, which is included in the grounds of the Roman Agora today. The excellently preserved octagonal tower, erected around 40 BC by the Syrian Andronicus, contained a water clock that displayed the time according to the height of the water in a cylinder. The tower took its name from the eight wind gods depicted in reliefs. Among them

Roman Agora

sundials have survived. The square has two gates, the Doric gate in the west, erected between 12 BC and AD 2, and the Ionic propylon, thought to date back to the time of Emperor Hadrian (2nd century), in the east. Inside there are colonnades and behind them rooms for shops and trading; on the south side there is a fountain. In the Turkish period, the **Fethiye Mosque** was built in the northern part of the market. Opening times: Apr–Oct daily 8am–7.30pm, Nov–Mar Tue–Sun 8.30am–3pm.

Lysikrates Monument

At the end of Lysikrates street the Lysikrates Monument stands in a little square. The walls of thise round structure are adorned with Corinthian columns. The narrow frieze below the roof shows scenes from the life of Dionysos. According to tradition the stone acanthus flower on the roof once bore a bronze tripod kettle which Lysikrates won in a tragedy contest in 334 BC and displayed here.

★

Little Mitropolis

To the north of Pláka on Mitropoleos Square stand the old and new main churches of the city. The Little Mitropolis, dedicated to Agios Eleftherios, is a beautifully proportioned 12th-century cruciform

The best place to end the day is a cosy taverna in Pláka.

domed church. Many ancient and medieval fragments were used in its walls, including two sections of a 4th-century calendar frieze. It is also decorated with pilaster capitals, above them coats of arms of the Villehardouin and de la Roche families (13th century) and under them Byzantine reliefs with Christian symbols (9th/10th century).

Modern Athens

To the east Ermou and Stadiou lead into the large square called Plateia Sýntagmatos, which has been called Sýntagma (»constitution«) since the revolution of 1843. The **palace** of King Otto I and his wife Amalia was built here from 1834 to 1838; since 1935 it has housed the Greek **parliament**. Built by **Friedrich von Gaertner** on the highest point on the square, it dominates the ministries, hotels, office buildings and banks that line Sýntagma. The Evzones keep watch at the Tomb of the Unknown Soldier in front of parliament and perform their picturesque »ballet« every hour.

Plateia Sýntagmatos

A stop for coffee in front of the famous Cafe Dionysus Zonar is an opportunity to take a look at Schliemann's House, which was built in 1879 in the style of the Italian Renaissance. This »Trojan palace« is where the archaeologist Heinrich Schliemann lived with his Greek wife Sophia. Today the numismatic collection of the National Ar-

★
Schliemann's House/ Numismatic Museum of Athens

! *Baedeker* TIP

Art in the Metro

Numerous remnants dating back to the Mycenaean, Classical and Byzantine periods were uncovered during the construction of the Metro between 1993 and 2000, and they are displayed very attractively at some Metro stations. When riding on the Metro, allow time to view these valuable artefacts. Ancient sculptures, gravestones, jewellery and household articles can be marvelled at in the Akropoli, Evangelismos, Panepistimiou and Sýntagma stations.

chaeological Museum is housed here. With 600,000 coins it is **one of the most important museums of its kind in the world**. Schliemann's coin collection, which comes mainly from Troy, is also on display. Opening hours: Tue–Sun 8.30am–3pm. The neo-classical building in Stadiou, designed by the French architect François Boulanger and built in 1858, was the seat of parliament until 1934. The **National Historical Museum** today housed here presents the history of Greece from the conquest of Constantinople by the Ottoman Turks in 1453 to the Italian invasion of Greece in 1940. The focal point is the 19th-century **fight for independence**. In front of the house is a monument to the war hero Kolokotronis. Opening times: Tue–Sun 9am–2pm.

University, Academy, National library

The main feature of 19th-century urban planning in this area was the elegant, yet quite academic-looking, so-called Athenian trilogy: the University (1837–52) by **Christian Hansen** from Copenhagen flanked by two elaborate buildings by his younger brother, Theophil, the Academy of Sciences (1859–85) and the National Library (1887–1902). The frescoes at the University and Academy were done by the Bavarian artist Karl Rahl. In front of the Academy are two columns with statues of Athena and Apollo, and on either side of the steps statues of Plato and Socrates seated. Panepistimiou is a street otherwise characterized by modern shops with a few remains of neo-classical two-storey buildings. The street ends at a roundabout, the noisy and bustling Omónia Square.

National Archaeological Museum

The National Archaeological Museum (Pattission 44) was built between 1860 and 1889 to plans by Ludwig Lange and Ernst Ziller. It holds **the largest collection of art of Greek antiquity in existence**, which makes it a must for every visitor to Athens. The wealth of its collections can only be explored with repeated visits. A project to renovate and reopen the museum departments one after another has been under way since 2004. The collections date from the Mycenaean (1600–1150 BC), Geometric (9th–8th centuries), Archaic (7th–6th centuries.) Classical (5th–4th centuries), Hellenistic (3rd–1st centuries BC) and Roman periods. The **finds of Heinrich Schliemann** in the mountains of Mycenae (1600–1150 BC) are in one department. On display is the famous gold mask of a king, known as the mask of Agamemnon (around 1580 BC). In the Cyclades department unusual finds from the 3rd and 2nd millennium BC are exhibit. Characteris-

Fresco of »Boxing Boys«

tic of the highly developed art of this culture are the **Cyclades idols** with folded arms, and Cyclades pans, part of the death and divinity cults. The most striking innovation of the Archaic era consists in monumental marble statues of **kouroi**, larger than life statues of youths that depict a powerful ideal image of masculinity. The Classical era is represented with masterpieces of sculpture and reliefs, including **Zeus** (460 BC) hurling a thunderbolt and the moving **gravestone of Hegeso** (around 400 BC). The colourful paintings from Akrotiri on Santorini (16th century BC) are enchanting. The superb **vase collection** includes an impressive variety of items from almost all epochs of Greek art. Opening times: Mon 1.30pm– 7.30pm, Tue–Sun 8am–7.30pm, holidays 8.30am–3pm. ⏱

Other Sights

Between Leoforos Vassilissis Sofias and Lykavittós lies the exclusive city district of Kolonaki, where ministries and embassies have found appropriate accommodation. There are trendy upscale shops and cafes around Plateia Filikis Eterias, as **Kolonaki Square** is properly called. Some of Athens' major museums are located in Boulevard Vas. Sofias.

Kolonaki

The Byzantine Museum (Vas. Sofias 22) is housed in a villa built by Stamatis Kleanthis in 1840 and has regular rotating exhibitions. The permanent exhibition is presented in a highly modern way in a new section that is largely underground. It presents the full spectrum of Byzantine art, from from everyday life and medieval technology through administrative and military structures to music, literature and architecture. Just how deeply early Christian art is rooted in antiquity is also presented in detail (opening hours: April–Oct Mon 1.30–7.30pm, Tue–Sun 8am–7.30pm, Nov–Mar Tue–Sun 8.30am–3pm; www.byzantinemuseum.gr).

★
Byzantine and Christian Museum

⏱

Right next door the War Museum (Vas. Sofias 24) has implements of war from the Stone Age until World War II. It covers wars in which Greece took part, e.g. the Persian Wars. Opening hours: Tue–Fri 9am–2pm; Sat, Sun 9.30am–2pm.

War Museum

⏱

The Benaki Museum (Kumpari 1) developed out of the private collection of **Antonios Benakis**, the son of a wealthy cotton merchant. In an old building and a modern wing it presents in an attractive

★
Benaki Museum

and informative manner about four and a half millennia of Greek cultural history from the Cyclades idols to icons and modern Greek painting. It also has exhibits from the Greek War of Independence of 1821, beautiful folk costumes and ancient ceramics. Opening times: Wed–Mon 9am–5pm, Thu until midnight, Sat until 3pm.

Museum of Cycladic Art

The core of the Museum of Cycladic and Ancient Greek Art (Neofitou Douka 4) is the **famous collection of the ship-owner Nikolaos Goulandris**. On display are masterpieces of Cycladic culture (3200–2000 BC), including the well-known, almost abstract marble figures known as the **Cycladic idols**, as well as pottery, bronzes and glass from the Geometric to the post-Classical period. The **Stathatos House** added in 1992 houses the academy's collection of ancient Greek art. Opening times: Mon, Wed, Fri, Sat 10am–5pm, Tue 10am–8pm, Sun 11am–5pm; internet: www.cycladic.gr.

✱ Lykavittós Hill

The way to the top of Lykavittós, the 277m/909ft »Wolf Hill«, leads from Dexameni Square, about 200m/200yd north of Kolonaki Square, between pines and cypresses (street and funicular railway from the top end of Plutarchou street). According to myth when Athena heard about the fate of the daughters of Cecrops, she dropped here the rock that she had intended to use to elevate the Acropolis. Thus the hill was formed. On its summit are a cafe and a restaurant, as well as a chapel to Agios Georgios which is visible from far and wide. In the **open-air theatre** jazz, rock and theatre performances are held during the Athens Festival. On the rare days when the air is clear there is a fantastic view from here to the sea.

National Garden

In 1836 Queen Amalia, the wife of King Otto I, initiated the laying out of a park in barren land south and east of the palace. This developed into today's National Garden. The botanist Karl Froos designed the garden and the chief court gardener Friedrich Schmidt built it by the 1860s. East of the National Garden, in Irodou Attikou, stands the **crown prince's palace**, which was built by Ziller in 1898; it was later the king's palace and is now the president's residence. To the south, the extension of the National Garden is **Zappion Park** with the exhibition and congress hall, which was built by Theofil Hansen and Ernst Ziller from 1874 to 1888 in Athenian neo-classical style.

Hadrian's Gate

Next to Leoforos Amalias, a busy road to the west of the Olympieion, Hadrian's Gate (AD 131–132), marks the boundary between ancient Athens and the Roman extension of the city, between the »city of Theseus« and the »city of Hadrian«, as the inscriptions on the outside and inside of the gate express it.

✱ Olympieion

When Odos Singrou was laid out from Piraeus to Athens in the 19th century, it was planned to terminate in two massive columns. These are part of the Olympieion, which dominates the area east of the

Acropolis. This, **the largest sacred structure in Athens**, dates back to the Peisistratid tyrants. The Seleucid king Antiochos IV (175–164 BC) resumed its construction, but it was Emperor Hadrian who had it completed in AD 130 after a total construction period lasting about 700 years. As an expression of the tastes of the times of the tyrants, a Syrian king and a Roman emperor, the Temple of Olympian Zeus was and remains at odds with the Attic sense of proportion. The Olympieion still stands today in the shadow of the Acropolis, even though the quality of its construction deserves greater consideration. Gone is the cella that once held a statue of Hadrian along with the cult image of Zeus; gone too are most of its 104 columns, for which 15,500 tons of marble were needed. However, the surviving 13 columns on the southeast corner are of imposing size. On the south side there are also two columns still standing and one that fell over in 1852. It is unclear whether the 13 extant columns are from the Hellenistic period and the three southern columns from the Roman structure, or whether they are all Roman. Opening hours: April–Oct ⊙ daily 8am–7.30pm, Nov–Mar daily 8am–5pm.

The Athenian stadium, nestled between two hills east of the Olympieion, is today called the »**Panathinaikos**«, the Panathenaic Stadium. The stadium of Pentelic marble with a seating capacity of 60,000 is modern, but has the same form and occupies the same site as its an-   **Stadium**

The Olympieion: the largest temple in Athens stands in the shadow of the Acropolis

cient predecessor in which the Panathenaic Games were held. Herodes Atticus, whose grave is on the hill adjacent to the north, had the stadium rebuilt in marble in AD 140–144. The stadium was again rebuilt for the **Olympic Games of 1896**, thanks to a wealthy private citizen, Georgios Averof, who thus continued the ancient tradition of benefactors (euergetes).

✶
Kerameikos

Bordering the Agora to the northwest is the **potters' quarter of ancient Athens**, which extends westward as far as the Academy and is named after Keramos, the patron of potters. From 479 BC, the city wall that Themistocles built after the attack by the Persians divided the area into an inner and an outer Kerameikos. The excavations include only the area of Kerameikos along the city wall between Odos Ermou and Odos Pireos. There were two gates here: the Sacred Way led through the Sacred Gate to Eleusis; within the excavation site another street turned off towards Piraeus (Street of Tombs). The larger dipylon (double gate) is the starting point of a 38m/125ft-wide street leading to the Academy. Monumental funerary amphorae (»Dipylon vases«, 8th century BC) are on display in the National Museum. Today complexes dating from the 5th–4th centuries BC dominate the scene. Many individual graves, burial precincts and terraces can be seen, as well as funerary monuments. Some are originals, but most are copies.

✶
Kerameikos Museum ▶

Ⓒ

The entrance to the Kerameikos Museum is on Ermou Street. The extensive collection of ceramics from the 10th to the 5th century BC is worth seeing. The museum also has some funerary sculptures: the relief of Ampharete with her grandchild (around 410 BC), the equestrian relief of Dexileos, who fell in 394 BC near Corinth, the Archaic funerary stele of Eupheros (around 500 BC), a sphinx as tomb guardian and an equestrian statue. Opening hours: April–Oct daily 8am–7.30pm, Nov–Mar daily 8.30am–3pm.

Piraeus · Pireás (Πειραιές)

Greece's main port

The port of Piraeus and Athens **have always formed one metropolitan area together**. Greece's main port – and one of the most important in the Mediterranean Sea – is also a major economic factor and a tourism hub. Shipping routes go from here to the rest of Europe and the Near East, as well as to most of the Greek islands. The city is a mixture of busy harbours, bustling urban life and a special atmosphere that can be experienced, for example, around the main harbour, Zea yacht harbour, Mikrolimano fishing and yacht harbour and on Korais Square.

✶
Piraeus Archaeological Museum

Piraeus Archaeological Museum (Charilaou Trikoupi 31) has exhibits, especially sculptures, which were discovered in Piraeus and along the Attic coast. On the ground floor in rooms 7 and 8 there are funerary monuments from the 4th century BC, including the mausole-

Excellent fish restaurants attract guests to Mikrolimano harbour in Piraeus

um of a merchant from Istria. **Hellenistic and Roman sculptures**, with two colossal statues of Emperor Hadrian (rooms 9, 10) can also be viewed. On the upper floor in the vestibule are naval exhibits, then pottery from various eras and a collection of musical instruments (room 2). The highlights of the museum are the famous bronze statues of Apollo and Artemis (4th century BC), which were discovered in the nearby harbour (rooms 3, 4). The Apollo is the oldest bronze statue ever discovered. There is also a major collection of marble funerary reliefs of the 5th and 4th centuries BC (room 6). Opening hours: Tue–Sun 8.30am–3pm.

✱
◀ Bronze statues

The Hellenic Maritime Museum, housed in a modern, semi-circular building directly on the Zea Marina below the street, provides an insight into the development of Greek seafaring since antiquity. The exhibit begins with models of Minoan and ancient ships, including an Athenian trireme (room B). The collection from the *Argo*, the yacht that belonged to Aristotle Onassis, includes ship models and nautical instruments from the 17th until the 19th century (room D). The theme of room E is the Greek War of Independence (models, flags, weapons), and room F examines the period from 1830 until the Balkan wars in the early 20th century. The **first Greek submarine** is on display here. The exhibition is rounded off by an interesting depiction of the Greek merchant marine and traditional shipbuilding (rooms H, I). Opening hours: Tue–Fri 9am–2pm, Sat, Mon 9.30am–1.30pm.

✱
Hellenic Maritime Museum

⊙

Salamis · Salamína (Σαλαμίνα)

Island with a famous battle

Salamis (population 38,000), the largest of the Saronic Islands, lies immediately west of Piraeus. The hills, partially of karst limestone, are sparsely wooded. There is modest agriculture, and many of the islanders work in Athens or regional industries (wharfs, refineries). Salamina Town is completely overrun at weekends by local trippers and not suitable for a vacation. Only the southern beaches are good for swimming (Paralia, Perani, Peristeria, Karakiani).

Phoenician settlers from Cyprus gave the island its name (»shalâm« meaning »peace, rest«). Long a bone of contention between Athens and Megara, it was conquered in 598 BC by Solon and Peisistratos for Athens. Salamis made history when, in 480 BC, the battle-weakened Athenians led by Themistocles with 378 triremes inflicted a devastating defeat on a far superior Persian fleet consisting of more than 1,200 ships at the Battle of Salamis, once and for all destroying the Persian king Xerxes' plans for expanding to the west. The **battle** took place in waters east of Salamis between the islands of Agios Georgios and Psyttaleia to the north and the Kynosoura peninsula to the south.

What to see

The unattractive island capital **Salamina** sprawls along the north side of a deep bay on the west coast. Around 3km/2mi to the east is the main port of **Paloukia**. The **archaeological museum** on Agios Nikolaos beach, 4km/2.5mi from Paloukia, has mainly funerary reliefs of the 4th century BC from the ancient necropolis. A very scenic road leads 6km/4mi west of Salamina to **the Convent of Faneromeni** with a highly revered icon of the Virgin Mary and a remarkable large fresco, the *Last Judgement*, on which more than 3,000 people are depicted. The convent was built in 1661 using materials from an ancient shrine on the same site. At the foot of the hill is the dock for the ferry to Neo Perama.

Chíos

O/P 7/8

Greek: Χίος
Area: 842 sq km/325 sq mi
Altitude: 0–1,267m/4,157ft
Capital: Chíos Town

Island group: North and east Aegean islands
Population: 51,000

The rugged island of Chíos, separated from Turkey by a strait 8km/5mi wide, attracts visitors with its varied landscape, unspoilt coves and medieval villages.

A huge, rugged limestone massif running north-south occupies the greater part of the island. It rises in the north to a height of 1,267m/

Chíos Map

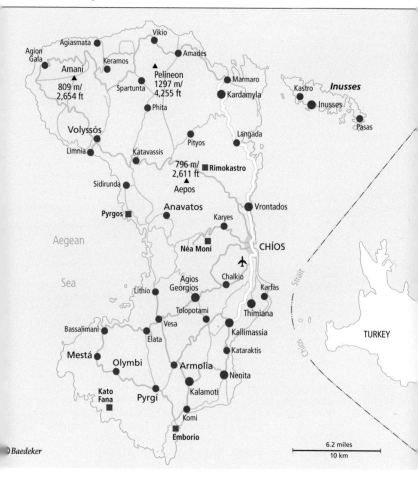

4,157ft at Mt Profitis Ilias and forms an impressive coastline, particularly in the east. In the fertile south, along with olives, wine, figs and citrus fruits, **mastic** trees are cultivated. The excellent aromatic resin of the mastic tree, known as mastic or mastix, was already exported in ancient times and helped to make the island wealthy. A bitter-sweet liqueur, masticha, and a very sweet confection, chewing gum and cosmetics are produced from mastic. About one third of the Greek merchant marine fleet is based in Chíos. Many ship-owners come from the island and still own magnificent villas there today. But Chíos is also popular among political leaders from Athens,

▶ VISITING CHÍOS

INFORMATION
Tourist information
Kanari 181
Chíos Town
Tel. 22 71 04 43 89

GETTING THERE
There are ships to Alexandroupoli, Kavala, Piraeus and Thessaloniki on the mainland, and to the islands of Fourni, Ikaría, Kos, Lesbos, Mýkonos, Rhodes, Samos, Sýros and Tinos.

WHERE TO EAT
▶ Moderate
Chotzas
Stefanous Tsouri 74
Chíos Town
Tel. 22 71 04 27 87
Rustic taverna with a cosy garden; traditional dishes, house-distilled ouzo and retsina from the barrel

WHERE TO STAY
▶ Luxury
Golden Sand Hotel
Karfas
Tel. 22 71 03 20 80
www.goldensand.gr
108 rooms. Directly on the beach; relatively new hotel: all rooms with terrace or balcony

▶ Mid-range
Aepos Touristic & Athletic Village
Vrontados
Tel. 22 71 09 22 66
www.aepos-village.gr
55 rooms. A cottage can be rented here for up to four persons; wonderfully situated in a pine forest, this holiday village offers all sorts of sports activities and, naturally, a pool.

whose beautiful holiday homes can be seen along the coast. Shipping brought great wealth not only to the ship-owners. The inhabitants of Chíos enjoy a living standard higher than in other parts of Greece. Shipping is still the main source of income, so that tourism plays hardly any role on the island. It has been said that the ship-owners and politicians want to keep this beautiful island for themselves, so they try to hinder the development of tourism. The people of Chíos rose up against the Turks in 1822, who retaliated with a **horrific massacre** in which 30,000 people lost their lives or were taken into slavery. This caused a wave of indignation in western Europe.

Chíos Town and Surroundings

✳
Chíos Town
The capital and main port, Chíos Town (population 30,000), is located approximately on the site of the ancient city in the middle of the east coast. The large semi-circular harbour basin is lined picturesquely by countless street cafes, which fill up in the evening. Little remains of the old town. The houses that survived the massacre of 1822 were destroyed in the earthquake of 1881, yet the town possesses a pleasant oriental atmosphere. In the background barren grey

The capital of Chíos borders a bay on the east coast

hills rise up like a mountain and form a charming contrast to the bright row of houses along the harbour promenade.

Vounaki Square

Vounaki Square, the centre of the town, is bordered by new office buildings, giant plane trees and many street cafes. The bus terminal, where local and overland buses arrive and depart, and the central taxi stand are nearby. The city park is northeast of the square. At the corner of Martiron Street near the park there is a pretty **Turkish fountain** of 1768. The former mosque with a minaret at Vounaki Square now houses the **Byzantine Museum**. Along with medieval exhibits there is a copy of the Delacroix painting *Massacre of Chíos* (closed for restoration).

Kastro

East of Vounaki Square is the main entrance, Porto Maggiore, to the medieval kastro, the fortified old town. It was originally built in the 10th century under Byzantine rule and fortified by the Genoese in the 14th century. During Turkish rule only Muslims and Jews were allowed to live within the city walls. The little Turkish cemetery with marble grave steles for dignitaries dates from this period. The **Giustiniani Museum** now occupies the 15th-century palace of the Venetian governor; it has a small collection of Byzantine art and early Christian floor mosaics. The Genoese church lies east of the Turkish cemetery. **Agios Georgios** (10th century) was converted into a mosque in 1566. In front of the church is a Turkish sarcophagus which was used as a basin for ritual ablutions.

Korais Library
On the southeast corner of the park the main shopping street Odos Aplotarias begins. At the end of the street turn left into F. Argentis to get to the Korais Library. The third-largest library in Greece is based on the important collection of books of the Chíos philologist Adamantios Korais (1748–1833). This building also houses the large **painting and folk art collection** of the Argentis family, which Filippos Argentis (portrait bust in front of the building) donated; along with engravings and cards there are beautiful embroideries and folk costumes.

Archaeological museum
From the harbour promenade turn in to Michalos Street to get to the archaeological museum of Chíos, which displays finds from Emborio and Fana and a stone from the year 332 BC with a »letter« from Alexander the Great carved into it.

Kampos
On the plain south of the city, the fertile Kampos, rich residents have built their **villas** in walled compounds. The residences usually have two to three storeys and are surrounded by high stone walls, which make it impossible to see them from the street. Imposing gates lead to lush gardens. Some of the old houses have been restored and transformed into beautiful traditional guesthouses. The best-kept of the historic residences belongs to Filippos Argentis; it is located in the middle of an orange grove on Argentis Street and is open to the public. It gives a good impression of the life of the Genoese and Greek nobility.

✱
Karfas
(Καρψάσ)
To get to Karfas, the island's tourist centre, leave Chíos Town heading south, pass the airport and continue for 6km/4mi; Karfas was only established in the 1980s. It offers all the conveniences of a modern seaside resort. The broad beach is flat and suitable for small children.

✱ ✱ Néa Moní and Surroundings

🕐
Opening hours:
April–Oct daily
7am–8pm
Nov–Mar Tue–Sun
8.30am–3pm

A panoramic road leads 15km/9mi from Chíos Town through the colourful village of Karyes northwest to Néa Moni, a monastic site in the midst of lush green mountain scenery, inhabited by a few nuns. It was founded by **Emperor Constantine IX Monomachos** (reigned 1042 – 55) on the spot where a miracle-working Madonna icon was found in a myrtle bush; its mosaics with gold backgrounds mean that it is certainly the work of artists from Constantinople. Next to the monastery churches of Dafni and Osios Loukas it is the third great achievement of Byzantine church art of the 11th century and is a **Unesco World Heritage site**. Like that of the monastery church of Dafni, the dome of the convent church rests on eight pillars and spans the full width of the church. The walls retain their original facing of red marble. The colourful **mosaics** were partly destroyed in the earthquake of 1881, specifically the ones in the dome, which col-

Néa Moní Monastery, one of the major examples of Byzantine architecture in Greece, is located in lush green mountains

lapsed. When the church was restored the dome was reconstructed and the remaining mosaics secured against further decay. They depict the Baptism of Christ, the Crucifixion, the Deposition from the Cross and the Resurrected Christ in Limbo. The archangels Michael and Gabriel are depicted in the left and right side apses and the Virgin Mary in the main apse. There are also major mosaics in the narthex: the Washing of Feet, saints of Chíos around the Panagia, Judas' Betrayal. All of these mosaics date from the time when the convent was founded around 1050. The frescoes in the porch (including the Last Judgement) were painted in the late Byzantine period (14th century). The rest of the buildings have been in a partially ruined condition since the Turkish massacre in 1822. The chapel next to the convent gate was built in memory of the victims of the massacre; there is also a charnel house here. The former trapeza (dining hall) and the large cistern are also worth noting; turn right a few metres after passing through the main gate. There is a beautiful view from the terrace in front of the new trapeza. A few miles higher lies the **mountain monastery Trion Pateron**. It is dedicated to three hermits who lived here; Néa Moní was founded from here. The dark impressive rock church is now accessible for women as well.

Further northwest a newly made road leads to the village of Anavatos, which has been almost deserted since 1822 and nestles impressively below a sheer rock with castle ruins. Some of the houses have been restored as holiday accommodation, as have the two churches near the upper castle.

Anavatos
(Ανάβατος)

The South of the Island

Pyrgi
(Πυργί) The pretty town of Pyrgi (population 1,300), some 30km/19mi southwest of Chíos Town, is at the centre of the Mastihoria, the 20 mastic-producing villages. The grey and white houses, whose geometric patterns are created by sgraffiti technique, are particularly charming. Bright red tomatoes strung on cords and hung up for drying on many of the balconies provide a colourful contrast. There is the tower of a Genoese castle above the village. **Agios Apostolos**, a 12th-century church with frescoes of 1665 that are worth seeing, follows the architectural model of Néa Moni.

! **Baedeker TIP**

Relaxing beach life
Many beautiful beaches are almost deserted during the off-season along the central west coast approximately opposite the Néa Moní convent.

Emboreios
(Εμπορίο) Near the picturesque little port Emboreios on the south coast a settlement of the 7th century BC and remains of a temple dedicated to Athena were discovered. The nearby black pebble beaches are the results of a volcanic eruption.

Houses decorated with sgraffiti are the special attraction in Pyrgi

The road from Pyrgi to the northwest passes the port of Bassalimani (43km/25mi from Chíos). En route the fortified medieval village of Olympi has kept its old appearance.

Olympi
(Ολύμποι)

Further on is Mesta, the prettiest and best-preserved of the fortified villages. The outer ring of fortified houses formed the city wall. It is worth looking inside the 18th-century **Palios Taxiarhe Church** to see the carved iconostasis. The road back to Chíos Town also passes through Elata and Vessa.

✶
Mesta
(Μεστά)

The North of the Island

The Voriohora begins north of Chíos Town. Compared to the fertile southern part of the island, the mountainous north is rather dry, but in the river plains, which usually dry out in summer, there are scattered oasis-like settlements with lush vegetation. The contrast to the picturesque, but mostly bare mountain backdrop gives these places the appearance of paradise.

✶
Rugged mountains with fertile spots

Langada (15km/9mi) is a popular and pretty village at the end of a bay. **Kardamyla** (27km/17mi) with the port of **Marmaro** (sandy beach) is the main town of the northeast and very popular among Greeks. The pretty tree-lined plateia in Kardamyla is the place to meet. Via Viki and the picturesque Keramos go on to **Agion Gala** (50km/30mi). The 13th-century Church of Panagia Agiogalousena stands directly at the entrance to a limestone cave. From Keramos continue south to **Volissos**, which climbs up a slope impressively and is topped by a Byzantine fortress. Another road leads from Chíos northwest along the northern slope of Marathovounos to Volissos (40km/24mi) and its port Limnia, where boats leave for the island of Psara.

Via Langada to the north coast

Corfu · Kérkyra

✶

A/B 5/6

Greek: Κέρκυρα
Area: 592 sq km/1,942 sq mi
Population: 112,000
Capital: Kérkyra

Island group: Ionian Islands
Altitude: 0–906m/2,972ft above sea level

Corfu – or Kérkyra as the Greeks call it – is one of the most popular islands in the Mediterranean Sea. Its gentle, rolling mountainous countryside with its ancient, silvery-gleaming, light-green olive trees and slender, dark cypresses, fabulous coves and, not least, the island capital with its Italian atmosphere are something special.

★★
Holiday island

The northernmost of the Ionian Islands is separated from the coast of Albania and the Greek region of Epiros by a channel between 2km and 20km (about 1–12mi) wide. Although Corfu is not the largest island in the archipelago, it is a good 60km/37mi long and up to 28km/17mi wide, and does have the largest population. Even back in the late 19th century, the picturesque island with its green landscape, peaceful villages and magnificent bays for swimming attracted holiday guests. **Empress Elisabeth** of Austria, niece of King Otto of Greece, and the German emperor **Wilhelm II** liked to spend the summer months here; today tourists come from all over the world, but especially from the United Kingdom. Hotels line up one beside the other on the east coast, while the west coast of the island has remained largely undeveloped. Here there are many beautiful beaches and still some more individual accommodation. The interior is delightful, particularly the mountainous north with its secluded towns and villages where time seems to stand still. The island's only »trademark« are its **ancient olive trees** that reach up to 25m/80ft in height and have formed real forests. In fact, during Venetian times a premium was paid for every new olive tree planted. **Kumquats**, dwarf oranges planted nowhere else in Greece, are a speciality of Corfu.

Mythology and history

Corfu is thought to be the Homeric Scheria, the land of the Phaeacians and their king Alcinous; **Ulysses**, who was stranded on the shores of Scheria during his Odyssey, was brought to Alcinous by Nausicaa. Colonized by Corinth in 734 BC, the island developed into a dangerous rival to Corinth itself. It became part of the Roman Empire (named Corcyra in Latin) in 229 BC. When the Roman Empire was divided in AD 395, it fell to Byzantium. The medieval name Corfu seems to have derived from the Greek word Koryphi, meaning »peak«. Corfu was under Venetian control from 1386 until 1797, when it became part of Napoleon's empire. After 1815, it and the rest of the Ionian Islands were ruled by Britain until 1864, when it passed to Greece. In 1943 German troops occupied the island. Corfu was repeatedly devastated during the course of its history, so that evidence of its ancient and medieval past has largely been destroyed.

★★ Corfu Town/Kérkyra

Lively island capital

The capital of the island, situated on foothills on the east coast, is Corfu/Kérkyra (population 28,000). Kérkyra has an especially beautiful **old town, the Kambiello**, a protected heritage area. It is the product of the Venetian, French and British occupations. It is a maze of lanes spanned by arches alternating with splendid palazzi and ornate wrought-iron balconies. There is no beach, so few tourists elect to stay in Corfu for long and it has been able to keep its charm.

New Fortress

The harbour lies on the northern edge of town, which is only used for small boats now. The massive New Fortress (Neo Frourio,

Corfu · Kérkyra Map

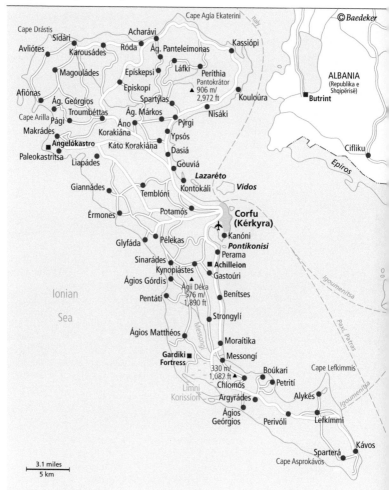

© Baedeker

Cape Agía Ekaterini

Cape Drástis
Sidári
Acharávi
Avliótes
Karousádes
Róda
Ág. Panteleímonas
Kassiópi
Magouládes
Epískepsi
Láfki
Períthia
ALBANIA
(Republika e
Shqipërisë)
Afiónas
Episkopí
Pantokrátor
▲ 906 m/
2,972 ft
Ág. Geórgios
Spartýlas
Kouloúra
Butrint
Cape Arilla Pági
Troumbéttas
Ág. Márkos
Nisáki
Makrádes
Áno
Korakiána
Pýrgi
Angelókastro
Káto Korakiána
Ypsós
Cifliku
Paleokastrítsa
Liapádes
Dasiá
Epiros
Gouviá
Giannádes
Lazaréto
Temblóni
Kontokáli
Vídos
Érmones
Potamós
Corfu
(Kérkyra)
Glyfáda
Pélekas
Kanóni
Pontikonísi
Sinarádes
Perama
Kynopiástes
Achilleion
Igoumenítsa
Ágios Górdis
Gastoúri
Agii Déka
576 m/
1,890 ft
Benítses
Pentáti
Strongylí
Ionian
Sea
Ágios Matthéos
Moraítika
Gardiki ■
Fortress
Messongí
330 m/
1,082 ft ▲
Boúkari
Cape Lefkímmis
Chlomós
Petrití
Limni
Korissíon
Argyrádes
Alykés
Ágios
Geórgios
Perivóli
Lefkímmi
Sparterá
Kávos
Cape Asprokávos

Italy

Paxí, Patrás

Igoumenítsa

3.1 miles
5 km

1546–88) towers over it. It is home to a gallery and a café, and is worth a visit for the beautiful view of the old town. Opening times in summer: daily 9am–9pm. ⊙

From the harbour, the main shopping street, Nikiforou Theotoki, leads to the Spianada (from Ital. »spianata«, »esplanade«), the large square between the city and the Old Fortress. After the Ottomans attacked in 1537 the Venetians tore down the houses that stood here

Spianada

Corfu Town Plan

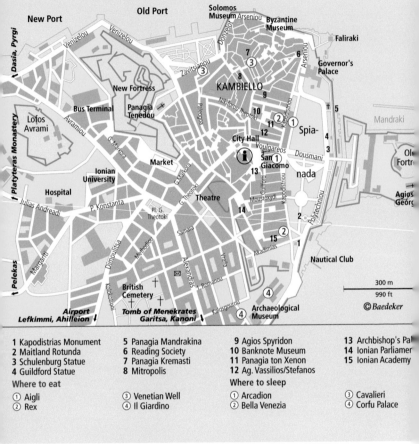

1 Kapodistrias Monument
2 Maitland Rotunda
3 Schulenburg Statue
4 Guildford Statue

Where to eat
① Aigli
② Rex

5 Panagia Mandrakina
6 Reading Society
7 Panagia Kremasti
8 Mitropolis

③ Venetian Well
④ Il Giardino

9 Agios Spyridon
10 Banknote Museum
11 Panagia ton Xenon
12 Ag. Vassilios/Stefanos

Where to sleep
① Arcadion
② Bella Venezia

13 Archbishop's Pal
14 Ionian Parliamer
15 Ionian Academy

③ Cavalieri
④ Corfu Palace

so that they would have a free field of fire. Today the northern part is used as a cricket field: a strange legacy of British rule, which lasted only half a century and ended 150 years ago, is that there are 13 cricket clubs on Corfu. The Spianada is flanked on the west by the elegant **Liston Arcades**, where there is a row of cafés; the southern part has been made into a beautiful park with tall trees. Baron Matthieu de Lesseps had the house fronts with arcades built in 1807 when he was the French governor of the island. On the east side of the esplanade a **monument** honours Count Johann Matthias von der Schulenburg (1661–1747), who defended the city against the Turks in 1716. The Venetian Antonio Corradini made this statue from Car-

► VISITING CORFU TOWN

INFORMATION
Tourist information
Evangelistrias/Dim
Kolla Alikes Potamou (outside)
Tel. 26 61 03 76 38
Fax 26 61 03 02 98
www.corfu.gr

Branch at airport

WHERE TO EAT
► Moderate
① Aigli
Kapodistriou 23
Tel. 2 66 10 3 19 49
Neat cafe-restaurant in the Liston
Arcades with international cooking;
pleasant atmosphere.

② Rex
Kapodistriou 66
Tel. 2 66 10 3 96 49
A restaurant steeped in tradition
behind the Liston Arcades with some
tables outside; good Corfiot cooking
and seafood at moderate prices.

③ Venetian Well
Plateia Kremasti
Tel. 2 66 10 4 47 61
Greek cooking with creative variety
and good local wines; posh prices.

④ Il Giardino
Vraila 4 B
Tel. 2 66 10 3 07 23
Outstanding Italian cuisine in elegant
surroundings (with garden); the restaurant is located in the museum of
archaeology; expensive.

WHERE TO STAY
► Luxury
④ Corfu Palace
Leoforos Dimokratias 2
Tel. 2 66 10 3 94 85

Fax 2 66 10 3 17 49
www.corfupalace.com
115 rooms. One of the most renowned hotels in Greece and »the«
hotel in Corfu Town; luxurious house
south of the Old Fortress; all rooms
with sea view; swimming pool, bar
and restaurant; regular barbecue par-
ties with Greek folklore.

► Mid-range
① Arcadion
Vlasopoulou 2/Esplanade
Tel. 2 66 10 3 01 04
Fax 2 66 10 4 50 87
www.arcadionhotel.com
32 rooms, 1 suite. Old-style hotel
combining historical surroundings
with modern comfort; from the roof
terrace and the rooms facing the front
there is the most wonderful view of
the Old Fortress.

② Bella Venezia
Zambeli 4
Tel. 2 66 10 4 42 90
Fax 2 66 10 2 07 08
www.bellaveneziahotel.com
32 rooms. Charming 19th-century
house, once a girls' school, quiet
location on the edge of the old city;
rooms with large windows are recommended.

③ Cavalieri
Kapodistriou 4
Tel. 2 66 10 3 93 36
Fax 2 66 10 3 92 83
www.cavalieri-hotel.com
50 rooms. Stylish 300-year-old palazzo on the south edge of the Spianada;
a fabulous view of the old town from
the roof terrace; generous English
breakfast.

The Liston Arcade: popular among tourists ands locals alike

rara marble while Schulenburg was still alive. The circular building at the southern end, the Maitland Rotunda, erected in 1816, commemorates a British Lord High Commissioner.

Governor's palace

Standing on the north side of the Spianada is the neo-classical former governor's palace. It is also called the Palace of St Michael and St George because the residence of the British Lord High Commissioner was also the seat of the Order of St Michael and St George, which was established in 1818. Between 1864 and 1913 it was also the **summer residence of the kings of Greece**. The main façade towards the esplanade is bordered by a Doric colonnade. There is a frieze of stone reliefs above the main part of the building. The centre tablet depicts Britannia, an allegorical figure that represents the benefits of the British protectorate – peace and wealth. To the right and the left are the coats of arms of six of the Ionian Islands. A tour of the palace includes the impressive state rooms (throne room, ballroom, dining room) and the **Museum of Asian Art**, which is mainly devoted to Chinese, Japanese and Indian art. The screens from Korea are especially beautiful. Opening hours: May–Oct Tue–Sun 8.30am–7.30pm, Nov–April 8.30am–3pm.

In a wing of the building the **Municipal Art Gallery** exhibits local 19th- and early 20th-century artists as well as works from the 16th to the 18th century, and some landscapes by Edward Lear, who often visited the island and proved that his talent was not limited to nonsense rhymes. Opening times: daily 9am–9pm.

Near the Schulenburg monument enter the **Old Fortress** (Palaio Frourio) via a bridge over the canal. The medieval city grew within the fortress walls, which were built in the 6th century. In order to defend themselves against attacks by the Ottoman Turks, the Venetians reinforced the fortress in the 14th and the 16th–17th centuries, but most buildings within the walls were constructed under British rule. This is also true of the **Church of Agios Georgios**, which was built in the style of a Doric temple around 1830 as the British garrison church. Concerts are now held in its grounds. Opening hours: May–Oct daily 8am–7.30pm, Nov–April Tue–Sun 8.30am– 3pm.

! **Baedeker** TIP

Views upon Views

Café Aktaion and Café En Plo at the former emigrants quay of Faliraki offer the best view of the Old Fortress on the Spianada. The roof garden bar of Hotel Cavalieri at the southwest corner of the Esplanade offers a fabulous panoramic view of the city from 6.30pm. The terraces of the Old Fortress Café in the Old Fortress are an excellent place to sit until well after midnight.

In the northern part of the Kambiello steps lead up to the 15th-century **Church of the Holy Virgin of Antivouniotissa**, which now houses the Byzantine Museum. It was renovated in 1994, when the nave was restored to its original appearance. The vestibules are used as exhibition rooms and display about 100 icons of various periods from the 15th to the 19th century. Opening times: Tue–Sun 8.30am–7.30pm. The Church of **Agios Spyridon** (1589) in the southern part of the Kambiello has a silver sarcophagus with a mummy of the city's patron saint, who was archbishop of Cyprus in the 4th century. Only a few steps to the west, the Orthodox **Cathedral of Panagia Spiliotissa** is the final resting place of Empress Theodora.

Byzantine Museum

West of the Spianada is the former Venetian theatre, which was built between 1663 and 1693 and has been the town hall since 1902. The Roman Catholic **Cathedral of St James** (17th century) with its neoclassical façade flanks the east side.

Town hall

The Corfu Archaeological Museum in the southern part of the city is worth a visit. The centrepiece of the collection is the **Gorgon Medusa pediment** (around 585 BC) of the Artemis sanctuary, one of the best-preserved Archaic Greek sculptures; it depicts the moment before Perseus cut off Medusa's head. The **recumbent lion** (7th century BC), which probably adorned the tomb of Menecrates, is also remarkable. When the Salvator Bastion was torn down in 1843 this tomb, a low round structure (7th–6th century BC), was found southwest of the museum in the garden of a police station. Opening times: Tue–Sun 8.30am–3pm.

★
Archaeological Museum

► VISITING CORFU ISLAND

GETTING THERE

There are boat services to and from Italy (Venice, Trieste, Ancona, Brindisi), to Igoumenitsa and Patras on the Greek mainland, and to the island of Paxi.

WHERE TO EAT

► Expensive
Nafsikaa
Nafsikas 11 Kanoni
Tel. 2 66 10 4 43 54
This restaurant on the Kanoni Peninsula is considered to be one of the best in the area; it has a pretty garden where its international and Corfiot specialties are also served.

► Moderate
Bella Vista
Gastouri at the Ahillion
The restaurant takes its name from its beautiful terrace and rightly so; the view over the east coast of the island is magnificent.

► Inexpensive
Il Pirata
Paleokastritsa town centre
Large selection of Italian and Greek dishes; terrace with a sea view.

WHERE TO STAY

► Luxury
Grecotel Corfu Imperial
Gouvia
Tel. 2 66 10 9 14 81
Fax 2 66 10 9 18 81
184 rooms, 126 bungalows
The most beautiful and luxurious hotel on Corfu, at the tip of Kommeno Peninsula between Gouvia and Dasia; choose from rooms in the main house, bungalows and villas; large variety of entertainment and sports, club for children.

► Mid-range
Sensimar Agios Gordis
Agios Gordis
Tel. 2 66 10 5 33 20
www.sensimar.com 246 rooms
This hotel, comprising a main building and some chalets, is on one of the island's most beautiful beaches; the roof garden with a bar greets its guests with a superb panoramic view.

Apollo Palace
Messongi
Tel. 2 66 10 7 54 33
Fax 2 66 10 7 56 02
www.apollopalace-corfu.com
260 rooms. Hotel complex on the beach opened in 1990; the buildings in traditional style are scattered around a large olive grove; prices are reasonable for this quality of surroundings; families looking for a variety of entertainment and water sports will like this place.

Grecotel Daphnila Bay
Dasia
Tel. 2 66 10 9 03 20
www.grecotel.gr
260 rooms. Hotel complex of the popular Grecotel chain in the midst of olive trees above its private beach; well-furnished terraced chalets are grouped below the main building; a broad range of sporting activities for guests.

Around Corfu Town

There are interesting attractions on the Analipsi Peninsula 4km south of the town centre. One of the most important churches on the island is located in the southern suburb of Anemomylos. It is dedicated to St Jason and St Sosipatros, who brought Christianity to Corfu around AD 70. This Byzantine domed cruciform church (11th–12th century) was built of undressed masonry and expanded in the 17th century. The **icons by Emmanuel Tzanes** on the iconostasis (*Christ as Ruler of the World* and the *Virgin with Child*, both around 1650) as well as the depictions of St Jason and St Sosipatros from 1649 in the vestibule are especially valuable.

★
Church of St Jason and St Sosipatros

500m to the south on the street leading to Kanoni, in the park with the remains of two ancient temples is the small castle Mon Repos, which was built in 1821. It was the birthplace of HRH Prince Philip (b. 1921). It now houses the **Archaeological Museum of Paleopolis**. Opening times: Tue–Sun 8.30am–3pm.The impressive ruins of the Basilica of Paleopolis, founded in the 5th century, rise up opposite the park entrance. Diagonally opposite are mosaic floors of a Roman therme (AD 200) that are protected by modern roofs. A five-minute walk further the foundation walls of an ancient Artemis temple (590/580 BC) can be seen in front of the convent Agii Theodori.

Villa Mon Repos

Cape Kanoni has a wonderful view of the nearby Vlacherna Monastery

✳
Vlacherna Monastery

The road that leads to Kanoni runs between the sea and Lake Halikiopoulos, which was partially silted up and later drained to build the airport's runway. The access road to the much-photographed Vlacherna Monastery turns off to the right. There is a causeway to the monastery island. Since the building is privately owned, only the inner courtyard and the small church of 1700 are open for viewing.

Pontikonisi

Boats leave regularly from the dock by Vlacherna Monastery for Pontikonisi (»Mouse Island«). It is considered to be the **model for Arnold Böcklin's painting** *The Isle of the Dead* (Böcklin was never on Corfu!). The ancient Greeks saw the island as the petrified ship of the Phaeacians, which brought Ulysses to Ithaca.

,

✳ ✳
Ahillion
(Αχίλλειο)

One of Corfu's major attractions is the magnificent Villa Ahillion (or Achilleion Palace), a good 10km/6mi south of Corfu Town near Gastouri, and about 145m/476ft above sea level. The elegant villa is surrounded by a superb garden and was the holiday residence of two crowned heads: **Empress Elisabeth of Austria** (▶ Baedeker Special p.180) and **Emperor Wilhelm II** of Germany. Since 1928 the villa has been the property of the Greek government; it was used as a casino for a time. Some memorabilia of Elisabeth and Wilhelm II are to be seen. In the park is a **sculpture of the** *Dying Achilles*, which Empress Elisabeth commissioned in 1881 from Ernst Herter. Wilhelm II preferred to identify himself with the victorious Achilles. There is a giant bronze statue of the Greek hero, armed and ready for battle.

🕐 Only the ground floor and the park are open to the public. Opening hours: May–Oct daily 8.30am–9pm, Nov–April 8.45am–3.30pm.

The trademark of the Ahilleion is the statue »Dying Achilles«

The South of the Island

Southwest of Gastouri, near Villa Ahillion, rises the 576m/1,890ft Mt Agoi Deka (»mountain of the ten saints«); the two-hour climb (there and back) is rewarded by a magnificent view from the summit.

Agoi Deka
(Αγιοι Δέκα)

C 3km/2mi south of Villa Ahillion lies Benitses, once a fishing village, now a holiday resort with a tiny pebble beach. On the northern edge of the village is the **Shell Museum**, a private museum that exhibits shells, seasnail shells and preserved fish. Opening times: daily 10am–6pm.

Benitses
(Μπενίτσες)

🕑

South of Benitses the coast road leads to the holiday resort Moraitika/Messongi. The hotels in the merged towns are mostly located away from the main road in green surroundings. While there is only a pebble beach here too, it much longer than at Benitses and enough entertainment is available in the form of bars, tavernas and restaurants.

Moraitika, Messongi
(Μοραΐτικα, Μεσογγί)

Make sure to stop in Lefkimmi, the largest town in the south. The eastern part of town along the little river Potami is the most picturesque quarter. At the southeast tip of Corfu the town of **Kavos** is one of the largest tourist centres on the island of Corfu and is especially popular among British holiday makers. The long sandy beach is the town's main attraction.

Lefkimmi
(Λευκίμμη)

Coming from the south, the west coast looks like untouched dune landscape with long sandy beaches. The area around Korission Lagoon is a good place to take long walk. More than 120 bird species can be observed here, including cormorants and grey herons.

★
Korission Lagoon (Λίμνη Κορισσίων)

The North of the Island

The east coast up to the unattractive town of Pyrgi is firmly in the hands of package tourism. Along the coastal road heading north the holiday resorts of Kondokali, Gouvia and Dasia have practically merged together.

East coast

Beyond Pyrgi the road to Spartylas (424m/1,391ft) and Strinylas branches off and leads up to Mt Pantokrator, at 906m/2,972ft the **highest mountain on the island**. It is named after the 14th-century monastery on its summit. The present church dates from the 17th century. The drive up to the peak, which is disfigured by antennas, is worthwhile mainly for the grand panoramic view of the whole island, the Othonian Islands offshore to the north and the mountains of Albania.

★
Pantokrator

Beyond Pyrgi the winding road along the coast runs past several villages and bathing bays. Kalami is located on a pretty bay; **Lawrence**

Kalami

I WOULD LIKE TO BE BURIED HERE!

Franz Joseph, the Austro-Hungarian emperor, was not exactly pleased when his wife Elisabeth (»Sisi«) told him in 1887 that she wanted to spend her last days on Corfu, »the only place on earth where I want to own a house«.

After all, the Hermes Villa in the Lainzer Tiergarten near Vienna, originally planned as the retirement home of the empress, was almost complete and the bills for the property were not yet paid. It also dismayed him that his wife wanted to live so far away from him and their homeland. But the Habsburg monarch, who had never denied his wife anything, submitted to her wishes, probably because he hoped she would finally find peace there.

Always on the road

Elisabeth (Sisi), the daughter of Duke Max of Bavaria, was born in 1837. At the beginning of their marriage the imperial couple still travelled together through the lands of the Austro-Hungarian Dual Monarchy, but from the age of 23, Sisi preferred to travel alone. She disliked Vienna, the capital of the monarchy, and hated the stiff Spanish court protocol even more;

her relationship to her mother-in-law, Archduchess Sophie, was also very strained. During her 44 years of marriage Sisi spent less than four years altogether in Vienna. She was introduced to Corfu in 1861 on one of her many trips. She was thrilled, and her enthusiasm remained for many years. »Corfu is the ideal place, climate, walks in the endless shade of olive trees, good roads and wonderful sea air, as well as the fullness of the moonlight.« She wrote to her youngest daughter Valerie once, »Even though I have seen many beautiful places, I prefer this one. When I return, no matter where from, I always say that this is the most beautiful place on earth.«

Ancient paradise?

But the beautiful empress was not only delighted with the lovely scenery and the mild climate. She loved Greek

Probably the best-known portrait of a legendary empress: Elisabeth of Austria in a magnificent gown

antiquity, Homer's *Iliad* and *Odyssey*, and Corfu was the ancient land of her dreams. Sisi was eager for knowledge, and got the Austrian consul on Corfu, **Baron Alexander von Warsberg**, an expert on Greek antiquity who had published *Landscapes of the Odyssey*, a description and history of Corfu, and *Kingdom of Odysseus*, to show her the island. She also began to learn classical and modern Greek. Even before Franz Joseph had given her permission, she told the baron to look for a suitable property for her on Corfu. The baron knew the island and soon found the right place: **Villa Vraila** (also written Braila) near Gastouri about 9km/5mi south of the island capital. The house, which was painted pink and decorated with colonnades, had been built by a Venetian a long time before, but it only had a few rooms. But instead of »leaving the house, which seemed »so cosy, sweet and small« to her, in its original form, Sisi decided to transform it into a fairy-tale castle. This is the origin of the **Ahilleion**, a rather inelegant classical Greek-style palace named after Achilles, the empress' favourite hero

from Greek mythology. In 1890 the empress, who was known to love shopping, brought several marble statues, busts of Greek thinkers, back from Italy. Unfortunately there were no art experts in her entourage to advise her. Most of the acquisitions were poor copies of works from Florentine and Neapolitan museums. The interior of the castle was decorated imaginatively and extravagantly. Marble bathrooms had gilded faucets, classical-style lounges were draped with leopard skins and goatskins, and everything from the bed and table linens to the stationery was adorned with the Austrian crown over a dolphin, the holy animal of Thetis, the mother of Achilles.

The »Train«

In March 1891 the empress showed her daughter Valerie the view of the sea from the completed palace terraces between two tall cypresses with the words: »I would like to be buried here.« Whenever she was tired of travelling she would return to her fairy-tale palace, where she would write somewhat stumbling poetry in

He also seems to be impressed by the Ahilleion

the style of Heinrich Heine, a poet whom she greatly admired, and explore the island on foot. Because of her quick walk, which always made her ladies-in-waiting out of breath, the residents of Corfu gave her the nickname »Train«, which was not meant to be pejorative since for rural Greeks a train was the epitome of everything great. The foreign monarch, who would often pay for a glass of milk with a gold coin, was very popular among the local people and they respected her wish to be left alone. Others, like **King George of Greece** and **Emperor Wilhelm II of Germany**, did not follow suit. She did not want to receive guests on Corfu since she had come for peace and quiet, and when the two rulers announced that they would come to visit her, she sent a message that she was not at home.

End of a dream

But Sisi soon ceased to take pleasure in the fairy castle on Corfu. It almost seemed as if the natural beauty of the place – the garden with a wonderful view of the sea and the Albanian mountains, the idyllic landscape with olive groves and lemon and orange trees – made the empress, who suffered greatly after the **suicide of her son Rudolph** in 1889, even sadder and more depressed. »When I came to Corfu the first time,« she told her Greek teacher in 1892, »I visited Villa Braila often. It was wonderful, completely isolated among its large trees. That attracted me so much that I turned it into the »Achilleion« … But I regret it now. Our dreams are always nicer when we don't make them come true.« She also had to accept that neither her daughter nor anyone else from her family would want to live on Corfu. In 1893 she admitted to her husband that the Ahilleion, which was barely completed, no longer gave her any joy. »Wherever I was, if someone told me that I had to stay there forever, then even paradise would seem like hell to me.« In order to appease the emperor, who had paid for part of the building costs privately, she suggested that the villa be sold. She imagined that some fantastically rich American would be willing to pay a fortune for it. But Franz Joseph advised her to think it over once more

Study decorated with cherubs

since the sale would not be well received in Austria, where the empress was criticized for being away so much and for spending huge amounts of money in other countries. Sisi spent some time on Corfu every year, but her **restless spirit** drove her on across the seas and through many lands. The island was no longer her choice for a last resting place. In 1897 she told Valerie that she wanted to be buried next to her son Rudolph. While staying in Geneva on 9 September 1898 she talked about future travel plans, including Corfu and the Ahilleion, which was now half empty and which she wanted to visit when it had been converted into a good hotel. This never happened: on the next day she was stabbed at a steamboat landing by the Italian migrant worker and anarchist Lucheni, who was actually targeting the Duc de Orleans but could not find him.

Wilhelm II

The Ahilleion stood empty for ten years and became run-down. In 1907 **Emperor Wilhelm II of Germany** bought it and used it as a holiday residence until the beginning of World War I. In 1924, after his abdication, Wilhelm remembered his court's first visit to the newly acquired residence: »Exclamations of astonishment, classical quotations and bright, happy enthusiasm evident on all faces for this paradise with its tranquillity and symphony of colours.« Among other things he had a desk chair in the form of a swivelling saddle installed, and the sculpture of the *Dying Achilles* was replaced by a giant martial statue of a victorious warrior.

Casino and James Bond

Thirty years later the American writer **Henry Miller** visited the Ahilleion: »I usually find palaces to be icy and dark, but this madhouse of the emperor is probably the worst kitsch I have ever seen. It would make an excellent museum for surreal art.« But it was used for other purposes, from 1962 becoming a casino for some years. In 1980 it served as the setting for the James Bond film *For Your Eyes Only*, in which 007 had to play poker for his life. Unlike Sisi, Roger Moore did not want Corfu to be his last resting place.

Durrell lived here for two years in the White House (taverna) while he wrote *Prospero's Cell*.

Kassiopi
(Κασσιόπη)

With the Albanian mainland as a backdrop, Kassiopi has a pretty setting but is overrun with tourists. The town differs from Corfu's other tourist centres in that its heart, centred on an idyllic harbour below the remains of a 13th-century Byzantine castle, still has an authentic feel. The road to the harbour bay, with the remains of a 13th-century castello that was destroyed by the Venetians, passes countless hotel and apartment complexes. The Church of Panagia Kassopitra (1590) stands not far from the harbour.

Northwest coast

The entire coastal region between the popular resorts **Roda** and **Sidhari** has been taken over by tourism. Miles of sandy beaches with good windsurfing are interrupted by picturesque cliffs. From the coastal road in the western part of town the way to the so-called **Canal d'Amour** is signposted. Here wind and water have cut the light sandstone cliffs into deep clefts. Single women who want to get married go to the canal early in the morning. If they swim through the Canal d'Amour as long as it is still in the shadows and think about the man they want to marry, it is said that they will get him.

✸
Cape Drastis ►

The short hike west of Sidhari (from the school about 30 minutes) down to the impressive cliffs of Cape Drastis, the northwestern tip of the island, is worthwhile. The beaches between Cape Drastis and Paleokastritsa can be reached by car. **Agios Georgios Bay** at Afionas is a pretty place.

✸
Angelokastro
(Αγγελόκαστρο)

A mountain road leads via Lakones and Krini to Angelokastro. The road ends below the picturesquely situated ruins of the once-mighty fortress Angelokastro. The walk there takes 15 minutes up a steep path. The view from the castle hill is even more impressive than the castle, which was presumably built in the 13th century. On the highest point within its walls is a chapel dedicated to the archangels Michael and Gabriel (1784). Around the church there are signs of tombs that were hewn into the rock. One cave has served as a chapel since the 18th century. The fortress was eventually razed under British rule and only the two chapels, the foundations and the remains of the cistern system are preserved.

✸✸
Paleo-
kastritsa
(Παλαιο-
καστρίτσα)

The heavily frequented town of Paleokastritsa, a tourist stronghold on the west coast in an exceptionally lovely setting, can be reached over the scenic Troumbeta Pass. Because of its beautiful site and monastery situated on a peninsula, it is one of the most popular tourist venues on the island. There are some larger hotels, restaurants and small pebbly bays for swimming. From the main road leading to the harbour there is a turnoff to **Panagia Theotokou Monastery**. The monastery was founded in the 13th century already, but the present buildings date from the 18th century. The monastery church at the

Cape Drastis: unusual rock formations at the northwest corner of Corfu

centre is surrounded by the wing with the monks' cells, stores and communal rooms as well as a pretty garden. The arcade with its lush floral decoration is also beautiful. Steps lead to a museum on the upper floor, where a collection of 17th- to 19th-century icons is on display; there are more icons in the monastery church. Opening times: April–Oct daily 7am–1pm, 3pm–8pm.

East of Paleokastritsa the road turns south and leads through relatively flat country to Corfu Town. After about 8km/5mi comes the turnoff to **Ermones** on the west coast. The town has a small sandy bay. In the neighbouring bay to the south, **Myrtiotissa**, there is a beautiful sandy beach below steep cliffs. 7km/4.5mi to the south **Glyfada** is an attractive holiday resort; its long sandy beach, **the most famous on the island**, is framed by picturesque rock formations. The shallow water is ideal for children and well visited all summer.

Middle west coast

Paxi (Παξοί)

Paxi (population 2,400) is the smallest of the seven larger Ionian Islands and thanks to its exceptionally picturesque scenery, beautiful bathing beaches and good diving, one of the most attractive venues in the archipelago. Paxi is only 10km/6mi long and up to 4km/2.5mi wide; it is easy to explore on foot or by moped. The island has thousands of olive trees and is known for its **excellent olive oil**. The west

Smallest Ionian island

coast has picturesque cliffs up to 185m/600ft high and numerous caves. Even a few of the highly endangered Mediterranean monk seals make their home here. The east coast slopes gently to the sea. There are some pebble beaches along the east coast. Mainly British and Italian tourists come to the green island for vacation, but many day guests come from Corfu and Parga (on the mainland) as well. **Tourism** is concentrated around the main town of Gaïos and in Lakka, while Loggos is quieter.

Gaïos (Γάιος) From the ferry pier Gaïos (population 560), located on a sheltered bay on the south coast, is a 15-minute walk away. There are lots of tavernas along the coast road and on the main square. The **folk art museum** shows household implements and folk costumes. On the uninhabited **island of Agios Nikolaos** to the east are the remains of a Venetian fortress (1423). The **islet Panagia** behind it has a church dedicated to the Virgin Mary, the destination of a boat procession at the feast of the Dormition of Mary (August 15). Taxi boats run to both islands from Gaïos.

Loggos In the quiet fishing village of Loggos 5km/3mi north of Gaïos it is possible to forget time in rustic fish tavernas. The nearby **Bay of Glyfada** is one of the most beautiful on the island.

Harbour in Gaïos

Lakka, in the extreme north of Paxi, is the water sports centre. Surfers, sailors and divers find what they are seeking in the sheltered bay with crystal clear water. There is a path from the lighthouse to the pebble beach of Plani; swimming is only possible when the sea is calm.

Taxi boats run to the cave of **Ypapanti** below the village of Vasilatika – used as a hiding-place for submarines in World War II – and further south to **Petriti Cave**, which is compared to the Blue Grotto on Capri because of its light effects.   **Caves**

To the southeast of Paxi is its smaller, rocky sister island Antipaxi; there are regular boat connections from Paxi during the high season. The island is only 6 sq km/2 sq mi in size and up to 107m/350ft high. The 20 or so permanent inhabitants raise sheep and produce a fine wine. Antipaxi has beautiful, isolated beaches, especially Vrika and Voutoumi on the northeast coast. There are tavernas or shops on the island but only private rooms and holiday cottages as accommodation.   **Antipaxi (Αντίπαξοι)**

★ ★ Crete · Kríti

K–P 11/12

Greek: Κρήτη
Altitude: 0–456 m/1,496 ft
Capital: Iráklio (population 116,000)
Area: 8,261 sq km/3,190 sq mi
Population: 750,000

Crete (Kríti in Greek) is the largest of the Greek islands. It also has a unique cultural and historical heritage as the first site of a European civilization during the Minoan period. It is an extraordinarily attractive island with its varied landscape, beautiful beaches and famous monuments of Minoan culture. The island varies between 12km and 57km (7.5–35mi) in width and extends over 260km/160mi in an east-west direction. The god Zeus was supposed to have been born here.

Crete is the **southernmost part of Europe** as well as a major link in the arc of islands that connects southern Greece to Asia Minor. It is segmented by three karst mountain massifs that are very rugged and almost barren. The snow-covered »White Mountains« (Lefka Ori) reach an elevation of 2,452m/8,045ft in the west, the Idi Oros, also with lots of snow, rise to 2,456m/8,058ft in the centre and the Dikti Mountains in the east to 2,148m/7,047ft. While the south coast is largely lined with cliffs, the northern coast is flatter and more indented. Here lie Crete's major cities – Hania, Iráklio and Rethymno – and here, too, are the longest sandy beaches on the island and thus most of the tourist centres. On the coastal plains, the Messara plain   **Mythical island**

Crete *Map*

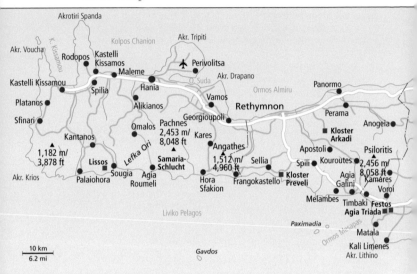

and in the high Omalos and Lasithi plateaus, intensive vegetable farming is practised, in places all year round in greenhouses made of plastic sheeting. Citrus fruits, wine and especially olives are the main products. Along with agriculture, tourism has been the most important source of income since the 1970s.

History The earliest traces of settlement, probably coming from North Africa, date from the 7th millennium BC. From the 3rd millennium BC, a proto-Greek Bronze Age culture emerged. It reached its apex between about 2000 and 1600 BC and is named **Minoan culture** after the legendary King Minos. As the first sea power in the Mediterranean, the cultural and economic influence of the Minoan empire reached all the way to the Iberian Peninsula. The downfall of Minoan society began around 1400 BC, allowing the invasion of the Mycenaeans, who ruled parts of the island. The final destruction of the palace of Knossos in 1200 BC ended Minoan civilization. A major part of the island was conquered by the Dorians around 1000 BC. Crete was taken between 69 and 67 BC by the Romans, who made it an important base in the eastern Mediterranean. After the partition of the Roman Empire, it belonged to Byzantium until AD 826. Arabian Saracens ruled over it from 826 until 961, when it again became a part of the Byzantine Empire. Venetian domination followed from 1204 until 1669. This brought the island a considerable cultural flowering, but was accompanied by a long and bitter struggle for independence. After the fall of Constantinople to the Turks in 1453 the

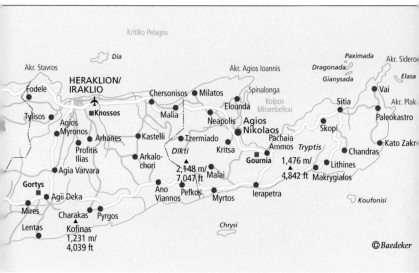

Cretan school of painting developed here. This school modified the strict Byzantine canon under Italian influence; Domenikos Theotokopulos, called **El Greco**, came out of this school (►Famous People). Following years of war (conquest of Hania 1645), Crete fell to the Ottoman Turks with the capture of Iráklio in 1669. It was not until 1898 that the Ottomans left the island. After a temporary period of autonomy, Crete was annexed by the Kingdom of Greece in 1913. The liberal politician and later Greek prime minister **Eleftherios Venizelos** (►Famous People), a native of Crete, played a paramount role in this move. On 20 May 1941, airborne German forces occupied the island, which was of great strategic importance because of its situation between southern Europe and Africa. They did not withdraw until October 1944. Since about 1970 Crete has developed into a popular destination for package tourism; a motorway along the north coast was built and countless hotel complexes mushroomed in Malia Bay, near Rethymno, Iráklio and Agios Nikolaos.

✹ ✹ Hania · Χανιά

Hania (population 62,000), Crete's second-largest city, lies in the bay of the same name on the north coast. It was founded in the 13th century by Venetians on the site of ancient Kydonia. This lively town is one of Crete's most attractive, and many cultures have left their mark here. Hania is an excellent base for exploring the scenic beauty of western Crete.

Second city of Crete

Venetian Port The idyllic Venetian Port is the centre of the city. Near the old light-house there is a wonderful view of the skyline, especially at evening, with its minarets, the white dome of the former Janissary Mosque built in 1645 and the white karst slopes of Lefka Ori in the background.

Old city To the west **Topanas**, an old part of town with small, stylish hotels, lies below the harbour castle. In the Venetian arsenal, which was built in 1497, the experimental **replica of a seaworthy Minoan ship** is on display. Opening hours: daily 10am–4pm, 6pm–9pm. **Kastelli**, another old quarter, spreads over the hill behind the Janissary Mos-

▶ VISITING HANIA

INFORMATION
EOT
Kriari 40
Tel. 282 10 929 43, fax 282 10 926 24
www.hania.gr

WHERE TO EAT
► Moderate
① *Aeriko*
Akti Miaouli/Nikiforou Foka
Restaurant with a quiet location on the bay east of the harbour; rare specialties are served here.

② *Tamam*
Zambeliou 49
Tel. 2 82 16 0 80 39
Housed in a former Turkish bath, serving delicious Greek cuisine at moderate prices. Along with the menu there are daily specials.

WHERE TO STAY
► Mid-range
① *Amphora*
Parodos Theotokopoulou 20
Tel. 2 82 10 932 24
Fax 2 82 10 932 26
www.amphora.gr
20 rooms. 13th-century building in the Venetian Port; furnished with Turkish and Venetian antiques; individually decorated rooms facing the harbour or the courtyard, some with a kitchenette, some with a balcony; it can get noisy at night; terrace with a beautiful view of the harbour; the restaurant serves traditional Cretan cuisine.

② *Dogis*
Kondilaki 14–16
Tel. 2 82 10 954 66, fax 2 82 10 960 20
www.dogehold.com
8 rooms. Dogis occupies a 13th-century Venetian house.

③ *Casa Delfino*
Theophanous 9
Tel. 2 82 10 930 98, fax 2 82 10 965 00
www.casadelfino.com
12 apartments. In the old quarter in a 17th-century Venetian nobleman's palace; view of the harbour from the roof terrace; the hotel has tastefully furnished studios with kitchenettes and a romantic green courtyard.

④ *Porto Veneziano*
At the fisherman's harbour
Tel. 2 82 10 271 00, fax 2 82 10 271 05
www.portoveneziano.gr, 51 rooms
Modern hotel in a beautiful location on the fishermen's harbour; most of the rooms have balconies facing the harbour; centrally located yet quiet.

Hania *Plan*

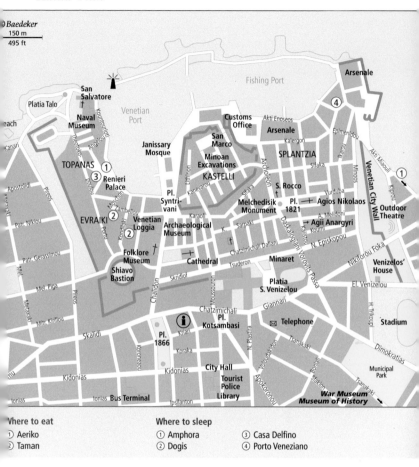

Ⓑ Baedeker
150 m
495 ft

Fishing Port

San Salvatore
Platia Talo
Naval Museum
Venetian Port
beach
Kanari
TOPANAS
Apostolidi
Renieri Palace
EVRAIKI
Venetian Loggia
Folklore Museum
Shiavo Bastion
Janissary Mosque
Customs Office
Arsenale
San Marco
Minoan Excavations
KASTELLI
Pl. Syntri-vani
Archaeological Museum
Cathedral
SPLANTZIA
S. Rocco
Melchedisik Monument
Pl. 1821
Agios Nikolaos
Agii Anargyri
Minaret
Platia S. Venizelou
Arsenale
Venetian City Wall
Outdoor Theatre
Venizelos' House
Venizelos' House
El. Venizelou
Stadium
Pl. Kotsambasi
Pl. 1866
Telephone
Municipal Park
City Hall
Tourist Police
Library
Bus Terminal
War Museum
Museum of History

Where to eat
① Aeriko
② Taman

Where to sleep
① Amphora
② Dogis
③ Casa Delfino
④ Porto Veneziano

que. Here are partially destroyed Venetian buildings (doors of palazzi, remains of the Church of San Marco) and Minoan excavations. In the former Jewish quarter of **Evraiki** a small Roman Catholic church (16th century) was converted into a **synagogue, Etz Hayyim**. Opening hours: Mon–Fri 10am–6pm.

The old town is surrounded by a 3km/2mi, 16th-century wall. The **Archaeological Museum** in the Gothic San Francesco church has outstanding exhibits from Neolithic to Roman times, including some mosaics. Note the masterly seal with the figure of a Minoan on a group of buildings. Opening times: April–Oct Mon 1pm–7pm, Tue–Sun 8am–7.30pm, Nov–Mar Tue–Sun 8.30am–3pm.

Highlights Crete

Samaria Gorge
A hiking tour through the 18km/11mi gorge should be part of every holiday in Crete.
► page 196

Iráklio
Iráklio Archaeological Museum contains amazing artefacts from the island's Minoan excavation sites.
► page 200

Knossos
The remains of the Minoan palace convey a vivid picture of Europe's first advanced civilization.
► page 205

The palm beach of Vai
Spend at least one afternoon on the famous palm beach of Vai on the east coast.
► page 219

Other attractions
Around the corner is a Venetian **Renaissance loggia** and in the southwest corner of the harbour in Odos Moskhon stands the **Renieri Palazzo**. On the northwest corner the harbour fort houses the **Naval Museum**, with model ships, nautical instruments and a comprehensive documentation of the »Battle for Crete« in 1941. Opening hours: April–Oct daily 9am–4pm, Nov–Mar 9am–2pm. On Plateia 1821 in the eastern part of the old city a monument under a plane tree commemorates a bishop who had rebelled against the Turks and who was consequently hanged on this tree. The Venetian **church of Agios Nikolaos** with a clock tower and a minaret is also on this square. The large **market building**, an iron construction (1911), is located on the southern edge of the old quarter.

Excursions from Hania

Souda Bay
About 4km/2.5mi southeast of the old quarter is Souda Bay, the largest and best natural harbour on Crete. It is Hania's trade and ferry port, and serves as a NATO naval base. The fortress on Souda Island at the entrance to the bay remained in Venetian hands until 1669. At the northwestern corner of the bay, 5km/3mi east of Hania and 3km/2mi north of the Hania – Rethymnon road, is a British and Commonwealth War Cemetery. The German military cemetery, with over 4,000 graves, mostly of paratroopers who were killed during the landing in 1941, is near Maleme (16km/10mi west of Hania).

Profitis Ilias
About 8km/5mi east of Hania, on the hill Profitis Ilias, there is a memorial with the graves of the **Cretan politician Eleftherios Venizelos** (►Famous People) and his son Sophocles. From here there is a wonderful view of the city and the Lefka Ori mountains.

Agias Triadas
Agias Triadas Monastery, the largest and most important on Crete, is 17km/11mi northeast of Hania. The church has a plain façade, built

in Italian Renaissance style in 1631 and a richly decorated iconostasis. A small icon museum displays works from the 18th and 19th centuries.

The setting of Gouverneto Monastery, 4km/2.5mi further north, is impressive. It was founded in 1548 and also has a Renaissance façade. An icon in the entrance hall depicts the legend of **St John of Gouverneto**, who, fleeing from the Near East, landed below the monastery and lived in a cave there with 98 companions. Opening hours: all year Mon, Tue, Thu 9am–12noon, Sat–Sun 5am–11am, from Orthodox Easter to Sept also Mon, Tue, Thu 5pm–7pm, Sat–Sun 5pm–8pm, from Oct to Orthodox Easter Mon, Tue, Thu 4pm–6pm, Sat–Sun 4pm–7pm.

Gouverneto

Below Gouvernéto is a spacious cave named »Bear Cave« after the shape of one of the stalagmites. It was probably a cult site as early as the Minoan period and in Classical times served the cult of Artemis, to whom the bear was sacred. At the entrance is the chapel of Panagia Arkoudiotissa (»Mother of God of the bear cave«). A narrow path then leads to the bridge of the Katholiko Monastery, which has a magnificent setting and was abandoned in the 16th century. Here St John the Hermit's cave can be seen to the left before the monastery doorway.

Bear Cave, Katholiko

Lying on a rock plateau 14km/9mi east of Hania are the ruins of the city of Aptera, which flourished from Dorian (1000 BC) down to Byzantine times. There is a fine view of Souda Bay and the Akrotiri Peninsula from the Turkish fortress (1868).

Aptera (Άπτερα)

8km/5mi west of Maleme the road to Kolimbari turns off right towards the 6km/4mi-wide Rodopos Peninsula, which extends to the north with magnificent, rugged landscape rising to 750m/2,461ft. The fortress-like Venetian **Gonias Monastery** north of Kolymvari was founded in 1618 and possesses some valuable 17th-century icons; a little further is an ecumenical academy that is subsidized by the independent church of Crete. At the northeast end of the peninsula, on Menies Bay near Cape Skala, the **sanctuary of the nymph Diktynna**, who is also the Cretan cave goddess Britomartis, was unearthed. She was the patron of fishermen and their nets (»diktyon« means »net«). The excavation site is best reached by boat from Hania or Kolymvari. From the landing follow a small valley with the ruins of an abandoned village and then climb up the left (south) slope to the excavation site to see the remains of a temple (2nd century AD) with an altar, cistern and other buildings.

Rodopos (Ροδοπού)

20km/12mi west of Kolymvari lies the wine-growing centre of Kissamos/Kastelli. A rewarding excursion goes from here to the island of **Gramvousa** off the peninsula of the same name in the extreme

Kissamos (Κίσαμος)

northwest of Crete. A 17th-century Venetian castle towers above the steep cliffs of the western coast. 9km/5.5mi west of Kastelli at the north end of a bay with a fabulous, miles-long dune beach lie the ruins of the ancient city of **Falasarna**, where the remains of buildings, the harbour, graves and sculptures can be seen. The town was founded in the 5th–4th century BC and presumably abandoned in the 6th century AD when the coast rose by 8m/26ft. There is a fine view of the Gulf of Kissamos from the ruins of the Dorian city **Polyrrenia** (6km/4mi south of Kastelli; a 30-minute walk from the village of Polirinia).

Moni Hrysoskalitissas A visit to the small, white 17th-century Hrysoskalitissas Monastery, 40km/25mi southwest of Kastelli Kissamos, is worthwhile because of its pretty location on a low cliff overlooking the sea. The modern-looking monastery has often been abandoned in its turbulent history. The Germans destroyed many of its buildings in 1944. Today only a few monks still live here and the empty cells are hired out as guest rooms.

! *Baedeker* TIP

Off to the »Caribbean beach«
Crete's most beautiful beach, Elafonisi, has the atmosphere of a lagoon; it is on the west coast, about 5km/3mi south of the village of Christóskalitissa. The multitude of blue and green hues in its water are reminiscent of the Caribbean.

Paleohora (50km/30mi south of Kissamos) lies on a cape in the Libyan Sea below the ruins of the Venetian castle of Selinu (1282); it is a popular seaside resort with a »taverna row« as well as long beaches of sand and pebbles, including the well-known Pahia Ammos beach in the west bay. Ferries leave from here for the little island of Gavdos.

To Sougia The first place on the way from Kandanos (63km/38mi southwest of Hania) to Sougia is **Anisaraki** with its four Byzantine chapels dating from the 14th and 15th centuries. South of the village of **Temenia** (11km/7mi) is the Sotiros Church (13th–14th centuries); it has remarkable architecture and superb frescoes. Continue 8km/5mi to **Moni** and its 13th-century Church of Agios Nikolaos; the free-standing campanile is unusual. The tour ends after another 25km/15mi at Sougia, which has developed into a popular holiday spot with its pebble beaches, in part bordered by caves.

Lissos **(Σισσός)** It is worth taking the 90-minute hike from Sougia over the western elevation to neighbouring Agios Kyrikos Bay, which is also accessible by boat from Paleohora and Sougia. This is the site of ancient Lissos, which was famous for its healing springs in ancient times. There are

A hike through the spectacular Samaria Gorge →
is a must for all nature lovers

still remains of a **temple from the sanctuary of Asclepius**: cella walls, floor mosaics, the base of the cult image and a receptacle for offerings. The water from the sacred spring flows under the floor to a well. Roman houses and Hellenistic and Roman grave sites can also be seen on the western slope. A Kyrikos chapel on the shore and a Panagia chapel west of the temple both stand on the remains of early Christian basilicas.

★ ★
Samaria Gorge
(Φαράγγι
Σαμαριάς)

42km/26mi south of Hania, at the edge of the fertile Omalos Plateau (1,050m/3,500ft), lies the village of Omalos. The road ends after another 6km/4mi at Xyloskalo (1,227m/4,026ft), the starting point for a six-hour hike through Samaria Gorge (Farangi Samarias). The gorge is 18km/11mi long, up to 600m/2,000ft deep and at the »Iron Gates« (Sideroportes) only 3–4m/10–13ft wide. This area, where Cretan wild goats (agrimi, or kri-kri) still live, was made a national park in 1962. Sturdy shoes and a good physical condition are essential for the hike – one of the highlights of a holiday on Crete, enjoyed on some days by more than 3,000 people. There are springs on the way for water.

The gorge can be entered from 7.30am to 4pm; it is closed from November to April. The southern exit of the gorge is at the abandoned village of **Agia Roumeli**; at the seaside is the modern town of the same name, which consists almost entirely of hotels and tavernas. Boats run from there to Hóra Sfakion in the east and Paleohora in the west.

Hóra Sfakion
(Χώρα Σφακίον)

Most Samaria hikers disembark at Hóra Sfakion and head straight for the waiting buses, to the detriment of the many restaurants in the town. 5km/3mi west of Hóra ferries land in the little bay of **Loutro**, which can also be reached on foot but not by car! Holiday-makers looking for peace and relaxation feel at home in Loutro with its blue and white houses. There are nice hikes up the flanks of the mountain to the villages of the freedom-loving Sfakia, where the men still wear their black folk costumes, or along the coast to the very attractive **Aradena Gorge** and the Church of Agios Pavlos by the dunes. Boats run from Loutro to sandy beaches. **Glikanera** is a very nice beach where fresh and salt water mingle.

Imbros Gorge

North of Hóra the wild Imbros Gorge cuts through the mountains; it is 7km/4.5mi long and even narrower than the Samaria Gorge. The hike from Imbros to Komitades takes about three hours.

Frangokastello
(Φραγγο-
κάστελλο)

Some 17km/10mi east of Hóra Sfakion, the mighty Venetian fortress Frangokastello (1371) with its massive walls stands at the edge of the headland. The Venetian lion of St Mark is mounted above the main entrance on the sea side. Beautiful sandy beaches and a small harbour for boats have made Frangokastello a holiday resort with many guest houses and holiday cottages, mainly for young people.

About 37km/22mi off the western south coast of Crete is the flat, wooded island of Gavdos, **Europe's southernmost point**. The island, inhabited by 80 people, is a paradise for ornithologists in the spring and with its beautiful beaches a great place for backpack tourists. Tour boats from Paleohora and Hóra Sfakion sail to the island in the summer.

Gavdos
(Γάυδος)

✷ Rethymno (Ρέθημνον)

Rethymno (population 20,000), the third-largest town on Crete, sprawls on the north coast with the Ida Mountains as a backdrop. Marked both by its Venetian and Turkish occupations, the city presents a charming cultural mix. Its 12km/7mi-long sandy beach, lined with many large hotel complexes, begins at the harbour and stretches eastwards.

Multicultural town

The old quarter, set on a peninsula, has a delightful atmosphere with its numerous Venetian buildings, Turkish houses with covered, latticed wooden balconies and mosques. The Venetian fortress (fortezza), built between 1574 and 1582, towers over the old town. Open-air cultural events are held here in the summer. The main meeting place is the romantic **Venetian harbour**, which is lined by cafes and tavernas. Work was started in 1646 to turn the Church of St Nicholas into the present mosque with its great dome.

✷
Old quarter,
Fortezza

The interesting archaeological museum in the former Venetian prison next to the fortezza presents Cretan finds from the Neolithic to the Hellenistic period, among them pottery, bronze sculptures, marble statues and clay figures from various periods. Among the coins is a remarkable **gold coin from Knossos** with a depiction of a labyrinth. Opening hours: April–Oct Tue–Sun 8.30am–5pm, Nov–Mar Tue–Sun 8.30am–3pm.

✷
Archaeological
museum

⊙

In the northeastern corner of the old quarter lies the little **Venetian harbour**, where the tavernas line up next to the other. The 17th-century **Venetian Loggia** (Arkadiou) can be reached from the southwest corner of the harbour; from there, Odos Paleologon leads to the pretty **Arimondi Fountain** (1623). Now head south to Vernardou Street, where the **Nerantzes Mosque** can be seen next to Venetian houses with Turkish superstructures of wood; this building was erected in the 16th century and later converted into a mosque. Go south on Odos Ethnikis Antistaseos past the former monastery church of San Francesco to **Megali Porta**, the Venetian city gate.

Other attractions

! *Baedeker* TIP

Extreme Bar

For rock music fans, young and old, the X-treme Bar (Odos Nearchou 27) in Rethymnon is just the right place. The DJs are Greek students.

Excursions from Rethymno

Arkadi (Αρκάδι)

23km/14mi southeast of Rethymno, the fortress-like complex of Arkadi Monastery is a Cretan national shrine and one of the most important historic sites on the island. In the **rebellion of 1866** some 1,000 Cretans – men, women and children – fled here and, after fighting a hopeless battle against 15,000 Turks, blew themselves up with a powder magazine on 8 November. The monastery was founded in the 11th century, but the present buildings date from the 17th century and were remodelled a number of times. Several monks still live there. The façade of the monastery church of 1587 has Italian Renaissance and Baroque elements; it is in the inner courtyard of the four-sided complex. Opening hours: daily 8.30am until sunset.

Preveli (Πρέβελη)

Preveli Monastery stands isolated on a rugged mountain on the south coast, 38km/24mi from Rethymno. Boats from Plakias and Agia Galini go there. The scenery is magnificent. Interesting features of the monastery are an old well in the courtyard, a richly decorated iconostasis in the church and ecclesiastical vestments and mitres in the museum.

Preveli Beach ►

Nearby to the east is **Preveli Beach** at the mouth of the palm-tree covered Megalou Potamou estuary, which was decimated by a forest fire in 2010. To get there go back on the road to the monastery for

Rethymnon harbour is a good place to end a wonderful day

▶ VISITING RETHYMNON

INFORMATION

EOT
El. Venizelou
Tel./fax 2 83 10 2 91 48

WHERE TO EAT

▶ Moderate

La Rentzo
Radamanthiou 9
Tel. 2 83 10 2 67 80
An elegant restaurant in a vaulted
room that is centuries old and
stylishly decorated with antiques;
Greek and international cooking;
reservations recommended during
high season.

Samaria
El. Venizelou 39–40
Tel. 2 83 10 2 46 81 Traditional old
taverna, popular among the locals;
excellent but expensive food.

WHERE TO STAY

▶ Mid-range

Grecotel Creta Palace
Tel. 2 83 10 5 51 81/3
Fax 2 83 10 5 40 85
www.grecotel.gr
154 rooms, 177 bungalows; 1 villa.
Right on a broad sandy beach 4km/
2.5mi from Rethymno, this hotel has
everything; Cretan architecture combined with modern design; great
variety of entertainment and sports
facilities; child care.

Palazzo Rimondi
H. Trikoupi 16
Tel. 2 83 10 512 89
Fax 2 83 10 5 10 13
www.palazzorimondi.com
Tastefully renovated residence in the
old quarter with apartments; pretty
patio with a small swimming pool.

Fortezza
Melissinou 16
Tel. 283 10 555 51
Fax 2 83 10 5 40 73
www.fortezza.gr
54 rooms. Modern hotel that fits
harmoniously into the old quarter,
with a swimming pool, below the
fortezza.

about 1km/0.5mi, turn right and drive to a parking lot on the plateau. Then cross the plateau on foot and go down into the gorge (20
minutes). The beach is also accessible by boat from Agia Galini and
Plakias.

The resort Plakias sprawls along the bay of that name; it is beautifully   **Plakias**
situated and bordered by high mountains 13km/8mi northwest of   **(Πλακιάς)**
Preveli Monastery on the south coast. The main attraction is the
mile-long sandy beach, which even has some dunes, but it is the
windiest place in southern Crete.

Unusual Preveli beach at the mouth of a river

Agia Galini
(Αγία Γαλίνι)
54km/32mi southeast of Rethymno lies Agia Galini (»Holy Rest«), which has changed from a quiet fishing village on the rocky coast to a lively holiday resort with a sandy beach. The two bays Agios Georgios and Agios Pavlos west of the town are best reached by excursion boat.

Lake Kournas
(Λημνη Κουρνά)
Crete's **largest lake**, a popular destination framed by magnificent mountains, lies not far from Georgioupoli Bay, 23km/14mi east of Rethymno. Swimming is allowed in the lake, which is also home to harmless water snakes and turtles. There are several tavernas for visitors.

✷ ✷ Iráklio (Ηράκλειον)

Island capital
Iráklio, Crete's largest city (population 130,000), is its capital and the **most important port on the island**. The city's historic fabric was largely lost in World War II, so that today it looks on the whole less attractive than it did 70 years ago. Still, Crete's tourist hub does have a few pretty spots and major sights. The old town, still enclosed within town walls that are mostly well preserved, is of interest. The best place to get a feel for the atmosphere of the bustling city is Platia

Iraklio Map

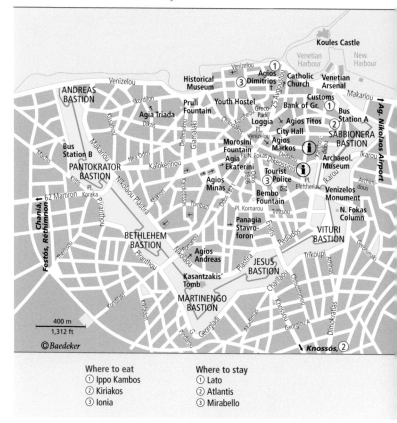

Koules Castle
Venetian Harbour · New Harbour

ANDREAS BASTION

Venizelou

Historical Museum

Agios Dimitrios ①

Catholic Church

Venetian Arsenal

Makariou

Ag. Nikolaou Airport

Skordilon

Pruli Fountain

Youth Hostel

Greco-Park

Customs

Bank of Gr. ①

Bus Station A

Agia Triada

Diktis

Glamalaki

Delimarkou

Koroheou

Chandakos

Loggia × Agios Titos ②

City Hall

SABBIONERA BASTION

Kissamou

Kastion

Venizelou

Bus Station B

Machis

Nea Odos

Kalokerinou

Morosini Fountain

Agios Markos

Agia Ekaterini

Tourist

Archaeol. Museum

Ikarou

Makariou

PANTOKRATOR BASTION

Kris

Pl.

Nikolaou Plastira

Dedalou

Dikeossinis

Police ③

Ikarou

Archimi-

Venizelos Monument

62 Martiron Koraka

Piranthou

Tombazi

Odos 1866

Bembo Fountain

Pl. Kornarou

Triffisou

N. Fokas Column

Chaniá, Rethimnon

Festós, Réthimnon

BETHLEHEM BASTION

Thensou

Piranthou

Romanou

Nikolaou

Panagia Stavro-foron

Evans

Pediados

VITURI BASTION

Gerohmak.

Agios Andreas

Plastira

JESUS BASTION

Trikoupi

Athinas

Kasantzakis' Tomb

Kordhaki

Kiriadon

MARTINENGO BASTION

Chariton

Knossou

Chrisostomou

Dimokratias

400 m
1,312 ft

©Baedeker

Georgladi

Piraeon

Georgiou A

↘ Knossós ②

Where to eat
① Ippo Kambos
② Kiriakos
③ Ionia

Where to stay
① Lato
② Atlantis
③ Mirabello

Venizelou with its Morosini Fountain and many restaurants and cafes. The city's main arteries begin here: Leoforos Dikeossinis with shops, office buildings and cafés; Odos 25 Avgoustou, which runs to the harbour, with banks and travel agencies; the pedestrian zone Odos Dedalou, the market street Odos 1866, and the main shopping street Odos Kalokerinou. The second central point in Iráklio, Plateia Eleftherias, is the site of a famous archaeological museum.

History   Iráklio – name comes from »Hercules« - was the harbour of Knossos in the Minoan period. It went into decline in Roman times but was given new life by the Saracens after 824. The Venetians started calling the town Candia in 1538, commissioned architect Michele Sanmicheli to build a long and massive fortified wall around it, and made it the island capital. In the 16th and 17th centuries Iráklio was the

▶ VISITING IRAKLIO

INFORMATION

EOT
Xanthoudidou 1
Tel. 28 10 39 93 99
Fax 28 10 22 71 80
www.interkriti.org

WHERE TO EAT

► Moderate

① *Ippokambos*
S. Venizelou 2–3
Cretan delicacies can be enjoyed on
two floors in this ouzerie on the
Venetian harbour.

② *Kiriakos*
Leoforos Dimokratias 53
Tel. 28 10 22 46 49 This modern eating
place with a cosy atmosphere, a bit
away from the centre of town, is
considered one of the best restaurants
in the city; they serve delicious Greek
dishes.

③ *Pantheon*
Odos 1866
Popular taverna centrally located near
the market, open almost round the
clock; serves a large selection of typical
local vegetable dishes and traditional
tripe soup (patsa).

WHERE TO STAY

► Mid-range

① *Aquila Atlantis*
Igias 2
Tel. 28 10 22 91 03

Fax 28 10 22 62 65
www.aquilahotels.com
160 rooms. Large hotel near the
archaeological museum; foyer and
restaurant in elegant designer decor.

② *Galaxy*
Dimokratias 67
Tel. 28 10 23 88 12, fax 28 10 21 12 11
www.galaxy-hotel.com.gr
140 rooms. Modern city hotel; large
pool in the inner courtyard.

③ *Lato*
Epimenidou 15
Tel. 28 10 22 81 03
Fax 28 10 24 03 50
www.lato.gr
50 rooms. Most rooms in this stylish
city hotel have fine views of the
harbour and sea.

► Budget

④ *Irini*
Idomeneos 4
Tel. 28 10 22 97 03
Fax 28 10 22 64 07
www.irini-hotel.com
59 rooms. Centrally located; rooms
facing the back are quiet.

⑤ *Mirabello*
Theotokopoulou 20
Tel. 28 10 28 50 52
www.mirabello-hotel.gr
25 rooms. The hotel is quiet, despite
its central location.

centre of a significant Cretan school of painting. Although the Ottoman Turks took Crete in 1648, Iráklio only fell in 1669 after a 21-year siege; the Turks made Hania the administrative centre. When Crete was annexed to Greece in 1913, Iráklio regained its role as the capital. During World War II most of the city was destroyed.

The most important attraction in the city is Iráklio Archaeological
Museum; the country's most significant museum after the National
Archaeological Museum in Athens. It exhibits wonderful finds from
palaces and residential buildings in Knossos, Phaestos, Agias Triadas
and other excavation sites and gives a comprehensive picture of the
unique Minoan culture from the 3rd millennium BC.

★★
Archaeological
Museum

Since the museum building, which opened in 1938, was too small
for the many new finds and no longer up to date in its presentation,
it was decided that the museum would be completely remodelled,
the building gutted and a new annexe built. Reopening is scheduled
for spring 2012, but might be delayed. Until then the museum's major objects are being shown in a special exhibition in a hall in the
southeast corner of the main floor of the
annexe. When the **remodelling of the
museum** is complete, these objects will
have to be integrated into the new displays and might possibly be missing from
the exhibition at some point. Some of
the pieces are described here; they will
be the highlights of a later tour of the remodelled museum as well.

The display case numbers refer to the
special exhibition. The outstanding finds
from the Neolithic age and Minoan Pre-
palatial period (5000–2100 BC) include **a
votive bowl** with sculptural decorations
depicting a herd of sheep and a shepherd
(display case 4). The famous clay **Disc of
Phaestos** from the Protopalatial (Old
Palace) period (2100–1700 BC, display
case 18) is one of the museum's most
valuable pieces. With its hieroglyphics
spiralling from the outer edge to the
centre, it is one of the world's oldest examples of stamped imprinting. The three
bare-breasted **snake goddesses** (display
case 14) are from the treasure-chamber
of the main shrine of Knossos. The **Steer
Rhyton** (ceremonial cup, display case
13), one of the most important finds
from Minoan culture, is a masterly work
in steatite. The eyes are of quartz and jasper; the golden horns are re-
constructions.

A beautiful quartz rhyton

Another of the museum's highlights is the **Reapers Vase** (display case
16) of steatite with a very lifelike depiction of men singing accompanied by musicians on the way home after harvesting grain.

Another masterpiece came from the palace of Kato Zakros from the
New Palace period (1700–1400 BC): a beautiful **quartz rhyton** (dis-

play case 12) with a handle of quartz beads and decorated with a gilt pearl wreath. The famous **sarcophagus from Agias Triadas** (*c* 1400 BC) is the only Minoan stone coffin; it probably contained the body of a king. The remarkably well-preserved frescoes show scenes of cult ceremonies with women recognizable by their white and men by their brown colour. A priestess is seen making an offering on an altar in front of a ceremonial building decorated with double horns. The bird on the double-headed axe next to it symbolizes the presence of the deity.

Another priestess is performing a bloody sacrifice of a bull, accompanied by a flute player. A further scene shows a funerary building with the deceased in front of it, recognizable by his lack of arms. Three men are bringing two animals and what appears to be a funeral barge. Opening times of the special exhibition: Mon noon–5pm, Tue–Sun 8.30am–3pm, in the summer possibly longer. Tel.: 28 10 22 60 92.

Harbour, Venetian Loggia

The attractive Venetian harbour and **Koules fortress** (1523–40; open-opening times: May–Oct Tue–Sun 8am–7pm, Nov–Apr 8.30am–3pm) are located north of the old quarter. The Venetian Loggia on Odos 25 Avgoustou, which leads south into the centre, was built from 1626 to 1628 by Francesco Morosini, the Venetian Generalproveditore. The 17th-century former **armoury** (Armeria) next to it is today the city hall.

Churches

The nearby Church of **Agios Titos** was named after Titus, the first bishop of Crete. A reliquary containing his skull (in the narthex on the left) was returned from Venice in 1966. The building dating from the 11th–12th centuries was made a mosque in 1862 and later an Orthodox cathedral. Further south on Plateia Venizelou note the **Morosini Fountain** (1628) with lions dating from the 14th century and the former **Church of Agios Markos** (1239). It was used as a mosque from 1669 until 1915; today it is a venue for events. Copies of major Cretan frescoes are on display here.

> ### Baedeker TIP
>
> **Religious painting**
> Anyone interested in icons should go to see the icon painter Voula Manousakis at 22 Chandakos Street. The smaller icons are affordable.

Bembo Fountain, Museum of Religious Art

Walk along the market street Odos 1866 in the morning when the market is at its busiest. The Bembo Fountain (1588) at its southern end has ancient spolia; the Turkish pump house next to it is used as a coffee house now. **Agios Minas Cathedral** (19th century) and the little 18th-century Church of Agia Ekaterini stand on St Catherine's Square. Today the church is the **Museum of Religious Art**, with six 16th-century icons by M. Damaskinos as the main attraction. They are exhibited on the south wall of the nave and were originally painted for the Vrondisi Monastery from 1580 to 1591.

The liveliest part of town is around the Morosini Fountain

The Historical Museum in the northern part of the old town documents Cretan history from late antiquity up to the present; it has an extensive ethnographical collection. Opening times: Apr–Oct Mon–Sat 9am–5pm, Nov–Mar Mon–Sat 9am–3pm; www.historical-museum.gr.

★
Historical Museum
⏲

The defensive wall designed and built by the Veronese architect Michele Sanmicheli, who came to Crete in 1538, has five bastions and two semi-bastions; there was a dry moat in front of the wall, which is still recognizable in places. Most of the eight city gates still exist. There is a good view of the city from the Martinengo Bastion in the south. The grave of the great Cretan **poet Nikos Kazantzakis** (▶ Famous People) is also here; the church refused to let him be buried in consecrated ground.

City wall

★ ★ **Knossos (Κνωσός)**

The palace complex of Knossos (5km/3mi southeast of Iráklio), the island's oldest capital, was excavated from 1899 by British archaeologists under the direction of Sir Arthur Evans. The complex is located on a slope and was once three to four storeys high; it was destroyed several times and rebuilt in three phases. It was in use from about 2000 until 1400 BC: the first palace from 2000 until 1800 BC, the second palace from 1800 to 1700 BC, the third palace from 1700 to 1400 BC. The remains visible today belong largely to the third palace, which was built after 1700 BC; even though it was changed and expanded in the following centuries the basic structure is the same as

⏲
Opening hours:
Opening times:
May–Oct
 daily 8am–7pm
Jan–Apr
Mon noon–5pm
Tue–Sun
8am–5pm
Nov, Dec Tue–Sun
8.30am–3pm

KNOSSÓS

✶ ✶ Knossós, the most important Minoan palace, is a vivid testimony to Europe's first civilization. With an area of 2 ha / 5 acres and consisting of more than 1,000 rooms, it was the largest palace of this unique culture. In its prime, more than 10,000 people are thought to have lived in the palace and its surrounding area.

⏱ Opening hours:
May–Oct daily 8am–7pm
Jan–Apr Mon noon–5pm
Tue–Sun 8am–5pm
Nov, Dec Tue–Sun 8.30am–3pm

① Throne room

Taking a central position in the Throne Room is an alabaster throne, flanked by benches and set off by frescoes depicting gryphons. Bordering the chamber are cult rooms in which a mother goddess was venerated.

② Tripartite Shrine

It is likely that earth and fertility gods were worshipped in this, the main sanctuary, illuminated only by torch-light. The double-axe symbols, or labrys, imbue the chamber with a special sanctity.

Along with bulls' horns, the labrys was a significant cult object of the Minoan religion. In addition, there were underground cysts holding treasure.

③ Northwest Wing

In the northwest wing are cult rooms decorated with beautiful and richly detailed frescoes.

④ Hall of the Double Axes

The Hall of the Double Axes – named after the double-axe symbols decorating it – probably served as the palace's official reception hall.

Knossós *Plan*

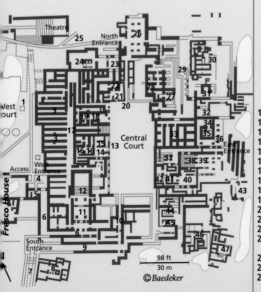

1 Altar base
2 Circular Pits
3 Magazines
4 West Propylaeum
5 Guard Rooms
6 Corridor of the Procession
7 Columned Stairs
8 South Building
9 Southern Corridor
10 Corridor
11 South Propylaeum
12 Staircase
13 Shrine
14 Anteroom
15 Main Sanctuary
16 Pillar Crypts
17 Magazine Corridor
18 Throne Room
19 Cult Room
20 North Ramp
21 Prison
22 Cult Room
23 Northwest Propylaeum
24 Cult Area
25 Royal Road
26 Customs House
27 Northeast Hall
28 Northeast Magazine
29 Potter's Workshops (?)
30 Ceramic Workshop
31 Magazine
32 Light-Well
33 Room with Water Basin
34 Pottery
35 Stonemason's Workshop
36 East Veranda
37 Grand Staircase
38 Hall of the Double Axes
39 King's Megaron
40 Queen's Megaron
41 Queen's Bathroom
42 Queen's Boudoir
43 East Bastion
44 Hall of the Double Axes
45 Cult Pond
46 House with the Sacred Podium
47 Southeast Building

98 ft
30 m
©Baedeker

Food w...
such pi...

in the 16th century BC. The complicated floor plan of the palace gave rise to the assumption that the palace was the legendary **labyrinth** of King Minos, especially since the symbol of the double axe (Greek »labrys«), a trademark of Minoan Crete, was often found here. Most researchers hold the traditional view that Knossos was a centre of power and administration.

Tour The palace is entered from the west court (to the left are the remains of a theatre). The Procession Corridor (named after the frescoes) leads to the large gateway of the south propylaea. Then walk along a large corridor past a large number of storage rooms with clay vessels to the spacious central courtyard, where bull-leaping was possibly performed. The grand staircase and the throne room with an alabaster throne are on the west side of the courtyard; on the east side are the utility and residential rooms with baths and latrines. Next to the hall named after the double-axe symbols carved on its pillars are the king's chambers and the queen's chambers. The numerous frescoes are copies; the originals are in Iráklio Archaeological Museum.

Around Iráklio

Fodele The village of Fodele is beautifully situated in olive and orange
(Φόδελε) groves 29km/18mi west of Iráklio, and can be reached by the coast road. The painter El Greco (▶Famous People) was probably born here. His father's house stands about 1km/0.5mi before the village near the church.

Tylisos Near Tylisos, which is about 15km/9mi southwest of Iráklio, there
(Τύλισος) are interesting remains of Minoan villas from the 17th–16th centuries BC. The walls were constructed meticulously of stone blocks and stabilized by vertical wooden beams. There are more remains of a Minoan residence 9km/5mi west of Tylisos in **Sklavokamos**. In the tourist village of **Arolithos** (about 2km/1mi north of Tylisos), which was established in 1987, old Cretan traditions are kept up, especially the production of handicrafts.

Anogia The village of Anogia (11km/7mi west of Sklavokamos) was com-
(Ανώγεια) pletely destroyed by the German army in 1944 as revenge for the abduction of General von Kreipe to Egypt. Today it is a popular excursion site and the starting point for tours of the Ida Mountains.

Idaio Antro From Anogia follow the road (22km/13mi) to the Nida Plateau (1,370m/4,495ft). The hike up to the Idaio Antro (»Idaean Cave«; 1,540m/5,052ft) takes about 30 minutes. According to myth **Zeus** was raised here by nymphs on goat's milk and honey. The cave was a cult site from the Minoan to the Roman period.

The climb up Mt Psiloritis, the **highest peak on Crete** (2,456m/ 8,058ft) is very rewarding; it is usually possible from June until September and requires good physical condition. For the ascent and descent from the Nida Plateau to the peak Timios Stavros plan about one day. It is part of the E 4 long-distance hiking trail, so it is adequately marked with black and yellow signs. Mt Psiloritis can also be climbed from Kamares (see below).

Psiloritis

About 15km/9mi south of Iráklio lies the town of Arhanes, the centre of Cretan wine-growing. On the town square, which is bordered by several cafes, the Panagia Church possesses valuable icons. The nearby Minoan excavation sites are worth a visit: the **Fourni necropolis**, the **archaeologically significant sanctuary of Anemospilia**, where there are signs of human sacrifice, and 4km/2.5mi to the south **Vathypetro**, a large Minoan villa in a beautiful location. South of Arhanes the **Church of Michail Archangelos**, all that remains of the village of Asomatos, has frescoes painted in 1315.

Arhanes
(Αρχάνες)

Baedeker TIP

Minoan wines

A visit to Minos winery near Arhanes is worthwhile. Try the Minos and Minos Palace wines. Opening hours: weekdays 10.30am–7pm; tel. 281074595.

It is possible to drive from Arhanes to the peak of Mt Jouchtas(811m/2,661ft). The views as far as Iráklio are worthwhile. Every year on August 6 a procession goes to the pilgrimage church of Afendi Christou (»Transfiguration of Christ«) on the southern peak.

Jouchtas

In Myrtia, 17km/10mi east of Arhanes, there is a small but informative **museum** dedicated to **Crete's greatest writer, Nikos Kazantzakis** (►Famous People), whose father lived in Myrtia. Opening hours: March–Oct daily 9am–5pm, Nov–Feb Sun 10am–3pm; www.kazantzakis-museum.gr.

Myrtia
(Μυρτιά)
⊙

From Iráklio to Matala

The 75km/45mi drive from Iráklio to the fertile plain of Messara and the south coast takes in attractive scenery and major historical sites. Leave Iráklio heading west on the road to Rethymno, then turn off after 2km/1mi towards Mires. The route first runs through the major Cretan region for the production of sultanas and near Siva one of the major wine-growing regions on the island.

Wine-growing region

A whitewashed rock in Agia Varvara (31km/19mi) marks the **geographical centre of Crete**. 6km/4mi north of Agia Varvara, the remains of ancient **Rizenia** command a spectacular view of the sea and surroundings.

Agia Varvara
(Αγία Βαρβάρα)

Kamares (Καμάρες), Ida Mountains

A side trip to Kamares (29km/18mi west) passes below the Ida Mountains (»forest mountains«) through superb landscape. In the first town on this route, **Gergeri**, there is a memorial to hostages shot in 1944 by the German army. The next town is **Zaros**, known for its trout farms that serve tasty trout dishes. From Agios Nikolaos Monastery above the town there is a clear view over the southern foothills of the Ida Mountains to the Messara Plain. **Valsomonero Monastery** near Vorizia (8km/5mi west of Zaros) stands out for its wonderful location. The frescoes here (14th–15th century) are of great art-historical interest. Opening hours: 9am–3pm. From Kamares it is possible to climb up to the **Kamares Cave**, a Minoan shrine where polychrome vessels from the Minoan period were found; they are now in Iráklio Archaeological Museum. Those who want to hike from here up Mt Psiloritis, the highest in the Ida range, have to sleep either in the cave, at the high-level pasture of Kotila or at the summit. The ascent takes 6–7 hours.

Messara Plain

The main route climbs up to the Vourvoulitis Pass at 650m/2,133ft; from here there is a wonderful view of the Messara Plain, the largest on Crete, where olives, citrus fruits and even sugar cane are grown.

Gortyna

The city of Gortyna was a one-time rival of Phaestos and Knossos and later the capital of the Roman province of Creta et Cyrenaica, which existed until the Saracens invaded in 826. In the north are the ruins of the 6th-century Basilica of Titus (6th century AD). The ancient agora leads to the odeon; twelve of what were once probably 20 Greek legal codes dating from the Archaic period (480 BC) are displayed in the colonnade that surrounds the odeon; they comprise the **oldest known European civil law code**. The *c* 17,000 letters of the civil and criminal law are inscribed on stone tablets in »boustrophedon« style (»as the ox ploughs«), i.e., in lines alternating from left to right and from right to left. Opening hours: May–Oct daily 8am–7.30pm, Nov–April 8.30am–3pm.

Lendas (Λέντας)

Near Lendas on the south coast (33km/20mi south of Gortyna) are the remains of the Graeco-Roman city of Lebena; it was once the harbour for Gortyna and was famous as early as the 4th century BC for its hot springs. The Temple of Asclepius stands on a terrace above today's town. It was built in the 3rd century BC and renewed in the 2nd century AD, with brick walls that are clad in rubble stone. Inside are two columns and the base of the cult figure. The beautiful mosaic in the room directly to the north depicts seahorses and palmetto decoration; temple treasures were stored in a room underneath. From there steps and a stoa lead to the east, where the well house of a spring that is supposed to have healing properties is still standing. Further to the east is the 11th-century Chapel of St John with frescoes of the 14th–15th centuries. The beautiful and inviting **sandy beach at Dyskos** is a 15-minute walk from Lendas.

The drive onwards offers many beautiful views of the Messara Plain. Vori, about 2km/1mi north of the road, has **Crete's finest and most interesting folk art museum**. The well-presented collection illustrates fishing, farming, forestry and handicrafts. Opening hours: May–Oct daily 10am–6pm. The road branches off towards Phaestos south of Vori.

✳
Vori
(Βώροι)

⏱

On a foothill of the Ida Mountains – with a wonderful view of the Messara Plain – lie the ruins of Phaestos, **after Knossos the most important Minoan palace on the island**. The new palace was built after 1700 BC on the site of a building constructed around 1900 BC. It

✳
Phaestos

Phaestos is the most important excavation site after Knossos

Phaestos *Plan*

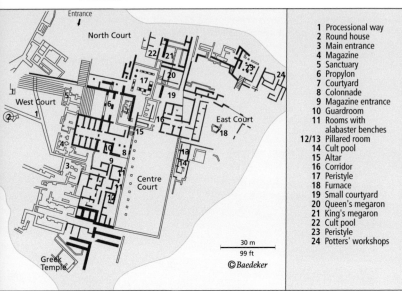

Entrance

North Court

West Court

East Court

Centre Court

Greek Temple

30 m
99 ft
©Baedeker

1 Processional way
2 Round house
3 Main entrance
4 Magazine
5 Sanctuary
6 Propylon
7 Courtyard
8 Colonnade
9 Magazine entrance
10 Guardroom
11 Rooms with alabaster benches
12/13 Pillared room
14 Cult pool
15 Altar
16 Corridor
17 Peristyle
18 Furnace
19 Small courtyard
20 Queen's megaron
21 King's megaron
22 Cult pool
23 Peristyle
24 Potters' workshops

was gutted around 1450 BC by a catastrophic fire. The surviving sections of the palace, which were grouped around a central court, are the ruins of the west and north wings, while the south and east wings collapsed during an earthquake. The remains of the old palace can be seen on the western and northern sides of the surviving sections. Opposite the entrance in the north courtyard a stairway descends. To the right the seating tiers of a theatre are recognizable, and to the left a monumental propylaea stairway leads to the palace with the royal chambers. Opening times: April–Oct daily 8am–7.30pm, Nov–Mar 8.30am–3pm.

★
Agias Triadas

About 2km/1mi west of Phaestos – and at one time linked to the palace by a paved road – lie the remains of the Minoan villa Agias Triadas, named after a Byzantine chapel standing on a neighbouring hill. Like Phaestos, it primarily dates back to the 16th century BC, but was rebuilt after a fire around 1450 BC and remained occupied into Doric times. There is a magnificent view of the sea and the Ida Mountains from the west side of the palace. The Venetian Chapel of Agios Georgios (14th century) with frescoes and interesting inscriptions is visible from to the south of palace; below it to the northeast are parts of a Late Minoan settlement (14th–11th century BC). At the foot of the hill is a necropolis with a large round domed tomb. Opening times: April–Oct daily 10am–4.30pm, Nov–Mar Tue–Sun 8.30am–3pm.

The onward drive to the Messara Plain passes the architecturally interesting **Church of Agios Pavlos** at the edge of the town of Agios Ioannis. The town of Pitsidia is reached by driving through a magnificent olive grove. From there a road leads to the excavation site of **Kommos**, once the harbour of Phaestos. The drive ends in Matala, which was the harbour of Roman Gortyna. Caves dug in the sandstone rock faces of the bay served as homes and tombs from Neolithic times. They were fenced off after hippies lived in them in the 1960s. Matala is a popular beach and day-trip resort. Its main attraction is the beautiful pebble and sandy beach with limestone rocks in the background.

Matala
(Μάταλα)

✳ Agios Nikolaos (Αγιος Νικόλαος)

The little town of Agios Nikolaos (population 8,000), charmingly set on the beautiful Mirambello Gulf, has an especially pleasant atmosphere. It has long been appreciated as a holiday resort because of the fine beaches and the many places to visit in the vicinity. Its life is concentrated mainly around the harbour and the picturesque **Lake Voulismeni**, which is fed with fresh water.

✳
Picturesque resort

Agios Nikolaos has an enchanting location

▶ VISITING AGIOS NIKOLAOS

INFORMATION

EOT
Marina
Tel. 2 84 10 8 23 84, fax 2 84 10 8 23 85

WHERE TO EAT

► Moderate

Itanos
Kyprou 1, tel. 0 84 10 2 53 40
Traditional restaurant in the town
centre, next to the cathedral, with
delicious food.

Pelagos
Strategou Koraka 10
One of the best restaurants in town in
a neo-classical villa with an idyllic
garden; its specialties are fish dishes;
large selection of wines.

WHERE TO STAY

► Luxury

Minos Palace
Tel. 2 84 10 2 38 01/8
Fax 2 84 10 2 38 16
www.mamidakishotels.gr
99 rooms, 9 bungalows, 39 suites.
Large hotel in a fabulous and restful
location on a small peninsula, surrounded by a beautiful garden; water
sports; all bungalows have a view of
the sea, some have their own pool.

► Mid-range

Coral
Akti Koundourou
Tel. 2 84 10 2 83 63, fax 2 84 10 2 87 54
www.hermes-hotels.gr
170 rooms. Upper mid-range hotel on
the harbour promenade

Sights The harbour is at pretty Lake Voulismeni. Odos Konstantinou Paleologou runs from the harbour to the **archaeological museum**, which
focuses on eastern Cretan artefacts from the Neolithic to the Graeco-
Roman period. Fabulous vases, extraordinary vessels and strange and
mysterious idolsmake it worth a visit. Opening times: Tue–Sun
8.30am–3pm. A folk art museum in the port authority building
shows beautiful woven textiles, costumes and Byzantine icons. The
10th-century **Church of Agios Nikolaos** gave the settlement its name;
it stands in the grounds of the Minos Palace Hotel (key at the reception) northeast of town and has rare frescoes from the time of the
Iconoclast Controversy.

Excursions from Agios Nikolaos

Kritsa
(Κριτσά)

Panagia Kera ►

11km/7mi southwest of Agios Nikolaos the pretty village of Kritsa,
spreading over a mountain slope in the midst of an olive grove, has
been taken over by souvenir shops. Kritsa became known through
the film *The Greek Passion*, based on the novel by Nikos Kazantzakis,
which was shot here in 1958. 1km/0.5mi before reaching Kritsa,
under tall cypresses, stop to see the beautiful Church of Panagia Kera

Restful atmosphere: Panagia Kera Church →

(12th–14th centuries) with its magnificent frescoes painted in the 14th and 15th centuries. The scenes of the Ascension in the nave and the frescoes in the north aisle are highly expressive. Opening hours: Tue–Sun 8.30am–3pm.

3km/2mi north of Kritsa are the ruins of the Dorian city of **Lato**, probably established between the 7th and 4th centuries BC. There is a beautiful view of the surrounding mountainside and Mirabello Gulf from the northern acropolis. 2km/1mi south of Kritsa, on the road to Kroustas, the Church of Agios Ioannis has a magnificent iconostasis; 4km/2.5mi south of Kroustas is another church dedicated to St John with outstanding frescoes (1347).

The 40km/25mi drive from Agios Nikolaos westward to the fertile, almost circular **Lasithi Plateau** (850m/2,789ft) is enjoyable. The thousands of windmills that once served to irrigate this intensively cultivated plateau have largely been replaced by motor pumps. The village **Agios Georgios** has an interesting folk art museum, with embroidery and household implements. Opening times: daily 10am–4pm. On the southwest edge of the plain, near Psyhro, is the dripstone cave **Diktaio Antron** (Diktaean Cave), according to myth the birthplace of Zeus. It is a very popular excursion site, and donkeys take visitors from the parking lot. Opening times: daily 10am–3pm, midsummer until 6.30pm.

From Lasithi Plateau to the coast

Just beyond Kera lies the atmospheric **Kardiotissa Monastery** (14th century). Opening hours: 8am–1pm, 3pm–7pm. In **Krasi** a huge cypress tree spreads over the main square and shades the tables at the taverna. From here drive to Malia via Mohos or directly on the new road. Continue to Hersonisos via **Avdou**, where there are several Byzantine chapels, especially the 14th-century Agios Antonios with its expressive frescoes, and via Potamies, where the abandoned **Gouverniotisas Monastery** dates from the 10th–14th centuries. **Hersonisos** consists of an old quarter away from the coast with a pretty square and the popular resort Limin Hersonisos. The **Lychnostatis Open Air Museum** by the sea illustrates rural life on Crete up to a few decades ago in a variety of ways. Opening hours: Mon–Fri 9am–2pm.

Thanks to its miles of sandy beaches, Hersonisos Bay up to **Malia** is one of the leading holiday regions on Crete, with a large number of hotels, restaurants, cafes and tavernas. Walk along the beach from Malia for about an hour to the remains of the Minoan **palace of Malia**, after Knossos and Phaestos the most important palace on Crete. It was built between 1900 and 1800 BC. Be sure to note the most significant find: a round sacrificial table. Opening hours: Tue–Sun 8.30am–3pm.

Eloúnda (Ελούνδα)

11km/7mi north of Agios Nikolaos, the hotel settlement of Eloúnda sprawls along the edge of a bay. There is an impressive view of the **Gulf of Mirabello** from the road leading there. At the entrance to the

Spinalonga island with a Venetian fortress: a popular destination for excursions from Elounda

village, a road heads off to the right onto an isthmus, site of the remains of the Dorian city Olous; part of it is under water. In Elounda **several of Crete's best hotels** can be found.

Pláka, once a fishing village, (5km/3mi north of Elounda) is an expanding tourist resort; it has two pebble beaches. The broad bays here are excellent for windsurfing. Pláka is also known for its fish tavernas.

Pláka (Πλάκα)

Off the northern tip of Spinalonga Peninsula lies the little rocky island with the same name. The Venetian fortress (1579–85) was the Greek leper colony from 1903 until 1957 and is now a popular site for day trips. Boats go to the island from Elounda, Pláka and Agios Nikolaos.

Spinalonga (Σπιναλόγκα)

22km/13mi northwest of Agios Nikolaos and 2km/1mi northeast of Neapolis there is a well-preserved Apollo sanctuary (7th century BC) among the remains of the Archaic settlement of Driros. Several bronze cult images found here are now in Iráklio Archaeological Museum.

Driros (Δρίρος)

The ruins of Gournia (20km/12mi southeast of Agios Nikolaos) give a good impression of how a Middle Minoan city (c 1500 BC) looked. The grounds consist of narrow, paved lanes and small homes, with a palace and a shrine on higher ground; it is one of the earliest examples of European urban planning Opening hours: Tue–Sun 8.30am–3pm.

★
Gournia (Γουρνιά)

⊙

Mohlos
(Móχλος)
11km/7mi northeast of Gournia, near Platanos, there is a wonderful view of the Gulf of Mirabello and Psira Island. 5km/3mi further to the northeast the charming fishing village of Mohlos has nice tavernas and pretty sandy bays, which however are only accessible from the sea. On the island of the same name off the coast (boat connection) funeral offerings were found in innumerable burial caves from the Early Minoan period.

Ierapetra
(Ιεράπετρα)
Ierapetra on Crete's south coast almost seems North African. It is **Europe's most southerly town**, 36km/22mi from Agios Nikolaos, and the centre of a rich area of vegetable cultivation with a particularly warm climate; swimming is possible even in January. In 1798 **Napoleon** is supposed to have slept here, in the house Spiti tou Napoleon north of the harbour. A former Koran school on Plateia Koupanaki now houses a small archaeological museum with finds from Roman and Venetian times (opening hours: Tue–Sun 8.30am–3pm). A mosque and a Turkish pump house stand on the town square. The shoreline promenade with tavernas and cafes along a beach of dark sand begins at the Venetian harbour fortress.

The town of **Myrtos** (12km/7mi west of Ierapetra) has a long sandy beach, and towards Tertsa there are isolated bays for swimming. About 18km/11mi off the coast of Ierapetra to the south (boat connections) lies the **island of Hrissy** with its magnificent dune beach. In the summer a taverna opens near the boat pier, but otherwise the island is not inhabited.

Things run at a slower pace in Sitia

Sitia (Σητεία)

Sitia, Crete's easternmost town (population 8,000), is a port with predominantly new buildings in a picturesque setting on a slope. The town was levelled in 1303 and 1508 by earthquakes. It was the home of **Vinzentinos Kornaros** (early 17th century–1677), who wrote the epic *Erotokritos*, which is still known in Greece today. After being destroyed by the Ottoman Turks in 1651, the town was not resettled until 1870.

Crete's eastern-most town

The harbour promenade with its restaurants is pretty. The centre of town is Plateia Iroon Politechniou with its palms and cafes. The **folk-lore museum** displays a collection of household items, costumes and tools in the city centre. Opening hours: Mon–Sat 10am–1pm. Steps lead up to **Fort Kasarma** (1631), which offers a grand view of the town and the surroundings. The **archaeological museum** on the road to Piskokefalou displays finds from eastern Crete dating from the Minoan to the Roman period. Opening hours: Tue–Sun 8.30am–3pm.

Sights

🕐

🕐

Excursions from Sitia

The fortress-like Toplou Monastery (14th–17th century), 15km/9mi east of Sitia, was a base for resistance against the Turks and a refuge from the Germans in World War II. It is **one of the most visited and most important monasteries on Crete**. In the northern aisle of the monastery church valuable 14th century frescoes have been exposed. The museum illuminates the role of the monastery in the fight for independence. Opening hours: daily 9am–1pm, 2pm–6pm, museum: April–October.

✱
Toplou (Τοπλού)

🕐

7km/4mi northeast of Toplou monastery, Crete's largest grove of palm trees grows in a sandy cove. The beach is overrun in the summer and the grove is fenced off except for a couple of trees. 3km/2mi further to the north near Erimoupolis are the remains of the port of **Itanos**. Three quiet and attractive beaches with coarse sand are a pleasant place to stop.

✱
Vai Beach

Located 7km/4mi south of Vai, the town of Palekastro lies on a hillside surrounded by olive groves; it is popular with young tourists travelling alone. Close to the beach are the ruins of the Minoan settlement of **Roussolakkos**.

Palekastro (Παλαίκαστρο)

The drive to Zakros, about 17km/10mi south of Palekastro, offers a magnificent panoramic view high above the sea. From there drive or hike through the »Valley of the Dead«, a gorge lined with oleander; it was named after the Minoan burial sites here. The excavated ruins of Kato Zakros on the bay of the same name are only a short distance

✱
Kato Zakros

away. This city was inhabited from the Early Minoan period. The palace stood from 1600 until 1410 BC and was the point of departure for trade with Egypt and the rest of North Africa. Opening hours: May–Oct daily 8am–7.30pm, Nov–Apr Tue–Sun 8.30am– 3pm.

★ ★ Délos · Dílos

N 10

Greek: Δήλος
Area: 3.6 sq km/1.4 sq mi
Population: 15

Island group: Cyclades
Altitude: 0–113 m/370ft

The small, uninhabited rocky island southwest of the holiday paradise of Mýkonos was not only the spiritual and cultural focus but also the economic centre of the Aegean in ancient times and today is one of country's most important excavation sites.

★ ★
Island of Apollo

Opening hours:
Tue–Sun
8.30am–3pm

Délos (Greek: »Dílos«), a ridge of almost barren rock 5km/3mi long and only 1.3km/1450yd wide, lies a little less than 3km/2mi southwest of Mýkonos. The only elevation worth mentioning, the 113m/370ft high Kýnthos, is at the centre of the island. Along the middle of the west coast lies the ancient sacred harbour, which is protected by two small promontories of rock. From here the main island plain extends to the northeast. The lower-lying northern part was flooded, and thus the sacred lake was formed. Even though it is one of the smallest of the Cyclades, Délos played a central role in antiquity, and the surrounding islands were named the »Cyclades« even in ancient times because it was believed they formed a circle (»cyclos«) around **the island on which the god Apollo was born**. A visit to the island is especially worthwhile for fans of Greek antiquity. Beyond that Délos offers nothing for vacationers. The only people living on the island are watchmen and their families.

Myth and history

According to myth the Titan **Leto**, Zeus' lover, gave birth to the **twins Artemis and Apollo** on Délos. The pregnant Leto wandered throughout Greece, fleeing from the jealousy of Hera, Zeus' wife. No one gave Leto refuge out of fear of Hera's revenge. Finally Délos (»visible«) rose up out of the sea and Poseidon, Zeus' brother, anchored it to the bottom of the sea with his trident. Leto gave birth to Apollo, the god of light, poetry and beauty, under a palm tree on the island. According to myth Artemis was also born on Délos. Its signifi-

▶ DELOS

GETTING THERE
Several ships sail daily to Délos from Mýkonos, occasionally also from Tinos, Náxos and Páros. Three to four hours' time is available for the tour. There is no overnight accommodation on the island. Telephone information 22 89 02 23 25

There is a sweeping view of the excavation site from Mt Kýnthos.

cance as a Panhellenic shrine played a major role in its history. In the 1st millennium BC Délos developed into a **centre of the Apollo cult**. In a first katharsis (cleaning) in 543 BC, Peisistratos ordered all graves to be removed from the area around the temple. In a second katharsis (426–425 BC) after the plague in Athens, births, deaths and burials were forbidden on the island and the graves were moved to the neighbouring island of Rinia. At the founding of the Ionian League, the Temple of Apollo was chosen as the site for the league's treasury; but already by 454 BC Athens had seized it, making Délos and the other islands dependent, a situation that lasted until the time of Alexander the Great. In the following period Délos became a **flourishing trading centre** of the archipelago. Foreign trading companies, the Hermaïsts (Romans), Poseidoniasts (Syrians from Berytos/Beirut) among others, had their seat on the island. The Romans, colonial administrators of Délos after 166 BC, once again made the island subordinate to Athens. As a result, Délos enjoyed its greatest period of prosperity, particularly after the destruction of Corinth, until the devastation of the island by Mithridates in 88 BC, which initiated its decline. Its complete destruction followed in the war against pirates in 69 BC. The island has hardly been inhabited since. In the Middle Ages and early modern times Délos was used as a stronghold of the Order of St John, later as a pirate hideout and finally as a stone quarry.

Sacred Precinct

The sacred harbour (the ferry landing is to the south) was on the west side of Délos, where delegates to the festivals once came on

Harbour

Délos: Ancient Sites *Plan*

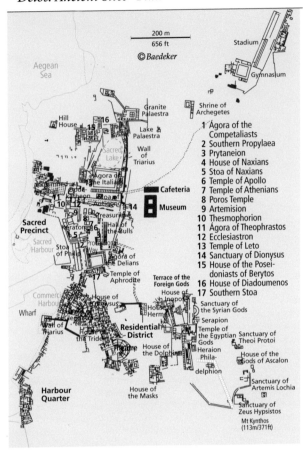

200 m
656 ft

© Baedeker

Aegean Sea

Stadium
Gymnasium

Shrine of Archegetes

Hill House

Granite Palaestra

Lake Palaestra

Wall of Triarius

Sacred Lake

Agora of the Italians

Cafeteria

Museum

1 Ágora of the Competaliasts
2 Southern Propylaea
3 Prytaneion
4 House of Naxians
5 Stoa of Naxians
6 Temple of Apollo
7 Temple of Athenians
8 Poros Temple
9 Artemision
10 Thesmophorion
11 Ágora of Theophrastos
12 Ecclesiastron
13 Temple of Leto
14 Sanctuary of Dionysus
15 House of the Posei-doniasts of Berytos
16 House of Diadoumenos
17 Southern Stoa

Sacred Precinct
Sacred Harbour
Stoa of Philip

Hall of the Bulls

Agora of the Delians

Temple of Aphrodite

Terrace of the Foreign Gods
House of Inopos

Commercial Harbour
Wharf

House of Dionysus
House of the Trident

Residential District

Theatre

House of Hermes

House of the Dolphins

Sanctuary of the Syrian Gods
Serapion
Temple of the Egyptian Gods
Heraion
Phila-delphion

Sanctuary of Theoi Protoi
House of the Gods of Ascalon

Sanctuary of Artemis Lochia

Sanctuary of Zeus Hypsistos

Mt Kynthos (113m/371ft)

Wall of Triarius

Harbour Quarter

House of the Masks

land. Further south was the commercial harbour. In the 2nd century BC the coastline from the Sacred Harbour down to the Bay of Foumi was equipped with quays and warehouses, the remains of which have survived under water.

Agora of the Competaliasts

Between the two harbours lies the Agora of the »competaliasts« (Roman slaves and freedmen), who gathered here for the cult of »lares competales« (the patron deities of crossroads). The agora is decorated with statues and small shrines. A 13m/43ft-wide processional way leads from here northwards to the Sacred Precinct. The 87m/285ft-long Stoa of Philip, a colonnade open to the east and west, was donated by Philip V of Macedon around 210 BC, according to the

Stoa of Philip ►

dedication on the architrave. East of the road stands a smaller stoa with a row of eight shops along its rear. The almost square South Agora (1st century BC), once the state market, lies beyond to the east. The area adjoining to the north up to Hall of Bulls was occupied by the fortifications of the Order of St John in the Middle Ages.

◄ South Agora

From the south propylaea (2nd century BC) with Doric columns and a three-tiered foundation, the Processional Way runs further to the north. Immediately to the right is the House of the Naxians (7th century BC) with columns along the length of the building. On the north side is a base for a 5m/16ft statue of Apollo. According to the 6th-century BC inscription, the statue and its base were carved out of a single block of stone. The dedication on the west side, »The Naxians to Apollo«, was added later. Their L-shaped stoa (c 550 BC) with Ionic columns is visible opposite the House of the Naxians. In the corner stood a bronze palm that the Athenian Nikias donated in 417 BC in memory of the palm tree under which Leto gave birth to Artemis and Apollo.

House of the Naxians

The island's »holy of holies« further north was the Keraton (4th century BC, dedicated to Apollo). The horned altar, around which rams' horns were attached and which was considered to be a wonder of the world, once stood there. In front of the entrance to the Keraton the bases of a number of equestrian statues have survived. The northernmost and smallest of them bore a statue of Sulla, as the inscription on the rear ramp indicates. The Keraton is thought to be older than the smaller Artemision. This Ionic prostyle temple with a granite foundation (4th–2nd century BC) is located to the north in the courtyard on the site of a 7th-century BC sanctuary. The torso and pelvis of a statue of Apollo from the House of the Naxians lie at the northwest corner of the Artemision. The **Thesmophorion** to the northwest of the Artemision was sacred to the cult of Demeter.

Keraton

Artemision

Three parallel temples dedicated to Apollo to the east of the Artemision formed the focal point of the precinct. The southern and largest temple was begun in 478 BC and completed in the 3rd century BC. The foundation walls are built of grey-blue slate and supported a peripteros of 6 : 13 columns. Of the structure little has remained apart from pieces of the triglyph frieze and the Doric columns; of the sculptures only palmetto ornaments and lion heads have remained. Adjacent to the north are the foundations, built of fine-grained »poros« limestone, of the second temple of the Athenians, which faced east and was dedicated in 417 BC. It was an amphiprostylos temple with a two-part cella in which seven statues stood on dark marble plinths. The treasury of the Delian League was stored in the 6th-century BC temple of poros limestone adjoining to the north. An 8m/26ft bronze statue of Apollo also once stood here. In front of the temple is a long base on which bronze statues once

Apollo Precinct

stood. A series of four little buildings that stood in a line to the north of the temples of Apollo are interpreted as **treasuries** because of their similarity to the buildings in Olympia and Delphi.

Prytaneion, Hall of Bulls

East of the House of the Naxians lies the Prytaneion (5th–4th century BC), the house of the chief magistrate, and the so-called Hall of Bulls, presumably a hall for a ship. This Hellenistic building is one of the best-preserved buildings on Délos. On the granite foundation three partially preserved marble steps lead up to the retaining wall of the building; the southern part consists of a vestibule and six Doric columns on the long side and two each on the short sides. Inside there is an elongated hall with a basin-like depression. Of the statuary only a nereid and a dolphin remain on site. At the entrance there are pillars with attached Doric half-columns, whose capitals are adorned by recumbent bulls.

Stoa of Antigonos Gonatas

The northern termination of the Sacred Precinct is the Stoa of Antigonos Gonatas, a colonnade with bull-head triglyphs (3rd century BC). Antigonos was an important Graeco-Macedonian king. The rooms that served as accommodation for delegates to the festivals lay behind the columns, which have fluted upper halves. In front of the stoa is a semicircular complex, the remains of the Mycenaean dome tomb of the Hyperborean Maidens, who assisted Leto during the birth of the divine twins, Apollo and Artemis. In the Sanctuary of Dionysos east of the stoa there are several marble phalluses. One of the bases has reliefs depicting the Dionysos cult (around 300 BC).

Sanctuary of Dionysos ►

Commercial district

A propylaeum leads into the commercial district. Here, behind an Archaic temple dedicated to Leto (6th century BC), is the Agora of the Italians (110 BC), a large four-sided court surrounded by a two-storey colonnade housing shops, workshops and niches for offerings. It was the business premises of a union of Roman merchants who named themselves Hermaïsts after their patron deity, Hermes.

Sacred Lake

Leto is said to have given birth to her son **Apollo** on a small island in the Sacred Lake, which has been filled in by the excavators. A terrace with five Archaic lions (7th century BC) of Naxian marble stood west of the lake on a terrace until 1999. In order to protect these important sculptures from deteriorating more – Aegean storms had literally »sand-papered« them – they were moved into the museum.

Lion Terrace ►

House of Diadoumenos ►

Behind the trading yard of the Poseidoniasts of Berytos (Beirut; 110 BC) northwest of the sea is the House of Diadoumenos, where a Roman copy of a famous statue by Polyclitus (around 420 BC; now in the National Museum of Athens) was found. North of the lake lay the old and new palaestras, and some distance to the northeast the shrine of the hero Archegetes, and a gymnasium and stadium were located.

The museum is a short distance from the Sacred Precinct. In the entrance area models of Délos give a good impression of the former magnificence of the buildings. It is worth noting the Archaic works of art, including a marble triangular base with a ram's head and gorgons (7th century BC), a sphinx made of marble from Náxos, several kouroi and korai (6th century BC), a hand from the colossus of Náxos and three seated women (7th century BC). The Archaic lion sculptures (6th century BC), which once stood on the so-called Lion Terrace, are masterpieces. The collection also includes fragments of the Temple of the Athenians, herms, funerary steles, small sculptures, terra cotta figures and ceramics, votive gifts from the Temple of Artemis and small finds that illustrate the lives and home furnishings of the inhabitants. The most important finds from Délos are in the National Museum of Archaeology and the Museum of the Cyclades in Athens.

✷ **Museum**

✷ ◄ Lions

Kýnthos District and Residential Quarter

A path leads up from the museum in a southeasterly direction to Mount Kýnthos. To the right of the path is the House of Hermes, a two-storey private home from the 2nd century BC named after a head of Hermes discovered there (on display in the museum).

Hermes House

This mosaic gave the House of the Dolphins its name

Terrace of the Foreign Gods
Egyptian and Syrian deities were worshipped on the somewhat higher-lying Terrace of the Foreign Gods. Next to the Doric temple to Isis are the foundations of the **Heraion** (around 500 BC), which was dedicated to Hera.

✴ Kýnthos
An ancient path of steps leads from here up to the 113m/371ft summit of Mount Kýnthos, with the ruins of the temples of Zeus Kýnthos and Athena Kynthia, both erected in the 3rd century BC. There is a **fantastic panoramic view** from Kýnthos.

Residential quarter
Between Kýnthos and the commercial harbour lay the residential district, which gives a vivid idea of living conditions during Hellenistic times (3rd–2nd century BC). The narrow streets are paved with slabs of slate. The houses, whose walls have often survived to a height of 4–5m/13–16ft, had at least one upper floor. The excellently preserved mosaic floors are impressive.

House of the Dolphins, House of Masks
Descending from Kýnthos, the House of the Dolphins is on the right. It gets its name from the beautiful mosaic floor in the columned courtyard. The House of Masks diagonally opposite is named after a floor mosaic depicting theatre masks.

The theatre of Délos once held 5,000 spectators

The theatre (3rd century BC), which seated 5,000 people, is located further west. The orchestra was surrounded by a narrow water canal, the stage building by a colonnade, whose east side served as a proscenium. Beneath the stage structure a huge **cistern** collects the rainwater that runs down the tiers of the theatre.

Theatre

Below the theatre is the **House of the Trident**, which gets its name from a mosaic depicting a trident decorated with a ribbon. The most important mosaic on Délos is in the **House of Dionysos** further to the north. Its motif is the winged Dionysos riding on a panther. In the **House of Cleopatra** opposite are the headless statues of the owners, Cleopatra and Dioskourides. From here it is not far to the ferry landing, where the tour of the excavation site ends.

Other houses

✴ Euboea · Évia

H–M 6–9

Greek: Ευβοια
Altitude: 0–1,743m/5,719ft
Capital: Halkída

Area: 3,897 sq km/1,500 sq mi
Population: 165,000

Greece's second-largest island remains to be discovered as a holiday destination. Only a small tourist zone has developed on the southwest coast; it is mainly visited by Athenians as a weekend getaway. The island is especially worth a visit for its scenery.

Evia, 170km/105mi long and 6km/4mi wide, is the second-largest Greek island after Crete. It lies off the northeast coast of Sterea Ellada and Attica. Together with the mainland, it encloses two lake-like bays that are linked to each other by the 35m/115ft-wide Evripous Channel in Halkída. The principal harbours face the mainland, while the rocky northeast coast drops abruptly into the sea in most places. The topography of the island is split: while the wooded north has characteristics of a region of low mountains, the barren and arid south is reminiscent of the islands of the Aegean. Rearing poultry is one of the major sources of income on the island.

Second-largest Greek island

The oldest inhabitants were immigrant Ellopians from Thessaly in northwest Evia, Abantes from Thrace in central Evia, and Dryopians in the southeast. Attic Ionians merged with the Abantes and brought prosperity and high standing to the island from the 8th to the 6th century BC. Halkída was subjugated by Athens in 506 BC, and possession of the fertile island, a source of lumber, grain and copper, soon became vital to her. The island regained independence towards the end of the Peloponnesian War (411 BC). Following the conquest of Constantinople in 1204, Évia fell to three noblemen from Verona, but the harbours went to the Venetians, who, after many battles with

History

▶ VISITING EVIA

INFORMATION

Tourist information
Karystos 7
Karystos
Tel. 2 22 40 2 62 00
www.euboea.de

GETTING THERE

There is a road link between the mainland and Halkída; boat connections with Volos, Arkitsa, Skala Oropon, Agia Marina and Rafina on the mainland and the islands of Alonissos, Skiathos and Skopelos.

WHERE TO EAT

▶ Moderate

Gouveris
Halkída
Tel. 22 21 02 57 69
This taverna by the sea serves tasty fish dishes.

Lalari
Kymi Tel. 2 22 20 2 26 24
Fine seafood and friendly staff.

WHERE TO STAY

▶ Luxury

Eretria Village Resort
Eretria
Tel. 2 22 90 4 10 00
www.eretriavillage.gr
205 rooms. Hotel complex with a good swimming pool

▶ Mid-range

Best Western Lucy
Halkída
Tel. 2 22 40 2 38 31
Fax 2 22 40 2 20 51
www.lucy-hotel.gr
92 rooms. Centrally located right on the Evripous Channel, 300m/350yd from the beach

▶ Budget

Beis
Northern part of the harbour
Kymi
Tel. 2 22 20 2 28 70, fax 2 22 20 2 26 04
www.hotel-beis.gr; 38 rooms. Nicely decorated rooms with balconies and there is a house-own taverna.

Frankish nobles, were able to subjugate the entire island. In 1470 the Ottoman Turks took possession. In the London Protocol of 1830 it was finally awarded to Greece.

Chalkís/Halkída

City and history Halkída (population 80,000), port and capital of Evia, is charmingly set on hills around the Evripous Channel. Its site at the crossing-point to the mainland led to the early development of a harbour. By 411 BC the town was connected to the mainland by a wooden bridge at the narrowest point of the straits. Today's bridge was constructed in 1962; both sides can be retracted under the access ramps. It had already been observed in antiquity that the current here changes its direction between six and 20 times a day; this is due to the interaction of the tides and waves. According to legend **Aristotle** drowned himself in the channel because he could not explain this phenomenon (in fact he died a natural death in Halkída in 322 BC). The Latin alphabet is based on the alphabet of Halkída.

From **Fort Karababa** on the mainland side, which was in use until 1856, there is a good view of the city and of the Bay of Aulis towards the south. From this bay the Mycenaeans set sail for Troy in mythical times, and Agamemnon is supposed to have sacrificed his daughter Iphigenia here. East of the bridge, the neo-classical town hall can be seen between hotels, restaurants and cafes. Behind them is the kastro, the Venetian and Turkish old quarter, whose walls have partially survived. The Church of **Agia Paraskevi** (second street left after the bridge) was remodelled by Crusaders in the 13th and 14th centuries in the Gothic style, which is very rare in Greece. Of the previous building (5th–6th century) only ancient columns made of Cipollino marble from Karystos are extant. The municipal jail is housed in the Venetian governor's palace. The old quarter is bordered on the north by bustling suburbs. **Halkis Museum** on Leoforos Venizelou (opening hours: Tue–Sun 8.30am–3pm) holds interesting archaeological pieces, especially from Eretria; on Plateia Koskou the **Byzantine Museum** is located in a mosque.

What to see

Northern Parts of the Island

The approximately 200km/120mi-long tour to the north part of the island starts in Halkída and first leads northeast along the Evripous Channel, reaching **Néa Artaki**, a friendly and busy seaside resort, after 7km/4mi. **Steni** lies 23km/13mi east of Néa Artaki; it is a pretty mountain village in lush surroundings with abundant water. From here, a strenuous but not difficult hike (seven hours both ways) goes to the impressive 1,743m/5,718ft summit of the Delphi Pyramid, the main peak of the Dirfys mountain range.

From Néa Artaki to Steni

Psachna, 7km/4.5mi north of Néa Artaki, is the gateway to the rougher, picturesque interior of north Evia; 3km/2mi to the north are the ruins of the Venetian castle Kastri. The resort **Politika** with its long pebble beach is 9km/5.5mi away. The monastery church Perivleptos with 16th-century frescoes is worth seeing. Travelling further on the main route there is a wonderful panoramic view from the pass between Kandylion and Pisaria. Continue through beautiful mountain scenery with plane trees and pine forests, past an ancient castle expanded by the Venetians, to the small **Agios Georgios Monastery** and then into the Kyrefs Valley, overgrown with arbutus and myrtle. Wealthy **Prokopi** in the verdant Klissoura Valley was founded in 1923 by refugees from Prokopio (today Ürgüp in Turkey). They brought along the miraculous mummy of Ioannis o Rosos (»John the Russian«), who served in the tsar's army, died in 1730 and was canonized in 1962. Every year on 27 March there is a pilgrimage to

From Psachna to Pefki

Enchanting, isolated coves glistening green and blue on Evia's east coast

the church, which was built in 1930. 4km/2.5mi beyond Prokopi along the road that passes over the suspension bridge there is a giant plane tree. After another 4km/2.5mi comes **Mantoudi**, a small industrial town whose main source of income is the mining of magnetite. About 8km/5mi beyond Strofylia lies the prosperous village of **Agia Anna**. At the nearby **Angeli** Mantoudi there is a long beach. From Agriovotano, south of Cape Artemisio/Amoni, there is a beautiful view to the island of Pontikonisi. **Artemisio** is known through the first naval victory of the Greek fleet over the numerically superior Persians in 480 BC. The remains of a Temple of Artemis Proseoa have survived nearby. The bronze Zeus of Artemisio (now in the National Museum of Athens) was found off the coast here. To the west pass the fishing village of **Pefki** (»firs«) with its long sandy beach.

Istiéa (Ιστεία)

The main town in the north of the island, Istiéa, is located in a fertile area. Its narrow streets are spanned by marble balconies. A Venetian castle divides the port, **Orei**. To the west of town is another castle, in which building materials from Hellenistic times were used. Next to the church of Orei a massive marble bull from the 4th century BC is displayed behind glass; it was found on the sea bed. From here there is a fine view across the channel to the Othris mountains.

16km/10mi further on is Loutra Edipsou, a **renowned spa** since ancient times with hot sulphur springs, some of them directly on the shore, at a temperature of 32–82°C/90–180°F. They are used to treat rheumatism, arthritis and gynaecological disorders. Anyone who wants to can have a warm bath in the sea. There is a modern spa, old hotels and a cafe on a pier. On the harbour promenade two outdoor cinemas help pass the time. The remains of Roman baths and the neo-classical pump house are also interesting.

Loutra Edipsou (Λουτρά Αιδηφσού)

> **? DID YOU KNOW …?**
>
> ■ … that the philosopher Aristotle came to Loutra Edipsou 2,500 years ago to have his arthritis treated?

A spectacular coastal road along the south coast leads to **Rovies**, site of the oracle of Selinuntian Apollo, where yet another Venetian 13th-century defensive tower stands. There is also a gravel beach and a campground. 10km/6mi to the northeast lies a 16th-century monastery, Osios David o Gerontas, with 17th-century frescoes. The next town is the pretty little port of **Limni**. The sights here are the remains of an early Christian church from the 4th–8th centuries with beautiful mosaics, and the church of Zoödóhou Pigis. A road heads southeast past a museum of marine biology on its way to **Galataki Convent**, which was built on the ruins of a temple dedicated to Poseidon. The present buildings date primarily from the 13th–15th centuries. The 16th-century frescoes in the katholikon (main church) are worth seeing.

From Rovies to Limni

South of the Island

The route from Halkída to the fertile south of the island leads 130km/80mi past beaches to Karystos. Some 3km/2mi down the road a chapel dedicated to Agios Stefanos stands on the site of ancient Halkída, with the Arethousa Spring, which was famous in ancient times. Vassiliko is located in the fertile Lelantian plain. Three Venetian watch towers line the road to the medieval castle of **Fylla** (2km/1mi). Above Fylla lies the well-preserved 13th-century Venetian castle Lilanto (today Kastelli).

Agios Stefanos (Αγιος Στέφανος)

21km/13mi further on, Eretria is a holiday resort and ferry port especially popular among British visitors. It has Evia's most important excavation sites. Eretria, a sea power and the seat of a school of philosophy in ancient times, was then the most important city on the island. Ionian settlers from Attica brought on its greatest period of prosperity in the 8th century BC. They supported Miletos in the Ionian rebellion against the Persian king Darius, who conquered and de-

Eretria (Ερέτρια)

Watch towers erected by the Venetians in the vicinity of Fylla

stroyed the city in 490 BC. However, it recovered quickly. In 411 BC the Eretrians destroyed the Athenian fleet, freeing Évia from the rule of Athens. In 198 BC the Romans conquered the city; in 87 BC it was destroyed by Sulla in the war against Mithridates, which ended the city's greatest phase. The modern city was founded in 1834 when refugees from Psara settled here.

Ancient remains ▶ Old foundation walls are visible everywhere between the houses. Lying in the centre of the ancient city are the agora and the foundation walls of a Temple of Apollo Daphnephoros, the »laurel bearer«. On the site of several preceding buildings the Doric peripteros temple with 6:14 columns, whose remains can be seen here, was built around 520 BC. The **pediment sculptures**, late Archaic masterpieces, are on display in the archaeological museum at the north end of town. The museum also has a ceramic gorgoneion, Pan-Athenean prize amphorae from the House of Mosaics and finds from Lefkandi, including a centaur (around 900 BC). Opening hours: Tue–Sun 8.30am–3pm. Adjacent to the museum are major architectural remains: the archon's palace, the Temple of Dionysos, a section of the city wall with the west gate and the sunken theatre. Its oldest part is a stone stage structure; in the 4th century BC a stone theatre with a wooden proscenium was built, and the proscenium was replaced in marble in early Roman times. Further east are the gymnasium and

✱ Archaeological museum ▶

🕑

the baths. The most important recent discovery is the House of Mosaics (*c* 370 BC), whose stately rooms are adorned with well-preserved mosaics.

The acropolis hill was fortified with polygonal walls. There is a tower with a beautiful view at the northern edge of the castle. At the east and west edges of the castle, walls that run down to the beach are still partially visible.

◄ Acropolis

9km/5.5mi east of Eretria is the small fishing harbour **Amarynthos**. Continue 6km/4mi northeast from there to the **Monastery of Agios Nikolaos** to see beautiful 16th-century frescoes with ceramic plates. 15km/9mi further on is **Aliveri**, a large industrial area (coal mining, power plant) with the Church of Panagitsa (1393) and Risokastro castle. Turn right before reaching Lepoura and pass a swampy valley floor that is often flooded, with the castle hill of ancient **Dhistos** rising above the eponymous village. Here 5th-century BC polygonal walls can be seen. The road now runs on to Karystos through rugged mountain scenery that rises to an elevation of 800m/2,600ft with sparse frygana vegetation. Near Zarakes the view west opens onto a deeply indented bay with the island of Kavaliani off the coast. Near Polypotamos there is a view of the east coast to Cape Kafireas and to the southwest over Styra Bay with the island of the same name. **Styra** sprawls up the slope of Mt Kliossi with its two peaks; its church, Gennisis tis Theotokou (»Birth of Mary«), has a screen and columns made of Karystos marble. Another 5km/3mi further to the northwest, Néa Styra, the tourist capital of southern Evia, has a fine sandy beach and hotels. The so-called **dragon houses** (drakospita) can be reached from Styra. They are three structures from early antiquity built of massive stone slabs that are thought to have been either temples or cottages for quarry workers. Climb about 30 minutes up a steep slope to a dip above the village, then past ancient stone quarries with incomplete column shafts and worked blocks; the walk to the foot of Mt Agios Nikolaos with the dragon houses takes about 15–20 minutes. On top of the mountain are the stately Frankish castle Larmena and a chapel dedicated to St Nicholas. There is a wonderful view from here. The turn-off to the ferry port of **Marmari** with its sandy beaches is 21km/13mi southeast of Styra. From the coast the **Petali**, a group of privately owned, partly inhabited islands, is visible. It is another 11 km before **Karystos** is finally reached. This pleasant fishing and holiday town in southern Évia was built in the 1840s as Othonoupolis according to the plans of a Bavarian architect named Bierbach. The remains of the 14th-century Venetian castle can be seen at the harbour,

**From Amaryn-
thos to Karystos**

Baedeker TIP

Have a beach to yourself
Romantic beaches can be found on the east coast near the jagged cliffs of Cape Ochthonia. Perhaps because they are exposed to the wind, they are usually deserted.

and there is a sandy beach behind it. 4km/2.5mi northeast of Karystos, near Myli, there are ancient marble quarries. Above the Church of Agia Triada there is the entrance to a dripstone cave. The energetic can take a four-hour hike to the 1,398m/4,613ft summit of **Mt Ohi** for a spectacular view of the surrounding area.

From Lepoura to Kymi

11km/7mi north of Lepoura turn off to Avlonari with its tile-roofed houses of rubblestone; ancient column shafts were used in the large 12th-century Church of Agios Dimitrios, which also has beautiful frescoes. From here go on to the village of **Agia Thekla** with its eponymous church (13th–15th centuries), which is decorated with precious frescoes. After more than 40km/24mi comes **Kymi**, a wealthy town set in fertile hills 250m/800ft above sea level with many fine houses and a wonderful view to Skyros. Make sure to visit the ethnology museum in a neo-classical house, which is dedicated to the pathologist George Papanikolaou, the town's famous son. A steep, narrow serpentine road leads to the harbour – the only one on the forbidding northeast coast. There are cafes here to pass the time while waiting for the ferry to Skyros.

★ Hydra · Ydra

J/K 10

Greek: Ύδρα
Area: 55 sq km/21 sq mi
Population: 2,700
Capital: Hydra Town

Island group: Saronic Islands
Elevation: 0–590m/1,936ft above sea level

Even though Hydra is barren, the 18km/11mi-long and 4km/2.5mi-wide island is very attractive to artists and intellectuals. Visitors appreciate the lack of cars and the capital, Hydra Town, is particularly pretty.

Traffic-free island

Even though the elongated island, which despite its name (»hydra« means »well-watered«) looks very dry and uninviting, entering the harbour is an experience. Around the harbour the stately houses of Hydra Town rise in terraces. Hydra became famous in 1957 through the film ***Boy on a Dolphin***, in which Sophia Loren made her Hollywood debut and played a Hydros sponge diver. In the following years other **famous actresses** like Brigitte Bardot, Audrey Hepburn and Elizabeth Taylor visited the island. The songwriter Leonard Cohen even bought a house here. The plans of large travel companies to build more hotels and restaurants on the island and to allow motorized vehicles were defeated more than once by the opposition of the Hydrians.
There are no paved roads on the island and travel between towns has to be done on foot, on a donkey or by boat. In the high season it can

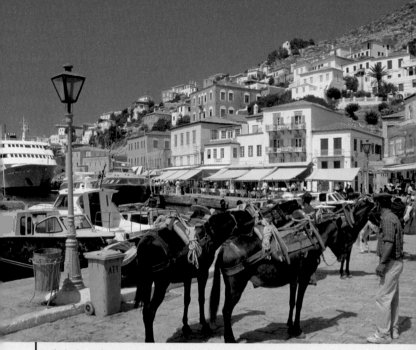

In the harbour of Hydra Town mules wait for their next load

happen that all of the beds are taken, but most guests stay only a few hours on the island, which is not exactly a cheap place. Yet the major source of income, alongside crafts (jewellery, ceramics, embroidery, hand-woven cloth and leatherwork) is tourism. Since the 15th century Albanian refugees have come to the island and helped it develop into an **economic and cultural centre** through shipbuilding, trade, seafaring and piracy. The Miaoulis, Koundouriotis, Vulgaris and Tombazis families, famous ship-owners as well as freedom fighters against the Turks, all come from Hydra. During the War of Independence Hydra used its merchant fleet as a navy and paid a large part of the costs of the war. In the 1930s the island was rediscovered by writers and artists.

What to See on Hydra

The colourful houses of Hydra Town (population 2,500) are nestled around the small harbour bay on the north coast. The town is a focus for artists, intellectuals and chic visitors or residents, who give Hydra its special atmosphere. Behind the quay is the marble bell tower of the **Church of Kimisis tis Theotokou**, which has a small Byzantine museum. Statues of the island's freedom fighters stand in the beautiful courtyard of the former Venetian-Genoese monastery (17th

▶ VISITING HYDRA

INFORMATION

Tourist police
Votsi 9, tel. 2 29 80 5 22 05
www.hydra-island.com

GETTING THERE

Boat services to and from Ermioni, Piraeus and Trizinia on the mainland as well as with the islands of Aegina and Spetses.

WHERE TO EAT

► Moderate

Douskas
Charamis, Hydra Town
The food is served on a small, pleasant square under shady trees, often with live music.

WHERE TO STAY

► Mid-range

Bratsera
Tombazi, Hydra Town
Tel. 2 29 80 5 39 70;
www.bratserahotel.com; 23 rooms
This hotel in a former sponge factory is considered to be one of the best in the Aegean.

Idra
Voulgari 8, Hydra Town
Tel. 22 98 05 21 02
Fax 22 98 05 20 91
12 rooms. An architecturally attractive hotel situated on the slope of the hill; rooms have high, wood-panelled ceilings.

century). The elegant mansions of wealthy ship-owning and merchant families of the 18th and 19th centuries were often built in the style of Venetian palazzi.

The most famous building is the **palazzo of the Tombazis family** at the western end of the harbour. The **Koundouriotis house** is an excellent example of late 18th-century architecture. The **Museum of History** near the pier informs on the Greek Wars of Independence.

Around Hydra Town
Walk westwards along the shore for 20 minutes to the quiet fishing village of **Kamini** with its pebble beach and tavernas. Further west, at the fishing village of **Vlyhos**, there are good tavernas and little-used pebble beaches. To reach **Mandraki**, the most popular beach on the island, walk eastwards from the Hydra harbour for half an hour. Above the bay is the **Convent of Agia Matrona** with a church dating from 1865.

Hikes to the monasteries
Beautiful hiking routes lead to monasteries in the mountains: three and a half hours (there and back) to the 15th-century **Monastery of Profitis Ilias** and **the convent Agia Efpraxia** nearby, where one nun still lives; from here there is a wonderful view of Hydra Town, the mainland and the surrounding islands. The hike to the 16th-century **Zourvas Monastery** on the eastern tip of the island takes six hours there and back. It once accommodated monks and is now a convent for nuns with a guesthouse for overnight guests.

A carriage is a comfortable way to explore Spetses

The little island of Dokos northwest of Hydra is used to pasture sheep; it can be reached by water taxi. Beach lovers can enjoy the sun and waves undisturbed on isolated beaches here.

Dokos
(Δοκός)

✳ Spetses (Σπέτσες)

Spetses (63 sq km/24 sq mi, population 3,900) was called **Pityusa** (»pine-covered island«) in antiquity and is a hilly, pine-forested island west of Hydra. In recent decades Athenians have built magnificent villas along the coast. Tourism has played a major role here since the end of World War I, when Spetses was already a popular **upper-class rendezvous**, and is today the major source of income for the traffic-free island, which has a mild climate and attractive, relatively quiet beaches.

»Pine-covered island«

 Baedeker TIP

Island speciality
Make sure to try the island's culinary speciality, the almond cake amygdalota.

After a failed revolution against the Turks, the Orlov Revolt led by Catherine the Great, the population was driven off the island in 1760 and the town laid waste.

However, the Spetsians soon returned and trade, seafaring and piracy made them wealthy. **Bouboulina** (Laskarina Pinotzis), an outstanding figure in the Greek liberation movement, lived on Spetses. In 1821 it was the first island to join the battle for independence.

Sights The only sizeable town on the island, **Spetses Town**, extends from the Paleo Limani and Dapia quarters along the seaside to the upper town of Kastelli. The town takes in almost half of the northern coast. The fine 18th- and 19th-century homes of shipbuilders and sea captains characterize the city, especially around the beautiful Old Harbour. The Spetses Museum inside the attractive Chatzigianni-Mezi mansion (1795) displays, along with its oldest pieces from the Hellenistic period, religious artefacts and a ceramics collection (18th century). The War of Independence of 1821 is also a theme; a sarcophagus with the mortal remains of **Bouboulina** is also on ⊙ display. Opening hours: Tue–Sun 8.30am–2.45pm. A separate museum housed in a mansion near the harbour has been dedicated to her. Along with personal effects the weapons of this female sea captain and a model of her ship are on display (admission only with a guided tour). **Agia Marina beach** near the city towards the southeast is very popular.

The best beach on the island, **Anargiri Beach**, 12km/7mi from Spetses Town, can be reached by bus or boat, or by hiking over Mt Profitis Ilias (244m/800ft). The **Bekiri sea cave** near the beach was used by islanders as a hiding place.

★ Ikaría

Greek: Ικαρία	**Island group:** Southern Sporades
Area: 255 sq km/98 sq mi	**Altitude:** 0–1,037m/3,402ft
Population: 8,300	**Capital:** Agios Kirykos

Until now, tourism has played a minor role on the island of Icarus – reason enough to come and explore this bare island.

Island of Icarus The largely barren island is 40km/25mi long and 8km/5mi wide. The 1,037m/3,402ft Atheras mountains cross the whole of Ikaría and divide it into a green northern part that has an abundance of rivers and a southern part that drops off sharply to the coast. Deep gorges cut through the massive, sparsely vegetated rock wall of the south. The somewhat gentler northern slopes are covered with oak and pine macchia, plane and chestnut trees. The best beaches are also to be found on the north coast between Evdilos and Armenistis. The main sources of livelihood here are agriculture (fruit orchards – Ikaría apricots are famous) and fishing. The rugged island was hardly known for a long time, except as a **place of banishment** for communists in the 1940s; the composer **Mikis Theodorakis** was imprisoned here. The island has always been sparsely settled, and lost almost one

▶ VISITING IKARIA

INFORMATION

In the travel agencies in
Agios Kirykos
www.island-ikaria.com

GETTING THERE

Boats to Piraeus on the mainland
and the islands of Chíos, Fourni,
Kálymnos, Kos, Léros, Lipsi, Mýkonos, Páros, Patmos, Samos and
Sýros.

WHERE TO EAT

▶ **Inexpensive**
Taverna
Karavostamo Large, friendly restau-
rant in the heart of the village.

WHERE TO STAY

▶ **Mid-range**
Kastro
Agios Kirykos
Tel. 2 27 50 2 34 80
E-mail: hotelkastro@internet.gr
22 rooms. Perched on the cliffs with a
superb view of the sea; there are a bar
and pool on the roof.

▶ **Budget**
Evdoxia
Evdilos
Tel. 22 75 03 15 02
www.evdoxia.gr

---

quarter of its population in a massive wave of emigration in the dec-
ade before 1991. Tourism only started to develop gradually after the
construction of a small airport in 1995. Ikaría is named after **Icarus
(Ikaros)**, the son of the Minoan inventor **Daedalus (Daidalos)**. According to legend, Icarus plunged into the water off the island and
drowned after attempting to fly with wings dipped in wax.

What to See on Ikaría

The peaceful port of Agios Kirykos, Ikaría's principal town (population 1,900), lies on the eastern part of the south coast. Apart from a
few traditional cafes and its relaxed atmosphere, it has little to offer.
The school houses an interesting **archaeological collection**. Irregular
opening times.

Agios Kirykos
(Αγιος Κήρυκος)

There are small bays for swimming along the rocky coast towards
Therma. This spa with its 53°C/127°F radium and sulphur springs is
3km/2mi to the northeast. The antiquated bathing facilities are only
used by Greek spa guests and are recommended for arthritis, skin
diseases and rheumatism.

Therma
(Θέρμα)

The 60km/35mi panoramic route between Agios Kirykos, Evdilos
and Armenistis runs through impressive mountain landscape in a
wide arc around Mt Fardi (1,037m/3,400ft). The village houses are
roofed with slate. The island's second ferry port, Evdilos, is also its

Evdilos
(Εύδηλος)

This fascinating section of coast lies near Therma

second-largest settlement (population 500), a picturesque fishing village that is mainly a stopping place for tourists.

Kampos
(Κάμπος)

In Kampos the ruins of a Byzantine palace and the 12th-century Church of Agia Irini can be viewed. The free-standing columns date back to a 4th-century structure. Next to the church there is a small museum with archaeological finds. There is a 400m/450yd-long sand and pebble beach below Kampos.

Armenistis
(Αρμενιστής)

The attraction in Armenistis (15km/9mi west of Evdilos), the island's tourist centre, are the beautiful sandy beaches. 3km/2mi to the west at the bay of **Nas** the remains of a 5th-century BC Temple of Artemis lie behind a pretty little pebble beach.

✴ Íos

Greek: Ίος
Area: 108 sq km/41 sq mi
Population: 1,800

Island group: Cyclades
Altitude: 0–713m/2,339ft
Capital: Íos Hóra

Apart from high life for the young, lively holiday crowds and extensive beaches the mountainous island also has beautiful landscape and historical sights to offer.

What to See on Íos

From the port of **Gialos** the main road of the island heads up to the main town **Íos Hóra** (population 1,600), the definitive Cycladean town with narrow alleys, small squares and many chapels. In the summer it transmutes into one large party venue that attracts younf people from all over Greece and Europe.

✴
Íos-Hóra

The **Archaeological Museum** is located right on the high street and displays finds from the early Cyclic settlement **Skárkos**, which flourished in the 3rd millenium BC. Opening times: Tue–Sat 8.30am until 3pm. This settlement was excavated on a low hill below Hóra; explanations and descriptions in English make it easy to explore. Opening times: Tue–Sun 8.30am until 3pm.

◷

▶ VISITING IOS

INFORMATION

Tourist information
Kiosk at the bus stop Íos-Hóra
Tel. 2 28 60 9 11 35
www.iosgreece.com

GETTING THERE

Boat service from Piraeus and to the islands of Anáfi, Crete, Folégandros, Kimolos, Kýthnos, Mílos, Mýkonos, Náxos, Páros, Santorini, Sérifos, Sífnos, Síkinos and Sýros.

WHERE TO EAT

▶ Moderate

O Lordos Byron
Íos Hóra
Tel. 2 28 60 9 21 25
Small restaurant with imaginative cuisine and house wine by the carafe.

WHERE TO STAY

▶ Luxury

Íos Palace
Mylopotas
Tel. 2 28 60 9 12 69
www.iospalacehotel.com
6 rooms, 60 suites, 1 apartment.
Hotel complex on the sandy beach of Mylopotas; spacious garden terrace with a seawater swimming pool; all rooms with sea view.

▶ Mid-range

Far Out Hotel & Spa
Mylopotas
Tel. 2 28 60 9 14 46, fax 2 28 60 9 17 07
www.faroutclub.com
45 rooms. Built in typical Cycladic style, the hotel has a marvellous sea view.

Crowded beach in the Bay of Mylopatas near the island's capital

A well-paved road leads to the north coast, first through a fertile plain then along barren, terraced slopes, to the so-called **grave of Homer**, an ancient but unidentified setting of stones. It is highly doubtful that it really is a kind of Heroon in honour of the poet, who according to Herodotus and Pausanias died on Íos, but the drive is worth it.

The drive on well-paved roads to the eastern side of the island also goes through spectacular landscape and leads to the especially child-friendly **beaches at Maganári** with there are even low sand dunes. The beach is much less crowded than the one at Mylopótas.

✳
Mylopotas beach

The beautiful long beach at Mylopotas, 2km/1mi south of Íos Hóra, extends along a wonderful broad bay. One of the most beautiful beaches in the Aegean, it is always crowded in the high season, mostly by young people.

Síkinos (Σίκινος)

Quiet island
(Continued on p.247) ▶

Síkinos (population 240) lies 6km/4mi to the southwest of Íos. 15km/9mi long and 5km/3mi wide, it is one of the smaller of the southern Cyclades. There is plenty of peace and quiet here and a largely undisturbed landscape, since there are few beaches. The island's barren north and northwest are mountainous and have a steep rocky coast, while vegetables, wine and grain are cultivated on terraces in the gentler southeast. The inhospitable island was always insignificant because it does not have a sheltered harbour. Many of the inhabitants emigrated to the USA or Australia after World War II.

The port of Alopronia is only in business during the high season. **Alopronia** The tavernas and lodgings open only during the summer. North of **(Αλοπρόνοια)** the harbour is the **sand and pebble beach Agios Nikolaos**, the most beautiful on the island. It is easier to reach by boat than on foot.

A road runs 4km/2.5mi from Alopronia to Síkinos Town, which con- **Síkinos** sists of Hóra (town) and Horió (village). The island's principal town **(Σίκινος)** can also be reached by foot on a 3km/2mi path through a deeply wooded gorge. On the plateia of the town's picturesque Hóra district stand two mansions and **the Church of Timios Stavros** (1787), which has a carved iconostasis and a post-Byzantine fresco. The abandoned Convent of Zoödóhou Pigis (1834) towers above Hóra on a steep ridge.

From Hóra the Heroon is a one hour's hike to the southwest. This ◄ Heroon, funerary monument was erected in the 3rd century AD in the style Episkopi of a Greek temple. In the Byzantine period it was converted into a church and in the 17th century incorporated into a monastery named Episkopi.

✴ Itháki

C/D 8

Greek: Ιθάκη   **Island group:** Ionian Islands
Area: 96 sq km/37 sq mi   **Altitude:** 0–808 m/2,651ft
Population: 3,000   **Capital:** Vathy

Despite its fame as the home of Ulysses, the island has so far been spared mass tourism. With its few but beautiful pebble beaches, Itháki (Ithaca) is regarded as a refuge for people seeking peace and relaxation.

Itháki/Ithaca is an extremely barren and mountainous island. It is **Island of Ulysses** considered – especially by the inhabitants – to be the **Ithaca that is mentioned in Homer's Odyssey**, the island of Ulysses, even though there is no evidence of this. The island has steep cliffs along its east coast and a green western side that is partially cultivated. The Gulf of Mólos divides it: to the north is the hill country of Ani with the 808m/2,651ft Mt Nerítos and to the south the 671m/2,201ft Stefani massif.

Dexia Bay: did the Phaeacians put Odysseus ashore here?

The adventures of Odysseus were also a popular subject for films

ON THE TRAIL OF ODYSSEUS

Was the kingdom of Odysseus (Ulysses) at one time on Itháki? Did the hero set off from there to fight for twelve years in the Trojan War and afterwards have to go through a perilous journey lasting ten years before he could take his wife, Penelope, in his arms again?

The actual location of the places described in the two great epics, **The Iliad** and **The Odyssey** by Homer, is an ancient question. For John V. Luce, professor at Trinity College, Dublin, the answer is clear. In his books *Homer and the Heroic Age* and *Celebrating Homer's Landscapes: Troy and Ithaca Revisited* – the latter with compelling photos and maps – he states that Homer wrote *The Odyssey* and the Ithaca of mythology is the same island as the one now known as Ithaki.

Facts and Myths

Although Itháki is smaller and more rugged than either Zákynthos or Kefalloniá, it is strategically much more important. The sea trade along the coast and the sea routes between Itháki, Kefalloniá and Lefkáda can be better controlled from it. Homer describes Odysseus' home island in *The Odyssey* as »low«, «narrow«, with islands »round about«, »clearly visible« and unsuitable for »steeds to romp« – descriptions that fit Itháki much better than any other of the Ionian Islands.

Odysseus' last stopover before he returned to Ithaca was the island of **Scheria**. Even in ancient times it was thought that this must be Corfu, named at the time Kérkyra. There he told the king of the Phaeacians, Alkinoos, and his daughter, Nausicaä, of his ten-year odyssey that included the adventures he experienced with the one-eyed Cyclops, Polyphemus, with the deadly Sirens and with Calypso, who held him captive on her island for seven years. With the help of the ruler of Scheria, Odysseus made it back to his home island, where, disguised as a beggar and with

the support of his son, Telemachus, he killed the suitors who had been besetting his wife, Penelope.

The Phaeacian ship that brought Odysseus to Ithaca deposited him while he was fast asleep in **Phorcys Bay** below the Cave of the Nymphs. When he woke up, he had lost his bearings and Athena, his protective goddess, appeared to him in the form of a shepherd boy and told him he was on Ithaca. John Luce identifies Phorcys Bay with today's Bay of Dexiá and the **Cave of the Nymphs** with a dripstone cave above the bay. It has two entrances, as described in *The Odyssey*, one for people and one reserved for the gods – the latter is an opening in the ceiling of the cave. After paying a visit to the cave, where he prayed and hid his treasures, Odysseus set off with Athena in search of Eumaeus, the swineherd. He left »the haven, and took the rough track up through the wooded country« – for Luce, a footpath leading along the eastern slope of Mt Merovígli that still

exists. »**Raven's Rock** above Arethousa Fountain«, where Eumaeus' hut was located, is at the north-eastern edge of the Marathiá plateau. There are still a lot of ravens at the rock, which slopes steeply down 60 m/200 ft over a length of 550 m/550 yd, and even today bears the name »stefáni tou korákou«, »Rock of the Ravens«. The **Arethousa Spring** has its source here. And the swineherd's hut and yards – »on a site which could be seen from far« – could have stood on the terrain 240 m/800 ft above the rocky shore. A nearby cave is displayed on Itháki as the place where Eumaeus lived. It was there that Odysseus met his son, Telemachus, who sent the swineherd to his parents' palace to inform Penelope.

The **palace** was probably near Stavrós on the opposite end of the island, some 24 km/15 mi away – Eumaeus needed a full day to march there and back. Luce found two other indications that the palace and the capital of Odysseus' kingdom was at Stavrós.

This Roman marble statue dating from around 50 BC shows Odysseus crawling out of Polyphemus' cave to escape

According to *The Odyssey*, »our« harbour and, a bit further away, the »harbour of Rheithron beneath wooded Neion« could be seen from the palace forecourt – the first would be Pólis Bay harbour, the second Frikes harbour and »Neion«, the mountain that Exogi is perched on. Both harbours can be seen from the ridge running to the north near Stavrós and at the intersection of both lines of vision, in today's Pilikáta, is where Odysseus' palace could have stood. Although Mycenaean potsherd and even traces of a fortification wall have been unearthed in excavations there, no remains of a palace have come to light. And yet, if Odysseus ever did have a palace, then it would have to be there – at least that is the conclusion of the professor, who is also convinced that Homer, whom he considers to have been well acquainted with Itháki's topography, must have visited the island.

An Ancient Mystery

Many researchers do not see it that simple. **Friedrich Schiller** once poked fun, saying (appropriately enough, originally in distichon verse), »Seven squabbling cities claim, Homer is their native son / Now that Wolf has torn him apart, each may have their piece of him!« In 1795, the German philologist, **Friedrich August Wolf**, had taken up the problem known in antiquity, namely how many poets were hiding behind the name Homer and when had the two epics, *The Illiad* and *The Odyssey*, been written. Today, it is widely held that the two great heroic songs had a number of authors who relied on an oral tradition of tales of seafarers dating from the Mycenaeans (c. 1300 BC) and wove them together with the social conditions and myths of their own eras. It is assumed that *The Iliad* was written around 730 BC and *The Odyssey* 50 years later. The mystery surrounding Homer will certainly never be solved, just as it will remain unclear as to which island was the legendary Ithaca. Maybe, after all, it was really Lefkáda, as the German archaeologist, **Wilhelm Dörpfeld**, maintained. Or maybe it was Kefallonia, as the British amateur archaeologist **Robert Bittlestone** claimed recently?

What to See in and around Vathy

The port of Vathy (population 1,800), also called Itháki, is the capital of the island. Charmingly nestled between two Venetian forts in a deeply indented bay, it is considered to be the harbour of Phorkys, where the Phaeacians set Ulysses on land (Odyssey XIII, 96 ff). According to a law passed in 1978, all new buildings have to be built in the traditional style. Thus the town presents a pretty picture with little pastel-coloured houses. Life is concentrated around a harbour street lined by cafes, restaurants and hotels. The neo-classical **Villa Drakoulis** on the harbour is worth seeing; it houses a popular cafe and a little **archaeological museum**. Opening times: Tue–Sun 8.30am–3pm. The old power station to the west of the harbour has been remodelled as a **maritime and folk art museum**. Opening hours: Tue–Sun 9.30am–3.30pm. The small **island of Lazareto** not far from the entrance to the harbour was a quarantine station in the 19th century. It is said that both Heinrich Schliemann (who excavated on Ithaki) and Lord Byron swam out to it every morning.

Vathy (Βαθύ)

There are beautiful beaches near Vathy. Little Loutsa beach to the northeast has a nice view to the island of Lazareto.

Beaches near Vathy

The South of the Island

West of Vathy there is a signpost at the edge of town to the Spilio Nymfo, the »Cave of the Nymphs« (Odyssey XIII, 107/8), a dripstone cave 2km/1mi away. There is a marble base on which a small statue

Spilio Nymfo (Σπήλαιο Νύμφων)

 VISITING ITHÁKI

The fabulous setting of the island's capital, Vathy

of a god once stood. It was supposedly in this cave that after his return Ulysses hid the precious gifts bestowed upon him by the Phaeacians (Odyssey XIII, 107 / 8).

Dexia Bay The main road leading to the north passes Dexia Bay, lined with olive trees, where there is a beautiful beach and a desalination plant.

Aetos (Αετός) Soon after there is a turn-off to the left to the harbour of Piso Aetos. On the slope along this road there is an excavation site with remains of a Hellenistic tower. It was part of a city wall built around Aetos mountain in the 7th century BC. Heinrich Schliemann thought that the city and **palace of Ulysses** once stood here. When American archaeologists discovered remains from the 14th and 13th centuries BC, it seemed that Schliemann's assumption might be true. It is more likely that the city Alalkomenes, mentioned by Plutarch, once stood here.

★
Perahori (Περαχόρι) About 3km/2mi south of Vathy the houses of Perahori cluster 300m/ 1,000ft high on the slope. Perahori was founded in the 16th century and soon became one of the most important settlements on the island. A signposted path leads up to the **medieval ruins** in about fifteen minutes. The houses of this village, which was abandoned in the 16th century, were fortified due to fear of pirate raids; they have small windows, large storerooms and cisterns. The ruins of the church, dedicated to St John the Evangelist, have lots of atmosphere; the roof has caved in so that the stone iconostasis stands out in the open. Sun and rain have damaged the frescoes of saints.

Arethousa spring Leave Vathy heading south to the **Marathia Plateau**. After about 5km/3mi a path turns off to the spring of Arethousa. According to myth the **nymph Arethousa** grieved here for her son Coryx and shed so many tears that a spring was formed. The walk to the spring is

Ithaki *Map*

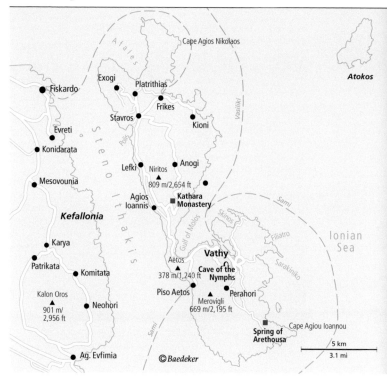

more worthwhile than the spring itself; from Vathy the hike takes about one hour. Further south the plateau of Marathia, covered by olive trees, affords a sweeping panorama. Here the swineherd **Eumaeus** is supposed to have watched his animals (Odyssey XIV, 6).

The North of the Island

After passing over the isthmus, the road sharply climbs to an elevation of 550m/1,804ft, where the Monastery of Panagia ton Kathara offers a superb view. The **monastery church** (1696) has a treasure: an icon of the Virgin Mary, which the apostle Luke himself is supposed to have painted. On 8 September a big festival is held with food, drink and dancing.

Kathara monastery

Next follow the main coast road past beautiful beaches. An ancient settlement (2200–1500 BC) uncovered on Pelikata Hill near Stavros in the northwest of the island supports the assumption that the **city**

Stavros (Σταυρός)

and palace of Ulysses are most likely to have been located here – at least Homer's description matches the site. In the **archaeological museum** at Pelikata the most significant exhibit is a pottery shard from the Hellenistic mask of a woman inscribed with the Greek words »dedicated to Ulysses«. The inhabitants of Ithaki during the Hellenistic period thus did not doubt that their Ithaca and the one in the Odyssey were identical. Opening hours: Tue–Sun 9.30am–2pm.

Polis
(Πόλις)
Below Stavros lies the picturesque Bay of Polis, the only significant harbour on the west coast of Ithaki (swimming not recommended). The collapsed **Loizos Cave** on the northwest side was a sanctuary of Athena and Hera in the Mycenaean period. The tiny **island of Daskalio** lies beyond the bay, not far from the coast of Kefallonia, and is supposed to be ancient Asteris (Odyssey XVI, 365).

★
Kioni
(Κιόνι)
The beautiful bays of the fishing villages of Frikes and Kioni lie on the northeast coast of Ithaki. Kioni is considered to be the prettiest town on Ithaki and is a popular destination and yacht harbour. Pastel-coloured houses with red tiled roofs line the bay; there are good tavernas as well. There are some pebble beaches between Kioni and Frikes right on the road.

★ Kálymnos

Q/R 10/11

Greek: Κάλυμνος	**Island group:** Southern Sporades
Area: 111 sq km/43 sq mi	**Altitude:** 0–678m/2,224ft
Population: 16,000	**Capital:** Kálymnos/Póthia

Kálymnos, known as the sponge divers' island, is a barren, mountainous island in the Dodecanese. Along with beach holidays the island offers good climbing.

Island of the sponge divers
It is separated from Léros to the north by the 2.5km/1.5mi-wide Diapori Channel. The coastline is predominantly sheer, rocky and punctuated by numerous coves. Most of the beaches and villages are to be found on the west coast. Since the decline of sponge fishing, brought about by over-fishing and the production of sponges from artificial materials, the importance of tourism has increased.

Kálymnos Town/Póthia

★
Kálymnos Town
The north is divided from the south part of the island, where the inhabitants have lived since antiquity, by a mountain that rises to 678m/2,224ft. At its foot, a fertile plain extends south to the bustling capital and major port Kálymnos/Póthia (population 10,000). The view of Póthia from the sea, spread picturesquely around a large har-

VISITING KALYMNOS

INFORMATION

Tourist information
On the harbour quay
www.kalymnosinfo.com

GETTING THERE

Ferries to Piraeus on the mainland and to the islands Agathonisi, Amorgós, Arki, Astypálea, Donoussa, Fourni, Ikaría, Kos, Léros, Lipsi, Mýkonos, Náxos, Nisyros, Páros, Patmos, Rhodes, Samos, Symi, Sýros and Tílos.

WHERE TO EAT

Uncle Petros
Platia Diamanti
Póthia, Tel. 2 24 30 2 96 78
There are many restaurants along the harbour promenade. This simple establishment at the east end of the promenade is recommended for its fresh fish.

WHERE TO STAY

▶ **Mid-range**
Villa Themelina
Enoria Evangelistrias
Póthia
Tel. 2 24 30 2 26 82
Fax 2 24 30 2 39 20
20 rooms. This villa, a protected monument with a luxuriant garden and a pool, lies on the northeastern edge of Póthia, opposite the Vouvalis Museum. It is tastefully furnished with antiques. The best rooms are those with a large roof terrace and a view of the whole town.

Plaza
Massouri
Tel. 2 24 30 4 71 34, fax 2 24 30 4 11 78
www.plazahotel.gr
60 rooms. A hotel with a large pool, right on the beach at Massouri; most rooms have a good view of the bay.

bour bay, is impressive. Its whitewashed houses are staggered terrace-like up to the foot of the towering, bare mountain that provides a romantic natural backdrop for the town. Tourists are only found on the harbour promenade with its countless sidewalk cafes, tavernas and fish restaurants. Dealers sell a large selection of natural and artificial sponges, which are popular as souvenirs.

Stately 19th-century **neo-classical houses**, including the town hall on the northeast corner of the harbour near the bus stop, testify to prosperity in times gone by. The Church of Christ (1861) next to the town hall is furnished with a screen by the sculptor Giannoulis Chalepas. The **nautical and folklore museum** at the harbour gives a good impression of the history of

 Sponges

- Kálymnos is the only island where people still fish for sponges. In order to satisfy tourists' demand for sponges, cheaper synthetic products are imported. They are softer, bleached a pale colour and only last two years at the most. Natural sponges from Greek waters are darker, rougher, round and with care last up to ten years. There are several factories in Pothis where the process of turning unattractive natural lumps into bathing sponges can be watched.

sponge diving and sailing on Kálymnos. Odos El. Venizelou, which runs across the town and on to Horió, starts here, too.

Follow the sign in the side street uphill tothe **archaeological museum** that was opened in 2009. On exhibit are a bronze statue and other parts of statues from the 2nd century AD, all of which were found on the floor of the sea in the 1990s. Among the displayed statues are a Kouros from around 530 BC and a larger-than-life statue of Asklepios, the god of medicine and healing. Opening times: Tue–Sun 8.30am–3pm.

The adjacent **Vouvalis villa** was once the home of a wealthy sponge dealer and is furnished in the style of the late 19th century. Opening times: Tue–Sat 8.30am–2.30pm.

Other Sights on Kálymnos

Horió
(Χωριό)
Horió and Póthia have merged. The highest point of the 9th-century Byzantine castle offers a good view of the whole valley to Póthia. At the western end of Horió are the ruins of the early Christian **Basilica of Christós tis Jerusalim**. It was built in the 6th century using ancient materials on the foundations of a sanctuary of Delian Apollo and is now a quiet and shady place.Opening times: Tue–Sun 8.30am–3pm.

West coast
A tree-lined road leads to Panormos on the west coast, where there is a sand and pebble beach. North of the road from **Myrties** to **Masouri** there is a fabulous view of the picturesque Masouri Bay, with Telendos island out in the sea. This section of coast with modern hotels, several travel agencies, bars, tavernas, and restaurants is the actual **tourist centre** of the island. While there are only narrow pebble beaches here that have been filled up with sand, the beautiful panorama of the bay, many cypress trees and modern comforts of the tourist facilities more than make up. Off the west coast lies the towering, 458m/1,502ft-high rocky island of **Telendos**. In high season boats sail from Myrties across to the sleepy island, which has some tavernas and accommodation. On Agios Konstantinos there is a medieval castle, with the ruins of Agios Vasilios monastery at its feet. In the quiet village of **Emborios** in the north there are good beaches for swimming.

Vathýs
(Βαθύς)
The island's second road runs northeast from Póthia to a deep bay that cannot be seen from the sea; at its end lies the quiet, pretty town of Vathýs. The so-called **Mandarin Valley** is the only part of the island that is still used for agriculture. Thousands of mandarin, orange and lemon trees are cultivated by irrigation here.

Léros (Λέρος)

»Crazy« island
Léros (population 8,500) has remained up to now a quiet island. This might have to do with its reputation; it was the site (near Par-

The west coast is the tourist centre of Kálymnos

theni) of a prison for those like Mikis Theodorakis who opposed the dictatorship of the colonels. Since 1957 the largest psychiatric hospital in Greece, near Lakki, has given the Léros the nickname »island of the insane«. The mountainous and fertile island, which has an abundant water supply, possesses an uneven coastline broken up by impressive coves and inlets. Tourism is an additional source of income to supplement agriculture and fishing.

Excursion boats and hydrofoils arrive at the old harbour **Agia Marina** on the east coast. The island capital Platanos merges seamlessly into the old port of Agia Marina. From Agia Marina follow a narrow street with many shops upwards. A 14th-century castle of the Order of St John towers over Platanos. The path leading up to the castle begins at the small town square. Opening hours: May–Sept 8.30–1.30pm, 6pm–8.30pm; Oct–April 8.30am–12.30pm, 3.30pm–7pm.

Platanos
(Πλάτανος)

🕐

Along wide Alinda Bay the coast road runs past a tamarisk-lined sand and pebble beach to the bathing resorts of Krithoni and Alinda. Constant winds make the bay ideal for windsurfers. In Krithoni there is a British military cemetery from World War II. A little further the so-called Bellenis Tower has one crenellated square and one crenellated round tower. It was built in 1925 by a wealthy Leriot and now houses a **folk art and historical museum**. Opening hours: May–Sept Tue–Sun 9am–12.30pm, June–Aug also 6.30pm–9pm.

Alinda
(λινδα),
Krithoni
(Κριθόνι)

🕐

A bay cuts deep into the west coast of the island some 3km/2mi south of Platanos. At its far end is the village of Lakki, with boulevards and buildings planned on a drawing board by an Italian urban planner. Léros was occupied by Italy from 1912 until 1943, when Lakki was the base of the **Italian fleet** in the eastern Mediterranean.

Lakki
(Λάκκι)

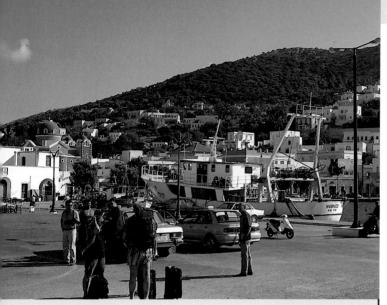

Finally arrived – Agia Marina harbour on Léros

Xerokambos
(Ξερόκαμπος)

Southeast of Lakki lies Xerokambos, a relaxed hamlet with a small sand and pebble beach, which is still relatively quiet. Above the village are the ruins of **Paleokastro fortress** (4th century BC).

West and north of the island

The **Bay of Gourna** on the west coast has beautiful beaches and is less frequented than Alinda. A causeway leads out to a small island with the Chapel of Agios Isidoros. Northeast of Partheni in the north of the island a side trip to the Chapel of **Agia Kioura** is worthwhile; the murals were done by political prisoners of the military junta, who were jailed in the former Italian barracks near Partheni. Further east at **Blefoutis Bay** tamarisk trees shade the beach.

★ Kárpathos

R 13/14

Greek: Κάρπαθος
Area: 301 sq km/116 sq mi
Population: 6,500

Island group: Dodecanese
Altitude: 0–1,220m/4,000ft
Capital: Pigádia/Kárpathos

In contrast to its larger neighbours, Crete and Rhodes, things are still quieter and more leisurely on this Dodecanese island. Favourable wind conditions make the south of the island a paradise for surfers in summer.

▶ VISITING KARPATHOS

INFORMATION
Tourist information
Info kiosk at Pigádia harbour
Tel. 22 45 02 38 35
www.karpathos.com

GETTING THERE
Boat service to and from Piraeus as well as to the islands of Crete, Halki, Kasos, Mílos and Rhodes.

WHERE TO EAT
▶ **Inexpensive**
Perigiali
Harbour bay

Pigádia
Popular with the locals, the taverna offers a large selection of starters.

WHERE TO STAY
▶ **Budget**
Olimbos
Main street Olympos
Tel. 2 24 50 5 12 52
7 rooms. Small hotel with nice, basic rooms

Together with its southwestern neighbour Kasos, Kárpathos forms the transition from Rhodes to Crete; the sea between Crete and Rhodes was named **Karpathian Sea** after the island. The narrow 48km/30mi-long island is the second-largest in the Dodecanese. A rugged, barren mountain range that reaches an elevation 1,200m/4,000ft traverses Kárpathos. The coastline is mostly steep with small sandy coves full of caves. The island lies far to the south and has a sub-tropical climate with hot, dry summers and rainy winters. Land on the island is still cultivated without modern machinery. Traditional sources of income are raising cattle, carpentry and woodcarving, weaving and embroidery. Package tourism only started after the airport was built. Apart from Pigádia and the beautiful beaches near Amoöpi and Lefkos, the island is still quiet. Kárpathos is famous for the traditional costumes of its women and its folk music. The north of the island has rugged and inaccessible landscape; the south was separated from it for a long time, so the two parts developed differently.

Island rich in tradition

What to See on Kárpathos

The island's young capital and at the same time its principal port spreads around a wide bay on the southern east coast on the site of ancient Poseidion. The town with about 2,500 residents is not exactly an attractive tourist centre, but is equipped with the necessary infrastructure. The 4km/2.5mi-long sandy beach runs along the entire bay to the north. A walk along the beach leads in fifteen minutes from a small fishing village to the ruins of the early Christian basilica **Agia Fotini** (6th century), which was built in honour of the female

*Pigádia/
Kárpathos
(Πηγάδια/
Κάρπαθος)*

martyr Fotini. Light grey marble columns and parts of the choir with reliefs can still be seen. From Pigádia a 30-minute hike also leads to the **Mili Valley caves**, which were used to inter the dead in ancient times. A more difficult hike 6km/4mi southwards leads to the **mountain church of Agia Kiriaki** and a beautiful view.

The South of the Island

A hike along an ancient path to the beautiful beaches near **Amoöpi** is also worthwhile. Amoöpi, 8km/5mi south of Pigádia, has developed into one of the most popular tourist centres on the island. There are several sand and pebble beaches here.

Surfing

As the south of the island near the airport is very flat and windy, its popularity with windsurfers is growing. Especially **Makrys Gialos Bay** northeast of the airport, where several hotels have been built recently, is considered by surfers to be one of the places in Europe where wind is guaranteed.

Menetes (Μενετές)

6km/4mi west of the island capital, the picturesque village of Menetes sprawls over the rocky ridge above Pigádia. A walk through its narrow and winding streets with colourful, neo-classical houses is worthwhile. In the Evangelistria Chapel there is a **museum of local culture** with old tools and agricultural implements.

West coast

The town of **Arkasa** on the west coast is developing into a holiday resort. Its major attraction is the sandy beach Agios Nikolaos 1km/0.5mi away. The ruins of the Agia Anastasia Basilica (4th–6th centuries) can be seen here. The mosaics that were discovered here in 1923 now adorn the courtyard of the archaeological museum in Rhodes. From the basilica a steep footpath leads to a cape in about fifteen minutes. Here the remains of the Venetian-Turkish Paleokastro castle and traces of ancient Arkesia can be seen. **Agios Nikolaos beach** lies to the south. Since the beach slopes very gently it is well suited for children. Only 3km/2mi north of Arkasa is the tiny secluded fishing village **Finiki**. Further north are the quiet, picturesque mountain village **Pyles** above the west coast, and **Lefkos** with its wonderful sandy beach, which is very popular in the summer.

Aperi, Othos (Απέρι, Οθος)

In the interior of the island northwest of Pigádia, the rustic mountain villages of Aperi, Volada, Othos and Pyles are fine places to undertake short hikes. Aperi was the island capital from 1700 until 1892. Returned emigrants have made it the wealthiest community on the island. A small folk art museum in Othos, the highest village on the island (510m/1,673ft), exhibits typical furnishings of a Karpathian home. Apella on the east coast has a dream beach (►photo p.258) with beautiful turquoise water.

◄ Beach of Apella

The North of the Island

Diafani, the harbour for the village Olymbos, was founded in the late 18th century on the east coast. The ferry pier, where excursion boats from Pigádia and other places now call, was only completed in 1995. Diafani, with its small pebble beach and some bays for swimming nearby, is a good place for a quiet holiday. An old footpath leads up to Olymbos in one and a half hours.

Diafani
(ΔιαΦάνι)

In the north of the island, on the slopes of the barren Profitis Ilias, lies **one of the most beautiful and original mountain villages in Greece**, Olymbos. Traditional houses and customs that are still practised – women wear their beautifully embroidered costumes on weekdays as well – have made the town popular among package tourists, but the visit is still worthwhile. Get to Olymbos by boat from Pigádia to Diafani and from there by bus or car on a long unpaved road. Thanks to its isolated location, centuries-old customs are still alive, for the access road was not built and electricity connected until 1980! Bread is still baked in common ovens fuelled by wood. Just after World War II about 3,000 people lived in Olymbos, but after a massive wave of emigration only 350 have remained today. Near the church a traditional house is open for viewing.

Olymbos
(Ολυμπος)

The **hike** from Olymbos to the outpost Avlona (about four hours round trip) is rewarded with a wonderful view of Olymbos and Profitis Ilias.

Kasos (Κάσος)

Kasos (population 1,100), 6km/4mi southwest of Kárpathos, is rocky and barren, with not one sheltered bay and almost no beaches. The few tourists who stay here take boats to the islands Armathia and Makra off the coast to sunbathe. The inhabitants of Kasos live from modest agriculture and boat building.

Forgotten island

The unattractive, partially deserted Fry (population 340) on the north coast has been the capital since 1840. The tiny fishing harbour Bouka and colourful domed churches have a certain charm. In the town hall an **archaeological museum** exhibits the island finds. 1km/0.5mi to the southeast lies the old port, **Emborios**, which is only used as a fishing harbour today.

Fry (Φρύ)

Almost half of the island population lives in pretty Agia Marina (1km/0.5mi southwest of Fry). Southwest of Arvanitohori (3km/2mi

Agia Marina
(Αγία Μαρίνα)

south of Fry) is the **cave of Ellinokamara**, where women and children hid during the massacre of 1824.

Scattered about the island are mountain monasteries, including **Agiou Georgiou** in the southwest (from Arvanitochori two and a half hours on foot) and – to the south of Fry – the abandoned **St Mamma** (one and a half hours from Fry). The three rocks in the bay below it are called »petrified Turkish ships«. St Mamma is supposed to have turned three Turkish ships that were attacking the island into rocks.

Mountain monasteries

The best beach, a pebble beach without facilities, is in the southwest near Agios Georgios in Helatros Bay.

Beach

Kastellorizo

Greek: Καστελλόριζο	**Island group:** Dodecanese
Area: 9 sq km/3 sq mi	**Altitude:** 0–271m/889ft
Population: 430	**Capital:** Megisti

Visitors to Kastellorizo discover island life that is barely contaminated by tourism, but also the difficulties that come with being isolated.

Greece's easternmost island outpost, a mere 7km/4.5mi long, lies 3km/2mi off Turkey's southern coast. Only about 250 people, mostly old, live on the dry, rocky island today; they live from fishing (some sponge fishing), modest livestock raising and some tourism. Many emigrated former inhabitants of Megisti return home for vacations; some even return permanently when they retire. The great distance to the Greek mainland and lack of an economic hinterland make life difficult for the islanders, even if the Greek state does provide aid. **Tourism** hardly exists because the island is so difficult to reach. While there are no beaches, the wonderfully clear waters along the rocky coast are just made for snorkelling.

Greece's eastern-most island

What to See on Kastellorizo

The only town on the island, Kastellorizo or Megisti, extends around a bay that cuts deeply into the northeast coast of the island. A good number of its colourful houses with their balconies are abandoned and dilapidated. Towering over the town is a **castle** that Juan Fernando Heredia, the Spanish Grand Master of the Order of St John from 1377 until 1396, built at the close of the 14th century on the remains of a Byzantine fortress. The castle's name »Castello Rosso«

Kastellorizo/ Megisti (Καστελλόριζο/ Μεγίστη)

← *Apella, a picture-postcard beach: as good as it gets*

(»Red Castle«) also gave the island its name. A 4th-century BC domed grave can be seen at the foot of the castle hill. The **former mosque** stands on the east side of the harbour; previously a church, it was later degraded to a storehouse by the Italian occupation forces. Above the mosque the **island museum** shows historical finds as well as jewellery, vases and coins. Opening times: Tue–Sun 8.30am–3pm.

Fokiali

The island's main attraction is the Blue Cave of Fokiali on the south coast; it is often compared to the Blue Grotto of Capri. It can only be reached when the sea is calm by tour boats out of Megisti, as the entrance to the cave lies only about a metre above the water's surface. The 35m/115ft-high cave, like a cathedral in the rock, shimmers with countless, marvellous shades of blue and turquoise.

Monastery, Paleokastro

Further up the slope lie the monasteries of Agiou Georgiou in the south and Agia Triada, which was abandoned in 1942, in the west, Mt Vigla with its military guard posts as well as remains of the ancient Paleokastro castle with Hellenistic walls, tower and cistern. On the inaccessible plateau in the east near Avlonia, Mycenaean rock tombs and an ancient workshop were found.

Picturesque location: Kastellorizo, the only town on the island

▶ VISITING KASTELLORIZO

GETTING THERE

Boats to and from Piraeus on the mainland as well as with the islands of Amorgós, Astypálea, Kálymnos, Kos, Náxos, Páros, Rhodes, Sýros and Tílos. Flights from Rhodes land several times a week at the small airport above the harbour.

WHERE TO EAT

▶ Inexpensive
Orea Megisti
Plateia Megisti
Diners can enjoy a large selection of dishes on a terrace covered with grapevines.

WHERE TO STAY

▶ Mid-range
Kastellorizo
Megisti, tel. 0 24 10 4 90 44
14 rooms. Traditionally furnished rooms in five historic houses on the harbour.

View from Kastellorizo Hotel

Kéa

L 9

Greek: Κέα
Area: 130 sq km/50 sq mi
Population: 2,400

Island group: Cyclades
Altitude: 0–570m/1,870ft
Capital: Kéa Hóra/Ioulida

The island of Kéa (also called Tzia), which can only be reached from the mainland from Lavrio harbour on the south coast of Attiki, possesses numerous pretty bathing coves. The most western of the Cyclades is a particular favourite of the Athenians as a holiday and getaway destination.

Livestock and terraced agriculture are declining because of emigration, and the traditional cultivation of acorns for leather tanning in the south of the island ended with the development of chemical products in the 20th century.

Island of the stone lion

What to See on Kéa

The harbour town of Korissia in the south of Agios Nikolaos Bay has hotels and a beach. It occupies the site of ancient Koresia, of which sections of the city wall and a shrine to Apollo have survived. The

Korissia
(Κορησσία)

▶ VISITING KEA

INFORMATION
Tourist information
Ferry landing at Korissia

GETTING THERE
Boat services to and from Lavrio as well as the islands of Amorgós, Kýthnos, Mýkonos, Sýros and Tinos.

WHERE TO EAT
▶ **Inexpensive**
To Steki
Ioulida

Taverna on the beach with a terrace decorated with plants and an ample selection of Greek dishes.

WHERE TO STAY
▶ **Budget**
Korissia
Korissia
Tel. 2 28 80 2 14 84
www.hotelkorissia.gr
16 rooms. The hotel is near the harbour in Korissia. All rooms have a balcony.

Kouros of Kéa (530 BC) found here is on display in the National Archaeological Museum in Athens.

Vourkari
(Βουρκάρι)
The main attraction of Vourkari yacht harbour is the beautiful **Gialiskari beach**, which slopes gently into the sea. The beach is shaded by tamarisk and eucalyptus trees. The **Vourkari Art Gallery** has rotating exhibitions by international artists. A Minoan-Mycenaean settlement (around 2800–1500 BC) has been excavated near Agia Irini Chapel on the northern part of Agios Nikolaos Bay. Of particular note are a large cellared building and the walls of a temple dating from the 15th century BC, the oldest so far found in Greece.

Otzias
(Οτζιάς)
Otzias is located 4km/2.5mi from Vourkari and has a beach shaded by tamarisk trees. A 5km/3mi unpaved road leads from Otzias southeast to **Panagias Kastrianis Monastery** (18th century), which has a picturesque site on a rock cliff and a beautiful view. A famous icon of the Virgin Mary in the older of the two churches is honoured in a procession on 15 August every year.

Kéa Hóra/Ioulida
The capital Kéa/Ioulida (population 700) lies at the foot of Profitis Ilias (560m/1,837ft). The whitewashed houses of the car-free village nestle along the slope. They have red roofs like the houses on the mainland. Kéa occupies the site of ancient Ioulida, of which the remains of a Venetian **kastro** (1210) fortress have survived. The **archaeological museum** on the main street displays local finds. The headless figures of women with bared breasts, which resemble Minoan figures from Crete, are remarkable. Opening hours: Tue–Sun 8.30am–3pm.

The major attraction of the island: the Lion of Kéa

A 10-minute walk leads northeast to the famous Lion of Kéa from the 6th century BC. The 6m/20ft-long lion was carved out of mica slate by an Ionian sculptor 2,500 years ago.

★
◀ Lion of Kéa

The massive terraces of the ancient city of Karthea on the southeast coast can only be reached on foot. The foundations of a Doric Temple of Apollo remain here; in the polygonal wall of the upper terrace an ancient inscription on a block as well as the foundations of another temple can also be seen.

Karthaia

The best beach on the island is located on the west coast (8km/5mi from Kéa) on Pisses Bay. The road here from Ioulida passes the abandoned **Agia Marina Monastery**, where there is a tower of the 4th century BC.

Pisses Bay

★ Kefallonia

Greek: Κεφαλλονιά
Area: 781 sq km/301 sq mi
Population: 36,000

Island group: Ionian Islands
Elevation: 0–1,628m/5,341ft
Capital: Argostoli

Kefallonia, the largest of the Ionian Islands, has delightful sandy beaches and varied scenery with interesting plants and animals. What makes a stay here even more pleasant is that tourism has hardly developed. The main tourist centres lie southwest of Argostoli (Makrys Gialos and Platys Gialos). For individual tourists, picturesque Fiskardo in the extreme north is a popular stop for short visits.

✱
Largest Ionian island
Kefallonia, the largest of the Ionian Islands, is about 45km/27mi long and up to 30km/18mi wide; it has a cleft coastline with two large **peninsulas** that reach far into the sea. The peninsula in the north is Erissos; in the west is Paliki, which borders on the Gulf of Argostoli. Mountains run north to southeast. The highest peak, in the Enos range, is forested and reaches 1,628m/5,341ft. Along with agriculture and fish farming, tourism is the main source of income on Kefallonia. The island produces good olive oil and white and red Robola wines.

What to See in and around Argostoli

Argostoli (Αργοστόλι)
Argostoli (population 9,000), founded in 1757 by the Venetians, lies on a bay that cuts deep into the east coast of the peninsula of Lassi. The harbour town, once quite handsome, was almost completely destroyed by an earthquake in 1953 and then rebuilt in the usual Greek style. While there are some hotels, few tourists spend any time in Argostoli. Plateia Vallianou is a good starting point for a stroll round the town. Many restaurants have set up tables on the square, which is adorned with flowers. South of the square on Rokkou Vergoti is the **archaeological museum**. Among the most significant finds are weapons and household articles from the Late Mycenaean period. There are also a Roman mosaic and bronze head (3rd century AD). Opening hours: Tue–Sun 8.30am–3pm. What life was like on Kefallonia before the great earthquake can be seen in the **Museum of History and Folk Art**, housed on the main floor of Korgialenios library (old books and manuscripts on the island's history). It also exhibits lace and embroidery, furniture, elaborate costumes, festive gowns and historical photographs, which give an impression of life in times gone by. Opening times: Mon–Sat 9am–2pm.

> ❗ *Baedeker* TIP
>
> **Captain Corelli's Mandolin**
> Kefallonia got publicity from this novel by Loùis de Bernières; it is a romance with the massacre of Italian soldiers by German troops in 1943 as the background. While the film, which was made on Kefallonia, flopped, the book is good holiday reading.

Katavothres (Καταβόθρες)
Leave the capital on the coast road and head north for 3km/2mi to visit one of Kefallonia's natural wonders: a **waterwheel** that used to be driven by seawater. The water flows inland through a channel and then drains into the karst ground through clefts (»katavothres«). It was later discovered that the water flows through underground passages from west to east under the entire island, is mixed with rainwater and after 14 days flows to the surface again on the east coast of Kefallonia in Melissani Cave, which lies above sea level, or into the Bay of Sami. Scientists explain these paradoxes as a consequence of currents and pressure in these underground channels. In the 1953

earthquake the ground level shifted so that the wheel, which was used to grind grain, now only turns slowly.

When standing at the waterwheel a small **lighthouse** in the form of an ancient round temple can be seen on the northern point of Lassi Peninsula. The tower, which was originally built in 1829, was rebuilt in its original form after the earthquake of 1953.

Lassi Peninsula

South of Lassi village the island's main tourist centre extends for several miles. It owes its existence to the picturesque bays of Makrys and Platys Gialos, each one about 500m/550yd long. The beautiful beaches framed by rock cliffs get very crowded during the summer.

Makrys Gialos, Platys Gialos

 # VISITING KEFALLONIA

INFORMATION
Tourist information
Provlita Teloniou Argostoli
Tel. 2 67 10 2 22 48
kefalonia-greece.biz

GETTING THERE
Boats to Astakos and Patras on the mainland and the islands of Ithaki, Lefkada and Zakynthos

WHERE TO EAT
▶ **Moderate**
Captain's Table
Harbour street Argostoli
Tel. 2 67 10 2 38 96
One of the decent restaurants on the waterfront; good selection of local dishes; the offshoot north of the main square (Rizospaston 3) is a bit posher and more expensive.

▶ **Inexpensive**
Saoulis
Harbour promenade Sami
Tasty grilled meat and fish dishes.

WHERE TO STAY
▶ **Mid-range**
Ionian Plaza
Argostoli

Tel. 2 67 10 2 55 81
Fax 2 67 10 2 55 85
www.ionanplaza.gr
43 rooms. Very attractive, elegant yet reasonably priced house on the central Plateia Vallianou; beautifully furnished rooms with balconies facing the square; cultivated Italian-style restaurant.

▶ **Budget**
Thalassino Trifilli
Lourdata
Tel. 2 67 10 3 11 14
www.trifilli.com
Idyllic hotel with a family atmosphere and its own taverna. 2- to 4-bed rooms and apartments with balconies.

An afternoon stroll through Lithostroto in Argostoli

Krane About 6km/4mi east of Argostoli are the remains of the ancient city of Krane. A mile-long track leads off the Argostoli–Sami road. The drive is worthwhile for the impressive remains of the ancient city wall (5th–4th century BC) and beautiful countryside.

Paliki Peninsula

Lixouri On the other side of the bay from Argostoli lies the second-largest
(Λιξούρι) town on the island, Lixouri, on the Paliki Peninsula. Ferries run almost every hour from Argostoli to this quiet harbour town (20-minute trip). On the western edge of town a 19th-century neo-classical villa houses the **Lixouri Museum**, where precious icons, old gospel manuscripts, priests' robes and antique furnishings are displayed. Opening hours: Mon–Fri 9am–1pm, Sat 9.30am–12.30pm.

Beaches The beaches in the south of Paliki Peninsula, near Megas Lakkos and Xi, are beautiful. Miles of fine red sand slope gently towards the sea and are edged by light-coloured limestone cliffs. There is some tourist infrastructure but the coast is hardly built up. There are also magnificent sandy beaches near Kounopetra on the southernmost tip of the peninsula.

Kipoureon The landscape changes on the drive from Kounopetra to the north-
Monastery west. At first the limestone is sparsely covered with vegetation, then it slowly changes into green hills that take in the entire western part

of the Paliki peninsula and drop off abruptly to the sea. Kipoureon Monastery, near the coast in picturesque landscape, is still in use. The first church was built here in 1759 and rebuilt after the earthquake of 1953.

The South of the Island

Agiou Gerasimou in the wine region of Omala southeast of Argostoli is the island's largest and foremost monastery. Pilgrims come here every day to ask the island's patron saint, Gerasimou, for intercession. His remains are interred in a silver sarcophagus in the old monastery church. An elaborate new church was built in the 1980s to cope with the crowds of pilgrims.

Agiou Gerasimou (Άγιος Γερασμος)

The south of the island is dominated by Mt Enos (a road runs up to the peak). In the higher elevations of Enos there are still extensive stands of the rare Apollo or Kefallonia pine (Abies cephalonica). The summit area is a national park.

★ Enos (Αίνος)

Near Travliata the road to the kastro turns off the road that connects Argostoli with Skala or Poros. In the 12th century fortifications were built on the 320m/1,000ft mountain ridge. The Venetians extended them in the 16th century. The **former island capital San Giorgio** grew up around the fort. After Argostoli became the capital in 1757, most residents of San Giorgio moved away. The outer walls of the fortifications are almost completely intact.

Kastro

Below the kastro lies the Convent of Agios Andreas, which was first documented in 1264. The monastery church was built around 1600 and is now part of a modern icon museum. In the church there are murals from the 13th and 16th–17th centuries. The museum is attractively arranged and displays Byzantine and Ionian religious art on two floors. Opening hours: Mon–Sat 8am–2pm.

Agios Andreas Milapidia

🕐

Villas and flower gardens give Metaxata – southwest of Agios Andreas monastery – a prosperous look. The memory of the **poet Lord Byron** is still alive here. He lived in Metaxata for four months in 1823 before travelling on to Mesolongi on the Greek mainland, where he died in 1824 of malaria. The house where Byron lived was destroyed in the earthquake of 1953; only a plaque commemorates his stay.

Metaxata (Μεταξάτα)

Even though it is not directly on the coast, neighbouring Lakithra has developed into a tourist centre. There are several attractive hotels and holiday apartment complexes here, some even with a view of the sea. Unfortunately Kefallonia airport lies in between. Near the church **Late Mycenaean graves** (1250–1150 BC) were discovered which still held rich grave goods. The south coast east of the airport

Lakithra (Λάκηθρα)

Kefallonia Map

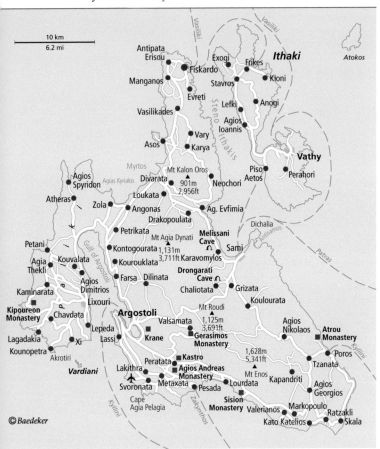

has some **coves for swimming**, such as Ammes, Lygia and Avythos, which are framed by rocks and have flat sandy beaches.

Skala (Σκάλα) Skala on the southern tip of the island welcomes visitors with many hotels, private accommodation and restaurants. The long, if not especially attractive red sandy beaches nearby and the charming hilly interior with pine woods and cypresses have made the town a popular tourist centre.

Other attractions in the south 13km/8mi to the north the harbour of **Poros** is not very pretty but bears the marks of tourism. Near Poros the pebble beaches are small and fairly unattractive; there are better ones further south. About 5km/3mi northwest of Poros, at an elevation of 535m/1,755ft, **Atrou Monastery** (1248) has a magnificent view over the harbour. Near **Tzanata** (4km/2.5mi west of Poros) a large domed burial site was discovered (1350 BC), the only one of its kind in Greece. Northwest, in the Atros range, **Lake Avythos** is set in picturesque mountain scenery.

The North of the Island

From the road that connects Argostoli with the north there are many fine views of the Gulf of Argostoli. The drive to one of the **loveliest beaches on the island** is not long: Myrtos Beach, in a beautiful bay bordered by high rock cliffs. Continue northwards on the main road for the best view of the bay.

✳
Myrtos Beach

Further on the town of Assos is dominated by a mountain. A side road leads off downhill in hairpin bends. Since there are no sandy beaches most tourists come here only for a day. A forest track accessible to cars leads up to a 16th-century Venetian **fortification**, which was considered to be impregnable.

Assos (Ασος)

Fiskardo is Kefallonia's model village in the north. It was named after the Norman leader Robert Guiscard, who died here in 1085. The village survived the earthquake of 1953 without damage. Picturesque, pastel-coloured houses, some of them dating from the 18th century, line the harbour bay. Elegant yachts stop here during the high season – Fiskardo has been a popular meeting place for sailors from all over the world for years. Heading south out of town, after 1km/0.5mi note a pretty tree-lined pebble beach. In the straits between the northeast coast of Kefallonia and Ithaki there is **one of the last colonies of monk seals in the Mediterranean**.

Fiskardo (Φισκάρδο)

From the road that connects Agia Evfymia with Sami lies the access road to Melissani Cave. A short tunnel leads down to the cave lake; part of the ceiling has caved in. The daylight streaming in creates an interesting play of colours. It is possible to take a boat ride on the underground lake with its bizarre rock formations. Opening hours: daily 9am–7pm.

✳
Melissani Cave

🕓

Sami is Kefallonia's most important ferry port. Ancient Same was located to the south on the slope of the double hill (signed »Kastro«). Besides the remains of the city wall, a 2nd-century Roman villa and a Hellenistic watchtower can be seen.

Sami (Σάμη)

The 100m/100yd-long Drogarati dripstone cave (3km/2mi southwest of Sami) has spectacular stalactite and stalagmite formations and is lit to great effect, and the cave has such good acoustics that concerts have been held here.

◄ Drogarati Cave

Small but state-of-the-art: Metaxas winery on Kefallonia

THE LEGACY OF CEPHALUS

Mavrodafne and Muscat are familiar varieties of grapes. But what about Robola, Goustolidi, Kakotrygis, Zakynthino? Wine lovers can discover new and interesting aromas on the Ionian Islands.

Wine growing on the Ionian Islands goes back a long way, for it was none other than **Cephalus**, the son of the god Hermes, who is supposed to have brought the first vines to Kefallonia – which was named after him. A document dated 1262 shows how important wine growing was for this island; another, which documents the conquest of Corfu by Venice in 1386, shows that wine was the most important product there.

Currants and wine

The production of wine lagged behind that of currants for centuries. Under the Venetians, from about 1540, currants became a lucrative branch of the economy, and in 1887 half of Greece's imports were financed by the export of **currants**. Towards the end of the 19th century Kefallonia had become the most important wine island in the Ionian archipelago.

Sweet Muscatel and Mavrodafne, which was often mixed with other wines in northern Europe because of its colour and spicy taste, were the most popular. But **Robola** was considered to be the island's best wine from early on, and in this period was often compared with white Bordeaux by wine experts. However, the two world wars and the catastrophic earthquake in 1953 dealt the wine industry a heavy blow, and tourism soon attracted attention at the expense of the production of high-quality wines.

Modern times

It was not until a transformation took place in the world of wine in the 1980s that production gained a new impetus. Wine was elevated to a lifestyle product that sells at high prices and has no lack of customers worldwide. Young members of wine-

growing dynasties changed their direction; people who entered the field from other businesses brought along new ideas and above all the finance for necessary investments. While some wine growers also planted »international« varieties like Chardonnay, the basic trend was to return to the older, more interesting, **local varieties of grapes**, a great treasure that can be exploited with new methods. Moreover the Ionian Islands were hardly touched by the phylloxera aphid, which is why there are still many old vines with original roots (even today there is hardly any grafting onto resistant roots). Instead of trying to compete in the international market with a tiny production of comparable wines, local wine growers are trying to create their own image. Depending on the circumstances, vineyards may be replanted in order to give each variety the ground and the location it needs to best bring out its own character. The Robola grape needs very dry, rocky mountain slopes, while lighter varieties like Zakynthino, which produce a fuller-bodied wine, need deep soil on flat land.

Wines, vines ...

30 varieties were documented for the year 1601 on Zakynthos, and Archduke Ludwig Salvator listed more than 80 in 1904. Only the major ones are listed here. Robola makes a lemony, fruity white wine with mineral tones reminiscent of a Riesling and is well-suited for fish and light meats. It is cultivated on the larger islands but it has OPAP status (V.Q.P.R.D., highest quality) only for an area of 350ha/865 acres on Kefallonia, while more than 1,400ha/3,500 acres in all are planted with Robola. It is not yet clear if it is identical with the northern Italian Ribolla (it was originally called Ribola). The freshly pressed juice ferments in cooled steel tanks, and after clarification the wine is bottled without any additional ageing. Accordingly it should be drunk young and well chilled. Other white varieties on Kefallonia are

Wine cultivation on Zakynthos

Tsaoussi, Perochoritikoand **Zakynthino** originally from Zakynthos.

Verdea, a specialty of Zakynthos, is classified as a »traditional wine« (onomasia kata paradosi). It is a blend of various old varieties, mostly Goustoldi (also called Vostilidi), Robola, Pavlos and Skiadopoulo. It gets its name from the Italian word »verde« for »green«. The grapes used to be picked very early and always included unripe ones, which gave the wine its typical greenish colour and acidity. Now they are picked later, but the wine should still be drunk fresh and young.

An exception is the Grande Reserve of Komoutos, which is aged for five years in oak barrels and resembles fino sherry. On Lefkada the dominant variety is **Vertzami** (known as Marzemino in Trentino), which produces a red wine that is rich in colour and extract, yet modest in quality. It is not the same as **Vertzamo**, a white wine that is also produced on Lefkada. On Corfu the main varieties are the white **Kakotrygis** and the red **Petrokoritho**, both of which are available in other colours as well. Red wines are grown mainly in the north and white wines in the south of Corfu.

The varieties Muscat (Moscato) and Mavrodafne are approved as OPE wines (controlled origin; second-highest category) but hardly ever produced as such any more. The **open country wine** from the Ionian Islands is very rustic and often has a unique sweet-sour aroma. This comes from the fact that the wine growers use residual sugar to make palatable the wine's crudeness, which derives from antiquated methods of production.

...and wineries

A trip through the Ionian Islands is not complete without a stop at a winery. Most of them are happy to present their products all summer, even if only on appointment.

Good wineries include **Livadiotis** in Chalikounas near Agio Mattheos on Corfu; on Kefallonia **Gentilini** in Minies near the airport, **Metaxas** in Mavrata, the **Kefalonian Robola Cooperative** in Omala near the Gerasimos Monastery on Kefallonia; and on Zakynthos **Komoutos** near Macherado.

✶ ✶ Kos

Greek: Κος
Area: 295 sq km/114 sq mi
Population: 21,000
Capital: Kos Town

Island group: Dodecanese
Altitude: 0–846 m/2,776ft above sea level

After Rhodes Kos is the second main tourist island in the Dodecanese. With miles of sandy beaches and sleepy, romantic coves, lively nightlife and tranquil rural seclusion, a famous Temple of Asclepius, a Roman villa and a powerful castle of the Order of St John, the resort island of Kos offers something new for each day of the holiday.

The Dodecanese island of Kos lies off the bay of the same name that cuts deep into the Turkish coastline. A ridge of mountains reaches an elevation of 846m/2,775ft and extends across the 51km/32mi-long island from east to west. Apart from this narrow mountain range Kos is, unlike the other Aegean islands, quite flat and well-suited for **cycling**. It is the only island in the Aegean that has bike paths. Its mild climate and fertile alluvial plain allowed a lush green landscape to develop that ancient travellers described as a »floating garden«. Agriculture used to be important here; today wine, olives, melons, barley and wheat are only produced on a small scale. **Tourism** has meanwhile become the main source of income for the islanders and Kos has developed into a venue for mass tourism. Nevertheless the architectural atrocities of other Mediterranean venues were not copied. The island is characterized by small bed & breakfast inns and apartment buildings scattered across the island. Tourism began around the island capital of Kos, where there are only narrow pebble beaches along the very busy coast road. The best beaches are along the north coast from Lambi to Mastihari, on the southern coast at Kardamena, and along Kefalos Bay in the southwest. The elongated form of the island and proximity to the beaches means that there are no longer any authentic mountain villages. However, there are numerous archaeological remains from antiquity, early Christian church ruins, medieval castles, mosques from the Turkish period and magnificent Italian buildings. The island enjoyed high esteem as the oldest **cult site of the god of healing, Asclepius**, and the site of a medical school, whose most famous representative was the native-born **Hippocrates** (►Baedeker Special p.279).

Island of Hippocrates

✶ Kos Town

The capital Kos (population 18,500) spreads around a wide bay on the northeast coast in the eastern part of the only large plain on the island. The Turkish coast seems close enough to touch from here.

Island capital

► VISITING KOS

INFORMATION
Tourist information
Vas. Pavlou 1
Kos Town
Tel. 2 24 20 42 44 60
www.kos.gr

HOW TO GET THERE
Boats to Alexandroupoli, Piraeus and
Thessaloniki on the mainland, as well
as the islands of Agathonisi, Amorgós,
Astypálea, Chíos, Donousa, Fourni,
Ikaría, Kálymnos, Léros, Lesbos, Lim-
nos, Lipsi, Mýkonos, Náxos, Páros,
Patmos, Rhodes, Samos, Symi, Sýros
and Tílos.

WHERE TO EAT
► Expensive
Hamam Oriental
Nissirou 3
Kos Town
Tel. 2 24 20 2 14 44

*Hamam Orien-
tal: historic
ambience for a
good restaurant*

The restaurant in a 16th-century
former Turkish bath serves Greek and
international cuisine.

► Moderate
Dionysos
On the island's main road at the edge

of Kamari, a large taverna directly on
the beach offering good, plain Greek
cooking with quick, friendly service

Baedeker recommendation

Serif
On the village square, Platani. A great place
to enjoy some Turkish specialties in the
shade of a plane tree after visiting the
Asclepieion.

WHERE TO STAY
► Mid-range
Kipriotis Village
5km/3mi south of Kos Town
Tel. 2 24 20 2 76 40
www.kipriotis.gr
340 rooms, 192 apartments, 98 suites.
This hotel village with its pool complex is surrounded by fantastic greenery; the energetic can let off steam
with tennis, football and fitness train-
ing.

Kos Aktis
Vas. Georgiou B' 7
Kos Town
Tel. 2 24 20 4 72 00
www.kosaktis.gr
48 rooms. Designer hotel on the beach
near the old city; all rooms have a sea
view.

► Budget
Porfyris
Mandraki, near Platia Ilikiomeni
Tel. 2 24 20 3 11 40
38 rooms. Family run, quietly situated
hotel in the town centre with medium-sized pool.

The earthquake of 1933 left some medieval, Turkish and Venetian-style buildings that give the town a pleasant atmosphere; reconstruction also left room for gardens, lawns, parks and boulevards lined by palm trees. Countless street cafes and restaurants, easily accessible ancient excavation sites, flowering oleander trees lining the streets and the colourful, bustling **harbour**, where only yachts and fishing boats moor during the daytime and are joined by excursion boats in the evenings, all make for a holiday atmosphere. Visitors enjoy the tangled labyrinth of lanes in the old town shaded by plane trees. One shop lines up one next the other and night owls find numerous bars and clubs.

Along Mandraki Harbour a palm-fringed promenade runs eastward to the castle of the Order of St John, which was built between 1450 and 1514. There are ancient sculptures and inscriptions in the walls and a Hellenistic relief above the entrance. Opening hours: May–Oct Mon 1.30–8pm, Tue–Sun 8am–8pm, Nov–Apr Tue–Sun 8.30–3pm.

Castle of the Order of St John

On Plateia Platanou stands the former Haji Hassan Mosque (1786). Under the so-called **Hippocrates plane tree** the great physician is said to have taught. In fact, the mighty tree, with a trunk 12m/39ft in diameter and now hollow, is »only« about 500 years old and is supported by a Roman sarcophagus, which the Turks used as a well house. The ancient **agora**, the marketplace, extends to the south. Like all ancient sites in Kos it is open free of charge. There is a beautiful view over the ruins and oleander trees to the minarets and church towers of the town.

Plateia Platanou

Mandraki Harbour is where the town's heart beats

Kos Map

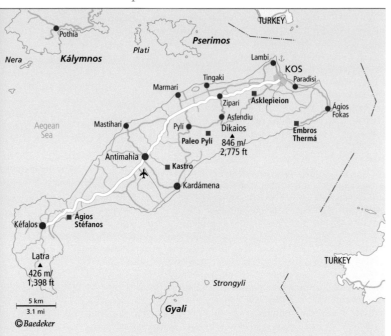

TURKEY

Pothia
Nera
Kálymnos
Plati
Pserimos
Lambi
KOS
Paradisi
Tingaki
Marmari
Zipari **Asklepieion**
Ágios Fokas
Asfendiu
Aegean Sea
Mastihari
Pylí
Dikaios
Embros Thermá
Paleo Pylí
846 m/ 2,775 ft
Antimahia
■ **Kastro**
■ Kardámena
Ágios Stéfanos
Kéfalos
Latra
▲ 426 m/ 1,398 ft
TURKEY
5 km
3.1 mi
◎ Strongyli
© *Baedeker*
Gyali

| Plateia Eleftherias | The Tax Gate on the west side of the agora leads to Plateia Eleftherias, »Freedom Square«, where the charming 18th-century **Defterdar Mosque** has Hellenistic and Byzantine columns. The interesting **archaeological museum**, a building with an interior like a Roman villa, is also here. It exhibits statues and sculptural fragments from the Hellenistic and Roman periods. The centrepiece is a beautiful 2nd- or 3rd-century AD mosaic in the inner courtyard depicting the arrival of Asclepius in Kos. Opening hours: May–Oct Mon 1.30–7.30pm, Tue–Sun 8am–7.30pm, Nov–Apr Tue–Sun 8.30–3pm. |

Excavations In the south and southwest of the town along Grigoriou Street extensive excavations are open to the public at no charge. From east to west: a Temple of Dionysos (3rd century AD), Roman baths, the reconstructed Casa Romana (3rd century AD) with beautiful mosaics, a Roman odeon, the house of Europa (mosaics), a gymnasium (2nd century BC) and the so-called Nymphaion, a public latrine (3rd century BC).

Beaches near Kos West of the city is the densely built-up tourist district **Lambi**, one of the most popular holiday venues on the island, especially for young people. Nothing shuts down at night in Lambi – anyone who comes here for peace and quiet is definitely in the wrong place. East of town the coast road runs along little beaches to **Psalidi beach** (3km/2mi), which is quieter than Lambi, and on to **Agios Fokas** (7km/4.5mi) and **Therma Loutra** (11km/7mi), where the thermal springs on the beach are often crowded.

Asclepieion

Southwest of Kos lies the little Turkish-style village of **Platani**. From here a pretty street lined with cypresses and plane trees runs to the sanctuary of Asclepius. These are the most important ruins on the island, in a wonderful location. The Asclepieion, erected in the early 3rd century BC, occupied three terraces. The higher the terrace, the more magnificent the view of the town, the straits and the Turkish mainland. On the lower terrace was the **treatment area** with a large square bordered by colonnades; behind the halls were several chambers and to the left of the entrance three private Roman or Hellenistic houses that are still extant. Baths were added on the northeast corner of the terrace later. Following the destruction of the Asclepieion by an earthquake in AD 554, a monastery was built here. The first terrace ends to the south with the retaining wall of the second terrace. On the left between the second and third abutment is the sacred spring. To the right in front of a wall is a naiskos (miniature temple), which according to the inscription was built by C. Stertinius Xenophon, the personal physician to Emperor Claudius, for Nero.

Opening hours:
Opening times:
May–Oct
daily 8am–8pm
NovApr, Tue–Sun
8.30am–3pm

◄ First terrace

On the second terrace, the **oldest cult site**, there is an altar right in front of the steps. It is not as old as the small marble Temple of

◄ Second terrace

Cleopatra enjoyed »beauty treatments« in the Asclepeion

Asklepieion Plan

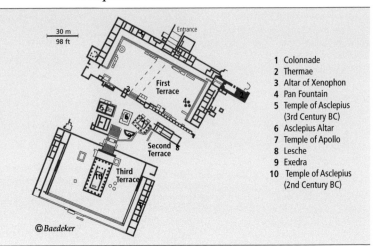

```
30 m
98 ft
```

Entrance

First Terrace

Second Terrace

Third Terrace

© Baedeker

1 Colonnade
2 Thermae
3 Altar of Xenophon
4 Pan Fountain
5 Temple of Asclepius (3rd Century BC)
6 Asclepius Altar
7 Temple of Apollo
8 Lesche
9 Exedra
10 Temple of Asclepius (2nd Century BC)

Asclepius (around 400 BC) to the west. Seven columns once belonging to an Ionian peripteros of 6:9 columns rise to the east of the altar. In the southwest stood a semicircular exedra; opposite it, behind the old temple, there was a Roman building.

Third terrace ▶ Between the two structures broad steps led up to the third terrace, with the large **newer Temple of Asclepius** (2nd century BC), a Doric peripteros of 6:11 columns. The black marble doorstep is still in place. Further up the hill is the Burinna well house, which supplied water to the ancient city.

Island Tour

On the northern slopes of the mountains the road runs southwest. In **Zipari** are the meagre remains of two early Christian basilicas on the south edge of town. 4km/2.5mi to the south is a charming mountain village, **Asfendiou**. The neighbouring picture-book village, **Zia**, has meanwhile been taken over by tourism. Nestled in a shady pine wood, the village consists almost entirely of terraced restaurants and souvenir stands. The view of the coastal plain is overwhelming especially at sunset, so that the trip here is worthwhile. Beyond Zia is the highest mountain on Kos, **Dikeos** (846m/2,776ft); the climb is rewarded with a beautiful view.

Beach resorts on the north coast ▶ On the north coast the sprawling resorts **Tingaki**, **Marmari** and **Mastihari** are merging. All three are near sandy beaches bordered in places by low dunes; only Mastihari has a historic town centre. Ferries depart several times a day from Mastihari for Kálymnos.

THE FATHER OF MEDICINE

Hippocrates is one of the best-known names in human history. And yet little is known of the life and work of this man of antiquity. Almost every physician in the last 2,500 years has had to swear an oath on his name, but Hippocrates did not even formulate the oath named after him. Nothing, however, can shake his reputation as the first »modern« physician.

Hippocrates was born around 460 BC on the island of Kos. He was descended from the Asclepiades, an ancient family of physicians who traced their lineage back to the healing god, **Asclepius**, and he was introduced to the healing arts at an early age by his father.

He came in contact with the most famous doctors

The statue of Hippocrates displayed in the archaeological museum in Kos Town was sculpted in the 4th century BC

of his time while travelling throughout Asia Minor and Greece practising as a physician and continued in further developing his methods of healing. After his return to the island of Kos he founded a medical school, which soon gained a high reputation. Hippocrates, whom **Plato** also mentioned as a famous doctor, died around 370 BC in Larissa, Thessaly.

Legendary Physician

Naturally, a great many legends have formed around the life and work of such an outstanding personality. For example, it is said he healed the Macedonian king, **Perdiccas II**, who was suffering from headaches and loss of appetite for some unknown reason. He found out that the monarch was having a love affair, unbefitting his station, with a pretty servant girl and,

Relaxing break beneath the venerable plane tree of Hippocrates

after the king had ended the relationship, he felt healthy once more, even feeling a desire for his own wife again. Hippocrates has also been falsely credited in scientific matters. Some 130 writings have survived under his name. Close to half of them are forgeries, with 58 of them forming the »Corpus Hippocraticum«, probably the most famous collection of writings in medicine. But not one of the works can be ascribed to Hippocrates with certainty. The works were written in the period from the 5th century BC down into the 1st century AD. The collection treats surgery, dietetics, epidemiology, pharmacology, prognostics, therapeutics and ethics. All of these treatises chiefly have in common a recognition of the healing power of nature or the body as being the physician's best helper, and particularly they stress high professional ethics. The »Hippocratic Oath«, which serves as a model for the physician's oath, also appears in these writings. Down to the present day, the oath is still, at least symbolically, administered upon graduation at quite a few universities. The oath begins with an appeal to the gods of healing, Apollo, Asclepius, Hygieia and Panaceia. In the first section, a kind of guild contract, the physician swears to his teachers to maintain the »secrets of the trade«. The second part dictates instructions on the behaviour of the physician, which have come down almost unchanged since the time of antiquity as the ethical foundation of the medical profession, such as the duty to maintain confidentiality and the obligation to always act in the patient's best interest. It is considered certain today, however, that the oath was not composed by the physician from Kos.

The Legacy

So Hippocrates wrote neither the oath named after him nor was he in all likelihood involved in the writing of the »Corpus Hippocraticum« and yet he is regarded as the **father of modern medicine**«, as the founder of medicine as an empirical science based on observations and the descriptions of the symptoms of illnesses. This new medical method was a conscious departure from the reli-

Medieval manuscript of the Hippocratic Oath from the Vatican Library

gious or magical conception of illnesses prevalent at the time; in other words, the sickness was no longer regarded as sent by the gods but could be traced back to explicable causes.

According to Hippocratic teachings, health was based on the correct blending of the four humours, blood, phlegm, and yellow and black bile, while illnesses were an imperfect mixture, with lifestyle and diet also playing a decisive role. Making exact observations at the patient's bedside and studying the patient's physiology were the most important medical activities of the **Hippocratics**. Therapy was essentially confined to dietary prescriptions and medicines in the form of herbal drugs. Hippocrates is said to have chastised contemporary martial arts for being a »school of deception« with its »force-feeding« of the athletes, who were not uncommonly fattened like animals for the slaughter in order to achieve the highest performance. On the other hand, the wine industry today likes to emphasize that the physician from Kos was said to have used wine »to strengthen the convalescents, as a

calming and sleep inducing agent, for headaches and states of ill temper and even for diseases of the eyes«.

Few Operations

Surgery played a subordinate role with the Hippocratics, being confined largely to bone-setting. The Hippocratic theory of humours dominated medical concepts in antiquity and the Middle Ages and in a slightly modified form even down into the 19th century. But while his science is no longer modern, Hippocrates' authority has not been shaken to the present day. The medical historian **Henry E. Sigerist** pointed out that every era has had a different image of Hippocrates, but what they all have in common, he said, was to see him as someone to appeal to if they thought that physicians needed putting back on the right path.

Antimahia
(Αντιμάχεια)

🕐

One of the last functioning windmills on Kos stands in Antimahia (5km/3mi south of Mastihari). In the **Traditional House** opposite there are exhibits on the life of farmers (opening times: Mon–Sat 9am–5pm, Sun 11am–3pm). Just before reaching the village look out for a path that turns off to the castle of the Order of St John, Palea Antimahia, which was rebuilt after the earthquake of 1493. The long row of battlements on this, the largest castle ruin on the island, can be seen from far off.

Kardamena
(Καρδάμαινα)

6km/4mi southeast of Antimahia a road turns off to the beach resort Kardamena with its long beach of light-coloured, fine-grained sand. The town is also popular as a shopping centre. With its many dance and music clubs it is a centre of nightlife on Kos for the young. From Kardamena boat trips leave for Nisyros every day. The road to **Kefalos** (17km/10mi) runs past the airport. Kefalos is a pretty village high up in the mountains with whitewashed, single-storey houses. Countless tour buses come here during the high season for the superb view of Kefalos Bay. North of Kefalos is one of the regions on the island with the most beautiful landscape: the **Bay of Limnionas**, a natural harbour with a few fishing boats, sheltered from the wind and nestling in a rugged, romantic coastal landscape. The almost untouched bays to the right and left of the harbour are ideal for undisturbed swimming. Below Kefalos lies **Kamari Beach**, where even the high season is quite restful. Off shore is the picturesque **Kastri rock** with the Chapel of Agios Nikolaos. Further northeast are the island's most beautiful beaches, including **Camel Beach**, **Magic Beach** and **Paradise Beach**. Building is prohibited on a stretch of broad, fine-grained sandy beaches amounting to more than 10km/6mi. South of Kefalos the road climbs steeply and runs through the untouched landscape of the southern tip of the island. **Theologos Beach** near the little Chapel of Agios Ioannis Theologos (4km/2.5mi west) is far from the bustle of tourism, with small, isolated bays bordered by dunes. Because of the relatively strong surf it is popular among surfers.

! **Baedeker TIP**

Outing to Bodrum
Bodrum on the Turkish Aegean coast, only a few miles from Kos, was formerly renowned under the name Halikarnassos. Its attractions are the Crusader castle of St Peter and the bazaar on the harbour, where high-quality leather goods and pretty gold jewellery can be purchased for reasonable prices. Boats sail for Bodrum from Kos Town.

✴ Nisyros (Νίσυρος)

Red island

The Dodecanese island of Nisyros (population 950) is a purely volcanic island, where boat trips from Kos stop. Its geology explains the low level of tourism, since there are only a few beaches of dark stones. Nisyros was formed when the volcano Diabates erupted in

Camel Beach: one of the many great beaches along the southern coast of Kos

1522. The floor of the crater is surrounded by mountains, which rise to 689m/2,260ft above sea level. While the southern half of the almost circular Nisyros is covered with lush vegetation, the moon-like volcanic landscape on the northern part is marked by small craters. Volcanic activity today is limited to sulphurous hot steam (solfatara). On the fertile pumice tuff in the south, which stores water, there is terraced agriculture (wine, citrus fruits, olives, almonds). There are two versions of the origins of the **name »red island«**. On the one hand, it is supposed to come from the reddish volcanic stone. According to another explanation it got its name from the red dye produced from the murex snails that live along the coast.

Mandraki, the island's principal town and port, lies on a lengthy seaside promenade lined by tavernas, sidewalk cafes and a few souvenir shops. Its shady village square is especially pretty. The dazzling white late Byzantine **cave church Panagia Spiliani** (around 1600) catches the eye at the western edge of town; next to it the remains of the **castle of the Order of St John** can be made out. On August 15 the church is one of the most important pilgrimage sites in the Dodecanes. On the southwestern edge of town there is the well-preserved remains of a city gate and about 100m/330ft of the ancient city wall.

Mandraki
(Μανδράκι)

Many of the exhibits in the modern archaeological museum in the centre of town are from there. Opening times: Tue–Sun 8.30am–3pm.

✳ Caldera

In the caldera (buses from Mandraki) there are four smaller craters and an accessible main crater, the **Stefanos crater**, 330m/1,083ft wide and 30m/100ft deep with colourful walls. Concentrated sulphurous gases (it smells of rotten eggs!) escape from the small, dark and hot holes of earth and mud.

Loutra (Λουτρά)

About 2km/1mi east of Mandraki lies the thermal spa Loutra. Sulphurous water runs right out of the caldera into bathtubs and is used to treat rheumatism and arthritis. There are also hot sulphurous springs (ancient remains of a thermal bath) about 1km/0.5mi to the east in Pali, the second coastal town of the island. For a wonderful view take a road from Loutra up to **Emborios**, a tiny wine village right on the edge of the crater.

Nikia (Νικιά)

Follow the edge of the crater to the attractively sited village of Nikia, where the cobbled square has a superb view of the sea and the crater. A path leads from the little volcano museum (opening times: Tue–Sun 8.30am–3pm) at the edge of town – interesting minerals and

A trail leads into the Stefanos Crater on Nisyros

good explanations of the volcano – down into the caldera in about an hour, passing the Monastery of Agiu Ioanni Theologou on the way.

Tílos (Τήλος)

On Tílos (population 500) tourism has not developed to any great extent, but is slowly increasing. Hikers appreciate the island for its varied and impressive scenery, with deeply indented coves and green, wooded valleys. Sun worshippers will find mainly pebble beaches. The island is best suited for those who seek quiet and rest.

Quiet island

The ferries dock at the small, unassuming port Livádia on the east coast. Almost all the hotels and other tourist facilities are here, as well as a pebble beach. From Livádia the road climbs northwest up to an OTE antenna, where there is a good view of the island, passing the village of **Mikro Horió**, which was abandoned in the 1970s. There is still a monastery here.

Livádia (Λιβάδια)

Megalo Horió (population 300) is located above Agios Antonios Bay on the north coast. The ancient settlement of Telos stood here once; remains of the wall can still be seen. A **castle of the Order of St John** crowns the 286m/938ft Agios Stefanos hill above the village; a ruined church dedicated to the Archangel Michael with interesting 16th-century frescoes stands here on the foundations of a sanctuary of Apollo and Athena. Tamarisk trees fringe **Eristos Beach**, which is 3km/2mi south of Megalo Horió.

Megalo Horió (Μεγάλο Χωριό)

5km/3mi to the southwest beneath a massive cliff, and not visible from the sea, lies the well-tended Agiou Panteleimona Monastery, which is only occupied sporadically. It was founded in the 14th century but the present building with its well-preserved frescoes dates from the 18th century.

Panteleimona Monastery

Kythira

H/J 12

Greek: Κύθηρα
Area: 285 sq km/110 sq mi
Population: 3,300
Capital: Kythira Hóra

Island group: Ionian Islands
Altitude: 0–506m/1,670ft above sea level

The sleepy island of Kythira with its pristine beaches is an ideal destination for holiday makers seeking peace and relaxation.

Kythira, about 15km/9mi south of the southeastern Peloponnese (Laconia), is counted among the Ionian Islands, but belongs admin-

Remote island

⏵ VISITING KYTHIRA

INFORMATION
www.kythira.info

GETTING THERE
Boats to Kalamata and Piraeus on the mainland as well as with the islands of Antikythira, Elafonisi and Crete

WHERE TO EAT
▶ **Moderate**
Sotiris
Avlemonas village square
Tel. 2 73 60 3 37 22

This taverna serves freshly caught fish and is extremely popular with the locals.

WHERE TO STAY
▶ **Mid-range**
9 Muses
Agia Pelaga
Tel. 27 36 03 31 55
www.9museskithira.gr
17 rooms. The spacious rooms with modern furnishings all have a balcony.

istratively to Attiki. The landscape is marked by coastal cliffs and karstified mountain ranges slashed by gorges. Meagre agricultural yields forced the inhabitants to emigrate in the mid-19th century; the preferred destination was Australia. Since descendants of the Australian emigrants love to come back for visits and support the island financially, Kythira is also called »**kangaroo island**«. Until a few years ago there was hardly any tourism on the island, so it can still be recommended to people who want to flee the stress of modern life.

What to See on Kythira

Agia Pelagia
(Αγία Πελαγία)
A wide bay on the northeast coast is the site of the friendly harbour of Agia Pelagia, where during the military dictatorship (1967–74) its political opponents lived in exile. South of Agia Pelagia, beautifully situated on the coast overlooking the sea, are the ruins of a medieval castle and the island's former capital, **Paliohora**, which was destroyed by the Turks in 1536 (access via Logothetianika). The drive there leads through **Potamos**, the island's commercial centre.

Mylopotamos
(Μυλοποταμός)
The attractions of the pretty hamlet of Mylopotamos in the centre of the west coast are Agios Haralambos Church and a waterfall. **Kato Hóra** and the Venetian castle can be reached from here on foot, as can the **dripstone cave Agia Sofia** with its lake. A chapel was built inside the cave in the 12th century.

Avlemonas
(Αβλέμονας)
The village of Avlemonas on the east coast has a small fishing harbour and a pebble beach. The beaches on Cape Kastri to the south are excellent.

Megalo Horió on Tílos is dominated by a fortress of the Knights of St John

The charming capital of the island, Kythira Hóra (population 600), in the shadow of a mighty 16th-century Venetian fortress, occupies the southern tip of the island, overlooking the bay and port of Kapsali. There is a breathtaking view of the island from the southern end of the fortress. The 17th-century **Panagia Myrtidion monastery** towers above the southwest coast. A procession is made on 15 August with a black icon that is venerated for its miraculous powers.

Kýthnos

Greek: Κύθνος
Area: 99 sq km/38 sq mi
Population: 1,600
Capital: Kýthnos Hóra

Island group: Cyclades
Altitude: 0–326m/1,070ft above sea level

Beautiful beaches make Kýthnos a popular holiday destination for the Athenians. Since the island also has healing springs, people come to the spas.

Kýthnos is a dry, rocky Cycladic island with a mostly steep and deeply cleft coastline. The inhabitants live mainly from agriculture and raising livestock.

▶ VISITING KYTHNOS

INFORMATION
Ferry pier,
Merichas
Tel. 2 28 10 3 22 50

WHERE TO EAT
▶ **Inexpensive**
To Kandouni
Merichas,
Tel. 2 28 10 3 22 20
On the sea front with a harbour view,
specializes in grilled fish

WHERE TO STAY
▶ **Mid-range**
Kýthnos
Merichas
Tel. 2 28 10 3 22 47, fax 2 28 10 3 20 92
The main hotel on the island, above
the harbour; rooms of reasonable
quality with balcony

What to See on Kýthnos

Merichas (Μέρχας)
The unattractive main port, Merihas, is dominated by a large and dilapidated hotel. 2km/1mi north, across the good beach at Episkopi,
on a rocky hill are the **ruins of the old capital, Vryokastro**. Holidaymakers come by boat from Merihas to the beautiful beaches further
north, including **Stin Kolona**.

Kýthnos Hóra
The capital Kýthnos (population 800) lies 8km/5mi northeast of
Merihas at an elevation of 160m/530m. Of the many churches in the
town Agios Savvas, Agios Sotiros (both 17th century) and Agia Triada are worth visiting for their carved iconostases and frescoes from
the Cretan school, but they are usually locked to prevent theft by
tourists. Above the town is a run-down wind energy park.

Loutra
On the north side of Agia Irini (5km/3mi north) are the mineral
springs (37°C and 55°C/99°F and 131°F) of **Loutra**, which were already known in Roman times. The Hotel Xenia Anagennisis was
founded on the initiative of Amalia, the wife of King Otto of Greece.
At the hotel beach the water is lukewarm. About 6km/4mi south of
Kýthnos the pretty village of **Dryopida** lies on two slopes of a tree-
covered valley. Its whitewashed houses have red-brown tiled roofs
like those on the mainland. In the southeast, 7km/4mi from Dryopida, is the holiday resort of **Kanala** on a promontory; the Panagia
Church (1906) with a miraculous icon is in the town centre. The
best beaches on the island are here.

Lefkada

Greek: Λεφκάδα
Area: 356 sq km/137 sq mi
Population: 23,000

Island group: Ionian Islands
Altitude: 0–158m/518ft above sea level
Capital: Lefkada

Until now, Lefkada has been little affected by tourism, although the island, with its magnificent mountain scenery and fantastic sandy beaches with bright turquoise water, can certainly compete with its neighbours.

Originally there was a land bridge between Lefkada and the mainland. It was broken already in antiquity, and today a shallow lagoon between 600m and 5km (650yd–3mi) wide separates Lefkada from mainland Greece. Road access to the mainland is by a causeway and most recently a pontoon bridge. Lefkada/Lefkas, the fourth-largest of the Ionian Islands, is 35km/22mi long and up to 15km/9mi wide. It is dominated by a mountain range, with Mount **Stavrotas** rising to an elevation of 1,158m/3,799ft. Along most of the western coast sheer cliffs fall to the sea. These pale cliffs reach a height of 500m/1,640ft and gave the island its name: »lefkos« means »white«. They

»White« island

 VISITING LEFKADA

INFORMATION
www.lefkada.gr

GETTING THERE
The island is connected to the mainland by a causeway and a pontoon bridge. There are boat connections with the islands of Ithaki, Kefallonia and Meganisi.

WHERE TO EAT
► **Moderate**
Sappho
Agios Nikitas
On the beach
A large selection of fish and seafood as well as various grilled dishes in Agios Nikitas' most beautiful dining place

► **Inexpensive**
Reganto
Dimarchou Verioti

Lefkada Town
Popular taverna near Agios Spyridon Church featuring good plain cooking

WHERE TO STAY
► **Mid-range**
Agios Nikitas
Agios Nikitas
Tel. 2 64 50 9 74 60
www.hotelagiosnikitas.gr
36 rooms and apartments. Pretty hotel with wooden balconies that blends in well with the local architecture; rooms have a refrigerator, apartments a kitchen.

Santa Maura
Vlanti 2 Lefkada Town
Tel. 2 64 50 2 13 08
19 rooms. Very pleasant family-run hotel; central and yet quiet; large rooms with balcony.

Lefkada Map

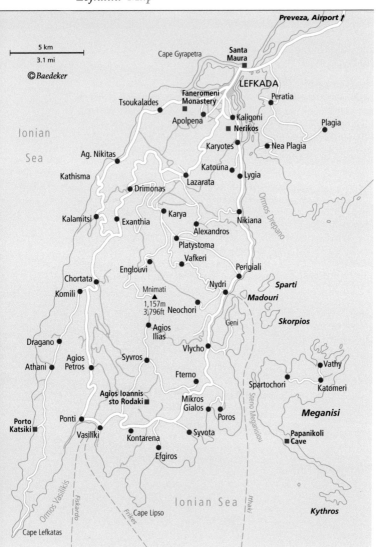

Preveza, Airport ✈

5 km
3.1 mi
©Baedeker

Cape Gyrapetra

Santa Maura

LEFKADA

Peratia

Faneromeni Monastery

Tsoukalades

Apolpena

Kaligoni
Nerikos

Plagia

Karyotes

Nea Plagia

Ionian

Ag. Nikitas

Sea

Katouna

Kathisma

Lazarata

Lygia

Drimonas

Karya

Ormos Drepano

Kalamitsi

Exanthia

Nikiana

Alexandros

Platystoma

Vafkeri

Englouvi

Perigiali

Sparti

Chortata

Nydri

Madouri

Komili

Mnimati
▲
1,157m
3,796ft

Neochori

Geni

Skorpios

Agios
Ilias

Dragano

Vlycho

Agios
Petros

Syvros

Vathy

Athani

Fterno

Spartochori

Katomeri

Steno Meganisiou

**Agios Ioannis
sto Rodaki**

Mikros
Gialos

Meganisi

**Porto
Katsiki**

Ponti

Poros

**Papanikoli
Cave**

Vasiliki

Kontarena

Syvota

Efgiros

Ormos Vasilikis

Fiskardo

Frikes

Ionian Sea

Ithaki

Kythros

Cape Lipso

Cape Lefkatas

provide an impressive backdrop for some of the **sandy beaches**, which **are among the most beautiful of the Ionian Islands**. The southern and eastern coastlines are deeply indented. Many small coves and offshore islands have fine views and ideal conditions for sailing. Tourism is modest and there are no large hotels. Lefkada has no major cultural sites but great scenic variety, and there are some largely untouched beaches on the west coast. Tourism is concentrated on the east coast, which only has small pebble beaches, however. The largest tourist centre on the east coast – and on the island – is the picturesquely located **Nydri**. Vasiliki in the south and Agios Nikitas on the west coast also have some tourist infrastructure. Agriculture is the other main source of income for the islanders. Fruit, vegetables and wine are cultivated on small fields, mostly for local consumption. Lefkada is known for its weaving and embroidery. Lefkada was the home of the German archaeologist **Wilhelm Dörpfeld** (1853–1940), who thought that the island – and not Ithaki – was the Homeric Ithaca, the home of Ulysses.

Lefkada Town and Surroundings

The capital Lefkada (population 6,900) on the northern tip of the island is bordered by the sea on three sides. Surprisingly not the harbour but rather the town centre is the focus of activity. The main axis, which is also the shopping street, is named Dorpfeld Street after the archaeologist Dörpfeld. The houses have upper storeys made of wood, which were not damaged in the earthquake of 1953. Today they are often clad with brightly painted corrugated metal. The brick church towers that caved in during the earthquake were given open belfries made with iron grilles. The modern **archaeological museum**

Island capital

Centrally located Spyridon Square is the heart of Lefkada Town

⊘ on the seashore to the west of the causeway displays finds from the island. Opening hours: Tue–Sun 8.30am–3pm. Post-Byzantine icons are exhibited in an **icon museum**. Along with several churches from the Venetian period, the 18th-century church of Agios Minas at the end of Mela Street deserves mention. Its Baroque iconostasis by artists from Zakynthos and ceiling paintings make it the most significant church in the town.

Surroundings About 3km/2mi north of the city is the Venetian **fortress of Santa Maura** (Agia Mavra), built in the 13th century by Giovanni Orsini and expanded in the 17th century. The **Faneromenis Monastery**, 4km/2.5mi southwest of Lefkada in a beautiful setting, was built in 1634 and reconstructed after a fire in 1886. From here there is a wonderful view of the city, the lagoon and the mainland. 3km/2mi to the south on a hill near Kaligoni the remains of the **ancient city of Leukas** with its acropolis, water system, city wall and theatre can be visited. The closest beaches are the dunes on the north side of the lagoon.

West and South Coast

Agios Nikitas
(Αγιος Νικίτας) Almost the whole length of coastline facing the Ionian Sea is sheer white rock up to 500m/1,650ft high. Agios Nikitas is a popular tourist resort that spreads along a wonderful bay. The picturesque town centre, an area of protected heritage, is closed to cars. There are quieter beaches to the north and south, for example near Kathisma.

Karya
(Καρυά) The southern coast is almost inaccessible and the road leads into the interior of the island. The large, peaceful village of Karya is located in the mountains. Its centre is a plateia shaded by plane trees and fringed by tavernas and restaurants. A little **folk art museum** provides an insight into the traditional art of embroidery. The main event of the year, held on 11–12 August, is a **festival** in which a traditional Lefkadian wedding is re-enacted.

✳
Porto Katsiki
(Πόρτο Κατσίκι) Below Athani lies the long **sandy beach of Engremni**, and about 14km/8mi further south the fabulous beach of Porto Katsiki lies (▶ photo p.293) below light-coloured, steep cliffs. This picturesque scene often appears on travel posters.

✳
Cape Lefkatas The drive ends at Cape Lefkatas/Cape Doukato at the southern tip of the island. Visitors are greeted by a lovely scene with steep cliffs. According to legend, the poet **Sappho** flung herself from the cliffs here out of unrequited love for the handsome youth Phaon, some say following the example of Aphrodite who jumped out of grief over Adonis' death. In antiquity the cape was used as a **seat of judgment**. Birds' feathers were tied to the condemned before they were thrown from the cliff (the Leucadian leap). Those who survived were set free.

Porto Katsiki: one of Greece's dream beaches

From the cape drive back to Komili, where a road leads to the rustic village of Agios Petra and on to Vasiliki, the most important holiday resort on the island after Nydri. Because of its ideal wind conditions, this harbour on the south coast is one of Europe's best windsurfing spots. To the west is a broad sand and pebble beach, but the **sandy bay of Agiofylli** south of Vasiliki is more beautiful.

Vasiliki (Βασιγική)

East Coast

When driving from Lefkada southwards along the east coast, the ruins of the **ancient settlement of Nerikos** (2nd millennium BC) appear first. Near Kariotes a section of the coast that is suitable for swimming begins with the towns of **Lygia**, with its pretty fishing harbour, and **Nikiana**.

After 16km/10mi Nydri, the largest tourist centre on the island, has an attractive setting and a magnificent view to the heavily wooded islands off the coast. Excursion boats leave for the islands Sparti with its sea caves, Madouri and Skorpios, which belongs to the heirs of Aristotle Onassis and is not open to the public. Among Lefkada's natural wonders is a waterfall in a narrow gorge 3km/2mi west of Nydri, which can be reached on foot in about an hour. A wild and romantic path leads further into the gorge.

Nydri (Νυδρί)

Romantic sunset at Cape Lefkatas

Geni peninsula South of Nydri a bay cuts far inland. In the town of Vlyho a road leads to the Geni peninsula. From the parking lot follow the signs to Kyriaki Chapel at the point of the spit of land; the path goes past the **villa and grave of the archaeologist Wilhelm Dörpfeld**. He excavated a necropolis at the southern edge of Nydri in 1912. Back in Vlyho it is another 7km/4.5mi to the charming mountain village of Poros. From here the road winds down to the coast, to a few tavernas at **Mikros Gialos pebble beach**. Another town on the southeast coast, worth visiting for its beautiful coastal scenery and good fish restaurants, is **Syvota**.

Nearby islands The largest island off the eastern coast of Lefkada is **Meganisi** (»large island«; 18 sq km/7 sq mi). It has a population of 1,500 and an elevation of 267m/876ft. Boat trips leave from there for two sea caves on the southwest coast. Apart from day trippers from Lefkada, tourists hardly ever come here. Accommodation and tavernas are in the main town Vathy. Southeast of Lefkada lies the mountainous, sparsely populated island (250 people) of **Kalamos** (24 sq km/9 sq mi, highest elevation 785m/2,575ft). The island consists partly of karst limestone and has a steep coastline. Kalamos on the southeast coast is the main town. To the south is **Kastos**, where only a few fishermen live.

✶ Lesbos

O/P 6/7

Greek: Λέσβος
Area: 1,630 sq km/629 sq mi
Altitude: 0–967m/3,173ft above sea level

Island group: North and east Aegean islands
Population: 91,000
Capital: Mytilini

Lesbos lies in a sweeping bay on the coast of Asia Minor, 15km/ 9mi to the northwest of Izmir. Holidaymakers will find quiet, flat sandy beaches, secluded mountain villages and picturesque little harbours.

Lesbos, after Crete and Évia the third-largest Greek island, is usually called Mytilini by the Greeks. It is one of the most fertile regions in Greece and is characterized by beautiful and varied landscape. Two narrow-necked bays, the Gulf of Kalloni and the Gulf of Yera, cut deep inland in the southwest and southeast respectively. The east and west of the island have clearly different landscapes: while the fertile, mountainous east has patches of woodland, the western part of the

Third-largest Greek island

Lésbos Map

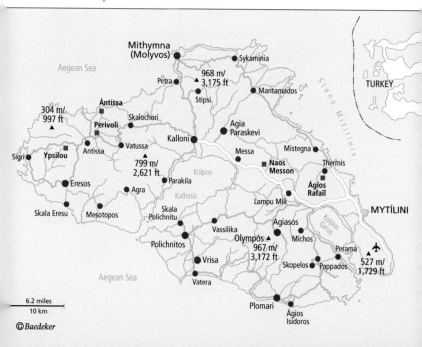

© Baedeker

▶ VISITING LESBOS

INFORMATION

Tourist information
Aristarchou 6 Mytilini
Tel. 2 25 10 4 25 11
www.greeknet.com

GETTING THERE

Ferries to Alexandroupoli, Kavala, Piraeus and Thessaloniki on the mainland, and the islands of Chíos, Kos, Limnos, Mýkonos, Rhodes, Samos, Samothraki, Skiathos, Skopelos and Tinos

WHERE TO EAT
▶ Moderate
① *Stratos*
Mytilini
Tel. 2 25 10 2 17 39
Taverna on the south side of the south harbour with tasty fish dishes

▶ Inexpensive
Panorama
Mythimna Magnificent view of the sea and countryside; serves solid, plain cooking.

WHERE TO STAY
▶ Mid-range
① *Lesvion*
P. Koundourioti 27 A
Mytilini
Tel. 22 51 02 81 77
Fax 22 51 04 24 93
www.lesvion.gr
34 rooms. Well-furnished rooms and a bar with a view of the harbour

Olive Press
Mythimna
Tel. 22 53 07 12 05
www.olivepress-hotel.com
45 rooms. The hotel, a converted olive press works at the edge of town in Mithymna, has a special ambience.

② *Blue Sea*
P. Koudourioti 91
Mytillini
Tel. 22 53 0 2 39 94
Fax 22 53 0 2 96 56
Large comfortable hotel at the ferry pier, with air-conditioning and sound-proofed windows

island is barren, becoming even desert-like around Eresos. Olive oil from Lesbos, the island's main source of income, is of high quality. After Crete Lesbos is the second-largest producer of Greek olive oil. The ouzo distilleries are also famous. **Tourism** has been increasing lately but is still within reasonable limits. The **best beaches** are in the south near Plomari, Agios Isidoros and Vatera. There are also nice beaches in Skala Eresou in the west and in Skala Kalloni. Lesbos was a spiritual and cultural centre in antiquity, the birthplace of **Sappho**, the greatest Greek poetess (►Famous People). **Aristotle** taught in the philosophers' school in Mytilene.

Mytilini (Μυτιλήνη) and Surroundings

Mytilini Town   Since the bustling capital Mytilini has no good beaches nearby, it is ignored by many tourists despite its many attractions. More than one third of the island population (30,000) lives in the town, which makes it the largest in the east Aegean. The town has always had two **harbours**. The north harbour was the major harbour in antiquity but is only used for fishing boats now. The big ferries arrive at the south harbour. The life of the town is concentrated around the south harbour, which is bordered by the Kountourioti promenade. The dome of the western-style **Agios Therapon Church** (1860), stands out among the houses, most of which are low, some colonnaded.

A canal once ran between the south and the ancient north harbour. Today the city's main axis, Odos Ermou with its oriental atmosphere,   **Odos Ermou**

The domes of the Church of Agios Therapon dominate Mytilini

ISLAND OF ANCIENT LYRIC POETRY

Long ago the head of Orpheus was washed up on the coast of Lesvos. This was said to be the reason why the island has produced such excellent poets and musicians – like Sappho, who influenced poetry thereafter and into the modern age.

Orpheus was the greatest musician of all times. With his captivating singing and playing of the lyre he moved plants and animals. He could even touch Hades with his music, but the underworld in the end refused to give back his beloved Eurydice. He met his fate in Thrace, where he was torn to pieces by enraged women. His head and lyre finally washed up on the beach of Lesvos. This is supposedly why the island has produced such excellent poets and singers. Orpheus' head washed up in Antissa on the northern coast of the island. The first great figure in the history of the music of antiquity also came from this town: **Terpandros** (7th century BC), who is considered to be a leading representative of early kitharody (songs accompanied on a kithara, a type of lyre). The invention of the lyre has also been attributed to him.

Saved by dolphins

No works of the poet and singer **Arion**, who was born in Methymna on Lesvos around 600 BC, have been preserved. He became known through the legend that when returning from a trip to Italy the sailors on his ship forced him to jump into the sea. He was given one last wish, namely to be able to play on his lyre and sing one last time. He sang and played beautifully, then jumped overboard and a dolphin that had been entranced by his music carried him to land on its back.

Some works by **Alcaeus** (around 600 BC) have been preserved. The only thing known about the life of this poet from Mytilene is that he fought on the side of the nobility against tyranny and thus was exiled several times. Alcaeus often used the Alcaic stanza, which was named after him

Today Sappho is considered to be one of the major female poets of world literature

(two lines of eleven syllables each, one line of nine syllables and one of ten syllables). The Alcaic stanza was adopted later in Latin verse, in French and English poetry of the Renaissance and by the German poets Friedrich Gottlieb Klopstock and Friedrich Hölderlin.

First female poet

Strabo considered **Sappho** (born around 600 BC) the greatest poetess of all times. A supposedly Platonic epigram calls her the tenth muse. The first known female poet in world literature came from a noble dynasty in Mytilene, was forced to flee to Sicily during political unrest and then returned to Mytilene. She gathered around her a circle of girls, whom she instructed until they were married in the way of life of a noblewoman, music, poetry and dance. Much has been speculated about this circle dedicated to poetry and education, for Sappho had close, passionate relationships with women. The term »Lesbian love« was already known in antiquity, but it has not been proved that Sappho's affection for her girls

was expressed sexually. Feelings, especially those expressed with her companions in their community of music and dance, are the main subject of Sappho's poetry. The language of her poetry is simple and reminiscent of folk songs, but it expresses all nuances of human emotion, especially happiness and the longing for love. Apart from a poem for Aphrodite, only fragments have been preserved: in 1038 the Church burned most of her works.

Sappho permanently influenced the literary world that followed her. Attic comedy made fun of her. A legend also grew up about her unhappy love for a beautiful young man, Phaon, for which she is supposed to have jumped off the Leucadian cliffs. For much of his poetry **Hórace** used the Sapphic metre, which also spread from Greece into Western literature. The effects of Sappho's poetry have thus lasted even into modern times.

Mytilini Map

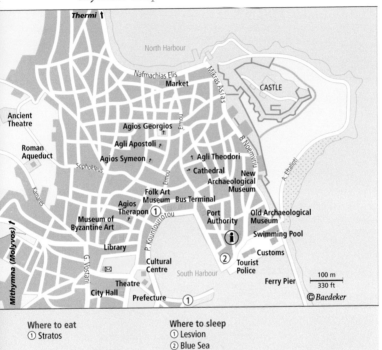

Thermi ↑

North Harbour

Nafmachias Elis
Market

Mikras Asias

CASTLE

Ancient
Theatre

Ermou

Roman
Aqueduct

Agios Georgios ↑

Agli Apostoli ↑

Agios Symeon ↑

↑ Agli Theodori

Sophokleus

↑ Cathedral

8 Noemvriu

A. Eftaliou

New
Archaeological
Museum

Folk Art
Museum Bus Terminal

Kanaris

Ermou

Agios
Therapon ↑

Museum of
Byzantine Art

P. Kountouriotou

Port
Authority

Old Archaeological
Museum

ⓘ

Swimming Pool

Library

G. Vostani

✉

Cultural
Centre

South Harbour

②

Customs

Tourist
Police

Ferry Pier

100 m
330 ft

Theatre

City Hall

Prefecture

Mithymna (Molyvos) ↑

①

© Baedeker

Where to eat
① Stratos

Where to sleep
① Lesvion
② Blue Sea

runs along here. On a quiet side street off Ermou stands the 17th-century **Athanassios Cathedral**. It has a beautifully carved altar and bishop's throne. Further north along Ermou the houses are more run down. This was once the Turkish neighbourhood.

Fortress East of Odos Ermou the ruins of a mighty fortress stand on the hill. It was built in the time of Emperor Justinian (6th century) and re-modelled by the Genoese Francesco I Gattelusi in the 14th century and later again by the Turks. The way to the fortress leads through a pine forest that is popular among picnickers. The large amount of ancient spolia built into the fortress is a reminder that the extensive complex includes the site of the ancient acropolis. Aeolian pottery found here suggests that there was a sanctuary to Demeter here from the 7th to 6th century BC. There are mosques and a Koran school from the Turkish period. Above the side door to the northwest is the double coat of arms of Gattelusi and his Byzantine wife, with a horseshoe and a double eagle and an inscription from 1377. The northern end commands a good view of the ancient north harbour and the remains of its jetty. Opening hours: Tue–Sun 8.30am–3pm.

The **old archaeological museum**, housed in a neo-classical house be-   Museums
hind the ferry terminal, exhibits rare Aeolian capitals and mosaics of
late antiquity from the Menander Villa (3rd–4th century AD). In order to have more room for its large collection, a **new archaeological
museum** was built at Odos Noemvriou 8. Opening hours for both
museums: Tue–Sun 8.30am–3pm. The **Byzantine Museum** behind
the domed Agios Therapon Church possesses an interesting icon collection – the oldest, of St George, dates from the 13th
century. Opening hours: Mon–Sat 9am–1pm. On the harbour, near
the monument to Sappho, a small **folk art museum** has been installed in the harbourmaster's house. The exhibits include traditional
costumes, household articles, pottery, weapons and paintings. Closed
temporarily.

About 5km/3mi south of Mytilini there are two museums worth vis-   Varia
iting in the upper-class suburb of Varia with its well-kept old villas.   (Βαρειά)
The **Theophilos Museum** is devoted to the naive painter Theophilos,
who was born on Lesbos. It was endowed by Stratis Eleftheriadis
(1897–1983) in 1964. Eleftheriadis was born in Mytilini and lived
under the name of Teriade as an art journalist and patron in
Paris. Opening hours: Tue–Sun 10am–4pm. He also provided the
funds for the neighbouring **Teriade Museum**, a collection of paintings by modern artists such as Joan Miró, Henri Matisse, Marc Cha-
gall, Fernand Léger and Pablo Picasso. Currently closed.

The road out of Mytilini follows the coastline to the north. After   Moria
4km/2.5mi is a turnoff for Moria, an impressive wealthy village with   (Μοριά)
several oil presses. In the post-Byzantine Basilica of Agios Vassilios
(1769) the wooden carved iconostasis and the bishop's throne are
worth seeing. The impressive remains of a 3rd-century Roman **aqueduct**, part of a sophisticated system that supplied the capital with
water, can be found some 600m/650yd west of the village.

The East and North of Lesbos

The last stop of the town buses from Mytilini is the resort Thermis a   Thermis
few miles to the north, which consists of four districts. It has a radio-   (Θερμής)
active thermal spring and a few small beaches. Some fortified, partly
dilapidated tower houses from the 16th–19th centuries still stand in
Pyrgi Thermis; they were built for protection against pirate raids.
The **village church Panagia Troulotis** (around 1100) is one of the
few churches from Byzantine times still standing on Lesbos. The
nearby prehistoric settlement of **Thermi** dates back to around 2700
BC. Most finds from the site are in the archaeological museum in
Mytilini.
About 3km/2mi southwest of Thermis is **Agios Rafail Convent**,
which was founded in 1963 and dedicated to St Raphael. The church
interior was painted in Byzantine style.

Mantamados
(Μανταμάδος)

The coast north of Thermis has so far been the preserve of Greek holidaymakers. The mountain village Mantamados, with its stone houses, cheese factory and pottery workshops, is interesting. About 1km/0.5mi to the north, an icon of the Archangel Michael in the **Taxiarchon Church** is considered to be miraculous. The icon is said to have been made in 1850 out of clay and the blood of a monk who was killed by pirates.

Sykaminia
(Σακαμινιά)

The mountain village Sykaminia with its steep lanes and old stone houses is the birthplace of the contemporary author **Stratis Myrivilis**. The Panagia Gorgona Chapel, which stands on the harbour of the attractive fishing town of Skala Sykaminias, plays a major role in his novel *The Mermaid Madonna*. Near the village, which has pretty tavernas along the harbour, there are several small pebble beaches. A path along the coast can be followed for a hike via Eftalou to thermal springs in Molyvos.

✱
Molyvos/
Mithymna
(Μόληβος/
Μήθυμνα)

The holiday centre of the island, Molyvos (officially Mithymna), has a delightful setting on the north coast. The tourist infrastructure here was developed back in the 1960s. The old harbour town lies on a slope beneath a mighty castle built by Gattelusi in 1373. The town is protected as a heritage site, and the house fronts facing the sea were once the city wall. While the romantic appearance of Molyvos is the main attraction, there is also an **archaeological collection** in the neo-classical town hall with historic photos of the town and a **gallery** which shows revolving exhibitions of works by Greek artists. Most of the beaches are small and pebbly, but there is a long **beach at Eftalou** (4km/2.5mi east of Molyvos).

Petra
(Πέτρά)

The village of Petra 7km/4mi to the south with its small harbour was only discovered by tourists 15 years ago. It was made popular by a women's cooperative that made headlines by letting rooms, and still lets accommodation today. In the middle of the village on a 27m/90ft-high rock (114 steps) that gave the city its name »petra« means »rock« stands the **Church of Panagia tis Glykofilousas** (»sweetly kissing mother of God«). It was built in 1747 and has a beautiful carved wooden iconostasis. At the foot of the rock is the 15th-century Church of Agios Nikolaos with interesting frescoes. The **Archontiko Vareltzidena**, a 17th-century mansion with wonderful ceiling paintings, is a beautiful example of Macedonian building with a protruding upper storey and unusual for Lesbos. Opening hours: Tue–Sun 8.30am–3pm. There is a long, well-kept beach right by the village with grey fine-grained sand.

Skala Kalloni
(Σκάλα
Καλλονή)

Drive south from Petra via the provincial town of **Kalloni**, the region's business district, to get to the fishing harbour of Skala Kalloni.

The small port of Mithymna is the most popular holiday resort on Lesbos →

It is popular as a holiday resort because of its long, gently sloping sandy beach. More and more bird-watchers are coming to watch the local wildlife.

✳
Limonos Monastery

Limonos Monastery, founded in 1523 and dedicated to the Archangel Michael, is the **largest and most important monastery on the island**. Under Turkish rule it ran an illegal school for the Greek language and thus helped preserve Greek culture. The monks are still active in social work and teaching. The monastery's main church is open only to men; women may walk around the outer monastery ring. It has a richly carved iconostasis and is decorated throughout with frescoes. A museum in new premises has icons, robes and liturgical items, and a library with valuable ancient books.

West of Lesbos

Antissa
(Αντισσα)

From Kalloni a winding road runs westwards into an increasingly barren volcanic landscape and up to Eresos. Drive via Filia and Skalohori to **Vatousa**, a mountain village that has managed to keep its original appearance. 5km/3mi beyond Vatousa on the right the abandoned **Convent of Perivoli** has 17th-century frescoes. Since the valley of the Voulgari River is almost completely dried out in the summer, it is possible to hike through it to the sparse remains of ancient Antissa. A road also runs the 8km/5mi away to the excavation site on the sea. The acropolis was protected by a double encircling wall. The village of Andissa has a beautiful square, where tavernas and cafes under plane trees make for a relaxed break.

To the west on the road to Sigri, on a steep promontory of Mt Ordymnos, lies the 9th-century **Ypsilou Monastery**. 12th-century manuscripts and liturgical vestments are on display in the monastery museum. There is a also magnificent view. The remote fishing and holiday village of **Sigri** on the west coast has a beautiful beach 3km/2mi to the north. The rugged and inhospitable area between Sigri, Antissa and Eresos is known for a **petrified forest**, tree trunks

Petrified tree trunk at least 1 million years old

that were buried under volcanic ash and petrified there. The trees are estimated to be 1–10 million years old. The standing or lying trunks are up to 12m/40ft long and have a diameter up to 1m/3ft. A museum of natural history in Sigri illustrates and explains this natural phenomenon. The access road to the petrified forest (Apolithomeno Dasos) is 5km/3mi west of Ypsilou monastery.

Baedeker TIP

Paradise for ornithologists

Some 280 species of bird nest on Lesbos or use the island as a stopping-off place on their long journeys between northern and southern climes. Good bird-watching areas are at Eresos, Petra, Skala Kallonis and Agiasos.

Continue 12km/7mi to the village of Eresos and beyond it the little holiday resort of Skala Eresou, where pretty tavernas await guests at the beach. This was the site of ancient Eresos, where the poet **Sappho** was probably born. The village's main attraction is its very beautiful long sandy beach. Right behind the new Church of St Andreas are the ruins of a **5th-century Christian basilica**. Next to it is a small museum with local finds such as coins with the head of Sappho.

Skala Eresou

The South of Lesbos

The forested south of the island between the gulfs of Gera and Kalloni has beautiful landscape. The main towns are the romantic mountain village of Agiasos, with its tiled-roof stone houses and narrow cobblestone streets, on the northern slope of Mt Olympus and the friendly coastal town of Plomari. In the centre of Agiasos is the most important pilgrimage site on Lesbos, the **Church of Kimisis tis Theotokou**. It was built in 1170 and remodelled in 1816. Thousands of pilgrims come on 15 August to see an icon of the Virgin Mary, which is supposed to have been painted by Luke the Evangelist, like several others in Greece. The church museum displays icons – including one painted on the head of a fish – and a collection of folk art. Pottery and woodcarving are still alive in Agiasos. A climb up Mt Olympus, which should take about five hours there and back from Agiasos (red-blue trail markings) is worth the effort. The hike goes through chestnut and beech forests to the 968m/3,176ft peak, from where there is a wonderful view. The peak can also be reached by car.

Agiasos
(Αγιασος)

◄ Olympus

Past the Tsingou springs, whose water is bottled as mineral water, drive on to the **hottest thermal springs in Europe** (91°C/196°F) at Polyhnitos. The island's largest spa facilities are under construction with subsidies from the EU. Presently there are two bath houses from the Ottoman period. About 4km/2.5mi to the north is **Skala Polichnitou**, a port where many birds, sometimes even flamingos can be seen in the salt flats. 5km/3mi to the south of Polyhnitos, in the village of **Vryssa**, the Church of Zoödóhou Pigis (1803) possesses a very interesting carved wooden iconostasis. The tour ends at the

Polyhnitos
(Πολιχνίτος)

★
Vatera (Βατερά) ►

sand and pebble beach of Vatera, almost 10km/6mi long and the **most beautiful beach on the island**. Numerous hotels, guest houses and tavernas have sprung up here in recent years.

Agios Isidoros, Plomari

From Mytilini follow the coastline of the Gulf of Yera to Plomari on the southern coast. The drive goes past Kato Tritos with its Byzantine Taxiarch Church and Mesagros with remains of a mosque. Further on the little holiday resort Agios Isidoros has almost merged with Plomari, 3km/2mi to the west. Both places are popular among Scandinavian tourists. Plomari has kept its original appearance, despite being overrun, and is known for its ouzo distilleries. The Barbagiannis distillery on the eastern edge of town was founded in 1860 and is open for tours. The tile-roofed houses of the town, which was founded in 1845, were built in a narrow valley that ascends a foothill of Olympus. An old soap factory that was converted into a **cultural centre** has displays on local history and soap-making.

> ! *Baedeker* TIP
>
> **Olive groves**
> Old trails that lead through olive groves are being restored at Plomari; they lead through beautiful vegetation, past springs and streams. The trails are between 1 km and 6km (about 0.5–3.5 miles) long and should be walked in the spring. Maps are available in Plomari and the surrounding villages.

Limnos

Greek: Λήμνος	**Island group:** North Aegean islands
Area: 476 sq km/183 sq mi	**Elevation:** 0–470m/1,542ft above sea
Population: 18,000	level
Capital: Myrina	

The landscape of Limnos is characterized by a craggy coastline and a gently undulating, fertile, hilly interior. Although the island boasts outstanding beaches, it has so far been spared from mass tourism.

★
Island with beautiful beaches

Limnos is agricultural; grain, cotton and wine, especially sweet moschatos, a muscatel wine, are the main products. Because of its strategic location on the Dardanelles, Limnos has a large naval and air base and much of the island is a restricted military area.

What to See on Limnos

★
Myrina (Μύρινα)

The main town is Myrina (population 5,100) on the west coast. This lively, pleasant town with its neo-classical buildings and half-timbered houses is dominated by a rock bluff with a massive castle, built around 1185 by Andronikos I and expanded by the Genoese in the

▶ VISITING LIMNOS

INFORMATION

Tourist information
Myrina town hall
www.lemnos.info

GETTING THERE

Ferries to Kavala, Piraeus, Thessaloniki and Volos on the mainland, and the islands of Agios, Efstratios, Chíos, Kos, Lesbos, Rhodes, Samos, Samothraki, Skiathos and Skopelos

WHERE TO EAT

▶ Inexpensive
O Platanos
Myrina

Tel. 2 25 40 2 20 70
Good, plain Greek food in a taverna shaded by spreading plane trees

WHERE TO STAY

▶ Mid-range
Poseidon
Myrina
Tel. 2 25 40 2 39 82
Fax 2 25 40 2 48 56
www.poseidonlemnos.gr, 20 rooms.
The spacious rooms of the Poseidon Hotel, which is located 200m/660ft from the beach, have a bathroom and a balcony.

15th century. From the top there is a beautiful view of the harbour in the bay to the south. In the bay north of the castle rock is a long but not especially attractive sandy beach. Here the **archaeological museum** displays finds from Poliohni, Hephaistia and the Kabeiroi sanctuary of Chloe. Opening hours: Tue–Sun 9am–3pm. Sections of ☉ coast that are suitable for a holiday with **sandy beaches** can be found around Kaspakas, to the south near Platy and further to the east near Thanos.

In Poliohni on the east coast archaeologists have unearthed the impressive remains of city and house walls and a gateway with ramp from a prehistoric settlement. The finds from four levels go back to the 3rd–4th millennia BC. The gold jewellery found there is in the National Archaeological Museum in Athens. The drive to **Agios Sozon Monastery** in the southern part of the peninsula and the picturesque **village of Skandali** is worthwhile. In the northeast of the island, on the Gulf of Pournia near Kontopouli, is the **necropolis of Hephaistia** (8th–6th century BC). At the **Cabiric shrine** on the other side of the bay are the ruins of two cult buildings from the 6th and 5th–4th centuries BC and a Hellenistic shrine with Doric columns where mystery rites took place.

Poliohni

Agios Efstratios, about 30km/20mi south of Limnos, has an area of 43 sq km/17 sq mi and an elevation of 303m/1,000ft above sea level. The origins of the rocky island are volcanic. Its beautiful, deserted beaches make it ideal for holidaymakers who want to get away from

**Agios
Efstratios
(Άγιος
Ευστράτιος)**

it all. A harbour town of the same name, which was practically destroyed during an earthquake in 1968, lies on a bay on the west coast. Above the town are a castle and some windmills. There are ferries to Limnos and also to Chíos, Lesbos, Patmos and Samos, among other places.

✳ Mílos

L/M 11

Greek: Μήλος
Area: 151 sq km/58 sq mi
Population: 4,700
Capital: Pláka

Island group: Cyclades
Elevation: 0–751m/2,464ft above sea level

The island of Mílos with its varied and picturesque scenery is one of the beauties of Greece – as is the world-famous *Venus de Milo*, which was discovered here.

✳
Island of Venus de Milo

Mílos is the original home of the famous **Venus de Milo**, which is now in the Louvre in Paris (▶ Baedeker Special p.58). Sulphurous thermal springs testify to the volcanic origins of the island, which are also the reason for its varied and lovely landscape with bizarre rock formations, and its main economic base. Mílos is open to the sea

▶ VISITING MILOS

INFORMATION
Tourist information
Ferry landing Adamas
Tel. 2 28 70 2 24 45
www.milos.gr

GETTING THERE
Boats to Piraeus on the mainland as well as to the islands of Folégandros, Halki, Íos, Kárpathos, Crete, Kýthnos, Páros, Rhodes, Santorinii, Sérifos, Sífnos, Síkinos and Sýros

WHERE TO EAT
▶ Moderate
Trapatselis
Coast road in Adamas
Tel. 2 28 70 2 20 10
Delicious fish and meat dishes are served here.

▶ Inexpensive
Varco
Adamas
Tel. 2 28 70 2 26 60
Nice eatery on the northern edge of town with Greek cooking and a beautiful terrace.

WHERE TO STAY
▶ Mid-range
Portiani
Adamas
Tel. 2 28 70 2 29 40
www.hotelportiani.gr
23 rooms. Hotel on the harbour bay with a magnificent view from the large roof terrace

Mílos *Map*

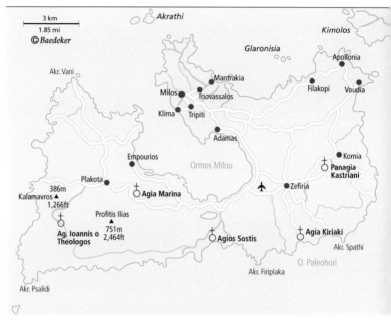

3 km
1.85 mi
© Baedeker

Akrathi

Kimolos

Glaronisia

Apollonia

Akr. Vani

Mantrakia

Filakopi   Voudia

Mílos
Triovassalos

Klima   Tripiti

Adamas

Empourios

Ormos Milou

Komia

† Ò Panagia
Kastriani

Plakota

386m
Kalamavros ▲
1,266ft

† Ò Agia Marina

Zefiria

Profitis Ilias
▲
751m
Ag. Ioannis o   2,464ft
Theologos

† Ò Agios Sostis

† Ò Agia Kiriaki

Akr. Spathi

O. Paleohori

Akr. Firiplaka

Akr. Psalidi

through an inlet in the north which **forms one of the best harbours in the Mediterranean**. The northeastern half of the island is flatter and more fertile than the mountainous southwest. The economy is based on rich mineral deposits, including pearlite, bentonite, kaolin and barite. Tourism is limited. The most beautiful beaches are on the south coast.

What to See on Mílos

The centre of tourism is the port of Adamas on the bay where ferries stop and the hotels, restaurants and travel agents are located. The centre of activity is the quay with its many tavernas. In the upper part of the town, which stretches up the hillsides, is a **church dedicated to the Kimisis (Dormition of Mary) and St Charalambos** with valuable icons. Its forecourt is decorated with a pebble mosaic depicting eagles flying to the east. In the courtyard of the **Church of Agia Triada**, which was built in the 11th century and remodelled in the 17th century, there is also a mosaic; it was created in 1937 by the Mílos artist Jagos Kavroudakis and depicts allegorical figures.

Adamas
(Αδάμας)

The capital Pláka (population 900) is 7km/4mi to the northwest. The 19th-century **Church of Panagia Korfiatissa** is notable for its gilded

Pláka (Πλάκα)

iconostasis, Creto-Byzantine paintings and a carved epitaph (*c* 1600). Along with a small folk art museum there is an **archaeological museum** with obsidian tools, Cycladic idols and a copy of the Venus de Milo. Opening times: Tue–Sun 8.30am–3pm. En route to the sparse remains of the 13th-century Venetian kastro (elevation 280m/918ft) is the Church of Panagia Thalassitra; on the peak is the Chapel of Messa Panagia with an icon of the Virgin.

Catacombs, Mílos

About 1km/0.5mi below Pláka, near Tripiti, the 3rd-century catacombs are signposted. This site, unique in Greece, has the grave of a saint in the middle of the main room and about 2,000 burial niches in all. Near the catacombs are the remains of the **Dorian city of Mílos** from the 1st millennium BC. A sign marks the **place where the Venus de Milo was found** (left). Part of the city wall and the tower are extant. Nearby in a beautiful location above the bay a few rows of marble seats remain from the Roman theatre that was built into the slope. To get to the shore follow the path that leads down to **Klima**. The ground floors of the two-storey houses here serve as boat houses. Opening hours for the catacombs and theatre: Tue–Sun 8.30am–3pm.

Filakopi
(Φυλακοπή)

Northeast of Tripiti lies the old settlement of Filakopi, just above the cliffs of the north coast. Settlements from the 3rd and 2nd millennia

The ground floors of homes in Klima serve as boathouses

BC and Mycenaean walls (around 1500 BC) were excavated here. Opening hours: Tue–Sun 8.30am–3pm.

The pretty port of **Pollonia** 2km/1mi to the northeast has a shaded sandy beach. Boats leave here for the »Seagull Islands« (Glaronisia), four bizarrely-shaped outcrops of basalt with the Sykia grottoes.

! **Baedeker TIP**

Around the island

A trip around the island is especially worthwhile on Mílos. The geological variety and the various colours of the beaches can be seen best from the water. The trip also gives a close-up look at the columnar basalt formations of the Glaronisia Islands.

The pretty bay of Paleohori on the southeast coast has warm sulphurous springs. There are good beaches on the middle section of the south coast and around the large Bay of Mílos, where the long beach shaded by tamarisks **Chivadolimni** is especially suited for families with small children because of its gentle slope. A nice boat excursion takes in the **Kleftiko** cliffs on the southwest tip of the island, where there are also small sandy beaches.

Paleohori

Kimolos (Κίμολος)

Kimolos (population 700) can best be visited on a day trip from nearby Mílos. The island is ideal for holidaymakers who are looking for rest and who want to experience authentic Greek village life. There are also some sand and pebble beaches for swimming. Kimolos, a flat volcanic island with little water, was already known in antiquity for its Kimolian earth. This mineral was used for washing and for spa baths and is still mined near Prassa today.

Milos' little sister

Ships dock at the small port of **Psathi** in the southeast. There is also a beach here. 1km/0.5mi from Psathi is the main town, **Kimolos Hóra**. The houses of the kastro formed a defensive ring and have no windows on the outward side. The main church, Panagia Odigitria (1873) at the edge of town, the Chrysostomos Church (17th century) with paintings by Skordilis and the Church of Christ (1592) in the kastro are all worth seeing. **Aliki Beach** is the most popular on Kimolos; it is a sand and pebble beach on the southern coast.

Sights

✳ Folégandros (Φολέγανδρος)

Elongated Folégandros (population 670; 13km/8mi long, 4km/2.5mi wide) is a Cycladic island straight out of a coffee-table book, with charming landscape and an idyllic town. The eastern part reaches an elevation of 415m/1,362ft and has cliffs along the coast; it is barren and dry. The milder western part has springs and modest terraced agriculture. Its main products are wine, vegetables, fruits and livestock.

Picture-postcard Cycladic island

Folégandros Hóra

✳ The capital Folégandros Hóra, **one of the most beautiful locations in the Cyclades**, is 4km/2.5mi from the ferry pier at Karavostasis in the east. The village with a population of 260 lies at an elevation of 200m/650ft on a cliff above the sea. The old quarter **Kastro** at the entrance to the village was built in 1212 by Duke Marco Sanudo. The narrow lanes with light-coloured mortar between the paving stones and whitewashed steps, which lead to the upper storeys and are often decorated with flowers, make a picturesque setting. It is worth visiting the Church of Eleoussa (1530) and the Church of Pantassa (1711) with its magnificent woodcarvings and icons of the Cretan school. The two newer districts of Folégandros, each has a tree-shaded plateia, are very pretty. A serpentine path leads up to the white **Church of the Panagia**, the island's emblem – a domed 19th-century church with a free-standing bell tower.

Ano Meria (Avo Μεριά)

5km/3mi northwest of Hóra is the largest village, Ano Meria, which is very rural. An old farmhouse in its eastern part is home to a small **folk art museum**.

The Panagia Church outside Hóra is the symbol of Folégandros

All beaches on the island – except for Angali – can be reached only **Beaches** on foot or by boat. **Angali**, which is framed by rocks and probably the most beautiful beach on Folégandros, lies on the narrowest part of the island. **Agios Nikolaos beach** to the north can be reached on foot in about 20 minutes. Behind the pebble beach tamarisk trees offer shade for the visitors.

★ ★ Mýkonos

Greek: Μύκονος
Area: 85 sq km/33 sq mi
Population: 9,300
Capital: Mýkonos Hóra

Island group: Cyclades
Elevation: 0–372m/1,220ft above sea level

The barren Cycladic island of Mýkonos, with its beaches of fine-grained sand, is *the* holiday island in Greece and is »open 24/7« during high season. Its visitors come here to spend the days and nights of their holiday partying on the beach and the dance floors of the clubs.

With Mýkonos, it is either/or: either you are looking for a party at **High-life island** the beach and in dance clubs – or you avoid the island. It is the **most popular holiday destination in the Aegean** and one of the most expensive in Greece. It is impossible to get lodgings between June and September without reserving long in advance. The barren island has little to offer in the way of scenery besides beautiful beaches. Among the cultural attractions are several small museums and, above all, the nearby island of Délos, to which boat trips run daily. The hallmarks of the attractive traditional architecture are white houses, contrasting blue and red windows and roads natural stone with white mortar.

★ ★ Mýkonos Town

The picturesque main town, Mýkonos Hóra (population 4,500), embraces a small bay with its whitewashed, cubic houses and many churches. The **best view** and the place to see a wonderful sunset is Boni windmill. Countless visitors push their way through the narrow streets, but this should not be a deterrent from visiting this beautiful place. In the evening all of Hóra is a bustle of shops, cafes and tavernas.

The major attraction in Kastro, the oldest still occupied part of **Kastro** Mýkonos, is the Church of **Panagia Paraportiani** (»near the gate«), whose name refers to its location between the sea and the gates of a former castle. It is actually a complex of four churches built between the early 16th and 17th centuries. The play of light and shade on the

⊙ VISITING MYKONOS

INFORMATION
Tourist police
Harbour
Tel. 2 28 90 2 24 82
www.mykonosgreece.com

GETTING THERE

Boat services to and from Kavala, Piraeus and Rafina on the mainland and the islands of Ándros, Chíos, Fourni, Ikaría, Kos, Lesbos, Limnos, Lipsi, Patmos, Rhodes, Samos, Sýros and Tinos. Daily excursions to the »island of Apollo«, Délos.

WHERE TO EAT

▶ **Expensive**
① *Philippi*
Kalogera Mýkonos Hóra
Tel. 2 28 90 2 22 94
High-class ambience and excellent Greek and international cuisine; very pretty garden.

▶ **Inexpensive**
② *Antonini's*
Plateia Manto
Mýkonos-Hóra
Tel. 2 28 90 2 23 19

This place serves excellent Greek cuisine.

WHERE TO STAY

▶ **Luxury**
Kivotos Clubhotel
Ornos
Tel. 2 28 90 2 40 94
Fax 2 28 90 2 28 44
www.kivotosclubhotel.gr
30 rooms, 10 suites. Member of »The Leading Small Luxury Hotels of the World« and »Small Luxury Hotels of the World«; this hotel on Ornos Beach has individually furnished rooms with many facilities such as a gym and spa area as well as swimming pools.

▶ **Mid-range**
① *Zorzis*
N. Kalogera
Mýkonos Hóra
Tel. 2 28 90 2 21 67
Fax 2 28 90 2 41 69
www.zorzis.com
10 rooms. In a historic house in the town centre with nicely furnished rooms

complex surfaces of the building delights the eye, not just for photographers.

★

Venetia, Alefkandra

Adjoining to the south is the Venetian quarter, whose picturesque front lies directly on the water. The houses were built from the mid-18th century by merchants and sea captains right on the rocky shore and have doors to the sea. The sea captains were presumably involved in piracy and could hide their booty easily by this means. **The-otokos Pigadiotissa Cathedral** and the **Catholic church** with the coat of arms of the Venetian Ghisi family above the door are in the Alefkandra quarter. To the southwest the symbol of Mýkonos can be seen: the defunct windmill on **Kato Myli**, the »lower mill mountain«.

Mykonos Hora Map

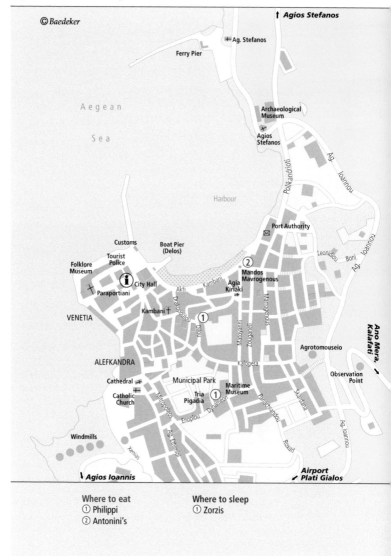

© Baedeker

Agios Stefanos

Ag. Stefanos

Ferry Pier

Aegean

Sea

Archaeological
Museum

Agios
Stefanos

Harbour

Polikandrioti

Ag. Ioannou

Port Authority

Leonidou Boni

Ag. Ioannou

Customs

Boat Pier
(Delos)

Tourist
Police

Folklore
Museum

②

Mandos
Mavrogenous

City Hall

Akti Kambani Agia
Kiriaki

Paraportiani

Mavrogenous

Drakopoulou

Kambani †

①

VENETIA

Pilou

Matoyianni

Zouganeli

Ano Mera,
Kalafati

Agrotomouseio

ALEFKANDRA

Kalogera

Observation
Point

Cathedral

Municipal Park

Maritime
Museum

Tria
Pigadia

①

Catholic
Church

Mitropoleos

Enoplou

Dynameon

Panachrantou

Skarpa

Ag. Efthimiou

Roxari

Ag. Ioannou

Windmills

Xenas

Agios Ioannis

Airport
Plati Gialos

Where to eat
① Philippi
② Antonini's

Where to sleep
① Zorzis

The archaeological museum, housed in a neo-classical house near to
the ferry terminal, shows significant artefacts found on Délos, Rinia
and Mílos. The centrepiece of the collection is a **neck amphora**

**Archaeological
museum**

Mýkonos Hóra is one of the prettiest towns in the Cyclades

🕐 (around 670 BC) with the first known depiction of the Trojan horse. Opening hours: Tue–Sun 8.30am–3pm.

Folk Art Museum

🕐 In the Kastro quarter the Mýkonos Folk Art Museum in an 18th-century captain's house displays everyday articles. Visitors are greeted by a stuffed pelican, Petros I, who lived in the harbour as a kind of living trademark for over 30 years. He died in 1985 and has been succeeded by other birds – to the pleasure of the visitors. Opening hours: Apr–Oct Mon–Sat 4.30–8.30pm, closed winters.

Maritime Museum

🕐 Near the Tria Pigádia, the »three fountains«, which provided water until 1956, the Aegean Maritime Museum occupies a former captain's house. It displays old model ships, maps and nautical instruments. The light of an old lighthouse has been set in the quiet garden. Next door **Lena's House** is a 19th century middle-class house with original furnishings, now a museum. Opening hours for both museums: daily 10.30am–1pm, 6.30pm–9pm.

Other Sights on the Island

Ano Mera (Άνο Μέρα)

In Ano Mera (8km/5mi east of Mýkonos Town) below the plateia is the fortress-like **Panagia Tourliani Monastery**. In its present form

Mykonos Map

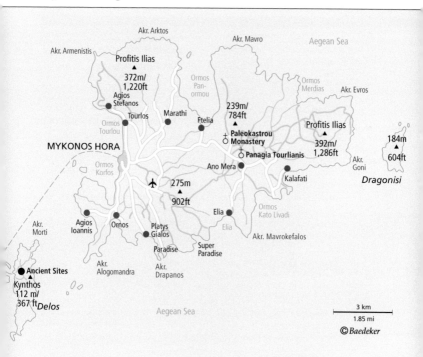

this monastery, founded in 1542 by monks from Katapoliani Monastery on Páros, dates back to 1767. Note the marble reliefs on the bell tower and the magnificently carved bishop's throne in the church.

The coast of Mýkonos has a variety of small and large bays. The nicest sections are in the south, where there are many wind-sheltered sandy beaches. Only 4km/2.5mi south of Mýkonos Town (regular buses), the gently sloping sandy beach **Platys Gialos** is ideal for families with children. From here either walk or take a kaiki (boat) to the equally family-friendly sandy beach at **Psarou**. The quieter alternative is **Agia Anna**, which is a 15-minute walk from Platys Gialos. **Paraga Beach** is a 20-minute walk from Platys Gialos along the beach or the road. A young crowd have taken over the wonderfully long and over-run beaches named **Paradise** and **Super-Paradise**; the noise level with music from all sides is as might be expected. **Elia**, with regular buses, is also an excellent beach.

★
Beaches

✳ Naxos

Greek: Νάξος
Area: 448 sq km/173 sq mi
Population: 18,000
Capital: Naxos Hora

Island group: Cyclades
Elevation: 0–1,001m/3,284ft above sea level

Naxos, the largest and most scenic of the Cyclades, is gaining in popularity as a holiday destination because of its beautiful beaches and outstanding places to surf.

Largest Cyclades island

Naxos is crossed from north to south by a range of mountains that reach an elevation of 1,001m/3,284ft. They fall off sharply to the east, and in the west slope down into gentle, fertile hill country and plains with an abundance of water. Besides growing wine on terraces, the island agriculture – an important economic factor – produces wine, citrus fruits, potatoes, vegetables, grain and fruit. Quarrying marble and emery has been a source of economic prosperity since antiquity.

Naxos Hora

✳ Town

Some distinctive scenes are immediately evident on arrival in the harbour of Naxos Hora (population 5,000): the little Myrtidiotissa Church on an islet and the Venetian kastro overlooking the town, which picturesquely spreads up the slopes of a cone-shaped rock. Numerous tavernas and cafes line the bustling harbour. Standing on an offshore peninsula is the famous 6m/20ft marble gate. It is part of a Temple of Apollo that was started in the 6th century but never finished. According to legend, Ariadne's palace stood there.

✳ Marble gate ▶

✳ Kastro

The Venetian kastro, which was built in 1207, stands at the highest point. The Trani Porta opens into a quarter of the town that seems like a museum. Roman Catholic aristocratic families lived here in houses decorated with coats of arms. In the 13th-century Cathedral of St Mary note the icon of the Virgin Mary at the main altar and the grave slabs with coats of arms. The **archaeological museum** is housed in a former Jesuit school behind the cathedral. Its impressive exhibits make it the most significant collection on Cycladic culture outside the National Museum in Athens. *Europa and the Bull*, a mosaic dating from late antiquity, can be seen on the terrace. West of the Orthodox cathedral the modern **Mitropolis Museum** is devoted to a Mycenaean settlement (14th–13th century BC); the area was used as a cemetery between 900 and 700 BC. In the **Museum Domus della Rocca-Barozzi**, at the north gate of the quarter, pictures, furniture, dishes and clothing give insights into the history of a noble

Marble gate: the symbol of Naxos →

family. Opening hours: daily 10am–3pm, end of May to mid-Sept 5pm–10pm.

Burgos The narrow lanes of the Burgos quarter extend behind the harbour; the colourful market street is especially pretty. While Orthodox Greeks lived in the Burgos, the neighbouring **Evraiki quarter** was inhabited by Jews.

Naxos *Map*

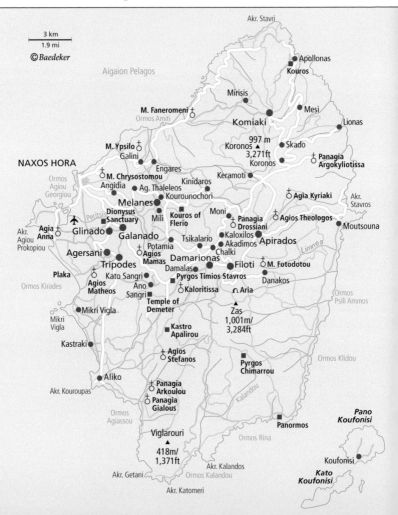

Akr. Stavri

3 km
1.9 mi
©Baedeker

Aigaion Pelagos

Apollonas
Kouros

Mirisis

Mesi

Lionas

M. Faneromeni
Ormos Amiti

Komiaki

Skado

M. Ypsilo
Galini

997 m
3,271ft
Koronos

Koronos

Panagia
Argokyliotissa

NAXOS HORA

Engares

Kinidaros

Keramoti

Ormos
Agiou
Georgiou

M. Chrysostomou

Ag. Thaleleos

Kourounochori

Agia Kyriaki

Akr.
Stavros

Angidia

Melanes

Moni

Mili

Kouros of
Flerio

Panagia
Drossiani

Agios Theologos

Moutsouna

Dionysus
Sanctuary

Agia
Agiou
Prokopiou

Glinado

Galanado

Tsikalario

Kaloxilos
Akadimos

Apirados

Akr.

Anna

Agersani

Potamia

Chalki

Limnes

Tripodes

Agios
Mamas

Damarionas

Filoti

M. Fotodotou

Plaka

Kato Sangri

Damalas

Danakos

Ormos Kirades

Agios
Matheos

Ano
Sangri

Pyrgos Timios Stavros

Kaloritissa

Aria

Ormos
Psili Ammos

Temple of
Demeter

Zas
1,001m/
3,284ft

Mikri Vigla

Mikri
Vigla

Kastro
Apalirou

Ormos Klidou

Kastraki

Agios
Stefanos

Pyrgos
Chimarrou

Aliko

Akr. Kouroupas

Panagia
Arkoulou

Panagia
Gialous

Ormos
Agiassou

Pano
Koufonisi

Viglarouri

418m/
1,371ft

Panormos

Ormos Rina

Koufonisi

Kato
Koufonisi

Akr. Getani

Ormos Kalandou

Akr. Kalandos

Akr. Katomeri

▶ VISITING NAXOS

INFORMATION

Tourist information
Naxos Hora
At the quay
Tel. 2 28 50 2 52 01, fax 2 28 50 2 52 00
www.naxosbest.com

HOW TO GET THERE

Boat services to and from Piraeus on the mainland and the islands of Amorgos, Anafi, Astypalea, Donoúsa, Folegandros, Fourni, Ikaria, Iraklia, Ios, Kalymnos, Kos, Koufonisia, Nisyros, Paros, Rhodes, Samos, Santorini, Sikinos, Symi, Syros, Tilos

WHERE TO EAT

▶ Expensive
Oneiro
Naxos Hora
Tel. 2 28 50 2 38 46
The best place to enjoy fine international cuisine here is the roof terrace.

▶ Moderate
Lucullus
Naxos Hora, tel. 2 28 50 2 25 69
Oldest taverna on Naxos, small and cosy

▶ Inexpensive
Manolis
Naxos Hora

Tel. 2 28 50 2 51 68
Tasty Greek cooking in a garden taverna

WHERE TO STAY

▶ Luxury
Kavuras Village
Agios Prokopios
Tel. 2 28 50 2 37 05
www.kavurasvillage.gr
111 rooms, 15 villas, 4 suites. The rooms are all in chalets; the hotel has a large swimming pool and a paddling pool.

▶ Mid-range
Anixis
Naxos Hora
Tel. 2 28 50 2 29 32
www.hotel-anixis.gr
18 rooms. This friendly hotel has nice rooms and a roof terrace with a fantastic view.

▶ Budget
Iria Beach
Agia Anna
Tel. 2 28 50 4 26 00
www.iriabeach-naxos.com
30 apartments. Lovely holiday resort, suitable for families with children, on the magnificent sandy beach of Agia Anna

There are good places to swim and beaches almost everywhere on Naxos, but the prettiest by far lie on the west coast, south of Naxos Hora, reaching down 16km/10mi to the village of Pyrgaki. From Naxos a coastal road runs to Plaka beach. The other beaches can be reached by side roads branching off from the main road heading inland. The stretches of beach close to town – **Agios Georgios**, **Agios Prokopios** and **Agia Anna** – have facilities for water sports, but are quite crowded. Those further south from Plaka are considerably quieter.

★
Beaches

Around Naxos Hora The 17th-century, blindingly white, fortress-like **Ioannis Chrysostomos Monastery** (not open to the public) is located 3km/2mi northeast of Naxos Hora. The **Faneromeni Monastery**, 10km/6mi to the northeast, was built in 1603. In the **marble quarry of Flerio**, 8km/5mi east of Naxos Hora and 2km/1mi east of Kourounochori – today an orchard with a kafenion – lies a famous incomplete **kouros** from the 6th century BC. Near the village of Yra (4km/2.5mi south of Naxos Hora) archaeologists have excavated the remains of an 8th-century BC **Temple of Dionysos**; some of its columns remain.

i **Culinary Naxos**

■ Along with wine Naxos has numerous culinary specialities: olives and olive oil, a lemon cordial called kitro which is distilled from fresh leaves of the citron lemon, as well as Naxian »marmalade«, various kinds of fruit in syrup. The three kinds of cheese produced on the island are also excellent: anthotiro, misithra and kephalotiri.

From Naxos Hora to Apollonas

Varied landscape The 50km/30mi drive across the Tragea Plateau to Apollonas in the north of the island provides a good picture of the island's varied landscape. A large number of ancient sanctuaries, Byzantine churches, Venetian fortresses and pyrgi, fortified tower houses, can be seen along the way. The drive back to Naxos Hora runs along the northwest coast (35km/21mi) with breathtaking views and side roads to beautiful swimming coves. From Naxos Hora drive 5km/3mi southeast through the town of Galanado on to **Pyrgos Belonis**, which once belonged to the island's Roman Catholic bishops.

The road then runs uphill in serpentines. A signposted road leads to a carefully reconstructed **Temple of Demeter** (6th century BC) with what is probably the oldest Ionic Greek temple. The little museum adjacent has a model of the temple. Opening hours: Tue–Sun 8.30am–3pm. On the main road in **Halki** (16km/10mi), the geographical and commercial centre of the plain, the Church of Panagia Protothroni, which dates from the 10th century and has beautiful frescoes, and the fortified Pyrgos Grazia of the Barozzi family with coats of arms are worth visiting. Off the route, 4km/2.5mi to the north at Moni, is the island's oldest church, Panagia Drossiani, dating from the 6th century. Some of the frescoes were painted at the time of its construction.

Filoti (Φιλότι) The main road then leads to Filoti (20km/12mi), which has a stunning location with Mt Zas as a backdrop. It pays to stop here and climb the white steps. They lead to the **Church of Panagia Filotitossa** with its old icons and a marble iconostasis as well as the Barozzi tower (1718).

From Agia Marina it is only a 90-minute hike to the peak of Mt Zas (1,001m/3,284ft); it was named after Zeus, the father of the gods. The reward for the climb is a fantastic view from the top.

Beyond the mountain ridge is **Apirathos**. The geological, archaeological and folk art museums, as well as a natural history museum on the marble-paved main road give an account of the island's history, both natural and cultural. From the road to Korónos there is an excellent view of the mountain ridge. **Korónos** (34km/21mi), impressively sited on terraces amidst vineyards, is the centre of marble quarrying and emery mining.

The tour ends at the restful holiday resort Apollonas (49km/30mi), which sprawls along a pretty bay with a little pebble beach. There are ancient marble quarries above the town – Naxian marble was used for sculptures, architecture and roof tiles. In the Ston Apollona quarry there is a large unfinished **kouros** (6th century BC).

Starkly beautiful landscape on the Tragea Plateau

Erimonisia (Ερημονήσια)

The Erimonisia (»lonely islands«), officially called the Lesser East Cyclades, are a chain of barren, but despite their name not lonely islands in the Naxos–Amorgos–Ios triangle. The islands have a quiet, simple beauty and broad sandy beaches.

»**Lonely**« **islands**

The centre of life on Donoúsa (population 160) is the main village Agios Stavros/Donoúsa, which is crowded in the summer with guests, most of them Greek. The **recommended hike around the island** takes about four hours. The route passes good beaches; the nicest ones are in the northern part of the island.

Donoúsa (Δονούσα)

The southern coast of Iraklia (population 150), at 6km/4mi the longest island in the group, falls sharply to the sea; the rest of the coastline consists of bays with sandy beaches.
The nicest beach, Livadia, stretches for 1km/0.5mi south of the harbour Agios Georgios.

Iraklia (Ηράκλεια)

The two islands Epano Koufonisia and Kato Koufonisia are separated by a 200m/650ft-wide sound. Only Epano Koufonisia (population 370) is inhabited; it is the **most visited island of the Lesser East Cyclades**.

Koufonisia (Κουφονήσια)

Pretty lonely – Kendros Bay on the island of Donoussa

Schinoúsa
(Σχινουσσα)
This relatively flat island (population 200) has two towns: Schinoúsa – also called Panagia after the church with a valuable icon of the Virgin Mary – and the run-down Mesaria. There are several pretty, uncrowded sand beaches here, like Psili Ammos in a bay with a cliff east of Mesaria.

✶ Paros

Greek: Πάρος
Area: 186 sq km/72 sq mi
Population: 13,000
Capital: Parikia

Island group: Cyclades
Elevation: 0–771m/2,530ft above sea level

Thanks to the sprucing up of its coastal villages and its wonderful beaches, Paros is now among the most frequented islands of the Cyclades. The coastal towns are naturally the busiest; the interior of the island is still quite unspoilt.

Marble island
The island has been known since antiquity for its marble, which was used for a large number of masterpieces. The famous Parian school of sculpture developed here in the 6th and 5th centuries BC. Much of the island consists of an undulating mountain ridge that rises to 771m/2,530ft at Agios Ilias. Three deep bays cut into the coastline: Parikia Bay in the west, Naousa Bay in the north and the shallow Marmara Bay in the east. The coastline is for the most part steep and

rocky, but interspersed with small sandy bays, There are also extensive beaches, mainly on the eastern side. Although Paros is largely bare, a significant amount of farming – wine, barley, fruit and vegetables – is possible on the well-watered, fertile soil. Marble is still quarried on a small scale.

Parikia

Town

Seen from the sea, Parikia (population 4,500) appears to have little to recommend it, but a stroll through the winding, picturesque lanes behind the harbour reveals its beauty. The main street is a feast for the eyes with its many shops and tavernas, pretty churches, marble fountains and flower-bedecked courtyards and balconies.

Kastro

The town is clustered around the kastro hill, site of the remains of a Venetian castle (*c* 1260), built using parts of a Temple of Demeter. The column drums and the marble slabs of the 10m/33ft-high tower are from the temple, which was never completed. Its foundation (*c* 530 BC) is nearby. A marble wall of the temple was incorporated into the Church of Agios Konstantinos, and a chapel with a beautiful three-columned portico built against it. The view from here is a lovely, especially at sunset.

Stroll through the picturesque lanes of the island capitol, Parikia

⏵ VISITING PAROS

INFORMATION

Tourist Information
Dock Parikia
www.parosweb.com

ARRIVAL

Boat services to and from Piraeus on the mainland as well as with the islands Amorgos, Anafi, Astypalea, Donoussa, Folegandros, Fourni, Ira-klia, Ikaria, Ios, Koufonisia, Milos, Naxos, Rhodes, Samos, Santorini, Schinoussa, Serifos, Sifnos, Sikinos and Syros.

WHERE TO EAT
► Expensive
Tamarisko
Parikia
Tel. 2 28 40 2 46 89
The »Tamarisko« serves excellent international cuisine.

► Moderate
Levantis
Parikia
Near the market street
Tel. 2 28 30 2 26 26
The terrace of this restaurant with its pretty greenery is a great place to enjoy Greek cooking.

WHERE TO STAY
► Luxury
Astir of Paros
Naousa
Tel. 2 28 30 2 26 26
www.astirofparos.gr
114 rooms, 46 suites. Located in a beautiful and expansive garden this hotel offers rooms with marble baths and balcony or veranda, a gourmet restaurant and lots of sports activities.

► Mid-range
Kalypso
Naousa
Tel. 2 28 40 5 14 88
www.kalypso.gr
35 rooms. This hotel is located on Agii Anargiri Beach; every room has a balcony or terrace.

► Budget
Captain Manolis
Tel. 2 28 40 2 12 44
Central yet quiet location in the old city; simple rooms; terraces face a small greened inner courtyard.

Katapoliani ✴ On the square east of the harbour is **one of Greece's oldest and most beautiful churches**, called Ekatontapyliani, or actually Katapoliani (»located in the lower city«), built between the 5th and 7th centuries AD. It was remodelled several times in the course of history, especially after the earthquake of 1773. The church is entered through an idyllic courtyard, where there is a small **Byzantine museum** and the tomb of the freedom fighter Manto Mavrogenous. The main church (*c* 600), a two-storey domed structure, has a barrel-vaulted gallery for women. Ancient materials were used in its construction: the altar is supported by two Doric column drums with egg-and-dart decoration (6th century BC). In the apse beyond is the

synthronos, with several tiers of seating for priests and a marble epis-
copal throne. A fresco illustrating the Akathistos Hymn cycle can be
seen. The oldest part of the church is the 4th-century St Nicholas
Chapel with Doric columns of Parian marble and a carved iconostasis. The baptistery on the right, with a cruciform font set into the
floor, dates from the 7th century. Opening hours: daily 7am–11pm,
museum daily 9am–10pm.

Near the church the archaeological museum with exhibits from Paros and the smaller surrounding islands, including funerary reliefs,
sculptures, idols and inscriptions – one refers to the poet Archilo-
chos, who lived here in the 7th century BC. A fragment of the »Marble Parium« is interesting. It is part of a marble tablet with a table of
Greek historical dates (336–299 BC on this fragment) that was found
here in 1627. Opening hours: Tue–Sun 8.30am–2.30pm.

Archaeological museum

Other Sights on Paros

The famous Paros marble, which was called »lychnites« (»shining«),
is purer and more translucent than any other. Highly valued in
antiquity, it was used for building in Delos, Epidauros and Delphi
during the imperial Roman period, and also for such sculptures as
the famous **Hermes of Praxiteles**, the **Venus de Milo** and the pediment sculptures in the Temple of Zeus in Olympia. The most important source, which was quarried from the Cycladic culture (3rd–2nd
millennia BC) until the 15th century AD, lies 5km/3mi east of Parikia in Marathi. The ancient mine shafts are still accessible (take a
flashlight and wear shoes with non-skid soles). The entrance is at the
western bench near a relief with nymphs in reddish marble.

★
Marathi marble quarries

The old island capital Lefkes, a large mountain village 6km/4mi
south of the marble quarries, is considered to be the prettiest town
on Paros. It has a picturesque centre with narrow lanes, idyllic corners, steep steps and typical Cycladic cube houses.

★
Lefkes
(Λεύκες)

The second-largest town, **Naousa**, is located on a wide bay the north
of Paros. Its idyllic **fishing harbour** lined with tavernas is one of the
most beautiful in the Cyclades. Unfortunately Naousa's Cycladic style
is being replaced more and more by
hotel and apartment buildings. The
remnants of a Venetian fort and a
chapel dedicated to St Nicholas are
at the harbour. There are many
good beaches on both sides of the
island. Thanks to its strong winds
the **beach of Agia Maria** on the east
side of the bay is very popular
among windsurfers.

! Baedeker TIP

Hiking ancient trails
A hike from the idyllic little plateia on Lefkes
down to Prodromos, mostly on a medieval
Byzantine road, takes about an hour. The breath
of history blows through untouched nature
here.

Most of the islands offer a variety of vehicles to rent

Petaloudes The tomb of the island's patron saint Arsenios is in the **Convent of Christou Thassou**, 7km/4mi south of Parikia. A big festival on 18 August honours the island's patron saint, Arsenios. The road leads further to lush green Petaloudes (»Valley of the Butterflies«), a habitat in summer of beautiful orange-red Jersey tiger moths (Euplagia quadripunctaria) with brown and white wings. Do not disturb them by clapping hands, calling or the like, as this makes them expend too much energy. Opening hours: June–Sept daily 9am–6pm.

Beaches on the east coast There are some nice holiday resorts with good beaches on the east coast too. Accommodation of all kinds borders the pretty sandy beach and fishing harbour in **Piso Livadi**. Near Drios to the south there is a view of the offshore islands from a beautiful and long sandy beach with dunes, **Golden Beach/Chrissi Akti**. This is the most famous beach on the island and is appreciated especially by families. Heaven for windsurfers is **Nea Chrissi Akti** beach in the north.

Antiparos (Αντίπαρος) Southwest of Paros off the coast is the island Antiparos (population 1,000), a popular holiday destination. Tourists and the island population are concentrated in the same place, in the **principal town** of the same name with a Venetian castle built around 1440. Precious icons and wood carvings decorate the white and blue **Church of Agios Ni-**

kolaos on the plateia. A beautiful **dripstone cave** 8km/5mi further south can be reached by bus; one of the inscriptions inside is supposed to have been made by King Otto I of Greece. As an alternative to the bus, come by boat and take a 30-minute walk to the cave. Despite the many tourists who come to visit Paros' sister island during the high season, there are still many quiet spots on the numerous beaches scattered along the coast. Off the tip of Antiparos on the **island of Despotiko** archaeologists have excavated the ruins of a city from the Archaic and Classical periods.

✦ ✦ Patmos

Q 11

Greek: Πάτμος
Area: 34 sq km/13 sq mi
Population: 3,000
Capital: Patmos Hora

Island group: Southern Sporades
Elevation: 0–269m/882ft
above sea level

Patmos is not only one of the most important pilgrimage sites in the Christian world; it also attracts sun worshippers and hiking enthusiasts with its bustling port of Skala, its beautiful bathing coves along a furrowed coastline and its in places bizarre scenery.

The most northerly island of the Dodecanese is at the same time one of the most thinly populated Greek islands. Patmos is considered to be a holy site not only in the Orthodox, but also in the Catholic and Protestant worlds. It has been regarded since the Middle Ages as the island of **St John the Evangelist**, who was banished here from AD 95 until 97. In a cave he is said to have had the visions that were added to the New Testament as the Book of Revelation. In 1983 Paros was officially given the title »Holy Island«. The monastery of St John and the Cave of the Apocalypse are popular destinations for day-trippers from Rhodes, Samos and Kos. The hotels are concentrated around Skala, Grigos and Kampos. Patmos is barren, rocky and craggy, but has an interesting coastline with beautiful bays and sandy beaches.

»Holy island«

What to See on Patmos

The island consists of three parts joined by narrow isthmuses. The busy port of Skala, the island's hotel and tourist centre, lies on the deepest bay on the east coast. Large cruise ships call at Skala several times a week. Despite the mass of day-trippers from the neighbouring islands, Skala itself never seems overcrowded in the high season. A pleasant atmosphere pervades the town, particularly in the evening, when the sidewalk restaurants on the harbour front and behind the first row of houses are filled with life. The Monastery of St John, which is illuminated in the evening, forms a harmonious ensemble

Skala
(Σκάλα)

Baedeker TIP

Beautiful hike

The one-hour hike from Skala to the Apocalypse Grotto and on to Patmos Hora is rewarding. From the town follow the old road, which is cobbled in parts, or the hiking trail, which sometimes leads through a shady pine wood. The walk offers wonderful views of the neighbouring islands.

✴
Apocalypse Grotto

with the picturesque harbour, where fishing boats bob at their moorings.

The **Moni tis Apokalypsis**, the »Apocalypse monastery«, with the grotto where St John received his revelations, is halfway between Skala and Patmos Hora. The iconostasis in the right-hand chapel in the grotto depicts the saint's visions. On the floor and the wall are marked the places where he was lying when he heard a voice »like a trumpet« and wrote down his visions, as well as three fissures in the ceiling through which the divine voice came. Many pilgrims come from all over Greece and overseas to pray in the chapel. Immediately above the monastery are the ruins of the influential **Patmias School**, founded in 1713 by the

John the Evangelist recounted his visions of the fate of mankind and the Last Judgement in this cave

VISITING PATMOS

INFORMATION

Tourist information
Main square
Skala
www.patmos-in-greece.com

HOW TO GET THERE

Boat connections to Piraeus on the mainland and the islands of Arki, Fourni, Ikaria, Kalymnos, Kos, Leros, Lipsi, Mykonos, Nisyros, Rhodes, Samos, Syros and Tilos

WHERE TO EAT

▶ Moderate

Aloni
Between Patmos Hora and Grigos
Tel. 2 24 70 3 10 07
Locals and tourists enjoy Greek food here and are entertained by live music and dancing.

▶ Inexpensive

To Balkoni
Patmos Hora
Tel. 2 24 70 3 21 15
There are nice views of Skala from outside the restaurant.

WHERE TO STAY

▶ Mid-range

Romeos
Skala
Tel. 2 24 70 3 19 62
www.hotelromeos.com
56 rooms. Romeos is 400m/450yd from the heart of the village and very close to the beach; the hotel has a large pool and a quiet garden.

Golden Sun
Grigos Bay
Tel. 2 24 70 3 23 18
Fax 2 24 70 3 14 19
www.hotel-golden.sun.gr
25 rooms. Very good hotel near the beach, on a hill above the bay with a fantastic view.

▶ Budget

Australis
Northern part of the bay
Skala
Tel. 2 24 70 3 15 76, fax 2 24 70 3 22 84
www.patmosaustralis.gr, 18 rooms.
Friendly hotel with a large terrace, garden and spacious rooms.

monk Makarios, in which spiritual as well as secular subjects were taught. Opening hours: daily 8am–1.30pm, Tue, Thu, Sun also 4pm–6pm.

The principal town, Patmos Hora (population 600), is a fine sight. The stacked-up whitewashed houses, narrow steps and cobbled alleys are reminiscent of the Cyclades islands. The crenellated monastery fortress of Agios Ioannis Theologos can be seen again and again when wandering through the village. Some of the **old mansions** were built by refugees. Spread out to the west of the monastery is the so-called Constantinople district, and to the east, the Cretan district with the Natalis house (1599), the Pankostas house (1606) and the Stefanos house (1636). The Simandris house (1625) can be toured. Nearby is the Zoödochos Pigi monastery, dating from 1607 and dec-

★
Patmos Hora

orated with frescoes. The **best view of the Monastery of St John**, the whole island and its surroundings, is from the windmill on the road to Grigos.

★ ★
Monastery of St John

The Monastery of St John rises above the old city of Patmos Hora like a mighty fortress. It was founded in the year 1088 by the monk Christodoulos. It was given its present form with the sloping fortification walls and battlements in the 17th century. A ramp leads into a beautiful courtyard lined by loggias and spanned by arched buttresses. The **katholikon** (main church, 1090), built during the lifetime of the founder, stands to the left. The 17th-century outer portico, the exonarthex, contains paintings from the 17th and 19th centuries on the life of St John, and columns and other pieces of marble taken from a 4th-century basilica. The narthex (12th century) is decorated with frescoes from the 12th and 17th centuries. Note especially the parable of the foolish and wise virgins (around 1600). The Russian tsar paid for the church furnishing in the 19th century. The iconostasis of 1820 is decorated with richly detailed carvings. The

Like a strong castle, the Monastery of St John towers over the island's principal town, Hora

paintings of the 17th to 19th centuries have many representations of St John and his apocalyptic visions. The silver-plated sarcophagus (18th century) of the founder of the monastery, the Blessed (Osios) Christodoulos, is in the first chapel to the right. Important 12th-century murals dedicated to the Panagia were discovered in the second chapel, beneath frescoes from 1745, which were removed and can be seen in the trapeza, the old dining hall. They include subjects like the enthroned mother of God, the three angels with Abraham, Christ and the Samaritan woman, the healing of the lame and the blind man, as well as the presentation of Mary in the temple. The painted wooden iconostasis (Cretan, 1607) and the ancient parts of the building (steps, columns) are noteworthy. In the **trapeza** the marble table tops have indentations for utensils; there are also frescoes from the 12th or 13th century and the murals taken from the Panagia chapel.

Icons and precious liturgical items, most of them from the 17th century, are stored in the monastery's treasury. The **library** has some unique materials: 890 codices and 35 parchment scrolls, some 2,000 old printed works and an archive with 13,083 documents. Of the once rich collection of ancient literature, only a manuscript of the history of Diodorus Siculus is still here. The library and the treasury, probably the most important ecclesiastical collection outside the Holy Mountain of Athos, are not open to the public. Some pieces, however, can be seen in the monastery museum, including Alexios I Komnenos' golden bull of 1088, said to have been over 5m/15ft long, 33 pages of the Gospel of St Mark (Codex Purpureus, 6th century; most of it is in St Petersburg), an 8th-century manuscript of the Book of Job with 42 miniature illustrations and a collection of sermons by Gregory of Nazianzus dating from 941.

✷ ✷
◄ Monastery museum

The roof terraces of the monastery have a **wonderful view** of Patmos and the islands. Opening hours: daily 8am–1.30pm, Tue, Thu, Sun also 4pm–6pm.

🕓

North of Skala are the **beaches** Meloi (2km/1mi) and Agriolivado (4km/2.5mi). The beautiful bay of Kampos, in the northern part of the island, has a gently sloping pebble beach. Tourists from the cruise ships are usually brought here for two hours of sunbathing. Grigos, southeast of Hora, is the second-ranking tourist spot after Skala and has **the best beach on the island, Psili Amos**.

Other sights

The island of Lipsi (population 600), 8km/5mi long, is 12km/7mi east of Patmos. It has no special attractions besides a modest but pretty harbour on the south coast. Hiking over the low hills is not strenuous, as the bay that is furthest from the main town can be reached in about an hour. Lipsi is an **island for individual tourists** who are looking for rest away from the crowds. The few islanders live mainly from farming and fishing. The island specialities are a fine type of cheese and a strong, »black« wine.

Lipsi
(Λειψοί)

Platys Gialos Beach on Lipsi

Lipsi Town, reminiscent of the Cyclades, has two pleasant squares and an odd local museum with archaeological and folk art exhibits. **The best beach**, the sandy **Platys Gialos**, is about an hour's walk to the northwest; other beaches are closer.

Arki
(Αρκί)

The 7 sq km/3 sq mi barren island of Arki lies 14km/9mi northeast of Patmos. Its 50 or so inhabitants live very modestly, essentially from fishing and raising cattle. There are some private guestrooms and beaches for people looking for peace and quiet; the **most beautiful beach** with fantastically blue water is **Tiganaki**. Arki is surrounded by numerous smaller islands and rocks, some of which are used to pasture goats.

Poros

Greek: Πόρος
Area: 33 sq km/13 sq mi
Population: 4,300
Capital: Poros

Island group: Saronic Islands
Elevation: 0–390m/1,280ft above sea level

Poros in the Saronic Gulf is separated from the Peloponnese only by a 1km/0.5mi-wide sound. Tourism is concentrated mainly between Neorion and Askeli.

Poros is covered with sparse woodlands and macchia. The inhabitants, some of whom are of Albanian descent, live from the products of the fertile coastal plains on the mainland that belong to Poros and from tourism. The best means of transportation on the little island are bicycle and motor scooter. There was a city already in Mycenaean times on the grounds of the later Temple to Poseidon. The **ancient city, Kalaureia**, was abandoned after the Roman period; the present city was only established in the Middle Ages. In his *Hyperion* the poet **Friedrich Hölderlin** praised »the forests and secret valleys« of Kalaureia.

Praised by Friedrich Hölderlin

What to See on Poros

Poros, the only town on the island, is charmingly located on a small peninsula that is connected with the main part of the island by a narrow spit of land. The relaxed town with its white houses is a popular weekend destination. From the clock tower with its blue dome there is a beautiful view of the mountains of the Argolis on the Peloponnese. The little **archaeological museum** (Plateia Korizi) on the harbour street with finds from the Temple of Poseidon, Classical and Hellenistic statues, grave steles and vases is worth a visit. Opening hours: Tue–Sun 8.30am–3pm.
Northeast of Poros is **Askeli beach**, which is crowded in the high season.

Poros Town

About 5km/3mi northeast of town – the hike is enjoyable – there are a few traces of the Doric Poseidon sanctuary from the 6th century BC, which was the focal point of the »Kalaurian Amphictyony« (cult

Temple of Poseidon

Charmingly located on a peninsula, Poros Town is a favourite weekend destination for Athenians

▶ VISITING POROS

INFORMATION

Tourist police
Paraliaki (Harbour street)
Tel. 2 29 80 2 24 62
www.poros-island.com

WHERE TO EAT

▶ Moderate
Karavolos
Poros Town
Tel. 2 29 80 2 61 58
This taverna behind the Diana cinema
with a little terrace has a selection of

imaginative starters and daily specials
as main dishes.

WHERE TO STAY

▶ Budget
Theano
Poros Town
Tel. 2 29 80 2 25 67
Fax 2 29 80 2 45 08
www.poros-theano-spiros.com
24 rooms. Guesthouse opposite the
naval school; simple rooms, some
with a balcony, and restaurant.

community) of the maritime cities on the Saronic and Argolian
Gulfs. Because many remains of building were found in the area, the
ancient city of Kalaureia is presumed to have been here. There is a
beautiful view of Methana and Ae-
gina from here.

The 18th-century monastery Zoö-
dohou Pigis in **Askeli** (4km/2.5mi
east of town) has a beautiful gilded
iconostasis from Asia Minor. There
is an attractive taverna next to it
for a break after the tour, and below it in the bay the beautiful **Mo-
nastirion Beach** for a swim.

! *Baedeker* TIP

Beautiful beach
Just like Askeli beach, the broad bay of Neorion
is crowded because of the hotels nearby. Anyone
looking for a quieter place should go to Russian
Beach, one of the most beautiful on the island,
west of Neorion.

★★ Rhodes

S/T 12/13

Greek: Ρόδος	**Island group:** Dodecanese
Area: 1,398 sq km/4,587 sq mi	**Elevation:** 0–1,215m/3,986ft above sea
Population: 117,000	level
Capital: Rhodes Town	

**Rhodes has superb scenery, excellent beaches and restored build-
ings from the time of the Knights Hospitaller, which give an impressive picture of Western culture in the eastern Mediterranean
area; all this makes it an extraordinarily rewarding place to visit.**

Rhodes Map

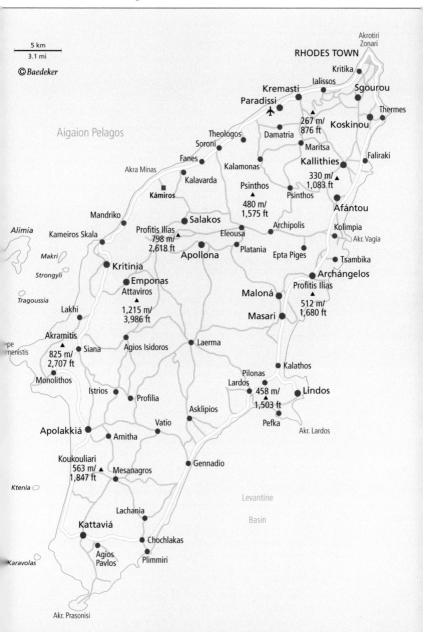

5 km
3.1 mi
© Baedeker

RHODES TOWN

Akrotiri Zonari

Kritika

Ialissos

Kremasti

Sgourou

Paradissi

Thermes

267 m/
876 ft

Koskinou

Aigaion Pelagos

Theologos

Damatria

Soroni

Maritsa

Fanes

Kalamonas

Kallithies

Faliraki

Akra Minas

Kalavarda

Psinthos

330 m/
1,083 ft

Kámiros

Psinthos

480 m/
1,575 ft

Afántou

Mandriko

Salakos

Kameiros Skala

Profitis Ilias

798 m/
2,618 ft

Eleousa

Archipolis

Kolimpia

Akr. Vagia

Alimia

Apollona

Platania

Makri

Epta Piges

Tsambika

Strongyli

Kritinia

Archángelos

Tragoussia

Emponas

Attaviros

Maloná

Profitis Ilias

Lakhi

1,215 m/
3,986 ft

512 m/
1,680 ft

Masari

Akramitis

Laerma

Kalathos

pe
menístis

825 m/
2,707 ft

Siana

Agios Isidoros

Pilonas

Lardos

Líndos

Monolithos

Istrios

458 m/
1,503 ft

Profilia

Asklipios

Pefka

Akr. Lardos

Apolakkiá

Vatio

Arnitha

Koukouliari

563 m/
1,847 ft

Mesanagros

Gennadio

Ktenia

Levantine

Basin

Lachania

Kattaviá

Chochlakas

Agios
Pavlos

Plimmiri

Karavolas

Akr. Prasonisi

Highlights Rhodes

Old quarter of Rhodes Town
Winding, romantic alleyways lead through old town, designated by UNESCO as a World Heritage site.
▶ page 339

Grand Master's Palace
The imposing 14th-century residence of the Knights of St John (Hospitallers) has today opened its gates to everyone.
▶ page 344

Lindos
The village, in a fabulous location high on a rock on the east coast, is one of the island's really great attractions.
▶ page 353

Symi
Take a tour boat and spend at least one day visiting one of the Aegean's most picturesque islands.
▶ page 356

Rose island In mythical times the sun god Helios is said to have claimed the rocky island that rises sharply out of the sea and woken it to life with his warming rays so that fragrant roses covered Rhodes. Rhodes is the largest of the Dodecanese, 18km/11mi from the Turkish coast, 78km/48mi long and up to 30km/19mi wide. A long mountain range runs across it and reaches an elevation of 1,215m/3,986ft at Mt Attaviros. The land, with an abundance of water and woods, falls gradually to the coasts and is used for farming, particularly in coastal regions. **One of the largest concentrations of hotels in Greece** has been built in and around Rhodes Town and between there and Lindos. But away from the tourist attractions, particularly in the south, the island is still relatively unspoiled.

History The cultural heyday of Rhodes began after its colonization by Dorian Greeks; their three cities, Lindos, Ialysos and Kamiros, belonged to the Hexapolis (»Six Cities«) that fell under the domination of the Persians around 500 BC. About 408 BC, the famous town planner **Hippodamus of Miletos** laid out a plan for the new capital, which in the 4th century BC became a trading hub that surpassed even Athens. The landmark of this wealthy, independent island state, the **Colossus of Rhodes** (▶3D p.342), a bronze statue of the sun god Helios, was one of the Seven Wonders of the World. With the expansion of Roman domination in the Orient, Rhodes' economic importance declined, but the city continued to be a cultural centre with **well-known schools of rhetoric** – attended by Cicero and Caesar – and a **major school for sculptors**. The famous **Laocoön group**, which can be seen today in the Vatican Museum in Rome, was produced here during the reign of Emperor Tiberius (AD 14–37). Rhodes was fought over during the Middle Ages by Arabs, Greeks (1204–46), Byzantines (1246–1309), Venetians and Genoese until the **Knights of St**

John finally took it in 1309. The »Knights of Rhodes« made Rhodes Town into a huge fortress and defended the island in the 15th century against the Egyptians and Ottoman Turks until they were forced to relinquish it to the Ottoman sultan, **Suleiman the Magnificent**, in 1523. After almost 400 years of Ottoman rule, the island was occupied by Italy in 1912 during the Italo-Turkish War and in 1947 was made a part of the Kingdom of Greece.

✳ ✳ Rhodes Town

The town of Rhodes (population 50,000) has been the capital of the island since its founding in 408 BC and is today also the administrative centre of Nomos Dodekanissou. It was once generously laid out according to the principles of **Hippodamos of Miletos** with a grid of streets intersecting at right angles. The Colachium, which was the district of the knights in the Middle Ages, with the Grand Master's Palace, their hospital and domiciles, occupied the approximately rectangular northern section of town. The larger southern section of the walled city was home to the Greeks. The western part became the Turkish quarter and the eastern part was the Jewish quarter, which existed until World War II. The fortress-like old town, a UNESCO World Heritage site, presents a unique image of a medieval town with its impressive Knights Hospitaller buildings. Turkish buildings, above all the mosques, add a further charming note. Despite mass tourism the old town, with its pleasant restaurants, well-stocked shops and beautiful squares, possesses a fascinating atmosphere.

City

The impressive **town wall**, dating from the 15th and 16th centuries, with its towers, bastions and moat, encircles the old town, where no Christian was allowed to live during the Turkish occupation from 1523 to 1912. The **Amboise Gate**, built in 1512 in the northwest under Grand Master Emery d'Amboise, and the **Harbour Gate** of 1468, with reliefs of St Mary, in the northeast at the commercial harbour are particularly beautiful. Defence of the individual sections of the town wall was assigned to the eight »tongues«, the geographical or cultural sub-groupings of the order. The city wall is closed until further notice because of the danger of collapse, but the walk around the outside of the wall is also worthwhile and takes a good hour.

✳ ✳ Old quarter

Souvenir hunting in the old town

► VISITING RHODES TOWN

INFORMATION
Tourist information
Alexandrou Papagou 31
Rhodes Town
Tel. 2 24 10 4 43 38; www.rodos.gr

WHERE TO EAT
► Expensive
Casbah ①
Platonos 4–8
Tel. 2 24 10 7 36 36
Even local people enjoy the food in
this beautifully restored Ottoman
house; it serves an accomplished
mixture of Mediterranean and Arab
cooking.

► Moderate
② *Romeo*
Menekleous 7–9
Tel. 2 24 10 7 44 02
Idyllic atmosphere and fine food in a
500-year-old house with a beautiful
courtyard.

► Inexpensive
③ *Oasis*
Plateia Dorieos
Diners enjoy the good, plain cooking
in this eatery opposite the Redjeb
Pasha Mosque beneath shady trees.

*The small Andreas guest house
in the middle of town*

Baedeker recommendation

► Inexpensive
④ *Socratous Garden*
Socratou 126
Tel. 2 24 10 2 01 53
Pretty garden restaurant, a tranquil atmosphere for a coffee break or a drink in the
evening.

WHERE TO STAY
► Luxury
① *Grand Hotel Rhodes*
Akti Miaouli 1
Tel. 2 24 10 5 47 00
www.mitsishotels.com
400 rooms, 10 suites
A hotel with a long tradition. Spacious rooms, a well-tended garden, a
generously-sized swimming pool, a
shopping arcade and a nightclub
across from the beach on the coastal
road in the new part of town.

► Mid-range
② *Andreas*
Omirou 28 d
Tel. 2 24 10 3 41 56
www.hotelandreas.com; 11 rooms
This little guesthouse is distinguished
by its lovely setting in a medieval
house and a view out over the roofs of
the old town from the breakfast
terrace.

► Budget
③ *Via-Via*
Pythagoras 45
Tel. 2 24 10 7 70 27
www.hotel-via-via.com
Small, quietly situated guesthouse
with individually furnished rooms,
attractive roof terrace and sumptuous
breakfast buffet.

Rhodes Old Town Map

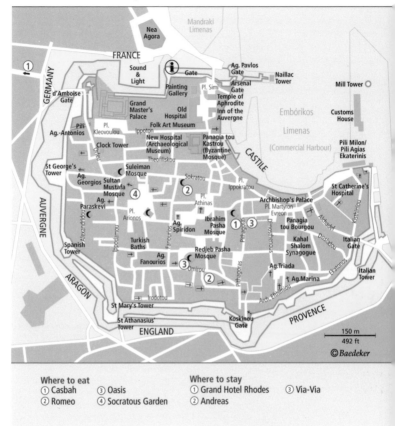

Where to eat
① Casbah ③ Oasis
② Romeo ④ Socratous Garden

Where to stay
① Grand Hotel Rhodes ③ Via-Via
② Andreas

Eleftherias or Arsenal Gate leads into the bustling old town with its maze of narrow lanes, its domes and minarets set between palms and plane tree. Simis Square with the remains of a **Temple of Aphrodite** (3rd century BC) and a **gallery** with a collection of contemporary Greek paintings in a historic building (opening hours: Tue–Sat 8am–2pm) is the starting point.

Plateia Simis
☉

Adjoining to the south is picturesque Argyrokastrou Square. The small fountain at its centre is made from pieces of an early Christian baptismal font. On the west side is the 14th-century **Old Hospital**, which now houses the archaeological institute. The **Hotel de la Langue d'Auvergne** (15th century) has a romantic inner courtyard. A passageway leads southeast to the 13th-century Church of Panagia

Plateia Argyrokastrou

THE COLOSSUS OF RHODES

✳ ✳ **The gigantic statue of the sun god Helios that the Rhodians erected in 292 BC in their capital's harbour was counted as one of the Seven Wonders of the Ancient World. It was a victory monument commemorating the heroic defence of their island against the greatly superior numbers of the army of Demetrius, the son of Antigonus, one of the Diadochi, in 305 BC. But the Colossus had already collapsed in an earthquake by 223 BC and the remains were taken to Syria in the 7th century and melted down. Thus the exact appearance of the statue and its precise location remain to this day a much debated issue among historians and archaeologists.**

① The Statue

It was said to have been 32m/105ft tall – according to the accounts of Pliny and Philo of Byzantium – and in addition, it was supposed to have stood on a 10m/33ft pedestal. That would mean the head alone would have been 4.30m/14ft in height and the raised arm about 10m/33ft long. It was erected within 12 years by the sculptor, Chares of Lindos.

② The Framework

Iron bars were anchored deep in the foundation. A basket-like mesh with crosswise braces is likely to have formed the framework. A skin of bronze 1– 2cm/0.4 – 0.8 in thick was put in place round about the frame. 45 tons of iron and 75 to 150 tons of bronze were used. The inside was filled with stones as ballast. Probably a mound of earth was piled up around each finished bronze section for standing on to complete the next section.

③ The Steel Crown

The hair of the sun god and his crown of sun-rays were gilded. Approaching ships are said to have seen them glistening in the sunlight from afar. Each sun-ray had a length of about 1.7m/6 ft.

④ The Nose

In order once more to gain an idea of the size of the Colossus, the nose alone was said to have been 90cm/3ft long.

⑤ The Location

Where it may have stood has long been a matter of discussion and dispute. Some proposed that it was even in the middle of the old town, a theory that has been disproved today. Whether it stood on the steep incline of the old naval harbour (today's Mandráki Harbour) or on the harbour mole – the most likely theory – is hard to prove because no remains have been found to date.

Classical depiction of the god Helios driving the sun chariot across the sky (vase painting)

Even the film industry has tackled the Colossus. Sergio Leone produced the monumental film »The Colossus of Rhodes« starring Rory Calhoun.

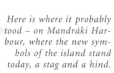

Here is where it probably tood – on Mandráki Harbour, where the new symbols of the island stand today, a stag and a hind.

Down through the ages, the Colossus has been a favourite subject of artistic depiction – lacking a real model, it is possible to allow the imagination free reign.

Coin from the 3rd century BC with the head of the king of the Macedonians, Demetrius the »Besieger«, 294–287 BC. He besieged Rhodes in vain. The Colossus was erected after his withdrawal.

tou Kastrou, home of the **Byzantine Museum**, which exhibits icons and wall paintings. Opening hours: Tue–Sun 8.30am–3pm. On the south side of the square, the **Museum of Decorative Art** is devoted to ceramics, weaving and carvings from the Turkish period in the Dodecanese. Opening hours: Tue–Sun 8.30am–3pm.

ew Hospital/ chaeological Museum

The massive hospital of the Knights of St John on the west side of Platia Mousiou is **one of the most beautiful and best-preserved buildings of the Crusader period**. It dates back to the year 1440. From the inner courtyard, a staircase leads up to the imposing infirmary on the upper floor, where tombstones of knights can be seen. The building now houses the archaeological museum. Among the most significant exhibits in the museum are finds from Ialissos, Kamiros and other places on the island, including the two Archaic kouroi (6th century BC) and the grave stele of Krito and Timarista (late 5th century BC), a life-size Aphrodite (2nd century BC), a famous Hellenistic head of Helios (2nd century BC) and a small **crouching figure, the Aphrodite of Rhodes** (1st century BC). Rooms VIII to XXII around the inner courtyard have a good collection of vases representing all periods of art from the Mycenaean period onwards. Opening hours: May–Oct Mon 1.30–6.40pm, Tue–Sun 8am–6.40pm, Nov–April Tue–Sun 8.30am–3pm.

venue of the Knights

One of the major attractions on Rhodes is Odos Ippoton, the Avenue of the Knights, which begins north of the new hospital. The street still looks much as it did in the 15th and 16th centuries. Most of the **inns**, the meeting houses of the individual »tongues« of the order, were in this street. Here the knights ate together, held meetings and received official guests. In the Turkish period wealthy merchants who lived here added screened wooden oriels to the façades so that their wives could look out onto the street. The most beautiful is the Auberge de France, built between 1492 and 1503 by French knights. Above the door with a pointed arch are the coats of arms of the order and the grand master, Emery d' Amboise.

Grand Master's Palace

The rebuilt Grand Master's Palace of **Grand Master Pierre d' Aubusson** towers on the highest point of the town, at the end of the Avenue of the Knights. The palace was almost completely destroyed in 1856 when gunpowder stored in the neighbouring Church of St John exploded. The palace was reconstructed during the Italian occupation (1912–43), but not true to the original plans. Nor do the furnishings correspond to their original state. Two exhibitions on the ground floor and the basement are dedicated to life on Rhodes during its 2,400-year history. Note especially some of the floor mosaics from the island of Kos on the upper floor. In one room there is also a copy of one of the most famous works in the tradition of Rhodian sculpture, the **Laocoön**

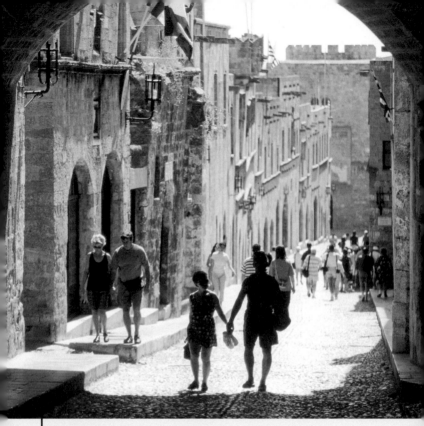

Pure Middle Ages without neon advertising – the Avenue of the Knights with the former hospice of the Knights Hospitaller

Group (1st century AD). Opening times: May–Oct Mon 1.30pm– 7.40pm, Tue–Sun 8am–7.40pm; Nov–Apr Tue–Sun 8.30am–3pm. 🕐

South of the Grand Master's Palace is the largest mosque on the island, the Suleiman Mosque, with a beautiful Renaissance door. Suleiman the Magnificent had it built after the conquest of Rhodes (1522). Opposite is the Turkish **Hafiz Ahmed Agha Library** (1794), which holds priceless Turkish, Persian and Arabic manuscripts. Opening hours: Mon–Sat 9.30am–4pm.

Suleiman Mosque

🕐

Agios Georgios, west of the mosque, is one of the most beautiful churches on Rhodes. It was constructed in the 14th century with four apses and is remarkable for the typical Rhodian niches in the tambour both inside and out. The Turks used the church as a madrasah (Koran school).

Agios Georgios

*Ippokratou Square, the heart of the old town,
lies in the Turkish quarter*

Plateia Ippokratou

Odos Sokratou, one of the town's most beautiful and popular shopping streets, leads from the Suleiman Mosque to Platia Ippokratous. The square, dominated by the two towers of the Naval Gate, is the pulsating heart of the old town with its tavernas and cafes. Note the **Castellania**; it was built in 1503 and once housed the market office and a commercial court; today it is home to the municipal library.

Plateia Evreon Martyron

Further southeast is the atmospheric Plateia Evreon Martyron, the »Square of the Jewish Martyrs«. It was given this name to commemorate the Jews deported from Rhodes during World War II. In the middle of the square is a modern fountain with three bronze seahorses. The 15th-century **Palace of the Admiralty** on the north side of the square was probably the residence of the metropolitan (archbishop).

Kahal Shalom Synagogue, in Dosiadou Street south of Evreon Martyron Square, was once in the heart of the Jewish quarter. It was probably constructed in the 16th century. To the right of the entrance there is a memorial plaque for the 1,673 Jews who were deported to German concentration camps. Of the 6,000 Rhodian Jews at the beginning of World War II, 4,000 emigrated. Only a few Jewish families remain today. Opening hours: Mon–Fri, Sun 10am–5pm. In the adjacent little **Jewish Museum** documents from the time of the Nazi persecution and from emigrants are on display.

Kahal Shalom Synagogue

⊕

South of Sokratous Street is a picturesque maze of lanes around Fanouriou Street, Omirou Street (both spanned by arches) and Pythagorou Street. Numerous mosques provide a Turkish atmosphere, e.g. the **Ibrahim Pasha Mosque**, the oldest in the city (1531), and the **Sultan Mustafa Mosque** (1765) on the attractive Plateia Arionos. The magnificent **Bath of Suleiman** opposite is now the municipal baths. On Fanouriou Street the small, partly subterranean Orthodox Church of **Agios Fanourios** is interesting; it was founded in 1335 as a Byzantine church and later used as a mosque by the Turks.

Southern old quarter

The trading port (Emborikos Limenas) is the main port and the dock for ferries. To the north lies the old Mandraki harbour, whose jetty is marked by three disused windmills. It has been in use since its establishment in 408 BC and today serves mainly as a yacht harbour and dock for excursion boats. At this lively harbour, which is also a traffic hub (bus terminal and taxi stand), stands the massive **Nea Agora** (New Market) with shops, fish restaurants and cafes. At the tip of the jetty stands **Fort Agios Nikolaos** (1400). The harbour entrance is flanked by a **hart and hind** on columns, the heraldic animals of the town.

Mandraki Limenas

There is a fine view of the town, the island of Symi and the coast of Asia Minor from the 110m/360ft-high hill Agios Stefanos, southwest of the old town. The remains of the ancient acropolis with the remnants of a temple, a stadium and a reconstructed theatre can be found here.

Acropolis

To the southwest of town is picturesque Rodini Valley, a green oasis for the town, with a park, a small zoo and pleasant paths (via Odos Stefanou Kazouli, bus from Mandraki harbour). Above the valley lies an ancient necropolis with the so-called **Ptolemy tomb** (3rd century BC).

Rodini Valley

From Rhodes Town via Kamiros to Apolakkia

From Rhodes Town the road to Apolakkia is 82km/50mi long and runs along the west coast. Leave the town heading southwest. In the **holiday resort Ialissos**, the largest hotel zone on the island, a road

★
Filerimos

The old Mandraki harbour: landing for yachts and excursion ships

runs to Mt Filerimos (»friend of loneliness«). The 267m/876ft mountain is a popular recreational area, also reached by bus from Mandraki harbour. It is the site of the acropolis of the ancient city of Ialysos. Filerimos was developed as a fortress several times, starting in the Mycenaean period around 1500 BC. In 1248 the Genoese occupied the mountain, in 1306 the Knights of St John followed and in 1522 the Turks used it to lay siege to Rhodes Town.

Broad steps once led up to the acropolis. On the plateau are the foundations of a **Temple of Athena** (3rd century BC), which was replaced by a church in early Christian times; the cross-shaped baptismal font set into the ground dates from this time. South of the entrance a stepped path leads down to a Doric **well house** (4th century BC) on the slope. Opening hours: May–Oct Mon 1.30–7.30pm, Tue–Sun 8am–7.30pm, Nov–April Tue–Sun 8.30am–3pm.

Petaloudes
(Πεταλούδες)

Near Kato Kalamon a road turns off south (7km/4mi) to Petaloudes (»butterfly«) Valley, where thousands of orange and black dotted **Jersey tiger moths** (Callimorpha quadripunctaria), a rare type of moth, once lived in the summer. In order to see them better, people used to startle them by clapping hands, which drove many of the moths away. However, the tranquil, shady valley is still worth a detour. In the small **nature museum** there is a butterfly collection. Opening hours: Mid-June to mid-Sept 8am–7pm, otherwise until sunset.

Near Kalavarda turn off towards the interior to Mt Profitis Ilias and return to the coastal road via Embonas. The 796m/2,612ft peak, the second-highest on Rhodes, has flora unusual for Greece, including pine trees, spruce and oak, with cyclamen, arbutus and orchids. The summit is a restricted military area.

Profitis Ilias
(Προφίτις Ηλίας)

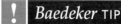

! Baedeker TIP

Donkey trails
One of the nicest hikes on Rhodes is from Salakos to the mountain Profitis Ilias. It starts at the bus stop about 50m/165ft from Hotel Nymphi (first towards the nymph spring and then turns right immediately to Profitis Ilias) and leads for two hours through unusual landscape along old donkey trails and shady forest paths up the mountain. There is a magnificent view from the plateau.

Along the road from Profitis Ilias to Eleousa stands one of the most beautiful churches on Rhodes, Agios Nikolaos Fountoukli. It got its soubriquet »fountoukli« (»hazelnut«) from the surrounding hills, which probably used to be covered with hazelnut bushes. The harmoniously designed structure was built in the 14th and 15th centuries as a monastery church; the belfry was added later. The sad occasion for building the church can be seen from the frescoes: the donor lost his three children, probably to the plague.

✸
Agios Nikolaos Fountoukli

About 4km/2.5mi west of Kalavarda take the turnoff (1.5km/1mi) to the **excavation site of ancient Kamiros**, which existed between the 6th century BC and the 6th century AD. The temple precinct, agora, cisterns, baths and residences of the wonderfully sited terraced city are clearly visible. From the acropolis there is an impressive view of the grand complex. Opening hours: May–Oct Mon 9.30–7.30, Tue-–Sun 8am–7.30pm, Nov–April Tue–Sun 8.30am–3pm.

✸
Kamiros
Κάμειρος

☉

About 4km/2.5mi to the northwest stands the best-preserved castle of the Knights of St John on the island, **Kastellos Kritinia**. Further south in the mountains is the pretty **village of Kritinia**. The Church of Agios Ioannis Prodromos offers a good view of the castle. Drive on past the magnificent backdrop of Mt Attavyros.

Kritinia
(Κρητηνία)

A detour (7km/4.5mi from the turnoff) to Embonas, the »wine capital« of Rhodes will not disappoint. It is a popular place for folklore evenings and wine tasting. There are lots of souvenirs for sale at the plateia. ►Tip p.350

Embonas
(Εμπωνας)

Continue along a panoramic road above the coast with some magnificent scenery to the dying hamlet of Monolithos. In a spectacular location (280m/920ft above sea level) – about 2km/1mi southwest of the town – stands an imposing castle of the Knights of St John (1476). The tour ends at a quiet village, **Apolakkia**. South of here isolated, wild coastal landscape begins.

✸
Monolithos
(Μονόλιθος)

High up on Monolithos are the remains of a large knights' castle

From Rhodes Town via Lindos to Kattavia

Route
From Rhodes Town the route runs along the east coast to the southern tip of the island. The distance to Kattavia without side trips is 88km/53mi. Along this coast, especially to Arhangelos, there are beautiful beaches with large hotel complexes.

Thermes Kalithea (Θέρμες Καλιδέαα)
Leave the town heading south. Turn off to the left 7km/4mi outside Rhodes Town to the former hot springs and seaside resort of Kalithea (3km/2mi) with its oriental atmosphere. The hot springs, highly valued since ancient times, have now dried up, but the spa, built in the 1920s by Italian architects and partially destroyed in World War II, is being renovated and is worth seeing. The hot springs overlook a small, beautiful **sandy beach** framed by rocks.

! *Baedeker* TIP

Good wine
Lovers of good wine should visit the Emery winery on the northern edge of Embonas. Taste and buy the mostly dry or semi-dry wines on the premises (opening hours: daily 9.30am–3.30pm or by appointment: tel. 2 24 10/ 412 08, www.emery.gr).

From here drive on along the coast bordered by large hotels or via the village of Koskinou, located picturesquely on a hill, to the island's tourist stronghold, **Faliraki**. It is a hotel city, built in the 1980s, with miles of child-friendly beaches and offers everything a tourist's – and a night owl's – heart can desire.

Near the village of Ladiko, south of Faliraki, the pretty little bay of the same name with a sandy beach surrounded by rocks is an inviting place to stop for a swim.

✷
Ladiko Bay

Immediately to the north lies the small and enchanting Anthony Quinn Bay, with a small pebble beach. It once belonged to the American actor.

✷ ✷
◄ Anthony Quinn Bay

East of the village of Afantou with its popular sand and pebble beach is the **Church of Katholiki Afantou** with early Christian parts. The village has the **only golf course on the island**. 4km/2.5mi from the beach resort Kolymbia, with its sand and pebble beaches, a side road leads 3km/2mi to **Epta Piges** (»seven springs«), a tranquil green valley with a stream and a taverna (footpath from the parking lot on the road Kolymbia–Arhipolis).

Afantou
(Αφάντου)

The enchanting Anthony Quinn Bay once belonged to the movie star

Tsambika (Τσαμπίκα) ✱ Tsambika beach ▶	3km/2mi after Kolymbia turn left to the abandoned **Tsambika Convent**. A spectacular view of the coast and interior are the reward for climbing the steep steps to get there. Below the convent to the south Tsambika beach with its fine-grained sand is one of the most beautiful on Rhodes.
Arhangelos (Αρχάγγελος)	Arhangelos, the second-largest town on Rhodes, is a picturesque place dominated by the »gingerbread towers« of Michail Arhangelos Church. To the south the ruins of a castle of the Knights of St John stands on a hill. Traditional crafts like pottery and weaving are still practised here. East of the village near **Stegna** there are beautiful beaches. The pretty village of **Malona** nestles among orange and lemon orchards a little further inland from the coastal road. North of the village the Church of Agia Irini (1728) is worth a visit. Continue via **Masari**, where the 14th-century Church of Agios Georgios Lorima should be seen for its frescoes in folk-art style. In **Harkin**, 8km/5mi south of Arhangelos, the pleasant town beach has not yet been overrun. The tour continues to Lindos (see below). After leaving Lindos the roads leads through picturesque

> **❗ Baedeker TIP**
>
> **Trip to an ostrich farm**
> About 2km/1mi before coming to Petaloudes, a road leads off to the right to an ostrich farm less than a mile away. There you can not only see the huge birds, but try an ostrich burger and purchase goods hand-made from ostrich leather, such as handbags and belts. Opening times: daily 9am–7pm.

resque landscape to the not exactly idyllic tourist resort of **Pefki**, which nevertheless has a sandy beach and many little coves for sunbathing, then on to Lardos and finally southwest towards Gennadion.

Asklipeio (Ασκληπείοο)	From **Kiotari**, with its beautiful long pebble beaches, a side trip north to Asklipeio and the impressive church Kimisis tis Theotókou (Dormition of Mary), built on the ground plan of a Latin cross (13th–14th centuries) is worthwhile.
Lahania (Λαχανιά)	3km/2mi beyond Gennadi take the time for a side trip to Lahania, which was discovered by foreign dropouts in the 1980s. The atmospheric plateia and the Church of Agia Irini, with a Baroque tower and early Christian baptismal font (6th century) on the southern edge of town, are worth seeing. About 6km/4mi south of Lahania, **Plimmyri** sprawls along the edge of a bay with a beach of dark sand.
Kattavia (Κατταβιά)	Pass the abandoned monastery of Agios Pavlos on the way to Kattavia, the southernmost town on Rhodes. Note the Church of Kimisis tis Theotokou, whose oldest parts date from the 14th century. **Prasonisi** (9km/5.5mi to the south) is a fabulous sand beach with white dunes. Wind surfers love the strong winds.

✷ ✷ Lindos (Λίνδος)

Lindos is one of the major attractions on Rhodes, and for good rea- **Fabulous**
son. The town, with its low, white houses below a medieval castle **location**
and an ancient acropolis, is stunningly situated on a high rock between two bays. During the high
season the town, which has been a
protected heritage site for years, is
understandably overrun.

The route from Rhodes Town
crosses a mountain ridge just before Lindos; beyond it there is a
fascinating view of the bay, town
and acropolis. Vehicles have to be

> ### *i* Shopping paradise
>
> ■ During high season, Lindos resembles one
> huge shopping arcade. Fashion, pottery,
> jewellery – almost anything can be purchased
> here. But keep in mind that most things can
> be bought more cheaply in Rhodes Town.

left at Plateia Eleftherias at the edge of town; continue on foot or by
donkey from here. Odos Akropoleos, which is lined by cafes, souvenir shops and travel agencies, leads into town. The houses in its romantic lanes all date from the 17th and 18th centuries. The Captain's
House, with its natural stone façade decorated with characteristic reliefs in the southern part of town, is a landmark. On the way to the
acropolis there is a beautiful view to the left of the harbour and a

Lindos looks grand in the evenings too

⏵ VISITING LINDOS

INFORMATION
▶ Tourist information office
Plateia Eleftherias
Tel. 2 24 40 3 19 00

WHERE TO EAT
▶ Expensive
Symposion
Apostolou Pavlou
Tel. 2 24 40 3 12 60
This gourmet restaurant in a restored old house is one of the best in Lindos; its menu includes Greek, Cypriot and international specialities like lobster, sea food and good steaks.

▶ Moderate
Calypso
Tel. 2 24 40 3 16 69
Greek, Caribbean and Turkish dishes are served in the inner courtyard or inside this wonderful old sea captain's house.

Dimitri's
The little garden restaurant below the main square has set up its tables in the shade of lemon trees; good food at moderate prices.

WHERE TO STAY
In Lindos itself there are almost no hotels, only private rooms that should absolutely be reserved in advance. The following hotels are in the neighbouring town of Vlyha.

▶ Luxury
Lindos Mare
Vlyha
Tel. 2 24 40 3 11 30, fax 2 24 40 3 11 31
www.lindosmare.gr
Modern hotel with a view of Vlyha Bay; modern rooms with a balcony or terrace. Club for children, entertainment programme, water sports.

▶ Mid-range
Electra
Tel. 2 24 40 3 12 66
Little guesthouse on the lane leading to Pallas beach; no meals but nice rooms with a sea view; garden and terrace.

round grave to the north, the so-called **tomb of Kleoboulos**. The grave is probably Hellenistic; the enjoyable walk there takes about 45 minutes.

Panagia   Along the way to the acropolis is the beautiful Panagia Church. It was built in the 14th century and in 1490 extended by the grand master of the Order of St John, Pierre d'Aubusson. Its richly decorated and gilded iconostasis and its hohlaki (pebble mosaic) floor are magnificent. The barrel vaulting and dome were decorated with paintings in 1779.

Agios Georgios Hostos   Not far to the northeast stands the oldest church on Rhodes, Agios Georgios Hostos. It dates from the 8th–9th centuries and has very rare frescoes from the time of the Iconoclastic Controversy (in the mornings get the key from the house to the right). South of the plateia (and difficult to find) is the impressive rock tomb of Archocrates (around 200 BC), which once had an imposing false front.

★★
Acropolis

A stair just inside the entrance to the acropolis leads to a small square with three cisterns and a Byzantine tower on its south side. Next to it is an exedra with a plinth on which a consecrated figure probably stood (3rd–4th centuries). The relief of a warship next to it on the right was created in honour of Admiral Hagesander Mikkion in the 2nd century BC.

To the left of the modern steps are the remains of ancient ones, and further up those from the Crusader period. A vaulted gateway leads into the ground floor of the **Knights of St John building**. In the vault to the left are steps cut into the stone, dating from the Archaic period. Outside is another exedra (3rd century BC). The temple behind it (3rd century AD) is dedicated to the prophesying demon Psithyros. The long **stoa** (3rd century BC) is one of the outstanding Hellenistic structures in Greece. To its right is the 13th-century Byzantine Church of St John. A wide stairway leads to the propylaea built in the early 3rd century, with five doorways in its back wall opening into the sacred precinct. The precinct consists of a courtyard lined with columns, with an Ionic colonnade added in the 2nd century AD, and a comparatively modest, yet artistically significant **Temple of Athena Lindia**, which was rebuilt as an amphiprostyle temple on the site of a 7th-century predecessor after a fire in 342 BC.

From here there is a **fantastic view** of Agios Pavlos Bay. Opening hours: May–Oct Mon 1.30–7.10pm, Tue–Sun 8am–7.10pm, Nov–April Tue–Sun 8am–2.40pm.

Lindos Acropolis *Plan*

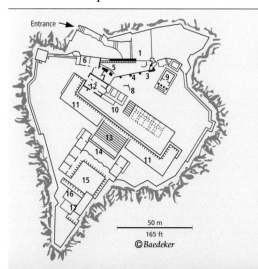

1 Cisterns
2 Byzantine tower
3 Exedra
4 Ship relief
5 Steps
6 Knights' building
7 Vaulting
8 Exedra
9 Psithyros Temple
10 Lower part
11 Stoa
12 Castle church
13 Steps
14 Propylae
15 Courtyard
16 Colonnade
17 Temple of Athena Lindia

50 m
165 ft
© Baedeker

The acropolis commands a wonderful view of the Bay of Lindos

Boukopion From the northern edge of town on Vigli Peninsula there is a beautiful view of the acropolis, the Temple of Athena Lindia and the Athena grotto. The sparse remains of the Boukopion, a sacrificial site probably for bull, are scattered around the grounds.

✳
Pallas Bay

✳ ✳
Agios Pavlos Bay

There is no reason to miss beach life in Lindos. Below the town lies the beautiful Pallas Bay, and on the other side of the acropolis the almost completely enclosed Agios Pavlos Bay with a small sandy beach. The **Apostle Paul** is said to have sought refuge here from a storm while sailing from Ephesus to Syria in AD 51. A small memorial chapel commemorates this event.

✳ ## Symi (Σύμη)

Popular excursion from Rhodes

The Dodecanese island of Symi, **one of the most picturesque in the Aegean,** is located 45km/28mi northwest of Rhodes in Symi Bay. Its 85km/53mi-long, steep and wild coastline is punctuated by numerous, deeply cut coves; the central part of the island is a rolling plateau, with Mt Vigla (616m/2,020ft) as the highest point. Tour boats with day-trippers arrive here several times a day from Rhodes. A hike through the interior is also pleasant. In the days when picturesque old houses were being torn down and replaced by faceless concrete structures all over Greece, the inhabitants of Symi renovated their houses or built new ones that match the local architectural style. On Symi there are also more than 100 churches, chapels, monasteries and many, mostly abandoned windmills. The island has been known for shipbuilding from antiquity until the present; sponge diving was also an important branch of the economy. When the two declined the community switched to tourism as a new source of income. Symi's history has been intertwined with that of Rhodes since ancient times.

✶
Symi Town

The island's principal town, a protected site, is **regarded as one of the most beautiful places in Greece**. Its white-and-earth-coloured houses spread up a slope at the end of a deep bay. The clock tower of 1881 greets guests from afar. In the lower part of town many cafés, restaurants and shops cluster around the harbour. Not only the usual souvenirs but also sponges and spices are on sale here. Many renovated mansions (arhontika) can still be discovered here, too. Several hundred steps lead from the heart of town at the rear end of the bay to the quieter upper town, Horio, where there is a nice view of the harbour. In Horio a small **folk art museum** displays costumes and crafts.

Nimborios Bay

About 2km/1mi northwest of Symi Town on a harbour bay lies the quiet summer resort Nimborios. Tavernas and accommodations are available for tourists. Fine mosaics can still be seen in the ruins of an early Christian basilica.

The principal town of Symi is one of the most picturesque places in Greece

Emborio on Halki is still a quiet place

Moni Panormitis Almost all boat trips head southwards for the 18th-century monastery dedicated to St Michael of Panormiti in the bay of the same name. It is **one of the foremost pilgrimage sites in the Dodecanese**. The focus of veneration is the richly carved and gilded iconostasis with an icon of the Archangel Michael. Pilgrims flock to the monastery in large numbers at Whitsun and on 8 November, a feast of St Michael in the Orthodox Church. The convent offers simple accommodation (500 beds).

From the southern tip of Symi **the lighthouse island of Sesklion**, which belongs to Panormitis, can be seen; excursion boats run there from Gialos and Panormitis.

Other neighbouring islands About 7km/4.5mi west of Rhodes are the two islands Alimia and Halki. **Alimia**, which is basically one giant fabulous sandy beach, is uninhabited; get there on a fishing boat from Halki. Boats go to **Halki** (population 530) from Rhodes Town and Kamiros Skala on the west coast of Rhodes. The rocky island is a nice place for a day trip. The sandy beach in Pontamos Bay, not far from Emborio, is popular. The old main town, Horio, is located 3km/2mi west of Emborio; apart from two very old churches everything else there is in ruins. There is a Crusader castle on a mountain south of Horio.

✶ Samos

Q/R 9

Greek: Σάμος
Area: 476 sq km/184 sq mi
Elevation: 0–1,433m/4,701ft above sea level

Island group: North and east Aegean islands
Population: 34,000
Capital: Samos Town/Vathy

Not only its sweet red wine has made Samos in the east Aegean a popular place to spend holidays. This green and wooded island with an abundance of water offers a wide variety of scenery with many places to hike and a rugged coastline with a large number of sandy and pebble beaches. Samos is also the site of one of the most important cult sites of antiquity, the Heraion of Samos.

Samos is separated from the Turkish coast by a strait just under 2km (just over 1mi) wide. Its highest point (1,433m/4,701ft) is Mt Kerkis in the west. Agriculture (wine-growing, olives, oranges, figs, tobacco, grain, fruit and vegetables), ship-building and fishing are the main sources of income. Tourism has increased strongly in the last two decades. **Samos wine** has been cultivated since ancient times and was the first Greek wine to be considered a quality product. The wine-growing region has 1,800ha/4,450 acres and is mainly used for white muscatel grapes; but the more popular dry wines are increasing now. Under the **tyrant Polycrates** the island reached its political and economic zenith in the late 6th century BC. Like other tyrants of his time Polycrates commissioned great buildings and furthered the arts. Samos was the birthplace of the mathematician and **philosopher Pythagoras** (*c* 570 to 496/497 BC), the **philosopher Epicurus** (341–271 BC) and the **astronomer Aristarchus** (*c* 310to *c* 230 BC), who anticipated the Copernican model of the solar system and attempted to determine the distance between the earth and the moon and sun.

✶
Wine island

Sámos Map

5 km
3.1 mi

Karlovasi
Ag. Konstantinos   Avlakia
Kolpos Vatheos
Zoodohos Pigi
SÁMOS (Vathý)
Vourliotes
Kokkari
■ Profitis Ilias
Karvouni
Kastania
1,253 m/
4,111 ft
Kallithea
Kerkis   Marathokampos   Mytilíni   Kervelis
Akr. Katavassi   ▲ Votsalakia   Stavros   Psili Ammos
1,437 m/   Ormos   Hora   Stene Samu
4,714 ft   Marathokampou
Mili
Spatharei   Pagontas   ✈   Pythagório
Heraion   TURKEY
Fourni
Aigaion Pelagos   Samiopoula
©Baedeker

▶ VISITING SAMOS

INFORMATION

Tourist information
Themistokli Sofoúli 107
(coastal road towards Kokkari)
Samos Town
Tel. 2 27 30 2 82 82

GETTING THERE

Boat services to and from Alexandroupolis and Piraeus on the mainland as well as the islands of Agathonisi, Chios, Fourni, Ikaria, Kalymnos, Kos, Leros, Lesbos, Limnos, Lipsi, Mykonos, Naxos, Paros, Patmos, Rhodes and Syros

WHERE TO EAT
▶ Moderate
The Steps
Samos Town
Pavlou Koundourioti
Excellent Greek food in a quiet locale with a good view.

There are many pretty tavernas on the island

To Kyma
Karlovasi
Tel. 2 27 30 3 40 17
Enjoy the delicious sea food platters accompanied by a wonderful sunset.

WHERE TO STAY
▶ Luxury
Proteas Bay
Pythagorio
Tel. 2 27 30 6 21 44/6
Fax 2 27 30 6 26 20
www.proteasbay.gr
92 rooms, 73 bungalows. This first-class hotel, 2km/1mi outside Pythagorio, has one main building and several out-buildings on a slope. Sunbathe either at an isolated small pebble beach or by the pool; taverna on the roof terrace, tennis court and indoor pool.

▶ Mid-range
Arion
Kokkari
Tel. 2 27 30 9 20 20
www.arion-hotel.gr
108 rooms. This attractive hotel, 600m/650yd from the beach, consists of a main building and bungalows.

Doryssa Bay
Pythagorio
Tel. 2 27 30 8 83 00
Fax 2 27 30 6 14 63
www.doryssa-bay.gr
155 rooms, 128 bungalows, 9 suites. This expansive holiday complex west of Pythagorio was made to look like a Samian village. Along with neo-classical villas and small fishermen's cottages there is a village square with a church and a coffee house. The hotel also has its own folk museum.

Samos Town/Vathy

Since 1832, when the town of Vathy (population 8,300) was founded, **Island capital** it has been the island's capital. It spreads in a semi-circle around the harbour bay of Vathy, which is bordered by the four-lane **Sofoúli road**. The numerous street cafes here are a good place to get refreshments. The centre of town is Plateia Pythagoria, where a large marble lion was set up in 1930 under tall palm trees in memory of the 100th anniversary of the battle for liberty from Turkish rule. Countless lanes of steps climb past rows of pretty houses up the mountain slope to the upper town, **Ano Vathy**. The village atmosphere of the historic town centre with its picturesque alleys and oriel windows has been preserved.

Likourgou Logotheti street runs parallel to the harbour promenade **✴** up to the city park and is Vathy's shopping street. The archaeological **Archaeological** museum is located here in the residence of the dukes of Samos and a **museum** new building. It displays finds from excavations in the Heraion. The major exhibit is the almost 5m/16ft-tall, colossal Archaic statue of a kouros (around 580/570 BC), a votive figure and the largest of its **✴** kind, which is on display in the enlarged main hall. Also note the **◄ Kouros**

View of Samos Town and Vathy Bay

larger-than-life statue of a woman from the Archaic period (around 570 BC). The base and three of the original six figures from an Archaic group by the sculptor Geneleos (around 560 BC) still exist. On the ground floor are sculptures from Hellenistic and Roman times, on the upper floor ceramic and ivory figures. The **large collection of bronze griffon heads**, which once decorated large cauldrons, is beautiful. Opening hours: Tue–Sun 8.30am–3pm.

Byzantine museum

The Byzantine museum is housed in the new bishop's palace. It displays valuable icons from the last six centuries, liturgical items and robes.

Other Sights on Samos

Mytilinii (Μυτιληνιοι)

Mytilinii (12km/7mi southwest of Samos Town) was founded in 1700 by settlers from the island of Lesbos, which was also called Mytilinii at that time. Today it has a very interesting **paleontological museum** displaying finds from excavations made in valleys and stream beds near the town. These include fossils of various kinds of mammals that came from Asia, with which Samos was connected about ten million years ago: rhinoceroses, mastodons (large elephants), dwarf ancestors of the horse, short-necked giraffes, antelopes and hyenas. The island of Samos was separated from Asia by tectonic shifts, and in time the animals died out on the island. Opening times: Tue–Sat 9am–2pm, Sun 10am–2pm.

Pythagorio (Πυθαγόρειο)

Follow the island road south from Samos Town for 15km/9mi to the pretty harbour town of Pythagorio on the eastern south coast. With its well-preserved centre and attractive harbour promenade, it attracts many tourists and now has the most guest beds on the island. It was called Tigani until 1955, when it was renamed in honour of the Samian **philosopher Pythagoras**. A modern bronze figure (1988) at the eastern harbour jetty commemorates the famous Samian. On the **kastro hill** in the western part of the town stand the city's main church, Metamorfosis, which was completed in 1932, and the castle of the freedom fighter Lykourgos Logothetis, which was built from 1822 until 1824 re-using ancient materials. From here there is a beautiful view of Cape Mykale in Turkey. A Hellenistic villa was unearthed next to it, on top of which a 5th-century Christian basilica had been built. On the road to Vathy on the right an archaeological museum that opened in 2010 exhibits finds from Pathagório. Opening times: May–Oct Mon 1.30–8pm, Tue–Sun 8am–8pm, Nov–Apr Tue–Sun 8.30–3pm

Northeast above the town centre is **Panagia Spiliani Monastery**. A rock grotto harbours a small shingled chapel. The water that drips from the rock wall is considered to be holy and to have miraculous properties (opening times: daily 9am–8.30pm). Below the monastery in a hollow are the remains of an ancient theatre.

Daylight fades – the blue hour in Pythagorio

Further to the north is the entrance to the Eupalinion, a 1,036m/ 1,130yd aqueduct designed by Eupalinos of Megara in 522 BC, a work of technical genius. The tunnel was built with a diameter of about 1.60–1.80m/5–6ft. A good 400m/450yd from the southern entrance, the spot can be seen where the two shafts, tunnelled in from either side, met almost precisely. Clay pipes laid in separate ditches channelled water into the city from the other side of the mountain. This ingenious water supply system was in operation for about 1,000 years. Accessible: May–Oct Tue–Sun 8.30am–8pm, Nov–Apr Tue–-Sun 8.30–3pm.

★
◀ Evpalinos

⊕

On the northern edge of Pythagorio near the shore are the well-preserved remains of extensive **Roman baths** (2nd century BC).

The famous Heraion (Irion) of Samos lies 9km/5mi west of Pythagorio. The Heraion and the ancient city of Samos were connected by a sacred way. At that time it was lined by giant kouros statues and other votive gifts. The large kouros that can now be seen in the archaeological museum in Vathy was also found here. The **Geneleos group** (now also in Vathy) was also found here; a copy stands in its original place. According to tradition, Ionian immigrants found a wooden cult image at the mouth of the river Imbrasos wrapped in the branches of a lygos tree. They recognized it to be a depiction of the goddess Hera. The first altar was built next to the lygos tree, fol-

★
Heraion of Samos

Samian Heraion – on the right is the base of the Genelaos group

lowed by others. The seventh was the partially reconstructed **Altar of Rhoïkos** (*c* 550 BC). The Samians built the **Temple of Hera** west of the altar. Polycrates ordered a new temple to be built on the site of a few preceding buildings. Covering an area of 112 x 55m/367 x 180ft, it was the largest temple ever designed by the Greeks, but – like other large-scale Ionic temples – was never finished. All but its massive foundations and the stump of a single column, which was originally twice its present height at 20m/66ft, has disappeared. In the altar area there are even remains of a lygos bush.

The Roman exedra south of the column commemorates the Quintus Tullius and Marcus Tullius Cicero. Nearby is the apse of an early Christian **basilica** (5th–6th century AD). Opening hours: May–Oct Tue–Sun 8am–7.30pm, Nov–April Tue–Sun 8.30am–3pm. After the tour relax on the beach at **Ireo**, a little resort not far from the excavation site.

Island Tour

The scenery of the north coast is particularly attractive, with narrow valleys, terraced slopes and isolated bays for swimming. First drive 11km/7mi from Vathy along the north coast to **Kokkari**, a pretty holiday town that stands out for its attractive location along a bay and its historic town centre. Having good beaches, it has developed into a lively resort in recent years and is especially popular among the young and among windsurfers. Turn left beyond Avlakia (20km/ 12mi) to the wine village **Vourliotes** (3km/2mi), a popular place for outings because of its pretty plateia and alleys.

After a short drive on the coastal route, a side road leads through an enchanting valley full of oleander shrubs to the picturesque mountain and wine village of **Manolates**. Back on the coastal road, the next stop is the second-largest town on the island, **Karlovasi** (32km/19mi).

> ## ! Baedeker TIP
>
> ### Hiking on Mt Kerkis
>
> A hike on 1,433m/4,701ft Mt Kerkis in the west of the island is strenuous but rewarding. The trail starts at the little resort of Votsolakia and leads past the still occupied Evangelistrias Monastery to the summit, where there is a broad sweeping view of a large part of the Aegean and the mountains of Asia Minor. The ascent takes about four hours, the return about three. The descent by way of Marathokampos, which is not as steep but takes an hour longer, is recommended.

This very extensive but rather sober port stretches out for several miles along the coast and also deep into the interior. It is the economic centre of the west of the island. Most hotels are along the harbour. The steep hill behind it with the old quarter is crowned by a small church. The paved road ends a few miles beyond Karlovasi. The picturesque but isolated **west coast** is only accessible with off-road vehicles and on foot over steep paths. Return to Samos Town through the mountainous interior by way of Marathokampos, Koumaradei and Hora.

The largest town in the interior of the island, **Marathokampos**, seems to cling above the coastal plain like an amphitheatre and offers wonderful views of the sea.

✱ Samothraki

Greek: Σαμοθράκη
Area: 178 sq km/69 sq mi
Elevation: 0–1,611m/5,285ft
above sea level

Island group: North and east Aegean islands
Population: 2,700
Capital: Samothraki Hora

Samothraki, Greece's most northeasterly island, is dominated by the mighty 1,611m/5,285ft Mt Fengari. The wild and rugged mountain country is ideal for hiking tours.

Samothraki has great natural beauty even though it lacks a rugged coastline. The visitor can expect to find mountains with dense forests and many streams in the north as well as endless olive groves in the drier south with its sparser vegetation. There are few beaches, and tourists find entertainment only in the lively port of Kamariotissa. Lovers of ancient art, on the other hand, will be satisfied, since the

Furthest northeast of the Greek isles

▶ VISITING SAMOTHRAKI

INFORMATION

Tourist information
Main street
Samothraki Hora
www.samothraki.com

GETTING THERE

There are ferries to Alexandroupolis and Lavrio on the mainland and the islands of Agios Efstratios, Lesbos and Limnos.

WHERE TO EAT

▶ Moderate

I Plateia
Main square
Samothraki Hora
Tel. 2 55 10 4 12 24
If you like unusually prepared seafood, this is the place.

Klimitaria
Coast road
Kamariotissa

Tel. 2 55 10 4 15 35
Pleasant taverna popular with the locals offering a large selection of dishes.

WHERE TO STAY

▶ Mid-range

Aelos
Kamariotissa
Tel. 2 55 10 4 15 95
56 rooms. Quiet hotel with a swimming pool, a short distance above the town.

▶ Budget

Niki Beach
Kamariotissa
Tel. 2 55 10 4 15 45
Fax 2 55 10 4 14 61
40 rooms. On the beach heading north; small but tidy rooms with balconies, some with a sea view.

Sanctuary of the Great Gods is one of the most impressive in Greece. The islanders' income is based on agriculture, especially grain, fruit and vegetables. There is **hardly any tourism** on the island. The few hotels have limited capacity and in the high season are all but taken over by Greek tourists. Apart from the pretty beach at Pachia Ammos on the southern coast of the island, most beaches are pebbly, like the nearby Vatos or the shady Kipos in the extreme southeast. The narrow beaches in the north are not very inviting.

What to See on Samothraki

Samothraki Hora

The harbour town **Kamariotissa** on the west coast has most of the hotels and tavernas on the island as well as a long shoreline promenade; there is also some night life. The capital Samothraki Hora is located 5km/3mi to the east in a bizarre rock landscape, climbing up two steep slopes and dominated by the ruins of a kastro. It has remained entirely in its original state, with white tile-roofed houses and narrow lanes, making it the most beautiful village on the island.

Only about 1,600 people live here. There are guest houses and private rooms for tourists. From the castle ruins there is a beautiful panorama.

The ruins of the Sanctuary of the Cabeiri, the Great Gods, are above the island's ancient capital, Palaiopolis, 5km/3mi north of Hora. They are impressively located in a scenic setting in an ascending valley cleft. The one-hour hike there from Hora along the slope of Mt Fengari with a wonderful view of the sea is not to be missed. Despite extensive research little is known about the **mysteries of the Cabeiri cult**; the initiates were committed to strict secrecy and in the course of centuries various cults were superimposed on each other. The cult arrived from Phrygia in Asia Minor in the pre-Greek period. Even the ancient Greeks no longer knew the meaning of the word »Cabeiri«, and the deities it referred to were never determined exactly. It is at least clear that it focussed on **Cybele**, the »Great Mother« of all life, an ancient fertility goddess. On Samothraki other gods were added, as inscriptions show, including the Thracian mother goddess Axieros as a goddess of nature, along with Axiokersos and Axiokersa,

★
Sanctuary of the Great Gods

The rituals performed in the Sanctuary of the Great Gods were wrapped in mystery

a pair of underworld deities (equated with Pluto and Persephone by the Greeks) and the youthful Kadmilos, god of vegetation and the phallus. They were venerated as protective gods of nature and later increasingly became patrons of sailors and those in distress at sea. Initiation into the mysteries, which took place in two steps, was open to all, Greeks and non-Greeks, men and women, free men and slaves – which undoubtedly cleared the way for the later spread of the cult.

Anaktoron ▶ A signposted walk leads southeast from the museum past a viewpoint to the Anaktoron (c 550 BC), the »House of the Lords« or »House of the Gods« where believers received the first degree of initiation. The northern part was sectioned off as the holy of holies. To the southeast is a walled sacrificial site. Adjoining to the south is the »sacristy«, in which a list of the names of the initiated was kept.

Arsinoion ▶ The Arsinoion, a place for sacrificial offerings, was built with a donation by the later queen of Egypt, Arsinoe II, between 289 and 281 BC and, with a diameter of over 20m/65ft, was **the largest roofed rotunda in ancient Greece**. It was built on an earlier cult site, of which inside walls and a stone altar have been uncovered. On the slope above the Arsinoion are the remains of an ancient road and a rotunda.

Temenos ▶ Altars dating from the cult's early period can be found in the area between the Arsinoion and the Temenos adjoining to the south. The shrine, financed by the Philip II of Macedon and built about 350–340 BC, had an Ionic propylon with Archaic-style frieze of dancers, parts of which are in the archaeological museum. The Doric Hieron (around 325 BC) stands on the middle terrace; it has an apse that was provided with a crypt in the Roman period. The initiates received the second degree of consecration here, probably after they had confessed their sins in front of two marble blocks at the eastern side. Parallel to the Hieron are the Hall of Votive Gifts (6th century BC) and the Altar Court built between 340 and 330 BC, whose portico presumably served as the stage wall for a (destroyed) theatre built around 200 BC.

Winged Victory of Samothrace

Sanctuary of the Cabeiri Plan

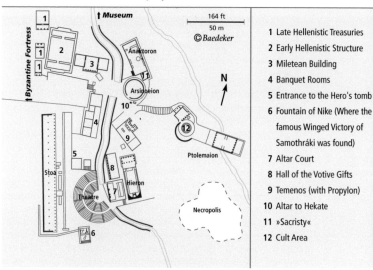

1 Late Hellenistic Treasuries
2 Early Hellenistic Structure
3 Miletean Building
4 Banquet Rooms
5 Entrance to the Hero's tomb
6 Fountain of Nike (Where the famous Winged Victory of Samothráki was found)
7 Altar Court
8 Hall of the Votive Gifts
9 Temenos (with Propylon)
10 Altar to Hekate
11 »Sacristy«
12 Cult Area

Visible to the south of the theatre is the Nike Fountain, where pieces of a famous winged victory made of Parian marble were found. This figurehead, a votive gift, was created in 190 BC, possibly the work of the Rhodian sculptor Pythekritos, to commemorate Rhodes' victory over Antiochos III of Syria. Today it stands in the Louvre in Paris and is one of the most famous Greek statues. Opening times: May–Oct daily 8am–7.30pm, Nov–April 8.30–3pm.

★
◄ Nike of Samothrace
⊙

Southeast of the sanctuary, south of the propylon built by Ptolemy II of Egypt in about 270 BC, are an ancient cemetery (7th–2nd centuries BC) and the **archaeological museum**, whose most interesting exhibit is a copy of the Nike of Samothrace. Opening times: summer daily 8.30am–8.30pm.

North of the sacred precinct lies Palaiopolis, the ancient city of the Aeolian colonists, whose colossal 6th-century BC wall extends up to the ridge of the mountain. Very little has been preserved inside. The ruins of a Genoese castle erected in the 15th century stand on the ancient acropolis hill.

Palaiopolis

Some 13km/8mi east of Palaiopolis a hot spring bubbles out of a sinter cone at 55°C/131°F. Loutra/Therma, the thermal spa that developed here, is pleasantly situated in the midst of chestnut and plane tree forests. It is a meeting place for elderly Greek spa guests and hiking tourists. The town is the starting point for the trek up the highest mountain on the island, Mt Fengari (1,611m/5,285ft), which takes six hours.

Loutra/Therma

✶✶ Santorini · Thira

Greek: Σαντορίνη/Θηρά	**Island group:** Cyclades
Area: 76 sq km/29 sq mi	**Elevation:** 0–566m/1,857ft above sea
Population: 13,700	level
Capital: Thira	

**Santorini or Thira, »the wild island«, the most southern of the larg-
er Cycladic islands, has unique volcanic landscape and towns with
spectacular locations which make it one of the most attractive
travel destinations in Greece.**

Unique volcanic island
One of the worst natural catastrophes in human history took place
on Santorini (»Santorini« in Italian for its patron Santa Irene; in
Greek Santorini), the southernmost of the large Cycladic islands
(►Baedeker Special p.372). Just the arrival in the giant, almost completely enclosed volcanic crater with white houses clinging to the
edge is an unforgettable experience. Santorini is not suitable for a
purely beach holiday, but the ancient sites are among the most important in Greece. There are hardly any trees because of the lack of
water. The islanders' income derives from the production and export
of wine and tomatoes, along with tourism.

The volcanic island does not have many good **beaches**. Popular resorts on the east coast, Kamari and Perissa, top the list. The beaches
at Monolithos and further north are much quieter. Probably the
most beautiful beach on the island, Red Beach, lies below Akrotiri.
Here imposing red cliffs frame a beach of grey sand and pebbles.

Geology
Santorini and its neighbouring islands, Thirasia and Aspronisi, are
part of a volcanic crater that sank into the sea. The rim of the caldera projects out of the sea to form a hollow ring with a diameter of
12–18km/7–11mi. At its centre is a bay or basin up to 400m/1,300ft
deep, out of which the peaks of a new volcano, the Kameni islands,
emerged. Hot springs and escaping gas testify to continuing volcanic
activity. The massive layers of ash, pumice and lava lie on a mountain of shale and greywacke, covered by limestone. The crater falls
away to the inner basin in cliffs of greyish-black lava that range in
height from 200 to 400m (660–1,300ft) and contain visible strata of
white pumice and reddish tuff. The outside of the crater with its
thick covering of pumice gently slopes down to the sea, forming a
fertile vineyard and garden landscape.

History
Santorini has been settled since the 3rd millennium BC. At **Akrotiri**
excavations testify to a golden age in the first half of the 2nd millennium BC; although the island was in contact with Minoan Crete, it
still developed its own culture. Akrotiri was probably not governed
through a central power, but rather by merchants and ship owners.

Santorini *Map*

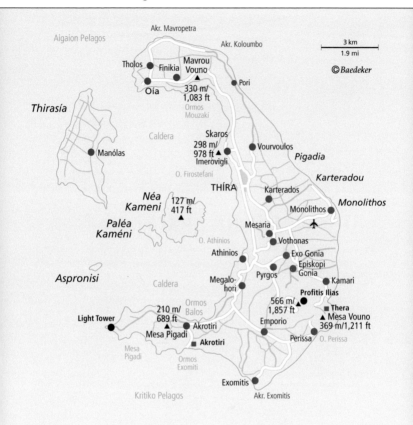

This is documented by wall paintings from Santorini, which are of excellent artistic quality. Most of them are in the National Archaeological Museum in Athens. The era of prosperity ended with the massive **explosion of Santorini's volcano** around 1645 BC. After the volcanic eruption, the island remained uninhabited for half a millennium. It was not resettled again until the start of the 1st millennium BC, this time by Minoan-Dorian immigrants from Crete. A certain degree of wealth was reached under the Egyptian Ptolemaic dynasty, who maintained a base there. Then the island became Roman, later Byzantine. In 1207, in connection with the Fourth Crusade, the Venetian Marco Sanudo, later Duke of Naxos, took over the island, which was then renamed Santorini. In 1537 it was conquered by

A volcano erupted in the caldera of Santorini in the 9th century (illustration from the »Illustrated London News«, 1866)

CATASTROPHE ON SANTORINI

What was most likely the greatest natural disaster in the history of mankind occurred on Santorini. It was not the last such event. Almost within living memory, there was another...

The explosion was enormous. The volcanic island flew into the air with the energy of 7,000 Hiroshima atomic bombs. In the process, a 20 cu km/4.2 cu mi cloud of ash, pumice and gas was hurled up to 80 km/50 mi into the atmosphere and two-thirds of the island was swallowed by the sea. 300 towns on the surrounding islands were destroyed and 36,000 peopled burned to death in the rain of fire or drowned in the tsunamis, tidal waves towering as high as 40 m/130 ft unleashed by the eruption, which reached Le Havre in France, 18,000 km/11,300 miles away, after 32 hours. The roar of the eruption travelled for four hours across the oceans and continents, the wave of air pressure raced around the globe several times and the ashes drifted visibly around the world for three years. The volcanic eruption of Krakatoa in the Sunda Strait between Sumatra and Java on 27 August 1883 was **one of the greatest natural disasters** in the history of mankind, but the eruption of Santorini, some 3,500 years earlier, was far worse. To gain an idea of what happened on Santorini, one has to imagine an explosion about four times as great as that on Krakatoa...

Enormous pressure

Before the eruption, Santorini was a small, round island; a number of seemingly extinct volcano cones fused together into a dome mountain that majestically rose out of the water and was covered with lush vegetation and forests. The island had been inhabited since around 3000 BC – until about 1645 BC when the volcano awoke again after a long period of dormancy. The catastrophe undoubtedly developed over a long period of time. It is likely that for weeks or months, gas explosions, fire and pumice rain and

earthquakes shook the island and, as living conditions became unbearable, the inhabitants probably fled, because no signs have been found that the subsequent eruption took any human lives. The natural spectacle culminated when the inside of the volcano was torn apart by the enormous pressure of the gas and steam. This was because, as in Krakatoa, cold sea water had entered the mountain through fissures in the rock and mixed with the broiling magma, a highly explosive mixture that could no longer escape through the few vents not plugged by lava.

Ash and pumice were probably also flung several miles into the sky in this eruption. What was left of Santorini volcano was covered with a 30 m/100 ft layer of glowing ash and even on the Dodecanese, on Cyprus and in the western part of Turkey, there is evidence of a layer of pumice up to 2 cm/0.8 in thick. After the magma chamber below the vents had been emptied by the blow-out of millions upon millions of tons of lava, the great volcano collapsed, creating an enormous **caldera** into which the ocean poured. Only the sections visible today, **Thira**, **Thirassia** and **Aspronisi**, were left standing with sheer rock walls. The crater of the collapsed volcano has a capacity of about 60 cu km/37 cu mi. Whether the collapsing mountain caused a gigantic tidal wave that devastated distant coastal regions, as happened with Krakatoa in the Sunda Strait, and was the cause of the fall of the Minoan civilization in the past, as many scientists assume, is still disputed. Perhaps the magma chamber collapsed slowly without creating tsunamis.

No rest

The volcanic activity has not ended, even after 3,600 years. The latest disaster on the island took place in 1956. On 9 July, an earthquake with a magnitude of seven on the Richter scale rocked the island for 45 seconds at five in the morning, destroying 2,000 houses, injuring 200 and claiming the lives of 50 people.

Khayr ad-Din Barbarossa, but onlybecame Ottoman in 1579. In 1834 Santorini passed to the Kingdom of Greece. Volcanic activity remained a problem in later times as well. The villages of Thira and Ia were destroyed in an earthquake in 1956.

What to See on Santorini

★★
Thirá/Firá
(Θίρά/Φίρά)

A bus service runs 17km/10mi from the ferry quay in Athinios to the beautiful capital, Thira (population 2,100). The way up to Thira (also called Fira) from the old harbour Skala is to climb steep steps, ride a donkey or take a cable car. The cable car was donated by a ship owner in the 1980s, and the donkey owners get part of the income.

Thira is extremely impressive. Its white houses built on the rim of the crater contrast with the dark stone, its winding lanes and squares constantly offer spectacular new views of the caldera, and its churches and chapels have turquoise domes. Intensive tourism with its ever-present jewellery and souvenir shops, tavernas and bars, especially in the most popular shopping street, Ipapantis, does not seem to spoil the town. Do not miss a **sunset walk** along the edge of the crater to the villages Firostefani and Imerovigli. The restaurants and bars along the edge of the crater also enjoy an overwhelming view.

Thira/Fira Map

Where to eat
① Kapari
② Naoussa

Where to sleep
① Kavalari

The magnificent Mitropolis Church of 1956 towers at the southern end of town. The **Archaeological Museum of Santorini** shows artefacts found at the excavation sites Thira and Akrotiri from Cycladic to Roman times, including beautiful Geometric and Archaic vases and vessels. The neck amphora with relief decorations is remarkable. Opening times: Tue–Sun 8.30am–3pm.

A little further to the north is the former Catholic quarter with the cathedral and a Dominican monastery. The Venetian mansion which now houses interesting exhibits from the island history and modern Greek art in the **Megaro Gyzi Museum** (Erithrou Stavrou) is also here. Opening hours: Mon–Sat 10.30am–1.30pm, 5pm–8pm, Sun 10.30am–4.30pm.

▶ VISITING SANTORINI

INFORMATION

Tourist information
In the travel agencies
Main square, Thira
www.santorini.com

GETTING THERE

Boat service from Piraeus and Thessaloniki and to the islands of Anafi, Crete, Folegandros, Kimolos, Kythnos, Milos, Mykonos, Naxos, Paros, Serifos, Sifnos, Sikinos, Skiathos, Syros and Tinos

WHERE TO EAT

► Expensive
Selene
Pirgos
Tel. 2 28 60 2 22 49, www.selene.gr
Santorini specialities and international cuisine

► Moderate
① *Kapari*
Thirá
Tel. 2 28 60 2 70 86
Excellent Santorin cooking in a friendly taverna atmosphere.

② *Naoussa*
Thirá, Shopping centre Lagoudera
Tel. 2 28 60 2 48 69
www.naoussa-restaurant.gr
Restaurant on the 2nd floor with a large selection of Greek starters

WHERE TO STAY

► Luxury
Katikies
Oia
Tel. 2 28 60 7 14 01
Fax 2 28 60 7 11 29
www.katikies.com
25 rooms. This elegant hotel, member of the »Small Luxury Hotels of the World«, stands out for its magnificent location on the edge of the crater; guests looking for quiet and a high level of comfort will find it here.

► Mid-range
① *Kavalari*
Thira
Tel. 2 28 60 2 24 55
Fax 2 28 60 2 26 03
www.kavalarihotel-santorini.com
19 rooms. Terraced hotel built into the edge of the crater with a wonderful view

Sunshine
Kamari
Tel. 2 28 60 3 13 94
Fax 2 28 60 3 22 40
www.hotelsunshine.gr
35 rooms. Family-run hotel with a pool terrace on the beach promenade

Large-scale replicas of many frescoes from Akrotiri can be seen in the old wine cellar in the **Nomikos Conference Centre**. Opening ⏱ times: high season daily 10am–8pm. New finds from Cycladic and Minoan culture can be seen in the **Museum of Prehistoric Thira** opposite the bus terminal. There are also exhibits on the geology of Santorini. The part of the museum dedicated to Akrotiri has a model of the excavation site and two of the famous frescoes (17th century

Thira's splendid location on the edge of the crater

⊕ BC). One unique find is a ram made of fine gold leaf. Opening hours: May–Oct Mon 1.30–8pm, Tue–Sun 8am–8pm, Nov–April Tue–Sun 8.30am–3pm.

Oia/Ia
(Οία)
The tidy little town of Oia spreads across the crater's rim on the northern tip of the main island. It was rebuilt after the earthquake of 1956. With its countless blue church domes, labyrinth of white-washed stepped alleys and white houses with flat roofs, Oia is the epitome of an idyllic Cycladic village. Meander along the shop-lined main street up to the castle ruins at the end, from where there is the best view of the town. This is also an ideal place to enjoy the **sunset**. The **Naval Maritime Museum** in an old mansion is worth visiting;
⊕ it shows nautical instruments, ship models and figureheads (opening times: Mon, Wed–Sun 10am–2pm, 5pm–8pm) and the **museum of historic musical instruments**, which opened in 2011.
From the Lontza castle, steps and a street lead down to dark **Ammou-di Beach** with a small harbour, where tasty fish dishes are served.

Art Space
At Exo Gonia (signposted on the Thira-Kamari road) the gallery Art Space exhibits works by artists living in Greece; it is located in a cave, an old wine cellar that was dug into the lava ash. The owner usually shows visitors around himself and explains how wine is made here
⊕ and marc liqueurs are distilled. Opening hours: daily 10am until sunset.

Pirgos, which was the capital during the Turkish period, is at 350m/ **Pirgos**
1,148ft the highest town on the island. The handsome, blinding- **(Πύργος)**
white houses are set along the
slopes among brilliant blue church
domes. Many steep stepped lanes
lead into the village.

i Wine tasting

- Mesa Gonia, about 2km/1mi east of Pyrgos, is
the centre of wine-growing on Santorini. In
September, anyone can take part in the
traditional wine pressing. Wineries here, and
in higher-lying Exo Gonia, offer tastings. The
Boutari winery has a visitor centre in
Megalohori, 10km/6mi south of Thira.

A road from Thira leads 12km/7mi
with magnificent panorama views
all the way and ends on the 566m/
1,857ft summit of Profitis Ilias, the
highest on the island, which is
spoiled by radio masts. However,
the view of the island and the Ae-
gean is magnificent. **Profitis Ilias Monastery** (not open) was the site **Profitis Ilias**
of a secret school, as was common during the Turkish period. The **(Προφίτις Ιλίας)**
church is open, allowing visitors to see a carved iconostasis and a
15th-century Cretan crown of Elijah. Opening hours: May–Sept ⊙
5am–9am, 4pm–7pm.

The **most popular beach resort on the island**, Kamari, sprawls along **Kamari**
the east coast north of the impressive, steep Cape Mesa Vouno. A **(Καμάρι)**
long beach of dark pebbles awaits visitors here. The shoreline promenade is shaded by tamarisks and lined with many hotels, bars and
tavernas. The second-largest beach resort on the east coast, **Perissa**,
has a fine sandy beach and many chic and unusual bars.

The ruins of ancient Thira are 3km/2mi south of Kamari on the Me- ★
sa Vouno mountain ridge, which drops off steeply on three sides. **Ancient Thira**
The city was founded about 1000 BC, prospered under Ptolemaic
rule (300–150 BC) and was inhabited into the 13th century.
The 3rd-century BC **Temple of Artemidoros**, a Ptolemaic admiral, is
at the start of the tour. A stepped path on the right leads to the barracks and gymnasium of the Ptolemaic garrison on the heights of
Mesa Vouno. The agora is surrounded by houses and workshops.
Standing on its southeast side is the **Stoa Basilike** (1st century BC), a
royal colonnade; the interior is divided lengthwise by a row of Doric
columns. A **Temple of Dionysos**, which was later dedicated to the
Ptolemies (2nd century BC) and finally also to the Roman emperor,
can be made out on the terrace above the northwest corner of the
stoa. There are foundations of some Hellenistic private homes with a
Delian ground plan on the main road, and the theatre with a Roman
stage is visible. A path branches off the main road at the theatre por-
tal to a rock shrine of the Egyptian deities Isis, Serapis and Anubis.
An artificially enlarged terrace (6th century BC) at the southeastern
end of the city is the site of the gymnopaedia square for cult celebrations honouring Apollo Karneios, as archaic inscriptions here, some
of an erotic nature, testify. The adjoining **Temple of Apollo Karneios**

to the northwest consists of a pronaos, cella and two chambers that may have been used as treasuries. On the southeast end of the ridge lies the **Ephebian Gymnasium** (2nd century BC) with the Grotto of Hermes and Heracles, as well as Roman baths. Opening times: Tue–Sun 8.30am–3pm.

**Akrotiri
(Ακρωτήρι)**

Large sections of an important city **destroyed by the great volcanic eruption (about 1645 BC)** have been uncovered at Akrotiri, 12km/7mi southwest of Fira. The archaeologist who led the excavations was killed by a collapsing wall in 1974 and buried here. The civilization that has come to light here appears to have combined ancient Cycladic culture with the innovations of Minoan society. The inhabitants of the city must have fled in time because no human remains have been found. The surviving buildings date from the 17th century BC and show traces of damage caused by earthquakes before the catastrophe, such as leaning walls that were held in position by the pumice sand that covered everything.

The city was a honeycomb of narrow cobbled streets. The houses had two, three or even four storeys. The ground floors were used as storerooms or workshops, the upper storeys as living quarters. The wonderful frescoes that were found here are on display in the National Archaeological Museum in Athens – apart from two that are in the Museum of Prehistoric Thira. The most important buildings of this second Pompeii have been provided with floor plans and explanations. Closed until further notice, reopening in 2010 at the earliest.

Red Beach ►

From the parking lot at the end of the road at the excavation site, a path leads down to Red Beach (Paralia Kokkini), **one of the most beautiful on Santorini**; the walk takes about 15 minutes. The beach is framed by imposing multi-coloured rock walls.

Kameni islands

Nea Kameni, which was first created by a volcanic eruption in 1707, is an impressively bizarre desert of black stone. From the quay St George's crater, which emits sulphurous steam, is a half-hour's walk away. Visitors can swim in warm ferrous and sulphurous waters on the northwest coast of **Palea Kameni**.

**Thirasia
(Θηρασία)**

From Skala harbour of Thira take a boat across to the island of Thirasia (population 270, 9 sq km/3.5sq mi), another part of the crater, and enjoy the view of Santorini. Steps lead up to the **main town Manolas** high above the east coast.

Anafi (Ανάφη)

The southeasternmost Cycladic island is Anafi (»the shining one«; population 300), 22km/13mi east

The Kameni Islands lie right in the middle of the caldera of Santorini

of Santorini. It is 12km/7mi long and at the most 7km/4.5mi wide. The island has charming, mountainous landscape and empty beaches. Below the **eponymous capital**, whose white houses impressively crown a rock promontory, there are a few **beautiful sandy beaches** towards the eastern cape, Kalamos.

Agios Nikolaos (Αγιος Νικόλαος)   The tiny harbour of Agios Nikolaos in the south of the island consists of a few houses in front of a cliff. Only fishing boats or kaikis can land here; larger ships have to transfer their passengers to smaller boats.

Anafi Hora   Follow the road or the footpath to the main town, Anafi Hora, impressively sited at 256m/840ft above sea level and dominated by a ruined 14th-century Venetian castle.

South coast   A pleasant hike leads eastwards from Agios Nikolaos, mostly right along the coast. Of several beaches here, **Megalos Roukonas** with its fine-grained sand is the best. After *c* 6km/4mi the **Zoödochos Pigi Monastery** is reached. It was built in 1807 on the foundations of an ancient Temple of Apollo making use of building material from the temple. Another hour to the east the **Church of Panagia Kalamiotissa** (1715) is visible from far off, perched 396m/1,300ft above the sea on the Kalamos promontory. From here it is possible to see as far as Crete. The islands Ftena, Pachia and Makra are to the southeast.

The harbour of Agios Nikolaos on Anafi with Hora high above

✴ Serifos

Greek: Σέριφος
Area: 73 sq km/28 sq mi
Population: 1,400
Capital: Serifos Hora

Island group: Cyclades
Elevation: 0–587m/1,926ft above sea level

This rocky island, divided by gorges, has beautiful beaches and, in places, lush green scenery. In recent years it has become increasingly popular with tourists.

Serifos, in the middle of the western Cyclades, is at first glance barren and rocky, but in fact is well supplied with water and has many green spots. The view upon approaching the island is impressive: a deep bay with a wonderful beach and the picturesque Hora on a steep cliff in the background.

Green rocky island

In mythology Serifos is the place where **Danaë** and her son **Perseus** found refuge after their father set them adrift at sea. Later Perseus came back to Serifos and turned King Polydektes, who had threatened his mother, to stone by showing him the head of Medusa.

What to See on Serifos

The harbour town of Livadi is the island's tourist centre. Most facilities are on the harbour bay and the adjacent **Livadakia** beach. There are more sandy beaches nearby, such as **Karavi** and **Psili Ammos**, a wonderful dune beach with fine white sand north of the peninsula.

Livadi (Λιβαδι)

 VISITING SERIFOS

INFORMATION
Krinas Travel and Tourism
Livadi
Tel. 2 28 10 5 14 88; fax 2 28 10 5 11 64

GETTING THERE
Boat service from Piraeus and to the islands of Folegandros, Ios, Kimolos, Kythnos, Milos, Naxos, Paros, Santorini, Sifnos, Sikinos and Syros

WHERE TO EAT
► **Expensive**
Takis
Sea shore, Livadi

Tel. 2 28 10 5 11 59
Very tasty Greek cooking, large selection of dishes and wines

WHERE TO STAY
► **Mid-range**
Maistrali
Livadi
Tel. 2 28 10 5 13 81
Fax 2 28 10 5 12 98
20 rooms. This small but nice hotel is 500m/550yd from the harbour and almost next to the beach; the well-furnished rooms all have a balcony.

There is a sweeping view of the Bay of Livadi from the island's chief town

Serifos Hora   From Livadi there is a 5km/3mi-long road or a short footpath up to Serifos Hora. The main town of the island has an enchanting location on a steep cliff, even though a large number of the houses cannot even be seen from the harbour. It consists of two parts: Kato Hora (»lower town«) with the interesting Evangelistria church and a small **folk art museum** (opening hours: Mon–Fri 6pm–9pm), and Ano Hora (»upper town«) with the former castle hill. From here there is a wonderful view of the harbour bay and the island – one of the most beautiful places in the Cyclades. In the neo-classical town hall next door a small **archaeological museum** shows artefacts from the Roman period. Opening hours: Tue–Sun 8.30am–1pm.

Panagia   In the pretty high-lying village of Panagia (5km/3mi to the north),
(Παναγία)   the **oldest church on the island**, founded about AD 950, possesses two ancient marble columns, frescoes from the 13th and 14th centuries and icons from the 18th and 19th centuries.

Taxiarchon   Another 4km/2.5mi north is the fortress-like Taxiarchon Monastery
Monastery ▶   (17th century), the island's major attraction. Its highlights are a richly decorated catholicon (1447) and **frescoes by Emanuel Skordilis** (around 1700), who depicted the torments of hell in great detail.

Other beaches   Along with the beaches of Livadi there are some on the north coast (Ormos Sikamia) and on the south coast in Koutalas Bay.

✴ Sifnos

Greek: Λίθνος
Area: 73 sq km/28 sq mi
Population: 2,400

Island group: Cyclades
Area: 0–680m/2,231ft above sea level
Capital: Apollonia

Attractive landscape, picturesque villages and beautiful beaches have made the island of Sifnos a popular holiday destination.

The northern part of Sifnos consists of stark, barren mountains, while the east and south have gentle hills with terraces where olive and almond trees flourish. In many places the scene is marked by dovecotes, white monasteries and churches. Along the deeply incised coast with steep cliffs there are still many Hellenistic, Roman and medieval watchtowers. The fertile land is cultivated: Sifnos olive oil enjoys an excellent reputation.

Pottery island

A good supply of clay has lead to a tradition of **ceramics craftsmanship**. In classical antiquity the island became wealthy through lead, silver and gold mining. After the mines sank into the sea the island lost its major role and wealth – since then it has been called »sifnos« (»empty«).

Panagia Chrissopigi Monastery:
one of the most-photographed views on Sifnos

▶ VISITING SIFNOS

INFORMATION
Tourist office
Opposite the quay
Kamares
Tel. 2 28 40 3 19 77

HOW TO GET THERE

Ferries to Anafi, Andros, Folegandros, Kimolos, Kythnos, Milos, Paros, Piraeus, Santorini, Serifos, Sikinos, Syros, Tinos

WHERE TO EAT
▶ **Moderate**
Boulis
Near edge of town, Kamares

Tel. 2 28 40 3 21 22
Creative Greek cooking in an old-established taverna

WHERE TO STAY
▶ **Budget**
Sifnos
Main street
Apollonia
Tel. 2 28 40 3 16 24
www.sifnoshotel.com, 9 rooms.
Family-run hotel with rooms of decent quality

What to See on Sifnos

Kamares
(Καμάρες)

The town of Kamares is where the ferries and excursion boats stop; in the summer tourists make it a lively place. There is a beautiful beach near the town, but boats also carry guests to other beaches on the island.

Apollonia
(Απολλωία)
🕐

The capital Apollonia, 6km/4mi southeast of Kamares, is a labyrinth of white houses on a fertile plateau. On the plateia the **folk art museum** displays embroidery work, old clothing, weapons and traditional ceramics. Opening hours: daily 7pm–10.30pm. The narrow main street is lined with souvenir shops, tavernas and cafes.

✱
Kastro
(Κάστρο)

It is worthwhile walking from Apollonia 3km/2mi eastwards to the picturesque town of Kastro, which is situated above a bay and for the most part abandoned. This well-preserved medieval town was the island capital from antiquity until 1834. The remains of the ancient wall (4th century BC) can still be seen. The outer town wall was formed by the outer walls of the houses. These all have outer steps, verandas and balconies, and are decorated with coats of arms. A small **archaeological museum**, the **Church of Theoskepasti** (1631) and the **Chapel of Efta Martires**, located impressively on a rocky point, can be visited.

Profitis Ilias
(Προφίτις Ηλίας)

From Apollonia it takes about two hours to climb the highest mountain on the island, the 680m/2,230ft Profitis Ilias; on top is an abandoned monastery of the same name, which goes back to the 9th century. There is a panoramic view of the island and the sea from here.

There are two sandy beaches in **Faros**, a little fishing harbour 4km/2.5mi south of Apollonia. The nearby **Chrissopigi Monastery** on a rocky promontory was founded in 1650 and is very photogenic. The main attraction of the popular holiday resort **Platys Gialos** further to the south is a 2km/1mi-long sandy beach. **Vathi Bay** in the southwest of the island also has an attractive sandy beach. The nearby 16th-century **Taxiarchis Monastery** is also worth seeing.

Other beaches

★ Skiathos

Greek: Σκίαθος	**Island group:** Northern Sporades
Area: 48 sq km/19 sq mi	**Elevation:** 0–438m/1,437ft above sea level
Population: 6,200	
Capital: Skiathos Hora	

Skiathos, with beaches of wonderfully fine sand and crystal-clear water that are considered to be the most beautiful in Greece, is a paradise for holidaymakers who enjoy a bustling night life. For those looking for a lively time, this is the right place.

Skiathos is a hilly, forested island of the Northern Sporades. Only the southern part of the island has been completely equipped for tourists; in the north with its pine and olive woods – along with tourism olives are the most important source of income for the islanders – there are still isolated churches and monasteries as well as secluded beaches. Skiathos has hardly any historic cultural sites, but to compensate more than 60 **beaches**, which are less crowded the further they are from Skiathos Hora and the more difficult to reach.

Fabulous beaches

Baedeker TIP

Cave trip

Three sea caves – Skotini Spilia, Galazia Spilia and Halkini Spilia – are located east of Lalaria beach on Skiathos. They can be explored by swimmers – a great experience! Tour boats also enter a few yards into the caves.

What to See on Skiathos

The main town and only significant settlement on the island is Skiathos Hora on the southeast coast. This idyllic town has white houses with red-tiled roofs and winding cobbled lanes as well as a pretty fishing and yacht harbour; it is completely given over to tourism. Chic boutiques and antique shops make it a veritable shopping paradise, and during the high season there is abundant night life. It de-

Skiathos Hora

▶ VISITING SKIATHOS

INFORMATION

Tourist information
At the ferry pier
Skiathos Hora
www.skiathos.gr

HOW TO GET THERE

Boats from Agios
Konstantinos, Thessaloniki and Volos
as well as Alonissos, Crete, Evia,
Lesbos, Limnos, Mykonos, Paros,
Santorini, Skopelos and Tinos

WHERE TO EAT

▶ Moderate

Psaradika
Old harbour, Skiathos Hora
Tel. 2 42 70 2 34 12
Taverna with good fish dishes and a
beautiful view of the bay

WHERE TO STAY

▶ Luxury

Atrium
Platanias
Tel. 2 42 70 4 93 45
Fax 2 42 70 4 94 44
www.atriumhotel.gr
75 rooms. Set on a pine-wood slope
with a fantastic view of the sea from
the rooms

▶ Mid-range

Alkyon
Skiathos Hora
Tel. 2 42 70 2 29 81
www.alkyon.gr
89 rooms. This hotel is ideal for
people who not only want peace and
quiet on the beach, but would like to
sample the nightlife on Skiathos as
well.

veloped after 1830 on the site of an ancient city, two low rocky ridges
around a harbour bay divided by the pine-covered Burdzi peninsula.
There are ruins of a Venetian fortress between the old and new harbour. Skiathos was the home of the poet **Alexandros Papadiamantis**
(1851–1911). A museum commemorates him in his former
residence. Opening hours: daily 8.30am–1pm, 5.30pm–8pm. There
is a monument in his honour at the harbour.

Beaches The beaches really are almost all beautiful. The most attractive are
Koukounaries southwest of Skiathos Hora, under umbrella pines,
and **Lalaria Beach** on the north coast with light grey pebbles, which
can only be reached by boat. Just offshore is a rock arch, through
which one can swim. Gialos Krassas, in a romantic bay with large
trees, on the west coast, known as **Banana Beach**, is the place for
nude bathing.

Kastro The ruins of the medieval village of Kastro, the island's capital from
1538 until 1829, have a spectacular setting on a high spur of rock on
the north coast, from where there is a **breathtaking view**. Kastro is
best reached by boat. Parts of the fortification walls with a draw-
bridge have survived, along with Turkish baths and three churches,

Attractive Koukounaries beach

including the Christos sto Kastro Church with a screen (1695) and beautiful frescoes.

The cave monastery **Evangelistria**, 4km/2.5mi north of Skiathos Hora, was founded in 1797 in a beautiful site overlooking a gorge. During the War of Independence it served as a hiding place for rebels. Frescoes dating from 1822 can be seen in the church. 8km/5mi northwest of Skiathos Hora lies the abandoned **Kechrias Monastery** (1540), the oldest on the island; it is decorated with beautiful wall paintings (1745). The 17th-century **Panagia Kounistra Church** (9km/5.5mi west of Skiathos Hora), is dedicated to the island's patron saint and is open for visitors. The murals (1742) have for the most part faded.

★ Skopelos

Greek: Σκόπελος
Area: 96 sq km/37 sq mi
Population: 5,000
Capital: Skopelos Hora

Island group: Northern Sporades
Elevation: 0–680m/2,231ft above sea level

Skopelos is a delightful wooded island with many excellent beaches. The island is trying to imitate its neighbour Skiathos, but still manages to keep a higher standard. Only the capital Skopelos gets lively during the high season.

Fertile and green Skopelos is one of the most scenically beautiful islands: large olive groves and almond orchards characterize the landscape. The steep northern coast is not inviting and, apart from broad Skopelos Bay, has a fairly straight coastline. The gentler southwest

Outstanding landscape

coast is also not much indented. Fruit is grown here, especially plums. Tourism is gaining in importance and not limited to visits to the picturesque capital, but it also profits from the **good beaches**. Almost all the beaches, with nearby hotels and tavernas, lie between Staphylos and Loutraki on the south and west coasts.

What to See on Skopelos

Skopelos Hora

The idyllic island capital Skopelos (population 3,800) is set attractively in a sweeping bay, its white houses with tile or slate roofs climbing up the castle hill along narrow, winding lanes. The **ruins of the castle**, which go back to Philip II of Macedon, were extended by the Ghisi family in the 13th century. The main attraction of the **old quarter**, which is a protected heritage zone, is the harbour, where tavernas line up in a row. In the small **folk art museum** a wedding room has been recreated. Opening hours: 11am–1.30pm, 7pm–9pm. The town has about 120 churches and chapels, which are almost always closed. **Agios Athanasios**, the oldest church, is especially interesting. It was built in the 9th century on the foundations of a temple and decorated with frescoes in the 17th century.

Beaches

The best beach is **Milia**, northwest of Panormos Beach. The most popular, about 5km/3mi from Skopelos Town, are the sand and pebble beaches **Stafilos** and **Velanio**.

Glossa
(Γλόσσα)

The houses of Glossa, in the northwest, the island's other town, are scattered prettily up the green slopes of the mountain overlooking the harbour of Loutraki. A fantastic view of Skiathos and Mt Pilion on the mainland can be enjoyed from this still authentic mountain village.

▶ VISITING SKOPELOS

INFORMATION
Tourist Office
Town hall
www.skopelosweb.gr,
www.skopelos.net

HOW TO GET THERE
Boat connections with Agios Konstantinos, Alonnisos, Kavala, Limnos, Samothraki, Skiathos and Volos

WHERE TO EAT
▶ **Moderate**
Finikas
Old quarter of Skopelos Hora

Pleasant restaurant with meat and fish dishes and a terrace

WHERE TO STAY
▶ **Mid-range**
Skopelos Village
Skopelos Hora
Tel. 2 42 40 2 26 18
Fax 2 42 40 2 27 70
www.skopelosvillage.gr
36 apartments. Not far outside Skopelos Hora, this very good hotel has apartments in bungalows; some of the rooms have a sea view.

A remarkable 350 churches, chapels and monasteries have been built on Skopelos. A visit to the monasteries some miles east of Skopelos Hora makes a good day's hike (three hours there and back). After 4km/2.5mi comes the **Evangelistria Monastery** (1712) with its extravagantly carved and gilded iconostasis and a 10th-century icon of the Virgin Mary encased in silver. Further east is the oldest monastery on the island, the abandoned **Metamorfosis** (16th century). The next site is a convent, **Timios Prodromos** (1721), with an inner courtyard decorated with flowers, and opposite it the abandoned **Agia Varvara Monastery** (1648).

Restful corner in Evangelistria Monastery

Alonnisos (Αλόηησς)

Alonnisos (population 2,700) is – unlike its sometimes very noisy neighbours Skiathos and Skopelos – a tranquil island with only a little tourism, where guests can always expect to find peace and quiet. A mountain ridge runs the whole length of the island. The northwest coast is steep and has few distinctive features, whilst the gentler southeast coast has more coves. Almost all residents live in the fertile south, where the modest tourist activity is also concentrated. The island is suitable for swimming, snorkelling and hiking, and is considered to have the **cleanest sea water in all of the Aegean**. There is a row of beaches in the southern half along the east coast, in the extreme south and in the west up to Ormos Megali Ammos.

The tiny port of Patitiri first came into being in the 1950s and is now the centre of tourism. It is sited on a round bay with steep cliffs. The only attraction is the small **monk seal museum** on the harbour promenade, where displays, photos and a 200-year-old monk seal skeleton inform about the local seal colony.

Patitiri (Πατίρι)

The former capital Alonnisos Horio (2km/1mi northwest) was all but abandoned after the earthquake in 1965, but has been rebuilt as a holiday resort. Many houses were bought and restored by wealthy foreigners, especially Germans and English. There is a magnificent view of the sea from this idyllic location.

Alonnisos Horio

Skyros

L/M 7

Greek: Σκύρος
Area: 209 sq km/80 sq mi
Population: 2,600
Capital: Skyros Hora

Island group: Northern Sporades
Elevation: 0–814m/2,671ft above sea level

Skyros lies off the beaten track and away from the tourist masses – an ideal holiday refuge for people seeking peace and relaxation. The donkey paths that crisscross the island make for ideal solitary hiking.

Peaceful island Skyros, the largest island of the Northern Sporades, is divided into two parts. The southeast is the rugged, arid Kochilas massif (814m/ 2,670ft). The quarries yielding variegated, coarse-grained marble that was much prized in Roman times are here. The more fertile northwest has gentler terrain, more water and is covered with pine forests. Between the two parts of the island lies a basin between Achilli Bay on the east coast and Kalamitsa Bay, which cuts deep inland in the west. At the foot of the steep, inhospitable cliffs on the coast are beautiful sandy beaches. Apart from agriculture and tourism, excellent **craftwork** (embroidery and weaving, carved furniture, ceramics and copper vessels) is an important economic factor. In the barren southeast there were once thousands of half-wild **ponies**, related to Shetland ponies. They are now endangered, but measures are being taken to save this species, which was already raised on Skyros in ancient times.

What to See on Skyros

✳
Skyros Hora The picturesque capital Skyros Hora (population 1,700) in the eastern part of the island makes an oriental impression with its cube-shaped houses. The elaborately and beautifully adorned houses rise in a semi-circle up a hill on which a fortified kastro once stood. **Theseus** is said to have been cast down from here; his remains, which were reportedly found later, were taken to the Theseion in Athens.

The statue of a nude man on Plateia Brooke commemorates the English poet **Rupert Brooke**, who was buried in an olive grove at Tris Boukes Bay in the south of Skyros in 1915. He died of septicaemia caused by an infected mosquito

A good way to spend a warm afternoon

▶ VISITING SKYROS

INFORMATION
Skyros Travel & Tourism
Skyros Hora
Tel. 2 22 20 9 16 00
Fax 2 22 20 9 21 23
www.skyrostravel.com

GETTING THERE
Boats from Evia

FESTIVAL
The carnival on Skyros is famous. On
the last two Sundays before Orthodox
Lent begins, men dress up in masks
and skins to look like goats; women
and children wear costumes, too.
They all process dancing and singing
through the streets.

WHERE TO EAT
▶ Moderate
Asterias
Central square, Skyros Hora

Tel. 2 22 20 9 13 80
Asterias serves delicious local specialities.

WHERE TO STAY
▶ Mid-range
Skyros Palace
Grismata, Molos
Tel. 2 24 40 3 19 00, fax 2 22 20 9 20 70
www.skiros-palace.gr
80 apartments
This hotel complex with its traditional
architecture and tasteful apartments
lies to the north of town near the
beach.

bite while en route to the Dardanelles. Behind the Brooke monument is the private **Faltaits Museum**, whose exhibits include excellent
Skyriot crafts, costumes, furniture, ceramics and photos. Opening ⊙
hours: 10am–1pm, 5.30pm–8pm.
The **archaeological museum** nearby has ceramics, vases, sculptures
and inscriptions from the Mycenaean to the Byzantine period as well
as traditional Skyriot furnishings. Opening hours: Tue–Sun ⊙
8.30am–3pm. To the left on the road to the castle the **Gialouri
House**, a typical Skyriot house, can be toured.

The long sandy beach north of Skyros Hora, one of the island's main **Beaches**
attractions, is divided into Magazia, Molos, Papa tou Coma, Vina,
Pouria and Gyrismata beaches. **Molos** beach, the best of them, has
developed into the island's tourist centre.

About 10km/6mi south of Hora, Linaria, the island's main harbour, **Linaria**
is located on the bay of the same name. The best beach on the island **(Λινάρια)**
lies to the east on **Kalamitsa Bay**. The fine-grained **sandy beach at
Pefkos** to the northwest is also good.

✳ Syros

M 9/10

Greek: Σύρος
Area: 86 sq km/33 sq mi
Population: 20,000
Capital: Ermoupolis

Island group: Cyclades
Elevation: 0–442m/1,450ft above sea level

Despite its importance as the administrative and commercial centre of the Cyclades, as well as being an important hub for shipping traffic in the Aegean, and because it is usually just a stopping-off point for island tours, tourism plays a relatively modest role on the hilly island.

»Capital« of the Cyclades
The hilly island of Syros is the political and economic centre of the Cyclades. Compared to agriculture (horticulture, dairy products), shipbuilding and textiles, tourism plays a minor role. In the more developed southern part of the island there are a few beaches, while the north is almost untouched. The island was taken over by the Duchy of Naxos in 1207 and has since had a strong Catholic influence. During the 19th century Ermoupolis grew to be the largest port in Greece and an important base between Asia Minor and western Europe. After the opening of the Corinth Canal in 1893 the economic growth of the city was stopped by the rising importance of Piraeus as a central port. Today the population is 40% Catholic and 60% Orthodox.

 VISITING SYROS

INFORMATION

EOT
Thimaton Sperchiou 11
Tel. 2 28 10 8 67 25; fax 2 28 10 8 52 75
www.syros.com
www.travel-to-syros.com

GETTING THERE

Ferries to Kavala, Lavrio, Piraeus, Rafina, Thessaloniki, Amorgos, Anafi, Andros, Astypalea, Chios, Donoúsa, Folegandros, Fourni, Iraklia, Ikaria, Ios, Kalymnos, Kea, Kimolos, Kos, Koufonisia, Crete, Kythnos, Leros, Lesbos, Limnos, Lipsi, Milos, Mykonos, Naxos, Nisyros, Paros, Patmos, Rhodes, Samos, Santorini, Schinousa, Serifos, Sifnos, Sikinos, Symi, Tilos and Tinos

WHERE TO STAY

▶ **Luxury**
Apollonos
Apollonos 8, Ermoupolis
Tel. 2 28 10 8 13 87, fax 22 81 08 16 81
www.xenosapollonos.gr
Small (3 rooms), but a very fine hotel; the owners have transformed a 19th-century house into a jewel.

▶ **Mid-range**
Omiros
Omirou 43, Ermoupolis
Tel. 2 28 10 8 49 10
www.hotel-omiros.gr, 11 rooms, 2 suites. Upmarket accommodation in a neo-classical mansion, ideal location, tastefully furnished with antiques; beautiful view of the harbour and the

Syros *Map*

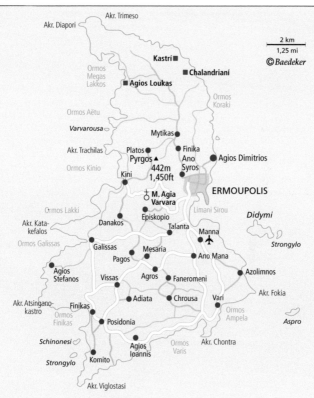

Akr. Trimeso
Akr. Diapori
Kastrí ■
■ Chalandriani
Ormos
Megas
Lakkos
■ Agios Loukas
Ormos
Koraki
Ormos Aëtu
Varvarousa ⌒
Mytikas ●
Akr. Trachilas
Platos ●
● Finika
Pyrgos ▲
Ano
● Agios Dimitrios
442m
Syros
Kini
1,450ft
Ormos Kinio
☩ M. Agia
Varvara
ERMOUPOLIS
Ormos Lakki
Episkopio
Limani Sirou
Didymi
Akr. Kata-
Danakos
Talanta
kefalos
Manna
Strongylo
Ormos Galissas
Galissas ●
Mesaria ●
✈
Pagos ●
● Ano Mana
Agios
Stefanos
Vissas ●
Agros ●
● Faneromeni
● Azolimnos
Akr. Atsingano-
Finikas
● Adiata
● Chrousa
Vari
Akr. Fokia
kastro
Ormos
Ormos
Finikas
● Posidonia
Ampela
Aspro
Schinonesi ⌒
Agios
Ormos
Akr. Chontra
Ioannis
Varis
Strongylo　Komito
Akr. Viglostasi

2 km
1,25 mi
© Baedeker

What to See on Syros

A striking picture greets visitors entering the harbour of Ermoupolis
(population 14,000) – named after Hermes, the god of trade. The
houses of the two parts of town, Ermoupolis and Ano Syros, spread
over two hills. The hill on the right is Vrontado, with the Orthodox
cathedral, that on the left Ano Syros, with the Roman Catholic St
George's Cathedral. The harbour front, as usual, is lined with cafes
and tavernas. The wharfs are adjacent in the south. The centre of
town is the elegant, marble-paved **Miaoulis Square** with its fine cafes.
A monument there commemorates Admiral Andreas Miaoulis, who
commanded the Greek fleet during the War of Independence. The
stately neo-classical city hall (1876–81) contains a small **archaeologi-**

★
Ermoupolis
(Ερμούπολι)

! *Baedeker* TIP

Sweet tooth?

For lovers of sweets we recommend the two island specialities: loukoumia, fruit jellies covered with powdered sugar, and chalvadopitta, wafers with honey and almonds.

cal museum with artefacts found on Syros and other Cycladic islands. The **Apollo Theatre** behind the city hall, a smaller version of La Scala in Milan, was built from 1861 to 1864 by the French architect Chableau. To the northeast is the neo-classical **Church of Agios Nikolaos** (19th century) with two high bell towers. The wealthy **Vaporia** (»steamship«) district, where rich shipping magnates built their neo-classical mansions, is here. The **Anastasis Church** stands above the town hall on a hill that offers a beautiful view of the city.

Ano Syros
(Άνω Σύρος)

The Roman Catholic town of Ano Syros (4km/2.5mi northwest of Ermoupolis) presents a typical image of a Cycladic town. It has existed since Venetian times and can be reached by a lane of steps. On the summit is the Catholic Cathedral of St George (1834), below it the Capuchin (1633) and Jesuit monasteries. For a superb view climb the highest mountain on the island, **Mt Pyrgos** (442m/1,450ft), from Ano Syros.

Plata Miaoulis in Ermoupolis with the elegant neo-classical town hall

Drive 4km/2.5mi from Ermoupolis along the winding road heading west into the interior to see **Agia Varvara Convent**, which cares for orphans and produces hand-woven textiles. The lively seaside resort of **Galissas** with its long, sandy beach shaded by tamarisk trees can be reached via the quiet fishing and holiday village of Kini, set in a round bay. The fishing village of **Finikas** (3km/2mi to the south) is just as popular and has some attractive beaches in the vicinity, as does **Posidonia** with its sand and pebble beach. Further along the coastal road **Vari**, above the bay on the southeast coast, is popular for its two sandy beaches. **South of the island**

✶ Thasos

Greek: Θάσος
Area: 379 sq km/146 sq mi
Elevation: 0–1,127m/3,698ft
above sea level

Island group: North and east
Aegean islands
Population: 13,800
Capital: Thasos Town/Limenas

Greece's most northerly island, with its magnificent beaches and many camping sites, is attracting increasing numbers of visitors.

Thasos, a fertile island with an ample water supply, lies only 8km/5mi off the coast. It is almost perfectly circular and despite destructive forest fires in recent years has remained a green island. The island mountain range, scored by deep valleys, reaches a height of 1,127m/3,697ft and is good hiking terrain. It is densely wooded on its northern and eastern flanks, which drop steeply off into the sea, while its southern and western slopes descend more gently. »Emerald green«

The population earns its livelihood from farming and mining copper and zinc. **Underground mining** of red chalk, an iron ore, took place as much as 20,000 years ago at Limenaria – the oldest mine in Europe so far discovered. White Thasos marble was also in great demand in antiquity and is still quarried south of Limenas. The painter **Polygnotus** (5th century BC), who worked in Athens and Delphi, came from Thasos. Now tourism is the main source of income. The finest bays with the best beaches are on the east coast, but there are bays with long beaches almost everywhere along the coastal road that circles the island.

Thasos Town/Limenas

In the modern capital and harbour Thasos (population 3,100), also called Limenas, holidaymakers create a lively atmosphere in the high season. The guests prefer the shopping street and the idyllic harbour, and keep numerous restaurants and cafes busy. There is entertainment of all kinds and the night life leaves nothing to be desired. The Town

Thasos Map

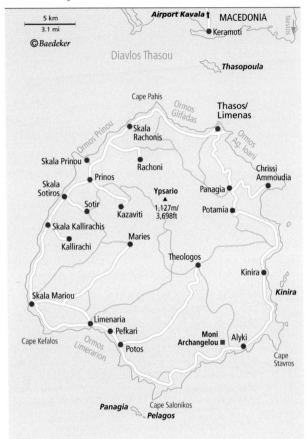

5 km
3.1 mi
©Baedeker

Airport Kavala
MACEDONIA
Keramoti
Nestos

Diavlos Thasou

Thasopoula

Cape Pahis
Ormos Glifadas
Thasos/ Limenas
Ormos Prinou
Skala Rachonis
Ormos Ag. Ioani
Skala Prinou
Rachoni
Chrissi Ammoudia
Prinos
Skala Sotiros
Panagia
Ypsario ▲ 1,127m/ 3,698ft
Sotir
Potamia
Kazaviti
Skala Kallirachis
Maries
Kallirachi
Theologos
Kinira
Kinira
Skala Mariou
Limenaria
Pefkari
Moni Archangelou
Alyki
Cape Kefalos
Ormos Limerarion
Potos
Cape Stavros
Panagia
Cape Salonikos
Pelagos

town itself is almost an open-air museum. It was built on the western part of the ancient capital, whose extent is marked by the surviving walls that enclosed the naval harbour (today a fishing harbour), sections of the city wall dating from the 7th to 5th centuries BC, and the foundations of residences and shrines. The excavated ancient city extends southeast from the harbour up to the heights of the acropolis, where the Genoese Gattelusi family built their castle in 1431.

✱
Agora

The agora (4th century BC to 1000 AD) with its colonnades lies behind the old harbour; some of the columns have been set up again. The **archaeological museum** on its west side contains artefacts found on the island, including its showpiece, a large kouros with a ram

⏵ VISITING THASOS

INFORMATION

Tourist police
Thasos Town
Near the bus terminal at the seafront
www.thassos-island.de

GETTING THERE

Ferries to and from Kavala and
Keramoti on the mainland

WHERE TO EAT

▶ Inexpensive
O Glaros
Alyki
Tel. 2 59 30 3 15 47

Fish and grilled specialities are best
enjoyed here on the shady terrace
with a view of the bay.

WHERE TO STAY

▶ Mid-range
Kipos
Thasos Town
Tel. 2 59 30 2 24 69
Fax 2 59 30 60 01 50
www.kipos-apartments.gr
8 studios, 8 apartments. Nice apartment complex with swimming pool;
apartments have a balcony, studios
have a terrace.

(*c* 600 BC). In front of the eastern corner of the agora, the gateway
of the theoroi (ambassadors) can be seen. The sanctuary of Artemis
Polo (6th century BC) lies to the southeast. South of the agora there
is a paved courtyard, and beyond the ancient Roman road an odeon
(2nd century AD); to the southwest are the remnants of a triumphal
arch erected in honour of the Roman emperors Caracalla and Septi-
mius Severus in AD 213–217, as well as a Temple of Heracles (6th
century BC). In the northern section of the ancient city are the sanctuaries of Dionysos and Poseidon (both 4th century BC), the theatre
(3rd–2nd century BC), a sanctuary to foreign gods, and, at the
northernmost point, a shrine to the »Patrooi Theoi« (6th century
BC).
During the summer, performances are held in the theatre. A path
leads up from there to the **castle** – an ancient relief of a funeral feast
can be seen at the southwest point – and to the foundations of a
Temple of Athena (5th century BC) on the hill adjoining to the
southwest. There is a magnificent view of the town from the highest
point of the acropolis.

Island Tour

Regular bus services run the 100km/60mi right around the island,
keeping close to the coastline, making all the beaches and villages
easy to reach. From Thasos Town drive south via the pretty mountain village **Panagia**, which is well visited in the summer for its characteristic houses with slate-tiled roofs and balconies, and further
along the southern slopes of Mt Ypsari.

The island's capital is surrounded by lush vegetation

Potamia
(Ποταμιά)
A museum in the mountain village of Potamia displays works by the sculptor P. Vagis, who came from there. There is a fine view of the wooded valley down to the sea and the long sandy **Golden Beach**, probably the best on the island. 3km/2mi east of Potamia lies **Skala Potamias**, once Potamia's harbour. Today the town with its fabulous beach is one of the island's major tourist attractions.

Alyki Peninsula
Past **Kinira**, whose main attraction is Paradise Beach, lies the small peninsula of Alyki with two idyllic sandy bays. The eastern bay is popular among naturists. A walk around the peninsula leads past the remains of a 5th century BC shrine to the Dioskouroi and two early Christian basilicas. There are also ancient marble quarries.

! | *Baedeker* TIP

Boat and barbecue
The boat *Eros II* tours around the island several times a week. It stops at good swimming beaches. A barbecue is included. It departs from the old fishing harbour in Thasos Town.

The road now runs westwards high above steep cliffs along the coast to the former fishing village of **Potos** with its long sand and pebble beach, which has been completely taken over by tourism. The road passes the **Convent of Arhangelou**, where an icon considered to be miraculous is preserved.

From Potos (or from Alyki) a worthwhile 10km/6mi-long side trip leads through a romantic valley to Theologos. This mountain village at an elevation of 240m/787ft was the island's capital in the 18th and 19th centuries. The beautiful old houses, mostly surrounded by walls and with slate roofs, are listed monuments.

Theologos (Θεολόγος)

The road leads past Pefkari, a fine beach, to the second-largest town on the island, Limenaria. It was founded in 1903 by a German company that mined ore and minerals on the island. Today Limenaria is a popular seaside resort. Above the harbour on a hill is the former Krupp family villa. Below it some crumbling blast furnaces can still be seen. Limenaria's beach is very small; the beach 500m/550yd to the west is better for sunbathing.

Limenaria (Λιμενάρια)

The pretty fishing villages of **Skala Marion**, **Skala Kallirahis** and **Skala Sotira** have hardly been touched tourism as yet. A recommended side trip runs up from Skala Kallirahis and Skala Sotira to the corresponding mountain villages. Although **Skala Rahonis** on the north coast is not very attractive, it has developed into a popular resort because of its long beach.

Resorts on the west coast

✶ Tinos

Greek: Τήνος
Area: 194 sq km/75 sq mi
Population: 8,600
Capital: Tinos Town

Island group: Cyclades
Elevation: 0–729m/2,392ft above sea level

Peace and seclusion on lonely beaches can still be found on this, the third-largest Cycladic island. Tourism is still low-key here.

Tinos is the southeastern continuation of the mountain massif extending from Evia past Andros. With a length of 30km/19mi and a breadth of 15km/9mi, this rocky green island is the **third-largest island** in the Cyclades chain. It is the »Greek Lourdes«, visited by thousands of pilgrims on festivals of the Virgin Mary, especially on 15 August, the feast of the Assumption (known in the Orthodox church as the Dormition). They not only take all of the hotel rooms, they also camp outdoors and eat their meals in the churchyards. Along with half a million pilgrims every year, the major sources of income are marble quarrying and vegetable farming. The island has been a centre of the Greek Orthodox religion since the 19th century. From 1207 until 1715 it was in Venetian hands, and thus had a longer period of Roman Catholicism than any other part of Greece, which gave it a large Catholic population. In 1822 – during the War of Independence against the Ottoman Empire – **a nun named Pela-**

»Greek Lourdes«

Tinos *Map*

gia had a vision that led to the discovery of a miraculous icon of the Virgin Mary. It soon became the object of pilgrimages (25 March and 15 August). The importance of the island, both ecclesiastically and nationally, only grew when an Italian submarine torpedoed the Greek cruiser *Elli* at anchor in the harbour on the Feast of the Dormition, 15 August 1940 – two months before Mussolini's declaration of war.

Tinos Town

Town ✱ Right upon arrival in the island's capital, Tinos (population 3,000), its significance as a **pilgrimage site** becomes apparent: the Church of Panagia Evangelistria commands the town, with a broad, steep pilgrimage way ascending directly to it from the harbour. This typical Cycladic town on a bay on the south coast developed from a modest

i Dovecotes

■ Tinos is famous for its tower-like dovecotes, which are imaginatively and artfully designed. There are about 800 of them all over the island. Especially beautiful examples, which go back to Venetian times and have been restored, can be seen at Kampos and Tarampados, north of Tinos Town. The delicate meat of the dove was prized and the droppings were used as manure.

coastal settlement to become the island capital after the destruction of the Exombourgo fortress by the Turks in the early 18th century. The harbour of Tinos is always busy, especially in the evenings when the many tavernas and cafes are filled with people. Devotional objects of every kind are sold in Evangelistria Street, which runs up the hill from the lively harbour parallel to the pilgrimage way.

The magnificent palace-like structure of Panagia Evangelistria was built between 1823 and 1830, using materials taken from the Poseidonion and the Temple of Apollo on Delos. The church is decorated with a large number of votive gifts and sacred treasures. To the left of the entrance is the **icon of Panagia Megalohori** (»Mother of God rich in grace«), which is more than 800 years old and venerated as miracle-working. Beneath the church is the site where the icon was found, as well as a mausoleum for the dead of the cruiser *Elli*. Baptisms are performed there and pilgrims draw »holy« water out of a spring.

Panagia Evangelistria

There are several **museums** on the site: a collection of late Byzantine art, a museum of Tiniot art with works by internationally known artists like Chalepas, a museum for votive gifts and an art gallery.

 VISITING TINOS

INFORMATION

Tourist information
Travel agencies in Tinos Town along the seafront
www.tinos.gr

GETTING THERE

Boat services to and from Piraeus and Rafina on the mainland as well as the islands of Amorgos, Astypalea, Donoúsa, Kalymnos, Kos, Leros, Naxos, Nisyros, Paros, Patmos, Rhodes, Symi and Syros

WHERE TO EAT

► **Moderate**
To Koutouki tis Elenis
G. Gagou 5
Tinos Town
Tel. 2 28 30 2 48 57
Small restaurant with character, good Greek dishes and its own specialities

WHERE TO STAY

► **Luxury**
Porto Tango Tinos
Agios Ioannis
Tel. 2 28 30 2 44 11
Fax 2 28 30 2 44 16
www.portotango.gr
55 rooms, 7 suites. The well-furnished rooms have a balcony or a terrace, some even have both; spa.

► **Mid-range**
Tinos Beach
Kionia
Tel. 2 28 30 2 26 26
www.tinosbeach.gr
164 rooms, 11 apartments, 5 suites. A beautiful hotel with many sports facilities; the rooms have modern comforts and a balcony or veranda.

Panagia Evangelistria is the destination of thousands of pilgrims each year

★
Archaeological museum
The archaeological museum beneath the church displays artefacts that were found on Tinos, mainly in the two large sanctuaries on the island: the sanctuary of Poseidon Amphitrite and the sanctuary of Demeter at Tripotamos. The highlights are huge vases from the 7th century BC, including a relief pithos, whose main picture is interpreted as the birth of Athena from Zeus' head. Opening hours: Tue–Sun 8.30am–3pm.

Beaches
There are good beaches east of Tinos Town – **Agios Fokas** and the long sandy beach at **Agios Kyriakis** – as well as the popular **Stavros beach** in the northwest.

Other Sights on Tinos

Kionia
In Kionia, 4km/2.5mi northwest of Tinos Town, a long pebble beach awaits its guests. In front of the Tinos Beach Hotel on the right there are the remains of the **Poseidon Amphitrite sanctuary**. Many people suffering from illnesses sought a cure in the shrine, which was established in the 5th century BC and rebuilt in Hellenistic times. The Poseidon cult on Tinos goes back to the 7th century BC. The god of the sea is supposed to have fought off a plague of snakes on the island. After that Poseidon was

! *Baedeker* TIP

Great walking
The hour-long walk from Tinos Town to Ktikados along a pretty footpath is rewarding. There is an impressive view from the idyllic mountain village with white houses and narrow lanes.

honoured as the god of healing. In the 3rd century BC the cult of Amphitrite, Poseidon's wife, was added. She was honoured as a healer of women's illnesses.

Mountain villages

Around the peaceful mountain villages **Kambos**, **Tarampados** and **Kardiani**, most of which is built out of marble, beautiful **dovecotes** can be seen.

◄ Isternia

A meander through the pretty mountain village of Isternia 4km/ 2.5mi northwest of Kardiani with its marble paved streets and church with faïence domes is also rewarding.

★
Pyrgos
(Πύργος)

A few miles further lies the second-largest town on the island, picturesque Pyrgos, known as a town of sculptors and painters. In the former home of the **sculptor Gianoulis Halepas** (1851–1938), who was born here, there is a museum. East of the plateia, at the highest point of the town there is a school for sculptors.

Kehrovounio

The nun Pelagia lived in **Kehrovounio Convent**, 9km/5mi northeast of Tinos, which originated in the 10th century. Pelagia's cell is shown in the atmospheric convent grounds, an other-worldly place with a magnificent view.

Exombourgo

A few miles to the north, a climb to the summit of the 540m/1,772ft granite cone is worthwhile just for the fantastic view. Take the road to the intersection outside Falatados, turn left and drive to the church. The path from here to the top of the rock takes about 20 minutes. On the cliff are the ruins of the Venetian citadel, including the remains of the medieval island capital, which was named Sant' Elena. In Loutra at the foot of the mountain is a Catholic convent of Ursuline sisters. **Kolimvythra Bay** in the north has a nice, uncrowded sandy beach that can be reached by way of Komi.

★ Zakynthos

D 9

Greek: Ζάκυνθος
Area: 402 sq km/155 sq mi
Population: 39,000
Capital: Zakynthos Town

Island group: Ionian Islands
Elevation: 0–758m/2,487ft above sea level

Zakynthos is one of the most popular places to visit in the Ionian archipelago because of its lush green vegetation, long sandy beaches and many romantic coves.

»Flower of the Orient«

The Venetians appreciated the scenic beauty of Zakynthos, which they named »Fiore di Levante«, »Flower of the Orient«. The island has been known since the time of Homer by one and the same name,

Zakynthos Map

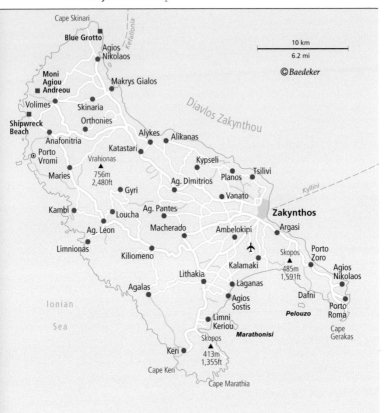

thought to be derived from the wild hyacinth. Zakynthos, the most southerly of the Ionian Islands, lies 16km/10mi off the west coast of the Peloponnese. The western part of the island is a plateau that rises to 758m/2,487ft, while the eastern part is a fertile and intensely cultivated plain where olives, citrus fruit, sultanas and wine are produced. Tourism has become the most important contributor to the economy. The north and west coastlines are wonderful high walls of rock that drop abruptly to the sea. Coves with sandy beaches are to be found in the east; the island's biggest holiday centre is in the **Bay of Laganas**, which opens up to the south. The sandy beaches in the south are still the nesting beaches of the endangered **loggerhead turtle** (Caretta caretta). Zakynthos was the birthplace of the poet **Dionysios Solomos** (1798–1857), who wrote the Greek national anthem and was the first poet to write in the vernacular (dimotiki), and of the Italian **poet Ugo Foscolo** (1778–1827). The historic, Venetian-influenced buildings of Zakynthos were almost completely destroyed in the earthquake of 1953.

✱ Zakynthos Town

The lovely capital (population 11,000) on the east coast of the island extends along the shores of the wide harbour bay. Stately buildings and broad squares, picturesque lanes and tidy lawns mark its appearance. Almost all buildings had to be rebuilt after the destructive earthquake of 1953. The shore is lined with hotels, restaurants and many shops. The arcaded Odos Alexandrou Roma is also a popular shopping street.

Island capital

A good starting point for a tour of the town is Plateia Solomou at the harbour, framed by imposing buildings; it is a popular meeting place in the evening. The square was named after the **national poet Dionysios Solomos** and a monument commemorates him; the **Solomos Museum** on Plateia Agiou Markou is dedicated to him. The Venetian **Church of St Nicholas**, originally built in 1561, is also near the shore. Its bell tower is also a lighthouse.

Plateia Solomou

The Zakynthos Museum on Plateia Solomou has a rich collection of icons, whole iconostases, wood carvings and frescoes from the Byzantine period up to the 19th century. At the same time, it presents an outstanding overview of the work of the **Ionian School** of painting. After the Ottomans conquered Crete in 1669 many Cretan artists fled to Zakynthos. While Byzantine painting was strongly oriented to formal models, the Cretan artists were influenced by Italian Renaissance art. They depicted the saints not as other-worldly mystical beings, but as people interested in normal life. The leading painters of the Ionian School are Panagiotis Doxaras (1662–1729), J. Strati Plakotos (1662–1728), Nikolaos Doxaras (1705–75) and Nikolaos Kantounis (1767–1834). In addition, interesting historic photographs of the city before and after the 1953 earthquake can be seen. Opening times: Tue–Sun 8.30am–3pm.

✱
Museum Zakynthos

! *Baedeker* TIP

Music with a view

The restaurants and cafes above the Church of Panagia Chrysopigí offer a magnificent view of the island capital and resound in the evenings to the sounds of poetic »kantades«, the typical Zakynthian songs.

Via Plateia Dimokratias walk north to **Plateia Agiou Markou**. Since the 16th century the three-sided plateia has been the centre of social life in Zakynthos; it is lined by cafés and some good restaurants. In the **Solomos Museum** (open daily 9am–2pm) the two greatest Greek poets of the 19th century are interred in marble sarcophagi: Diony-

Plateia Agiou Markou

▶ VISITING ZAKYNTHOS

INFORMATION
Tourist police
Lomvardou 62
Zakynthos Town
Tel. 2 29 80 5 22 05
www.zakynthos-greece.biz

GETTING THERE
Ferries to and from Kyllini on the mainland and the island of Kefallonia

WHERE TO EAT
▶ Moderate
To Spiti tou Lata
Bochali, Zakynthos Town
Good meals and a fantastic view on a terrace high above the city

▶ Moderate
Arekia
D. Roma
Zakynthos Town
Arekia is a small, simple taverna on the shore road to Kryoneri, known for the kantades and arekia music sung there in the evenings.

WHERE TO STAY
▶ Luxury
Villas Cavo Marathia
Marathia

Tel. 2 28 30 2 26 26
www.vcm.gr
In a magnificent setting in the far south, on the cape west of Laganas Bay; tastefully designed holiday residences with spacious studios and seawater swimming pools.

▶ Mid-range
Aquarius
Vasilikos
Tel. 2 69 50 3 53 00
www.hotelaquarius.gr
24 rooms. Small hotel in a quiet location in a grove of pine trees about 10 minutes on foot from Vasilikos; nice, well-furnished rooms, some with a balcony.

Liuba Bungalows
Vasilikos
Tel. 2 69 50 3 53 72
www.liuba-houses.gr
Pretty complex with apartments for 2 to 4 persons; in a wonderful location at the tip of Skopos Peninsula.

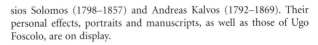

sios Solomos (1798–1857) and Andreas Kalvos (1792–1869). Their personal effects, portraits and manuscripts, as well as those of Ugo Foscolo, are on display.

Roma Mansion Museum The grand Villa Roma (Louka Karrer 19) shows how wealthy Zakynthos families lived a few decades ago. The house was completely destroyed in the earthquake of 1953; it was originally built by an English merchant in 1660. In the mid-1950s one of the wealthiest families on the island had it partially reconstructed. It has served as a museum since 2007. Portraits of family members, furnishings and photographs as well as a library of 10,000 books are on display. Opening times: April–Sept daily 10am–2pm, 7pm–9pm, Oct–Mar daily 10am–2pm; www.romas.gr.

Synagogue

The Jewish community on the island, which was founded in 1453, had a synagogue in the town centre (Tertseti 44) until the earthquake of 1953. It was not rebuilt. Two stones on the small plot of land commemorate the Orthodox island bishop and the mayor of Zakynthos during the German occupation during World War II. They defied the Nazis, refusing to give them a list of all Jewish citizens and thus saving them from German death camps.

Agios Dionysios

The southern part of the harbour is dominated by the bell tower of the church of the island's patron saint, Agios Dionysios (1948). Inside are numerous paintings from the 1980s with scenes from the life of the saint, who was born on Zakynthos in 1547. The saint's relics are preserved in a magnificent **silver sarcophagus** in a side chapel.

★ Museum of religious art

In a wing of the adjacent monastery is the museum of religious art; it shows silver plate, liturgical vestments, old manuscripts and books and some valuable works of art, including a metres-long depiction of a Dionysios procession (1766).

★ Bohali

On the road to the western suburb of Bohali, which is located on the mountain ridge that frames the town, stand the new cathedral (Mitropolis), the 19th-century **British cemetery** and the **Jewish ceme-**

There is a superb view of Zakynthos from Bochali Hill

ENDANGERED SPECIES

The long, flat beaches with fine-grained sand are the biggest attraction on Zakynthos – not only for holiday makers, but also for sea turtles that lay their eggs there. In this conflict the prehistoric reptiles are at a disadvantage.

The loggerhead turtle (Caretta caretta), which can achieve a shell length of 1.2m/4ft and weigh up to 140kg/310lb, is the only sea turtle that lays its eggs in Greece. Laganas Bay, which takes up almost all of the south coast of Zakynthos, is one of its most important breeding grounds.

Puzzling animals

Sea turtles, which have existed for 200 million years, are still a puzzle to science. Almost nothing is known about the life of the young turtles in the sea. The animals' most amazing characteristic is their **sense of direction**, since they can find the beach where they hatched after 20 years with an accuracy of 50–100m/165–330ft. Loggerhead turtles undertake journeys of epic length at a speed of 2–3km/h (1.2–1.8mph): animals that were marked in Florida were sighted one and a half years later off the Azores; a turtle marked off the Azores

was found again off Sicily. Zoologists at the University of Frankfurt in Germany were able to prove in 1998 that the animals' extreme **bond with their place of birth** is even anchored in DNA (how the information got there will remain a mystery for a long time yet), so that every beach, even every section of beach, has its own population. If a breeding ground is lost, an entire genetic line is destroyed.

Life on land

Between late May and late August the female turtles approach the beach in order to find a suitable nesting place. They climb up the beach in early evening using all of their strength – just far enough for the eggs to be away from the water for the entire hatching period. Then they dig a hole, about an arm's-length deep, and within 15 minutes deposit 100 to 120 eggs, which have a soft, leather-like shell

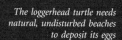
The loggerhead turtle needs natural, undisturbed beaches to deposit its eggs

and are the size of a ping-pong ball. Then the female turtle covers the hole with sand and presses it down firmly with her back legs. They visit the beaches two to three times in one season to lay eggs, but take a break lasting between two and four years, sometimes even up to nine years, before the next »campaign«. After 55 days of incubating in the warm sand, about 80% of the eggs produce little turtles about 6cm/2.5in in length. These then try to reach the water at night, using the brightest point – usually the horizon – for orientation. Only two of 1,000 young turtles survive to the age of reproduction, enough to maintain the population.

Humans

Humans are the greatest danger to Caretta caretta. The breeding grounds in Laganas Bay are popular beaches, often just as busy at night as during the day. The turtles can be injured or killed in the water by the **propellers of motorboats** that disregard the protected zone. On land they are frightened by the **lights and noise** of the hotels, restaurants and streets, return to the sea and drop their eggs there, where

they cannot hatch. **Parasols** stuck into the sand destroy the nests. **Vehicles** from scooters to bulldozers, as well as horses on which people gallop along the beach, make the sand so firm that the young cannot hatch out of the eggs. Sandcastles, loungers and other hindrances keep the young from reaching the water, and artificial lights lure them inland, where they die. Well-intended help harms as well, for the baby turtles have to find their way alone so that they can return later to their place of birth. Of course the animals are also exploited without mercy as a **tourist attraction**: »Go and see the turtles!«, visitors staying on Zakynthos are told. A boat ride from Laganas with a ranger from the national park service is definitely preferable to a trip on an excursion boat.

It is true that the Greek government has reacted to the massive protests of Greek and international environmentalists. The sea turtles have been classified as »endangered« in several declarations since 1980 and the expansion of tourism has been prohibited. In late 1999 the bay was made into a **marine national park** with three zones offering varying degrees of protection.

In the east part (zone A) building and boat traffic out to Pelouzo Island are prohibited in a large area between Cape Gerakas and Kalamaki. The land behind Sekania beach was bought by the **Worldwide Fund for Nature** in order to prevent development. In zone B, between Kalamaki, Laganas, Marathonisi and Pelouzo, boats may only travel at a speed of 6kmh (4mph); dropping anchor or beaching is prohibited. However, so little has changed that the **European Court of Justice** officially reprimanded the Greek government in 2002. Land-owners whose interests have been prejudiced for over 20 years by the laws blame the government for not recompensing them in the form of an exchange of property or financial compensation, which would involve large sums of money. Moreover, on Dafni beach seven buildings were constructed, including four restau-rants and bars, when the building prohibition was already in effect between 1984 and 1992. Meanwhile the number of female turtles laying eggs has remained stable at a high level. The management of the marine national park has done a good job in

the last years. It is supported by the state-employed park rangers and by volunteers of the **environmental orga-nization Archelon** (www.archelon.gr), who together inform holidaymakers on the beaches. On Sekania beach between 800 and 2,000 turtles are laying eggs again every year. In all it is estimated that there are between 1,600 and 4,000 layings every year on the Gulf of Laganas. This wide fluctuation is natural and not reason for concern. Anyone who insists on spending a holiday here should not fail to follow some **basic rules**:

– Beaches marked as nesting grounds are only open between 7am and 7pm; Sekania beach is off limits.
– No vehicles or horses are allowed on nesting beaches.
– Parasols may only be used in marked locations at Gerakas, Kalama-ki and Laganas, and only within 5m/16ft of the water line.
– Leave behind no waste of any kind.
– Do not dig in the sand or build sand castles.
– Do not touch baby turtles or carry them to the water.
– Do not touch the mesh that protects nests.

by the action of the waves. It shimmers in various shades of blue and consists of two chambers. Visitors experience a unique play of colours, especially in the morning hours, with a palette that extends from dark green to azure.

To reach the extreme northern point of the island, **Cape Skinari**, drive via the remote village of Korithi. The boats from here take only 10 minutes to reach the Blue Grotto. Trips also leave from here to Shipwreck Beach.

In Volimes an unpaved road turns off toward the abandoned St Andreas Monastery near the sea. The bell tower still testifies to its beginnings: 1641. Frescoes and icons from the modest church have been taken to the museum in Zakynthos Town. Only a few miles southwest of Volimes, the simple Monastery of **Agios Georgios Krimnon** lies in pretty scenery. The walls that surround the uninhabited complex were once white. The round tower was built in 1562 to protect it from pirates.

Ágios Andreos (Άγίος Ανδρέος)

To the north of the monastery a road leads to the beach; after about 2km/1mi there is a parking lot. A narrow path leads along the cliff to the north, and after about 500m/550ye a spectacular view of Shipwreck Beach. In the impressive sandy cove framed by high, white cliffs lies the wreck of a freighter that ran aground in the 1970s. The sea water shimmers an intense turquoise colour.

✷ ✷
Shipwreck Beach Navagio

The mountain village Anafonitria (7km/4mi south of Volimes), with its winding lanes and whitewashed houses, is one of the most popular destinations for excursions on the island, but the town is also visited because of the **Anafonitria Monastery** to the south. Walk through an archway into the wooded grounds of the monastery, which was founded in 15th century. Right next to the arch are the remains of a defensive tower. The basilica is the **oldest church on the island**. The silver-plated miraculous icon of the Virgin Mary is supposed to have been brought to Zakynthos from Constantinople in 1453 after the Ottomans conquered the Byzantine capital. The patron saint of Zakynthos, Dionysios, spent the last years of his life here as abbot.

From the monastery a road continues to **Porto Vromi**. A bay that cuts deep into the interior has created a wonderful harbour here. There are boat trips to Shipwreck Beach, which is only accessible from the sea.

Anafonitria (Αναφωνήτρια)

From Anafonitria drive via Maries to the village of Kambi near the southwest coast, which is situated among vineyards, fields and olive trees, to enjoy sunset from one of the tavernas. From the town of **Limnionas** a few miles to the south, boats excursions start on along the craggy coast, for instance to the small **island of Karakonisi** nearby.

Kampi (Καμπή)

Leave Agios Leon heading north into the isolated mountain region. **Island interior** In the two villages of **Louka** and **Gyri**, which have existed since the 15th century, time seems to have stood still. Many of the residents have left to look for better sources of income along the coast or on the mainland. On the drive from Kiliomeno via Lagopodo to Maherado, the road passes the Panagia i Eleftherotrias Convent, which was founded in 1961.

The town of **Maherado** is dominated by the tall Venetian bell tower of the church of Agia Mavra, which is considered one of the most beautiful on the island; it has very melodious bells. The church is unadorned on the outside but it has a richly decorated iconostasis; on a carved and gilded shrine is a 16th century icon of Agia Mavra. The distance from Maherado back to Zakynthos Town is about 10km/6mi.

← *Breathtaking scenery: Shipwreck Beach on Zakynthos*

INDEX

LIST OF MAPS AND ILLUSTRATIONS

PHOTO CREDITS

PUBLISHER'S INFORMATION

Illustrations etc: 181 illustrations, 50 maps and diagrams, one large map
Text: Dr. Bernhard Abend, Achim Bourmer, Birgit Borowski, Dr. Katja David, Astrid Feltes-Peter, Carmen Galenschovski, Wolfgang Liebermann, Helmut Linde, Reinhard Strüber, Andrea Wurth
Revision:
Klaus Bötig
Editing: Baedeker editorial team (Robert Taylor)
Translation: Barbara Schmidt-Runkel
Cartography: Christoph Gallus, Hohberg; Franz Huber, Munich; MAIRDUMONT/Falk Verlag, Ostfildern (map)
3D illustrations: jangled nerves, Stuttgart
Design: independent Medien-Design, Munich; Kathrin Schemel

Editor-in-chief: Rainer Eisenschmid, Baedeker Ostfildern

1st edition 2012
Based on Baedeker Allianz Reiseführer »Griechische Inseln« 11. Auflage 2012

Copyright: Karl Baedeker Verlag, Ostfildern
Publication rights: MAIRDUMONT GmbH & Co; Ostfildern

Printed in China

BAEDEKER GUIDE BOOKS AT A GLANCE
Guiding the World since 1827

- ▶ Andalusia
- ▶ Austria
- ▶ Bali
- ▶ Barcelona
- ▶ Berlin
- ▶ Brazil
- ▶ Budapest
- ▶ Cape Town •
  Garden Route
- ▶ China
- ▶ Cologne
- ▶ Dresden
- ▶ Dubai
- ▶ Egypt
- ▶ Florence
- ▶ Florida
- ▶ France
- ▶ Gran Canaria
- ▶ Greek Islands
- ▶ Greece
- ▶ Iceland
- ▶ India
- ▶ Ireland
- ▶ Italian Lakes
- ▶ Italy
- ▶ Japan
- ▶ London
- ▶ Mexico
- ▶ Morocco
- ▶ Naples •
  Amalfi Coast
- ▶ New York
- ▶ Norway
- ▶ Paris
- ▶ Portugal
- ▶ Prague
- ▶ Rome
- ▶ South Africa
- ▶ Spain
- ▶ Thailand
- ▶ Turkish Coast
- ▶ Tuscany
- ▶ Venice
- ▶ Vienna
- ▶ Vietnam

DEAR READER,

**We would like to thank you for choosing this Baedeker travel guide. It will be a reliable companion on your travels and will not disappoint you.
This book describes the major sights, of course, but it also recommends the best beaches, surfing and diving, cafés, as well as hotels in the luxury and budget categories, and includes tips about where to eat or go shopping and much more, helping to make your trip an enjoyable experience. Our authors ensure the quality of this information by making regular journeys to the Greek Islands and putting all their know-how into this book.**

Nevertheless, experience shows us that it is impossible to rule out errors and changes made after the book goes to press, for which Baedeker accepts no liability. Please send us your criticisms, corrections and suggestions for improvement: we appreciate your contribution. Contact us by post or e-mail, or phone us:

▶ **Verlag Karl Baedeker GmbH**
Editorial department
Postfach 3162
73751 Ostfildern
Germany
Tel. 49-711-4502-262, fax -343
www.baedeker.com
www.baedeker.co.uk
E-Mail: baedeker@mairdumont.com